Fitzhugh Lee

His Nephew and Cavalry Commander

GENERAL LEE

ARCADIA PRESS

TABLE OF CONTENTS

GENERAL LEE

PREFACE.

The occasion has been embraced to express the universal regret that General Lee never wrote anything concerning his career and campaigns. His statements would have settled conflicting opinions on all subjects contained therein. We know that it was his intention to record the deeds of his soldiers, but not to write his personal memoirs. He waited for a "convenient season," and waited too long. In this volume the attempt has been made to imperfectly supply the great desire to have something from Robert E. Lee's pen, by introducing, at the periods referred to, such extracts from his private letters as would be of general interest. He is thus made, for the first time, to give his impressions and opinions on most of the great events with which he was so closely connected. Except in a few instances, the scope of the book has not permitted the tactical details of the battlefield, or the mention by name of many of the officers and organizations whose superb courage contributed to their commander's fame.

F. L. Glasgow, Va., August, 1894.

CHAPTER 1

ANCESTRY.

Westmoreland is one of a group of counties in Virginia lying between the Rappahannock and Potomac Rivers. It was originally a portion of Northumberland County, and, though small in geographical extent, its historical record is great. Within a space of thirty miles in length and an average width of fifteen miles were born statesmen, soldiers, and patriots whose lives and characters adorn the pages of American history, and whose courage, genius, and learning are the proud inheritance of those who dwell to-day in the powerful republic of America. Here, from England, in 1665, settled the great-grandfather of the "Father of his country." Americanized, he became an extensive planter, soldier, magistrate, member of the House of Burgesses, and a gentleman whose virtue and piety were undoubted. In his will he expressed his "sorrow for his sins, and begged forgiveness from Almighty God, Saviour, and Redeemer." Here his son, Lawrence, and his grandson, Augustine, were born. The second wife of Augustine was Mary Ball, and their first child, born February 22, 1732, was named George Washington.

This son was destined to establish, with stainless sword, a free republic, and by great skill, unfaltering faith, and sublime patriotism transfer power from king to people. A grateful country acknowledged his illustrious services, and he was chosen the first President of the United States. This little county was not satisfied with the high honor. On April 28, 1758, James Monroe was born within its limits. He became a distinguished citizen, served as an officer in the Revolutionary War, was a member of the General Assembly of Virginia, of the Congress of Confederation, and the Virginia Convention called in June, 1778, to consider the Federal Constitution, a United States Senator, envoy to France, England, and Spain, twice Governor of his native State, Secretary of State in Mr. Madison's administration, and President of the republic for two terms from 1817 to 1825 — thus adding, by a long and meritorious public career, additional renown to the county of his birth, his State, and his country. James Madison, fourth President of the United States, was born in the adjoining county of King George seven years before Monroe, and but a few miles distant. To this section, from England, came, too, the Lees, who belonged to one of the oldest families in the mother country, its members from a very early date being distinguished for eminent services to sovereign and country. By the side of William the Conqueror, at the battle of Hastings, in 1066, Lancelot Lee fought, and a later descendant, Lionel Lee, followed Richard Coeur de Lion, taking part in the third crusade to Palestine, in 1192, at the head of a company of "gentlemen cavaliers," displaying great bravery at the siege of Acre.

The Lees of Virginia, "a family which has, perhaps, given more statesmen and warriors to their new home than any other of our old colonial progenitors," came of an ancient and distinguished stock in England, and neither country can boast a nobler scion than the subject of these memoirs. General Lee had never the time or inclination to study genealogy, and always said he knew nothing beyond his first American ancestor, Colonel Richard Lee, who migrated to Virginia in the reign of Charles I. He believed, however, from his inherited traditions and the Coat of Arms borne by his progenitors in this country, that his family came originally from Shropshire, England; and when the world rang with his name and fame, and he paid the usual penalty of greatness by being besieged with reiterated queries respecting his pedigree, this was all he would say. Others, however, took more interest in the subject; he was claimed by the Lees of Cheshire, Oxfordshire, Bucks, and Essex, as well as of Shropshire, and much was said and written pro and con both before and after his death.

In recent years his genealogy has been very persistently and thoroughly investigated by those learned in antiquarian research, and their conclusion is in favor of Shropshire, though in 1663 the first emigrant, Colonel Richard Lee, made a will in which he states that he was "lately of Stafford Langton in the county of Essex." Now, as we have every reason to believe that he was a younger son, the parental nest was probably full; neither was it such a "far cry" from Shropshire to the near vicinity of London, a remove preparatory, possibly, to the still greater one across the Atlantic. He certainly used the arms of the Shropshire Lees.

Colonel Lee's devotion to the House of Stuart was notorious, and had been often proved even by the manner of dating his will — viz., "The 6th of February, in the sixteenth year of the reign of our Sovereign Lord, Charles II, King of Great Britain, etc., and in the year of our Lord 1663." Being Secretary of State and Member of the Privy Council in Virginia, he had assisted that stanch royalist, Governor Berkeley,in holding the colony to its allegiance, so that after the death of Charles I, Cromwell was forced to send troops and armed vessels of war to reduce it to subjection. Unable to resist, they made a treaty with the "Commonwealth of England," wherein Virginia was described as an "Independent Dominion," this treaty being ratified in the same manner as with a foreign power.

Berkeley was then removed and another governor appointed; but the undaunted Colonel Richard Lee hired a Dutch vessel, freighted it himself, went to Brussels or Breda, surrendered up Sir William Berkeley's old commission — for the government of that province — and received a new one from his present Majesty, Charles II, "a loyal action and deserving my commendation." It is also said that he offered the exiled monarch an asylum in the New World. It is certain that on the death of Cromwell he aided Governor Berkeley in proclaiming Charles II in Virginia King of England, Scotland, France, Ireland, and Virginia two years before his "restoration" in England. In consequence, the motto to the Virginia Coat of Arms was "En dat Virginia quintam" until after the union of England and Scotland, when it was "En dat Virginia quartam."

The inscription on the tombstone of the second Richard Lee, at Burnt House Fields, Mt. Pleasant, Westmoreland County, describes him as belonging to an "ancient and noble family of Morton Regis in Shropshire." It is clearly established that the three earliest representatives of the family in America, Colonel Richard Lee and his two eldest sons, claimed this Shropshire County descent.

It is our purpose to trace the Lees in America, not in England. The first emigrant, Colonel Richard Lee, is described as a man of good stature, of comely visage, enterprising genius, a sound head, vigorous spirit, and generous nature; and when he reached Virginia, at that time not much cultivated, he was so pleased with the country that he made large settlements with the servants who accompanied him. To his credit it may be added that when he returned to England, some years afterward, he "gave away all the lands he had taken up, and settled at his own expense, to the servants he had fixed on them, some of whose descendants are now possessed of very considerable estates in that colony."

After remaining some time in England he again visited Virginia with a fresh band of followers whom he also established there. He first settled in York County in 1641, where he was burgess and justice in 1647, and when later he removed to the "Northern neck," between the Potomac and Rappahannock Rivers, he filled the offices of Secretary of State and Member of the Privy Council. Of his loyalty to the house of Stuart we have already spoken, and of his various voyages, indicating in themselves his "enterprising genius." When he made his will in London, in 1663, he was returning on what proved to be his last voyage. He had with him his large, young family, his eldest son John not yet being of age; but he was so determined to establish them in Virginia that he ordered an English estate — Stratford — worth eight or nine hundred pounds per annum, to be sold and the money divided between his heirs. He died soon after his return, and as John, the B. A. of Oxford, never married, Richard, the second son, succeeded to the homestead in Westmoreland. He also graduated at Oxford in law, and was distinguished for his learning, spending almost his whole life in study. On October 15, 1667, as "Major Richard Lee, a loyal, discreet person and worthy of the place," he was appointed member of the council. He was born in 1647, married Letitia Corbin, and died in 1714, leaving five sons and one daughter. His eldest son, Richard, the third of the name, married and settled in London, though his children eventually returned to Virginia. Philip removed to Maryland in 1700, and was the progenitor of the Lee family in that State. Francis, the third son, died a bachelor, but Thomas, the fourth, with only a common Virginia education (it could not have been much in those days), had such strong natural parts that he became a good Latin and Greek scholar, long after he was a man, without any assistance but his own genius. Though a younger son, with only a limited patrimony, by his "industry and parts" he acquired a considerable fortune, was a member of the council, and so well known and respected that when his house in Westmoreland burned down Queen Caroline sent him a large sum of money out of her privy purse, with an autograph letter. Stratford was rebuilt on an imposing scale, and, becoming the property of "Light-horse Harry," on his marriage with Matilda, daughter of Philip Ludwell Lee and granddaughter of Thomas, was eventually the birthplace of General R. E. Lee. On the recall of Sir William Gooch, Thomas became president and commander in chief over the colony, in which station he continued some time, until the King thought proper to appoint him governor, and he is always spoken of as the first native governor, though he died in 1750, before his commission could reach him. He married Hannah Ludwell, of an old and honorable Somersetshire family, originally of German extraction, and left six sons and two daughters.

Stratford is still standing in Westmoreland County, an object of much veneration and respect. Within its walls, in the same chamber, two signers of the Declaration of Independence were born, while the fact that Robert Edward Lee first saw the light there makes it yet more interesting. It is a large, stately mansion, built in the shape of the letter "H," and not far from the banks of the Potomac. Upon the roof were summer houses, with chimneys for columns, where the band played in the evenings, and the ladies and gentlemen promenaded. Thomas Lee was buried at Pope's Creek Church, five miles from Stratford. George Washington was baptized at this church, and in the early days his family, the Lees, Paynes, and other prominent families of the neighborhood worshiped there.

It has been said that as Westmoreland County is distinguished above all other counties in Virginia as the birthplace of genius, so, perhaps, no other Virginian could boast so many distinguished sons as President Thomas Lee. General Washington, in 1771, wrote: "I know of no country that can produce a family all distinguished as clever men, as our Lees." These sons in order of age were: Philip Ludwell, Richard Henry, Thomas, Francis Lightfoot, Henry, and Arthur. Matilda, the first wife of General Henry Lee, the father of General Robert E. Lee, was the daughter of the eldest son, Philip Ludwell Lee. Richard Henry Lee, the second son, is well known to students of American history. He has been generally styled "The Cicero of the American Revolution." He moved on June 10, 1776, that "these colonies are, and of right ought to be, free and independent States"; and with his brother Francis Lightfoot signed the Declaration of Independence. Having moved this declaration, according to parliamentary etiquette, he might have been appointed chairman of the committee to draw up the instrument, but the sickness of his wife called him home; or he might also have been the author of the Declaration of American Independence in place of Thomas Jefferson. His services to the cause of the colony were great, and their struggle for independence was sustained by his tongue and pen. He was a great orator, an accomplished scholar, a learned debater, and a renowned statesman in that period of our country's history. His father's brother, Henry Lee, the fifth son of the second Richard, married a Miss Bland, a great-aunt of John Randolph, of Roanoke. His only daughter married a Fitzhugh. His son Henry married Miss Grymes, and left a family of six sons and four daughters. Henry, the eldest, was the well-known "Light-horse Harry" of the Revolutionary War, the father of Robert E. Lee. He and Richard Henry Lee are frequently confounded, and their relationship has often been the subject of inquiry. Richard Henry Lee's father, Thomas, and Henry Lee's grandfather, Henry, were brothers. The former was therefore a first cousin of the latter's father. "Light-horse Harry" was conspicuous in the military and civil annals of his country as a dashing dragoon in the war between Great Britain and the colonies. His boldness and activity were frequently commended by Washington, and he came out of the war with a brilliant reputation. He possessed the love and confidence of the commander in chief, and it is possible that Washington's interest was first excited because he was once supposed to have had a tender feeling for Lucy Grymes, his mother, a friendship which was continued by reason of the attractive qualities of the son as soldier and statesman. This attachment was deeply appreciated by General Henry Lee, and throughout his career he was steadfast in his devotion to Washington.

"Light-Horse Harry's" father, Henry Lee, of Leesylvania, and Lucy Grymes were married at Green Spring, on James River, December 1, 1753. His mother was the daughter of Lucy Ludwell, who married Colonel Grymes, of the Council of Virginia. Bishop Porteus, of England, was her uncle. Their son Henry was born January 29, 1756, at Leesylvania, some three miles from Dumfries, a village built by Scotch merchants, and then the county town of Prince William. His brother, Charles Lee (not to be confounded with General Charles Lee, an Englishman, and no relation to this family), was subsequently Attorney General in Washington's second Cabinet. The future cavalry leader was educated at Princeton. Dr. William Shippen writes to Richard Henry Lee from Philadelphia, August 25, 1770: "I am persuaded that there is no such school as Princeton on this continent. Your cousin Henry Lee is in college, and will be one of the first fellows in this country. He is more than strict in his morality, has fine genius, and is diligent." The profession of law was thought best for the display of his talents, and he was about to embark for England to study it, under the direction of Bishop Porteus, of London, when stopped by hostilities between the mother country and her American colonies.

Possessing fine descriptive powers, application, great facility for public expression, and with character formed and mind trained by such a distinguished light of the Church of England, a great legal future would seem a safe prediction; but before the smoke cleared away from the first British gun fired in Massachusetts, its report was heard in Virginia. The English volley lighted patriotic fires in the hearts of the colonists with the rapidity electricity flies in this age from the touch of the button. The sword was substituted for the law book in the hands of Henry Lee, and we find him, at the age of nineteen, after the battle of Lexington, a captain of cavalry, being nominated for that position by Patrick Henry, the orator of American liberty. He rose rapidly in his new career. In the Northern Department at Brandywine, Germantown, Springfield, and in the operations in Pennsylvania, New Jersey, and New York, his address, cool courage, great ability, and unceasing activity as an outpost officer speedily drew the attention of his superiors. Congress recognized his services, promoted him, and gave him an independent partisan corps. Ever thereafter his position in the war was near the flashing of the guns. His duties kept him close to the enemy's lines, and his legion was what cavalry should be — the eyes and ears of the army. His communications to Washington were confidential, were sent direct, and he was ordered by the commander in chief to mark them "Private." When Washington was anxious to effect Arnold's capture he consulted the commander of the "Light horse," who planned the famous desertion of Sergeant Champe. He projected and executed the surprise and capture of Paulus Hook by a brilliant coup de main, and for prudence, bravery, and tactical skill was presented by Congress with a gold medal emblematical of his success — a distinction conferred on no other officer below the rank of general during the war. On one side of the medal was a bust of the hero, with the words: "Henry Lee, Legionis Equit.: Praefecto Comitia Americana," and on the reverse is translated: "Nothwithstanding rivers and intrenchments, he, with a small band, conquered the foe by warlike skill and prowess, and firmly bound, by his humanity, those who had been conquered by his arms. In memory of the conflict at Paulus Hook, 19th August, 1779."

In November, 1780, he was promoted to be lieutenant colonel of dragoons, and his corps is spoken of as the "finest that made its appearance in the arena of the Revolutionary War." Washington had it formed expressly for him of equal proportions of cavalry and infantry, both officers and men being picked from the army. Under its victorious guidons rode Peter Johnston, the father of the distinguished soldier, Joseph Eggleston Johnston, who joined the legion when only sixteen years old and led the forlorn hope at the storming of Fort Watson, and was publicly thanked. Afterward he became a judge, and was celebrated for his learning and ability. It is curious that the sons of Judge Johnston and General Henry Lee were afterward classmates at the United States Military Academy, and at the marriage ceremony of Lee, Johnston was a groomsman. These two eminent soldiers were in the front rank of the United States Army, and served with great distinction under the Southern flag, even as their fathers rode boot to boot in the days of the Revolution. When Henry Lee's legion was selected to assist in the defense of the Carolinas and the Virginias in the Southern Department, Washington wrote to Mr. John Matthews, a member of Congress from South Carolina, informing him of its march, saying: "Lee's corps will go to the southward; it is an excellent one, and the officer at the head of it has great reserves of genius." Lafayette held the leader of the legion in high estimation, and bears testimony to his "distinguished services," his "talents as a corps commander," and his "handsome exploits"; while one of the general officers of the army said: "He seemed to have come out of his mother's womb a soldier." General Nathanael Greene, his immediate commander, testified that "few officers, either in America or Europe, were held in so high a point of estimation," in a letter to the President of Congress, February 18, 1782, expressed himself as "more indebted to this officer [Lee] than any other for the advantages gained over the enemy in the operations of the last campaign," and in a letter to Lee himself writes: "No man in the progress of the campaign had equal merit with yourself, nor is there one so reported; everybody knows I have the highest opinion of you as an officer, and you know I love you as a friend." After the British colors were lowered at Yorktown Henry Lee began a civil career which proved to be as great as his military record. In 1778 he was a member of the convention called in Virginia to consider the ratification of the Federal Constitution. In the battle of intellectual giants composing that body, with eloquence and zeal he pleaded for its adoption. By his side, and voting with him on that important question, were such men as James Madison, John Marshall, afterward Chief Justice of the United States, and Edmund Randolph; while in the ranks of the opposition stood Patrick Henry with immense oratorical strength, George Mason, "the wisest man," Mr. Jefferson said, he "ever knew," Benjamin Harrison, William Grayson, and others, who thought the Constitution, as it came from the hands of its framers, conferred too much power on the Federal Government and too little upon its creator, the States. In 1786 he was a delegate to the Continental Congress. From 1792 to 1795 he was Governor of Virginia, and was selected by President Washington to command the fifteen thousand men from Pennsylvania, New Jersey, and Maryland, who were sent into western Pennsylvania to quell what was known as the "Whisky Insurrection," which he successfully accomplished without bloodshed. This rebellion grew out of a resistance to a tax laid on distilled spirits. Washington accompanied him on the march as far as Bedford, Pa., and in a letter, dated October 20, 1794, to Henry Lee, Esq., commander in chief of the militia army on its march against the insurgents in certain counties of western Pennsylvania, says at its conclusion: "In leaving the Army I have less regret, as I know I commit it to an able and faithful direction, and that this direction will be ably and faithfully seconded by all."

While Governor of Virginia, a section lying under the Cumberland Mountains, projecting between Kentucky and Tennessee, was formed into a separate county and named after him. It has since been divided into two, the eastern portion being called after General Winfield Scott. In 1779 General Lee was elected to Congress, and on the death of General Washington was appointed to deliver an address in commemoration of the services of that great man, in which occurs the famous sentence so often quoted: "First in war, first in peace, and first in the hearts of his fellow-citizens." In 1798-99, as a representative of the County of Westmoreland in the General Assembly, he took an active part in the debate upon Mr. Madison's famous resolutions of that date. In his opinion, the laws of the United States then under discussion were unconstitutional, and if they were, Virginia had a right to object; "but," he exclaimed, "Virginia is my country; her will I obey, however lamentable the fate to which it may subject me."

When he was Governor of Virginia, six years before, his native State occupied the first place in his heart. In reply to a letter from Mr. Madison, dated Philadelphia, January 21, 1792, asking him if he would relinquish his office and accept command of an army to be organized for the protection of the western frontier, he writes: "Were I called upon by the President to command the next campaign, my respect for him would induce me to disregard every trifling obstruction which might oppose my acceptance of the office, such as my own repose, the care of my children and the happiness I enjoy in attention to their welfare, and in the execution of the duties of my present station. As a citizen, I should hold myself bound to obey the will of my country in taking any part her interests may demand from me. Therefore I am, upon this occasion, in favor of obedience to any claim which may be made on me. Yet I should require some essential stipulations — only to secure a favorable issue to the campaign." After speaking of how formidable the enemy was, he adds: "One objection I should only have (the above conditions being acceded to), and that is, the abandoning of my native county, to whose goodness I am so much indebted; no consideration on earth could induce me to act a part, however gratifying to me, which could be construed into disregard or faithlessness to this Commonwealth."

His great son therefore inherited this doctrine. It was branded into his brain and flowed through his veins; so that later when he had to meet the question of serving under the flag of the United States or of obeying the will of Virginia, he drew his sword in defense of his mother Commonwealth. When the war was declared with England in 1812, Henry Lee was living in Alexandria, having moved there to facilitate the education of his children; he was offered, and accepted at once, a major general's commission in the army. Before entering upon his duties he went to Baltimore on business, and while there visited the house of Mr. Hanson, the editor of the Federal Republican. "When he was about to leave he found the house surrounded by an angry mob, who were offended with the editor for his articles in opposition to the war; as his friend's life was threatened, he determined to assist him in resisting the attack of the mob. The results of that night proved nearly fatal to General Lee, and were disgraceful to party spirit." The injuries he received at the hands of the excited mob prevented him from entering upon the campaign, obliged him to go to the West Indies for his health, and ultimately caused his death. While abroad, amid the fatal march of his disease, his heart turned ever to his home and family. His letters to his son, Charles Carter Lee, have been preserved, and are literary models, the object being to impress religion, morality, and learning upon his children, as well as to manifest his great affection for those left behind. "Fame," he writes, "in arms or art, is naught unless betrothed to virtue." And then: "You know I love my children, and how dear Smith is to me. Give me a true description of his mind, temper, and habits. Tell me of Anne. Has she grown tall? And how is my last, in looks and understanding? Robert was always good, and will be confirmed in his happy turn of mind by his ever-watchful and affectionate mother; does he strengthen his native tendency?" He wanted to know, too, whether his sons rode and shot well, bearing in mind a Virginian's solicitude always that his sons should be taught to ride, shoot, and tell the truth.

In his opinion, Hannibal was a greater soldier than Alexander or Caesar; for he thought an ardent excitement of the mind in defending menaced rights brings forth the greatest display of genius, of which, forty-four years afterward, his great son was an illustrious example. On June 18, 1817, from Nassau, he writes: "This is the day of the month when your dear mother became my wife, and it is not so hot in this tropical region as it was then at Shirley. Since that happy day, marked only by the union of two humble lovers, it has become conspicuous as the day our war with Great Britain was declared in Washington, and the one that sealed the doom of Bonaparte on the field of Waterloo. The British general, rising gradatim from his first blow struck in Portugal, climbed on that day to the summit of fame, and became distinguished by the first of titles, 'Deliverer of the Civilized World.' Alexander, Hannibal, and Caesar, among the ancients; Marlborough, Eugene, Turenne, and Frederick, among the moderns, opened their arms to receive him as a brother in glory."

Again he tells him "that Thales, Pittacus, and others in Greece taught the doctrine of morality almost in our very words, 'Do unto others as you would they should do unto you,' and directs his son's attention to the fact that the beautiful Arab couplet, written three centuries before Christ, announced the duty of every good man, even in the moment of destruction, not only to forgive, but to benefit the destroyer, as the sandal tree, in the instant of its overthrow, sheds perfume on the axe that fells it." The principles sought to be inculcated in these admirable letters will be found running through their lives, lodged firmly in their characters, and their constant reappearance in the life of one of them is an evidence of the impression made.

At the expiration of nearly five years, finding that there was no hope of his ultimate recovery, he determined to return to his family and friends. In January, 1818, he took passage in a New England schooner bound from Nassau to New Providence and Boston. On nearing the coast of the United States he became so much worse that he requested the captain to direct his course to Cumberland Island, lying off the coast of Georgia. He knew that his former trusted friend, General Nathanael Greene, had an estate there, and that there resided his married daughter, Mrs. James Shaw. Next to dying within the limits of his native State he preferred to furl the flag of a celebrated career under the generous roof and kindly influence of the hospitable daughter of a beloved brother soldier. He was landed at "Dungeness," known as the most beautiful and attractive residence on the Georgia coast, and here he was lovingly received and tenderly cared for. From the window of his sick-room "an extensive view of the Atlantic Ocean, of Cumberland Sound, and the low-lying verdant shores of Georgia could be seen upon the one side, while upon the other lay attractive gardens and groves of oranges and olives, while grand live oaks swayed solemnly to and fro loaded with pendent moss."

General Henry Lee's sufferings, consequent upon the injuries received in Baltimore, were intense. Mrs. Shaw, General Greene's daughter, said that after his arrival at "Dungeness" they still continued, and that a surgical operation was proposed as offering some hope of prolonging his life; but he replied that an eminent physician, to whose skill and care during his sojourn in the West Indies he was much indebted, had disapproved a resort to the proposed operation. His surgeon in attendance still urging it, he put an end to the discussion by saying: "My dear sir, were the great Washington alive and here, joining you in advocating it, I would still resist." His agony at times was very great, causing irritation to overcome his rarely failing amiability. At times he would lose self-control and order his servants and every one else from the room. At length an old woman who had been Mrs. Greene's favorite maid, and who was then an esteemed and privileged family servant, was selected to wait upon him. The first thing General Lee did as she entered his room was to hurl his boot at her head and order her out. Entirely unused to such treatment, without saying a word she deliberately picked up the boot and threw it back. The effect produced was marked and instantaneous. The features of the stern warrior relaxed, in the midst of his pain and anger a smile passed over his countenance, and from that moment to the day of his death he would permit no one except "Mom Sarah" to do him special service. In the presence of the angel of death he recognized and rewarded pluck and spirit in an old negro nurse, even as he did courage in the breasts of his soldiers.

Not the least among the recollections of "Dungeness" is the fact that the last days of one of the great heroes of the Revolution were passed there; and when the "flowers of spring could no longer charm by their beauty and fragrance, or the soft southern wind bring health and surcease of pain to the suffering and dying, it received into its hospitable bosom and folded in one long and affectionate embrace all that was mortal of the gallant, gifted, and honored dead." Henry Lee and Nathanael Greene now sleep but a short distance apart, where the "recollections of their brave deeds and the grateful songs of the true lovers of liberty are caught up by the billows of a common ocean." Two months after the sick soldier landed he was dead. Every token of respect was shown by the United States Navy vessels in Cumberland Sound; their colors were put at half-mast, as well as the flags at the military headquarters of the army on Amelia Island. Citizens from the adjoining islands united in paying their respects. Commodore Henley, of the navy, superintended the last details. A full army band was in attendance, and Captains Elton, Finch, and Madison, and Lieutenants Fitzhugh and Ritchie, of the navy, and Mr. Lyman, of the army, acted as pall-bearers. Upon the stone marking his grave is this inscription: "Sacred to the Memory of General Henry Lee, of Virginia. Obiit March 25, 1818, Aetat. 63."

Not long before the war of 1861-65 the Legislature of Virginia passed resolutions for the appointment of a committee who, with the consent of his sons, should remove the remains to the capital city of Virginia, where a suitable monument would be erected to his memory. The commencement of hostilities prevented the accomplishment of this purpose. The sad duty had not been performed before by his sons, because one, Major Henry Lee, was abroad, one was an officer of the army, another of the navy, the fourth a lawyer, and their respective duties kept them widely apart, so that the matter, though frequently referred to in their correspondence, had never been fully arranged. The remains of "Light-horse Harry," therefore, still rest amid the magnolias, cedars, and myrtles of beautiful "Dungeness."

In many respects this officer was one of the most remarkable men of his day. He was a patriot and soldier, whose personal courage was tested in the fire of battle; an orator, a writer of vigorous and terse English, with a happy facility for expression rarely equaled. His book, called the Memoirs of the War of "76," is the standard work to-day of events in the war in the Southern Department of the United States. Two editions of it had been exhausted, and in 1869 a third was issued by his son, R. E. Lee, who, forgetful of his own great deeds, was desirous only of perpetuating those of his distinguished father.

General Henry Lee was twice married: first to Matilda, the daughter of Philip Ludwell Lee, of Stratford, and afterward to Anne Hill Carter, daughter of Charles Hill Carter, of Shirley. Four children were born from the first marriage. The eldest was named after his beloved commander, General Nathanael Greene, and died in infancy. The second son died when ten years old. The miniature of this child he always thereafter wore, and it is still preserved in the family. The third son, Henry, was born in 1787, and died in Paris, France, January 30, 1837. He graduated at William and Mary College, and served with credit in the War of 1812. He was appointed by General Jackson Consul to Algiers in 1829. In journeying through Italy he met the mother of the great Napoleon, and, being an admirer of his Italian campaigns, determined to write his life; the book is well written, as are other works of his.

The daughter married Bernard Carter, a brother of her stepmother. The children by General Henry Lee's second marriage were Algernon Sydney, Charles Carter, Sydney Smith, and Robert Edward, and two daughters, Anne and Mildred. The first boy lived only eighteen months. The second, named after his wife's father, was educated at Cambridge. "We have just heard," writes his father from San Domingo, June 26, 1816, "that you are fixed at the University of Cambridge, the seminary of my choice. You will there have not only excellent examples to encourage your love and practice of virtue, but ample scope to pursue learning to its foundation, thereby fitting yourself to be useful to your country." Charles Carter Lee afterward studied law, and was a most intellectual, learned, and entertaining man. His social qualities were of the highest order, his humor inimitable; his classic wit flowed, as clear as the mountain stream, from a well-stored mind. He was a boon companion and the first guest invited to the banquet; around him all clustered, and from his vicinity peals of laughter always resounded. His speeches, songs, and stories are marked traditions in the family to-day. Gifted with a most retentive memory, and being a great reader, especially of history, his recollection of all he had read made him a most instructive and agreeable companion. Every subject received its best treatment from his genius. He was thoroughly conversant with biblical literature, and had been known to maintain the leading part in discussions of the Bible with a roomful of ministers whose duty it was to expound it. In every drawing-room his presence was most warmly welcomed. At every festive board his song or speech was hailed with enthusiastic greeting. He was clever, generous, liberal, and free-hearted. When paying visits with his brothers — and the three often went together — should wine happen to be offered, Smith and Robert with their usual abstemiousness would decline; Carter, however, would accept, remarking: "I have always told these boys that I would drink their share of wine, provided they would keep me generously supplied." He wrote, too, with beauty and fluency of expression, and once said to his brother Robert:. "The Government employs you to do its fighting; it should engage me to write your reports. I admit your superiority in the exercise of the sword and in planning campaigns. I am, however, as you know, the better writer of the two, and can make my pen mightier than your sword after the battle is over. We could thus combine and be irresistible." He died, and was buried at his country seat, Windsor Forest, in Powhatan County. The third son, Sydney Smith, entered the United States Navy at an early age, and served with marked distinction in that service for thirty-four years. When Virginia withdrew from the Union of States he accepted service in the Southern navy.

A daughter of General R. E. Lee writes of him: "No one who ever saw him can forget his beautiful face, charming personality, and grace of manner, which, joined to a nobility of character and goodness of heart, attracted all who came in contact with him, and made him the most generally beloved and popular of men. This was especially so with regard to women, to whom his conduct was that of a preux chevalier, the most chivalric and courteous; and, having no daughters of his own, he turned with the tenderest affection to the daughters of his brother Robert. His public service of more than thirty years in the navy of the United States is well known. He entered it as a boy of fifteen, and faithfully served his country by land and sea in many climes and on many oceans. He was in Japan with Commodore Perry, commanding his flagship, when that inaccessible country was practically opened to the commerce of the world. He was Commandant of the Naval Academy at Annapolis, and afterward in command of the navy yard at Philadelphia. When the war of secession began he was stationed in Washington, but when Virginia seceded he did not hesitate to abandon the comforts and security of the present and ambitions of the future and cast his lot with his native State in a war which, from the very nature of things, there could be but little hope for a naval officer. Uninfluenced then by hope of either fame or fortune, he sadly parted with the friends and comrades of a lifetime, including General Scott, who had been likewise devoted to him as he was to his brother, and for four years served the Southern Confederacy with the same ardor and energy and unselfishness that he had previously given to the whole country. When the end came he accepted the situation with characteristic resignation and fortitude."

The eldest daughter married Mr. William Marshall, and lived in Baltimore. When the war cloud overshadowed the land, Judge Marshall was ardently devoted to the cause of the Union; their only son was educated at West Point, and remained in the army of the United States during the war which followed. It was natural, therefore, that the wife's sympathies in the pending struggle should be with husband and child. For many years she was a great invalid and rarely left her couch. Sick and tortured with conflicting emotions, her days were days of trial. It is said she would smilingly agree with her husband in the hope that the armies of the United States would gain victories over the troops of the South, and then into a thousand pieces dash all former arguments by shaking her head and saying: "But, after all, they can't whip Robert." It was the triumph of ties of consanguinity over all other bonds. Mildred, the youngest daughter, married Mr. Edward Vernon Childe, of Massachusetts, who removed to and lived in Paris, where she died, where her children were brought up and educated. The eldest son, Edward Lee Childe, possessing an excellent education, fine literary ability, and a love for the memory of his great uncle, wrote a life of him in French, which has been well received by the people of that country, and was translated into English, in 1875, by Mr. George Litting, of London.

CHAPTER 2

BIRTH. — CAREER AS OFFICER OF ENGINEERS, UNITED STATES ARMY.

Seventy-five years after the birth of Washington, Robert Edward, the fourth son of General Henry Lee and Anne Hill Carter, was born at Stratford, Westmoreland County, Virginia, on the 19th of January, 1807. If he inherited much from a long and illustrious line of paternal ancestors, he no less fell heir to the strong characteristics of his mother's family, one of the oldest and best in Virginia. The unselfishness, generosity, purity, and faithfulness of the Virginia Carters are widely known, and they have always been "true to all occasions true." In his mother was personified all the gentle and sweet traits of a noble woman. Her whole life was admirable, and her love for her children beyond all other thoughts. To her watchful care they were early confided by the long absence and death of her distinguished husband.

Robert was four years old when his father removed the family to Alexandria, six when he visited the West Indies for his health, and eleven when he died. If he was early trained in the way he should go, his mother trained him. If he was "always good," as his father wrote, she labored to keep him so. If his principles were sound and his life a success, to her, more than to any other, should the praise be given. This lovely woman, as stated, was the daughter of Charles Carter, of Shirley, who resided in his grand old mansion on the banks of the James River, some twenty miles below Richmond, then, as now, the seat of an open, profuse, and refined hospitality, and still in the possession of the Carters. Mrs. Henry Lee's mother was Anne Moore, and her grandmother a daughter of Alexander Spottswood, the soldier who fought with Marlborough at Blenheim, and was afterward sent to Virginia as governor in 1710, and whose descent can be traced in a direct line from King Robert the Bruce, of Scotland.

Robert Edward Lee could look back on long lines of paternal and maternal ancestors, but it is doubtful whether he ever exercised the privilege; in a letter to his wife, written in front of Petersburg, February, 1865, he says: "I have received your note. I am very much obliged to Mr. — for the trouble he has taken in relation to the Lee genealogy. I have no desire to have it published, and do not think it would afford sufficient interest beyond the immediate family to compensate for the expense. I think the money had better be applied to relieving the poor…"

He felt a natural pride in their achievements, but no one knew better than he that in a republic, and in a great war, a man's ancestry could not help him, but that place and promotion depended upon individual merit. His lineage has been traced because the descent of a celebrated man excites attention, just as it is interesting to discover the source of a noble river whose blessings to commerce cannot be measured. In consequence of the absence of the elder brothers, the ill health of one sister, and the youth of another, to Robert's care, in a measure, his mother was committed. After his father's departure to the tropics she watched over his daily life with tender solicitude, and he was, she said, both a daughter and a son to her. With filial devotion to her comfort his hours out of school were given. He waited on her, nursed her when sick, drove with her, obeyed her every wish, and this reciprocal love was a goodly picture in old Alexandria to those who saw mother and son in those days. As Robert grew in years he grew in grace; he was like the young tree whose roots, firmly imbedded in the earth, hold it straight from the hour it was first planted till it develops into majestic proportions. With the fostering care of such a mother the son must go straight, for she had planted him in the soil of truth, morality, and religion, so that his boyhood was marked by everything that produces nobility of character in manhood. The handsome boy was studious and sedate, was popular with other boys, stood high in the estimation of his teachers, and his early inspiration was good, for his first thoughts were directed upon lofty subjects by an excellent mother.

His birthplace and that of Washington were not only in the same county but only a short distance apart. The landscape of that section of Virginia was the first that greeted the eyes of each. The Potomac River, in all its grandeur and beauty, flowed past Stratford as well as Pope's Creek. Alexandria afterward became his town, as it had before been the town of Washington. The married life of the two was respectively passed at Mount Vernon and Arlington, the same river rolling at their feet, while the old town stood dignified and historic between the mansions proudly connecting the name and fame of their occupants.

Robert went first to the Alexandria Academy, being under the tuition of Mr. Leary, who was ever after his firm friend. Later he attended the famous school of Mr. Benjamin Hallowell, in Alexandria, whose house, still standing, is yet conducted as a popular school. Ben. Hallowell was a Quaker of the Quakers. His school stood high; so did he as a teacher. "Brimstone castle" the boys called it, on account of its color. Mr. Hallowell says that young Lee was an exemplary student, perfectly observant and respectful, and those who knew him, either in the charm of the domestic circle or amid the roar of battle, knew that good old Mr. Hallowell's opinion must have been correct.

The time had now arrived to select a profession, and to the army his inclination pointed — a direction which probably resulted from a son's desire to follow in his father's footsteps, especially when that father had been so distinguished in the profession. He was now a modest, manly youth, in his eighteenth year, who resolved to take care of himself and relieve his mother to that extent. His father's career had reflected credit upon his country; could he not hope to do the same? Sydney Smith Lee, his next oldest brother, had already entered the navy, and was supporting himself; so he decided to go in the army. The application for an appointment to the United States Military Academy was successful, and in 1825 his name was entered upon the rolls of that celebrated institution. He had now four years of hard study, vigorous drill, and was absorbing strategy and tactics to be useful to him in after-years. His excellent habits and close attention to all duties did not desert him; he received no demerits; was a cadet officer in his class, and during his last year held the post of honor in the aspirations of cadet life — the adjutancy of the corps. He graduated second in a class of forty-six, and was commissioned second lieutenant in the Corps of Engineers. It is interesting to notice that his eldest son, George Washington Custis Lee, also entered the Military Academy twenty-five years after his father, was also the cadet adjutant, graduated first in his class, and was assigned to the Engineer Corps. During his whole course at West Point Robert was a model cadet, his clothes looked nice and new, his crossbelts, collar, and summer trousers were as white as the driven snow mounting guard upon the mountain top, and his brass breast and waist plates were mirrors to reflect the image of the inspector. He conscientiously performed his tours of guard duty, whether the non-commissioned officer of the guard was approaching his post or sleeping in his quarters. He never "ran the sentinel post," did not go off the limits to the "Benny Havens" of his day, or put "dummies" in his bed, to deceive the officer in charge as he made his inspection after taps, and at the parades stood steady in line. It was a pleasure for the inspecting officer to look down the barrel of his gun, it was bright and clean, and its stock was rubbed so as to almost resemble polished mahogany.

Cadet Lee in 1829 became Lieutenant Lee of the Engineer Corps of the United States Army. The cadets who graduate in each class with first honors are assigned to it, and its ranks are kept full of first-class material; its members are composed of students who obey the regulations, are proficient in their studies, and receive few demerits. From this scientific corps distinguished men and great soldiers have issued, and to be an officer of the United States Engineer Corps is a passport everywhere.

A short time previous to the late war a number of officers of the different arms of service were assembled in one of the rooms at West Point. The conversation turned, as it often did, upon the relative merits of the different arms of services, each officer contending for his own branch; finally an officer of infantry, who afterward became a distinguished major general in the army of the United States, said: "You gentlemen who graduate at the head of your respective classes are of opinion that you are the most talented, and possibly will make the best soldiers and most intelligent officers of the army; you will find, however, that should war actually take place between the Northern and Southern States, and you get in a tight place on the field of battle, you cannot work yourself out with equations." All of which is very true. A courier has been known to tell his superior officer how to extricate his troops in a perilous position under fire, because he had more military perception, though less education and engineering skill.

Great soldiers, like poets, are born, not made. Military training, discipline, the study of strategy, and grand tactics are powerful re-enforcements to natural genius. All the army commanders from 1861 to 1865, on either side, were West Point graduates; but many West Pointers were indifferent officers; on the other hand, others climbed high on Fame's military ladder who never attended a military school. Generals Logan and Terry on the Northern, and Generals Forrest and Gordon on the Southern side, were distinguished examples; but if to their soldierly qualifications a military education had been added, their ascent to distinction would have been greatly facilitated.

Lieutenant Lee entered upon the usual life of a young officer of engineers; his chosen profession had his earnest attention, and every effort was made to acquire information. He knew his studies at West Point were only the foundation upon which to build the life edifice. Without continued application to the principles of engineering and study he could not hope to rise above the ordinary level of the military graduate. So his army career began with the fixed determination to put aside daily pleasures of life where they conflicted with daily hours of duty. Officers in this branch of the service had pleasant stations, necessarily near or in the cities. Fortifications for the defense of harbors, forts for the protection of seaports, streams whose currents made bars at wrong places, and other similar works must receive the attention of the engineer. His location was therefore near the centers of civilization. Cavalry and infantry graduates of West Point were ordered to posts where the sun goes down behind the western hills; guarding long lines of frontier, scouting, and fighting hostile tribes of Indians were their particular duties. The temptations incident to city life did not lie so much in their course as in the path of the engineer. The pleasures and fascinations of social life everywhere surrounded him. As soon as he unbuckled sword belt there was but a step to take to get into the gay world. It is not to be wondered at, therefore, that sometimes the engineer drank wine when it was red, and did not seek his quarters till the sun had gilded with its first glance the spires of the neighboring church. The artillery officer enjoyed with his comrades his mess table; the infantry officer occasionally had moistened lips from a canteen of frontier fire water; while the "bold dragoon who scorned all care" rode far and sometimes drank deep.

Lee was naturally exposed to an engineer's temptations, but was careful and abstemious. He went much in the society of ladies — always most congenial to him. His conversation was bright, his wit refined and pleasant. Cement, mortar, lime, curves, tangents, and straight professional lines disappeared then. He enjoyed a dress parade of this kind, was happy in the drawing-room in the evening, and happy in his work on the parapet next day. He was in love from boyhood. Fate brought him to the feet of one who, by birth, education, position, and family tradition, was best suited to be his life companion. Mary Custis, the daughter of George Washington Parke Custis, of Arlington, and Robert E. Lee, were married on the 30th of June, 1831, only two years after he had emerged from his Alma Mater. They had known each other when she was a child at Arlington and he a young boy in Alexandria, some eight miles away. It is said she met him to admire when he came back to Alexandria on furlough from the Military Academy. It was the first time any one in that vicinity had ever seen him in his cadet uniform. He was handsomer than ever; straight, erect, symmetrical in form, with a finely shaped head on a pair of broad shoulders. He was then twenty years old and a fine specimen of a West Point cadet on leave of absence. The impressions produced were of an enduring nature, and the officer, upon graduation, followed up the advantage gained by the attractive cadet.

G. W. P. Custis was the adopted son of Washington and the grandson of Mrs. Washington. Lee was therefore to marry a great granddaughter of Mrs. Washington, and was a fortunate man, not so much, perhaps, from these ties, but because of the great qualities of head and heart possessed by Mary Custis, his affianced bride. It is difficult to say whether she was more lovely on that memorable June evening when the Rev. Mr. Keith asked her, "Wilt thou have this man to be thy wedded husband?" or after many years had passed, and she was seated in her large armchair in Richmond, almost unable to move from chronic rheumatism, but busily engaged in knitting socks for sockless Southern soldiers. The public notice of the marriage was short:

Married, June 30, 1831, at Arlington House, by the Rev. Mr. Keith, Lieutenant Robert E. Lee, of the United States Corps of Engineers, to Miss Mary A. R. Custis, only daughter of G. W. P. Custis, Esq.

The modesty of the newly married couple was spared the modern newspaper notice of what the bride wore at her wedding and what she had packed in her trunks, and her presents and trousseau are in happy oblivion. Beautiful old Arlington was in all her glory that night. The stately mansion never held a happier assemblage. "Its broad portico and widespread wings held out open arms, as it were, to welcome the coming guest. Its simple Doric columns graced domestic comfort with a classic air. Its halls and chambers were adorned with the patriots and heroes and with illustrations and relics of the great Revolution and of the 'Father of his Country,' and without and within, history and tradition seemed to breathe their legends upon a canvas as soft as a dream of peace."

At the expiration of the usual leave of absence granted officers who marry, Lieutenant Lee returned to his duties as assistant engineer at Hampton Roads. For four years he labored to make the harbor defensible, and to construct there strong works, little dreaming that it would be his fate to study how to demolish them twenty-seven years afterward. While stationed there the negro insurrection in Southampton took place, and the young lieutenant writes to his mother-in-law about it, telling her that it is at an end, and adding that the troops returned to Fort Monroe last night "from Jerusalem, where they did not arrive until the whole affair was concluded. Colonel Worth says that, from all he can learn, he is satisfied the plot was widely extended, and that the negroes, anticipating the time of rising by one week, mistaking the third Sunday for the last in the month, defeated the whole scheme and prevented much mischief. It is ascertained that they used their religious assemblies, which ought to have been devoted to better purposes, for forming and maturing their plans, and that their preachers were the leading men. A man belonging to a Mrs. Whitehead, and one of their preachers, was the chief, under the title of Major Nelson, and his first act was to kill his mistress, five children, and one grandchild. However, there are many instances of their defending their masters, and one poor fellow, from the inconsiderate and almost unwarrantable haste of the whites, was sadly rewarded. He belonged to a Mr. Blunt, and himself and two others, assisted by his master and his son, nobly fought with them against twenty of the blacks; after beating them off and running in great haste after horses for them to escape on, a party of whites suddenly came up and, thinking the horses were for other purposes, shot him dead. The whole number of blacks taken and killed did not amount to the number of whites murdered by them."

From that point he was ordered to Washington and made assistant to the chief engineer, an agreeable change, for it brought him near the home of his wife. A fine horse carried him every morning from Arlington to his Washington office and back every evening. He loved his chosen profession, and was rising rapidly in it. Now he could combine equestrianism with engineering, and he was happy, and must have been sometimes merry, for his late lamented military secretary, General Long, narrates an incident of his inviting Captain Macomb, a brother officer, to get behind him on horseback one evening on his return to Arlington. Macomb accepted the invitation, and the two gayly rode along the great public avenue in Washington, passing by the President's house, bowing to Cabinet officers, and behaving in rather a hilarious way generally. It is difficult for a soldier of the Army of Northern Virginia to picture his commanding general in a scene such as has been described.

Five years after leaving his Alma Mater he was promoted from second to first lieutenant of engineers, and in two years more reached a captaincy. In 1835 he was made assistant astronomer of the commission appointed to lay the boundary line between Ohio and Michigan. Two years afterward he bade adieu to Arlington to obey an order to proceed to St. Louis to make estimates, prepare plans, and devise means to prevent the "Great father of Waters" from leaving his legitimate channel and overrunning property upon which he had no claims, for the Mississippi had threatened to leave the St. Louis side and become a flowing citizen of Illinois. In the performance of this duty he came prominently into notice again; he was so active, so indefatigable, and worked so intelligently and successfully, that the system of river improvements first introduced there is to this day followed. Some of the citizens of that section did not understand his methods, and threatened to drive him and his working parties away, and at one time actually brought cannon to accomplish their purpose. They did not comprehend the labors of this quiet, methodical engineer, or understand the reason why piles were driven and cofferdams made at acute angles to the shore; nor did they understand that the flow of the waters being retarded in these angles, sediment was deposited, land made, and the river, in consequence, forced back and confined to its channels on the St. Louis side.

While thus professionally engaged it occurred to him that he would like to possess a seal with the family's Coat of Arms, and he writes to an Alexandria cousin about it:

St. Louis, August 20, 1838.

My Dear Cassius and Cousin: I believe I once spoke to you on the subject of getting for me the Crest, Coat of Arms, etc., of the Lee family, and which, sure enough, you never did. My object in making the request is for the purpose of having a seal cut with the impression of said Coat, which I think is due from a man of my large family to his posterity, and which I have thought, perhaps foolishly enough, might as well be right as wrong. If, therefore, you can assist me in this laudable enterprise I shall be much obliged, and by enveloping it securely, directed to me at this place, and sending it either by mail or some safe hand to the Engineer Office, Washington City, without any word or further direction, it will come safely to hand. I once saw in the hands of Cousin Edmund, for the only time in my life, our family tree, and as I begin in my old age to feel a little curiosity relative to my forefathers, their origin, whereabouts, etc., any information you can give me will increase the obligation.

So sit down one of these hot evenings and write it off for me, or at any rate the substance, and tell my Cousin Phillippa not to let you forget it. I wish you would at the same time undeceive her on a certain point, for, as I understand, she is laboring under a grievous error.

Tell her that it is the farthest from my wish to detract from any of the little Lees, but as to her little boy being equal to Mr. Rooney, it is a thing not even to be supposed, much less believed, although we live in a credulous country, where people stick at nothing from a coon story to a sea serpent. You must remember us particularly to her, to Uncle Edmund, Cousins Sally, Hannah, and all the Lloyds.

I believe I can tell you nothing here that would interest you, except that we are all well, although my dame has been a little complaining for a day or two. The elections are all over, the "Vanites" have carried the day in the State, although the Whigs in this district carried their entire ticket, and you will have the pleasure of hearing the great expunger again thunder from his place in the Senate against banks, bribery, and corruption. While on the river I cannot help being on the lookout for that stream of gold that was to ascend the Mississippi, tied up in silk-net purses! It would be a pretty sight, but the tide has not yet made up here. Let me know whether you can enlighten me on the point in question. And believe me,

Yours very truly, R. E. Lee. C. F. Lee, Esq., Alexandria, Virginia.

And to Mrs. Lee he writes:

St. Louis, September 4, 1840.

A few evenings since, feeling lonesome, as the saying is, and out of sorts, I got on a horse and took a ride. On returning through the lower part of the town, I saw a number of little girls all dressed up in their white frocks and pantalets, their hair plaited and tied up with ribbons, running and chasing each other in all directions. I counted twenty-three nearly the same size. As I drew up my horse to admire the spectacle a man appeared at the door with the twenty-fourth in his arms. "My friend," said I, "are all these your children?" "Yes," he said, "and there are nine more in the house, and this is the youngest." Upon further inquiry, however, I found that they were only temporarily his, and that they were invited to a party at his house. He said, however, he had been admiring them before I came up, and just wished that he had a million of dollars and that they were all his in reality. I do not think the eldest exceeded seven or eight years old. It was the prettiest sight I have seen in the West, and perhaps in my life…

On the completion of his great services here he was sent to New York and stationed at Fort Hamilton to perfect the defenses of the splendid harbor of that great city. A letter to his wife from that point gives a glimpse of the humor which constantly found vent in his private life. He writes:

Fort Hamilton, New York, January 14, 1846.

This week I have been closely occupied here. I have kept "Jim" and "Miss Leary" (his servants) constantly moving, cleaning up, and fear I will wear them down. I do not know whether it was your departure or my somber phiz which brought Miss Leary out Sunday in a full suit of mourning. A black alpaca trimmed with crape and a thick row of jet buttons on each sleeve, from the shoulder to the wrist, and three rows on the skirt, diverging from the waist to the hem; it was, however, surmounted by a dashing cap with gay ribbons.

He was now a captain of engineers, and his mettle was soon to be tried in the fiery furnace of war, for his country and the Republic of Mexico were daily growing more angry with each other. Mexico, from 1519, when Hernando Cortez marched through the causeway leading into its Capital City to the present period, has been an object of much interest to other countries. Commencing with the Indian Emperor Montezuma's costly presents to Cortez, the land has been associated with inexhaustible supplies of gold and silver. The Spanish commander, from his quarters near the temple of the Aztec god of war, dreamed of infinite wealth for himself, his soldiers, and his country.

A fascinating interest in Mexico has always kept pace with the progress and growth of the contiguous American Republic. Upon the final overthrow of the Mexicans by the Spaniards, the adjoining sections were settled by the latter, and a permanent location was made in Texas, at San Antonio de Bexar, in 1692. France, in selling to the United States Louisiana, claimed the boundary line to be the River Rio Grande del Norte, and assigned this boundary claim to the United States. It was, however, relinquished by the American Republic to Spain, in a treaty made with that country in 1812. When Mexico, in 1820, threw off the Spanish yoke, she obtained at the same time the domain of Texas. Afterward Stephen F. Austin obtained from the Mexican Government large tracts of land in Texas and established colonies on them. Citizens of the United States were naturally attracted there, and as they grew in numbers wanted a government similar in form to the one they had left. Stephen Austin was sent to Santa Anna, then Emperor of Mexico, with petitions praying for a separate state organization, and to be no longer united with Cohahuila, the neighboring Mexican province. Austin's petition, it seems, was more than Santa Anna could stand, and he threw him into prison and kept him there over a year. The American Texans, some ten thousand in number, were indignant, and determined to resist the Mexican Emperor's authority. A war ensued, and the redoubtable Santa Anna was finally overthrown and captured at the battle of San Jacinto, April 21, 1836. Texas was later an applicant for membership to the union of American States. Her independence had been acknowledged by Great Britain, the United States, and other Powers; but Bustamente, who succeeded Santa Anna, repealed the treaty Mexico had with Texas and declared war. In the United States opinion was divided between annexation and war. President Van Buren, a citizen of New York, would not entertain annexation, while a successor — John Tyler, of Virginia — favored it. A treaty made to carry out the provisions of annexation was rejected by the Senate. In 1844 it became a party question, and by the election of James K. Polk, of Tennessee, who was in favor of it, over Henry Clay, of Kentucky, whose adherents were opposed to it, the people of the United States practically decided in favor of annexation. It was then natural and proper that the United States Government should look closely after the interests of her new possessions, and to General Zachary Taylor they were confided. A Virginian by birth, he was appointed a lieutenant in the Seventh Infantry, United States Army, in 1808, being one of the new regiments authorized by Congress, upon the recommendation of President Thomas Jefferson. He became conspicuous in the Indian contests, and was especially famous after winning the battle of Okeechobee in the Seminole War. Promoted to be a brigadier general in 1837, three years thereafter he was assigned to the command of the Southern Division of the Western Department. He was in place, therefore, to defend Texas against the Mexicans, to insist on the Rio Grande boundary line, and to prevent Mexican authority from being extended to the River Nueces, which was claimed as the proper line. He was the right man in the right place, and when Arista, the Mexican general, crossed the Rio Grande with six thousand men, near Fort Brown, Taylor, being in the vicinity, promptly attacked with two thousand men and defeated him, assumed the offensive, crossed the Rio Grande, and war with Mexico became an accomplished fact. Palo Alto, Resaca de la Palma, Matamoras, Monterey, and Buena Vista are the stars in the military crown on the brow of "Old rough and ready," as he was called. Calm, silent. stern, possessed of military genius, this soldier at once became a favorite with the American people, and for his services was afterward elected to be the twelfth President of the United States. When Mexico's capital was decided to be the objective point of the campaign, Taylor's base of operations was too distant and his line of communication too long. It was thought advisable to select as the base of future operations Vera Cruz. General Winfield Scott, then commander in chief of the United States Army, was assigned to the command of the army to be concentrated for its reduction. The new army commander, Scott, was born near Petersburg, Va., in June, 1786, and was sixty-one years old when he began the siege of Vera Cruz on the 19th of March, 1847. He was an alumnus of William and Mary College, Williamsburg, Va., and a lawyer for two years before he was appointed to a lieutenancy in the artillery of the United States Army. His services in the war of 1812, and especially in the battles of Chippewa and Lundy's Lane, had made him famous. With a grand physique and imposing presence in full uniform, he was a splendid specimen of the American soldier. Being in command of the whole army, and in active charge of the army of invasion, his requests for the best officers, as well as ordnance, quartermasters' and commissaries' supplies, were promptly acceded to. A war with a foreign country was highly exciting and new to most of the army and navy officers, so that applications for service in Mexico rapidly rained upon the War Department, and the Secretary of War had no difficulty in sending to Mexico the most capable officers.

Engineers are as necessary to an army as sails are to a ship; they locate lines of battle, select positions for the artillery, make reconnoissances, and upon their reports the movements of the army are based. They draw topographical maps, construct roads and bridges, and guide troops in battle to positions they had previously reconnoitred. Scott soon drew to him from this branch of the service Totten, J. L. Smith, R. E. Lee, Beauregard, McClellan, Foster, Tower, Stevens, G. W. Smith, and others, and at once placed Captain Lee on his personal staff. This officer, when Scott was assembling the army at Tampico, for the purpose of investing and capturing Vera Cruz, was with General Wool, who had been assigned the duty of invading Mexico from the north, while Taylor advanced from Matamoras, and General Kearny from New Mexico.

In a letter to Mrs. Lee, dated Rio Grande, October 11, 1846, Captain Lee says: "We have met with no resistance yet. The Mexicans who were guarding the passage retired on our approach. There has been a great whetting of knives, grinding of swords, and sharpening of bayonets ever since we reached the river."

It seems on the eve of active operations Captain Lee's thoughts were ever returning to his family and home. In a letter to his two eldest sons (one thirteen and the other nine years of age), written from Camp near Saltillo, December 24, 1846, he says: "I hope good Santa Claus will fill my Rob's stocking to-night; that Mildred's, Agnes's, and Anna's may break down with good things. I do not know what he may have for you and Mary (his daughter), but if he only leaves for you one half of what I wish, you will want for nothing. I have frequently thought if I had one of you on each side of me riding on ponies, such as I could get you, I would be comparatively happy."

The little fellows had been writing to their father asking about his horses and the ponies in Mexico, etc. In reply he tells them "the Mexicans raise a large quantity of ponies, donkeys, and mules, and most of their corn, etc., is carried on the backs of these animals. These little donkeys will carry two hundred pounds on their backs, and the mules will carry three hundred on long journeys over the mountains. The ponies are used for riding and cost from ten to fifty dollars, according to their size and quality. I have three horses. Creole is my pet; she is a golden dun, active as a deer, and carries me over all the ditches and gullies that I have met with; nor has she ever yet hesitated at anything I have put her at; she is full-blooded and considered the prettiest thing in the army; though young, she has so far stood the campaign as well as any horses of the division." He then tells them about his other two — a dark bay, deep-chested, sturdy, and strong, that his servant Jim rides, and says that Jim has named him after himself; he goes on to say that he has ridden them all very hard, sometimes fifty or sixty miles a day.

He was still at Saltillo the next day: it was Christmas, and he had arranged a campaign in his own heart, which would result in his taking advantage of the holiday to write a letter to his wife. He tells Mrs. Lee that he had put aside that Christmas day to write to her, but just after breakfast orders were received to prepare for battle, intelligence having reached General Wool that the Mexican army was coming. "The troops stood to their arms and I lay on the grass with my sorrel mare saddled by my side and telescope directed to the pass of the mountain through which the road approached. The Mexicans, however, did not make their appearance. Many regrets were expressed at Santa Anna's having spoiled our Christmas dinner for which ample preparation had been made. The little roasters remained tied to the tent pins wondering at their deferred fate, and the headless turkeys retained their plumage unscathed. Finding the enemy did not come, preparations were again made for dinner. We have had many happy Christmases together. It is the first time we have been entirely separated at this holy time since our marriage. I hope it does not interfere with your happiness, surrounded as you are by father, mother, children, and dear friends. I therefore trust you are well and happy, and that this is the last time I shall be absent from you during my life. May God preserve and bless you till then and forever after is my constant prayer."

The American commander promptly availed himself of the talents of the engineer and summoned Lee to his side, and in the memorable campaign which followed, Lee was his military adviser and possessed his entire confidence. The high estimation and cordial friendship which the army commander ever thereafter displayed for his subordinate was born at Vera Cruz.

The city of Vera Cruz was surrounded by a wall and strengthened by forts, the castle of San Juan de Ulloa, its fortress, was defended by four hundred guns and five thousand men under General Morales. The soldierly genius of Scott at once told him there were but two ways to capture the city — either by storming or by the scientific principles of regular siege approaches. In his "Little Cabinet," as he called it (it appears he was even then thinking of a future presidency) — consisting of Colonel Totten, Chief Engineer; Lieutenant-Colonel Hitchcock, Acting Inspector General; Captain R. E. Lee, Engineer; First-Lieutenant Henry L. Scott, Acting Adjutant General — these questions were taken up. A deathbed discussion could hardly have been more solemn, the army commander tells us. To his Cabinet he said: "We, of course, gentlemen, must take the city and castle before the return of the vomito, and then escape by pushing the contest into the healthy interior." He was "strongly inclined to attempt to capture the place by laying siege to it, not by storming it." The first method, in his opinion, "could be accomplished with moderate loss on his side. The second method would, no doubt," said Scott, "be equally successful, but at the cost of immense slaughter on both sides, including non-combatants, Mexicans, and children, because the assault would have to be made in the dark, and the assailants dare not lose time in taking or guarding prisoners without incurring the certainty of becoming captives themselves, until all the strongholds of the place had been captured." The council determined upon a siege. In two weeks the army and navy were ready to open fire, and one week's bombardment resulted in the capitulation of Vera Cruz, and the adjacent forts on the 29th of March, 1847. In the preparatory two weeks Lee spent nights and days in incessant labor, and his enterprise, endurance, energy, and intelligent arrangement of all the necessary details of the siege were most conspicuous, and to him has been ascribed much credit for the victory.

At Vera Cruz Captain Lee met his brother, Lieutenant Sydney Smith Lee, of the United States Navy, and the soldier and sailor fought together. In a letter written from Vera Cruz at the time, after describing a battery which had been placed in position by him, Captain Lee adds: "The first day this battery opened, Smith served one of the guns. I had constructed the battery, and was there to direct its fire. No matter where I turned, my eyes reverted to him, and I stood by his gun whenever I was not wanted elsewhere. Oh! I felt awfully, and am at a loss what I should have done had he been cut down before me. I thank God that he was saved. He preserved his usual cheerfulness, and I could see his white teeth through all the smoke and din of the fire. I had placed three 32- and three 68-pound guns in position... Their fire was terrific, and the shells thrown from our battery were constant and regular discharges, so beautiful in their flight and so destructive in their fall. It was awful! My heart bled for the inhabitants. The soldiers I did not care so much for, but it was terrible to think of the women and children… I heard from Smith to-day; he is quite well, and recovered from his fatigue."

And to his naval brother he writes on March 27, 1847, when it seems he wanted some liquors, in all probability for his guests, as his own abstemiousness was well known:

My dear Smith:

I tried to see you the night you went on board, but failed. I was too thankful you were saved through that hot fire. I felt awful at the thought of your being shot down before me. I can't get time to see you, nor have I time to attend to anything for myself. There is a French bark anchored by your fleet, and detained at Anton Lizardo — or was — from Bordeaux. She has some wines, etc. Can you, through any of your comrades, get me a box or two of claret, one of brandy, and four colored shirts. The latter are seventy-five cents each (I have two of them), and the brandy thirty-seven and a half cents per bottle. God bless and preserve you. Your battery (naval) has smashed that side of the town. I have been around the walls to examine. The Quartet Battery has been silenced. I grieve for the fine fellows that were killed there.

Very affectionately your brother, R. E. Lee.

P. S. Can you buy me a good telescope from the fleet? I have lost mine and am woefully at a loss.

Before leaving for the interior with the army, Captain Lee sought his brother to say good-by. In one of his letters he writes: "Went on board the Mississippi, and passed the night with Smith. I had scarcely been able to see him before, and wished, ere commencing work, to have one night with him. He was very well, but what a place is a ship to enjoy the company of one's brother!"

When Scott set out, on the 12th of April, from Vera Cruz, to join his advanced divisions under Patterson and Twiggs, in front of the heights of Cerro Gordo, Lee accompanied him. It was the reconnoissance of this officer at the head of the pioneers which found a possible route for the troops and their light batteries, by which the Mexican left could be turned. Santa Anna, who commanded the Mexican army, said he did not believe a goat could have come from that direction. In his final report Scott thus speaks: "The reconnoissance, begun by Lieutenant Beauregard, was continued by Captain Lee, of the engineers, and a road made along one of the slopes over chasms — out of the enemy's view though reached by his fire — was discovered, till, arriving at the Mexican lines, further reconnoissance became impossible without an action. I am compelled to make special mention of Captain R. E. Lee, Engineer. This officer greatly distinguished himself at the siege of Vera Cruz; was indefatigable during these operations in reconnoissances, as daring as laborious, and of the utmost value. Nor was he less conspicuous in planning batteries and in conducting columns from stations under the heavy fire of the enemy." General Lee thus describes the battle of Cerro Gordo:

Perote, April 25, 1847.

The advance of the American troops, under Generals Patterson and Twiggs, were encamped at the Plano del Rio, and three miles to their front Santa Anna and his army were intrenched in the pass of Cerro Gordo, which was remarkably strong. The right of the Mexican line rested on the river at a perpendicular rock, unscalable by man or beast, and their left on impassable ravines; the main road was defended by field works containing thirty-five cannon; in their rear was the mountain of Cerro Gordo, surrounded by intrenchments in which were cannon and crowned by a tower overlooking all — it was around this army that it was intended to lead our troops. I reconnoitered the ground in the direction of the ravines on their left, and passed around the enemy's rear. On the 16th a party was set to work in cutting out the road, on the 17th I led General Twiggs's division in the rear of a hill in front of Cerro Gordo, and in the afternoon, when it became necessary to drive them from the hill where we intended to construct a battery at night, the first intimation of our presence or intentions were known. During all that night we were at work in constructing the battery, getting up the guns, ammunition, etc., and they in strengthening their defenses on Cerro Gordo. Soon after sunrise our batteries opened, and I started with a column to turn their left and to get on the Jalapa road. Notwithstanding their efforts to prevent us in this, we were perfectly successful, and the working party, following our footsteps, cut out the road for the artillery. In the meantime our storming party had reached the crest of Cerro Gordo, and, seeing their whole left turned and the position of our soldiers on the Jalapa road, they broke and fled. Those in the pass laid down their arms. General Pillow's attack on their right failed. All their cannon, arms, ammunition, and most of their men fell into our hands. The papers cannot tell you what a horrible sight a field of battle is, nor will I, owing to my accompanying General Twiggs's division in the pursuit, and being since constantly in the advance. I believe all our friends are safe. I think I wrote you that my friend Joe Johnston was wounded the day before I arrived at the Plano del Rio while reconnoitering. He was wounded in the arm and about the groin; both balls are out, and he was doing well and was quite comfortable when I left; the latter wound was alone troublesome. Captain Mason, of the rifles, was badly wounded in the leg, and General Shields was wounded in the chest; I have heard contradictory reports that he was doing well and that he was dead. I hope the former. Jalapa is the most beautiful country I have seen in Mexico, and will compare with any I have seen elsewhere. I wish it was in the United States, and that I was located with you and the children around me in one of its rich, bright valleys. I can conceive nothing more beautiful in the way of landscape or mountain scenery. We ascended upward of four thousand feet that morning, and whenever we looked back the rich valley below was glittering in the morning sun and the light morning clouds flitting around us. On reaching the top, the valley appeared at intervals between the clouds which were below us, and high over all towered Orizaba, with its silver cap of snow. The castle or fort of Perote is one of the best finished that I have ever seen — very strong, with high, thick walls, bastioned fronts, and deep, wide ditch. It is defective in construction and is very spacious, covers twenty-five acres, and although there is within its walls nearly three thousand troops, it is not yet full. Within the fort is a beautiful chapel, in one corner of which is the tomb of Guadalupe Victoria. There are various skulls, images, etc., in the sanctuaries. This morning I attended the Episcopal service within the fort. It was held on the parade. The minister was a Mr. McCarty, the chaplain of the Second Brigade, First Division. Many officers and soldiers were grouped around. I endeavored to give thanks to our heavenly Father for all his mercies to me, for his preservation of me through all the dangers I have passed, and all the blessings which he has bestowed upon me, for I know I fall far short of my obligations. We move out to-morrow toward Pueblo. The First Brigade — Duncan's battery, light infantry and cavalry form the advance. I accompany the advance. General Worth will remain a day or two with the remainder of his division till the Second Division, under General Twiggs, shall arrive. General Scott is still at Jalapa, Major Smith with him. I have with me Lieutenants Mason, Tower, and the Engineer Company. In advance, all is uncertain and the accounts contradictory. We must trust to an overruling Providence, by whom we will be governed for the best, and to our own resources.

And in another letter to his eldest son, dated same day and place, he writes: "I thought of you, my dear Custis, on the 18th in the battle, and wondered, when the musket balls and grape were whistling over my head in a perfect shower, where I could put you if with me to be safe. I was truly thankful that you were at school, I hope learning to be good and wise. You have no idea what a horrible sight a battlefield is." The writer then describes to him the battle of Cerro Gordo, and tells him about the dead and dying Mexicans; how he had them carried to a house by the roadside, where they were attended by Mexican surgeons; of his finding by the side of a hut a little Mexican boy who had been a bugler or drummer, with his arm terribly shattered, and how a large Mexican soldier, in the last agonies of death, had fallen on him; how he was attracted to the scene by the grief of a little girl; how he had the dying Mexican taken off the boy, and how grateful the little girl was. "Her large black eyes," he said, "were streaming with tears, her hands crossed over her breast; her hair in one long plait behind reached her waist, her shoulders and arms bare, and without stockings or shoes. Her plaintive tone of 'Mille gracias, Signor,' as I had the dying man lifted off the boy and both carried to the hospital, still lingers in my ear. After I had broken a way through the chaparral and turned toward Cerro Gordo I mounted Creole, who stepped over the dead men with such care as if she feared to hurt them, but when I started with the dragoons in the pursuit, she was as fierce as possible, and I could hardly hold her."

From Cerro Gordo to the capital of Mexico, Captain Lee at every point increased the reputation he was acquiring. At Contreras, Churubusco, Molino del Rey, and Chapultepec he was constantly in the saddle, performing with alacrity and courage the duties of a trusted staff officer. "Before the battle of Contreras," wrote one of the most distinguished soldiers of that war, "General Scott's troops had become separated in the field of Pedrigal, and it was necessary to communicate instruction to those on the other side of this barrier of rocks and lava. General Scott says in his report that he had sent seven officers since about sundown to communicate instructions; they had all returned without getting through, but the gallant and indefatigable Captain Lee, of the engineers, who has been constantly with the operating forces, is just in from Shields, Smith, Cadwalader, etc…"

Subsequently Scott, while giving testimony before a court of inquiry, said: "Captain Lee, of the engineers, came to me from Contreras with a message from Brigadier-General Smith. I think about the same time (midnight) he, having passed over the difficult ground by daylight, found it just possible to return on foot and alone to St. Augustine in the dark, the greatest feat of physical and moral courage performed by any individual to my knowledge, pending the campaign."

His deeds of personal daring, his scientific counsels, his coup d'oeil of the battlefield, his close personal reconnoissances under the scorching rays of a tropical sun, amid the lightning's flash or thunder's roar, did much to mold the key which unlocked the gates of the Golden City. The reports of his commander are filled with commendations of his bravery: "That he was as famous for felicitous execution as for science and daring"; that at "Chapultepec Captain Lee was constantly conspicuous, bearing important orders" from him, "till he fainted from a wound and the loss of two nights' sleep at the batteries." This veteran general, in referring afterward to this campaign, was heard to say that his "success in Mexico was largely due to the skill, valor, and undaunted courage of Robert E. Lee," and that he was "the greatest military genius in America, the best soldier that he ever saw in the field, and that if opportunity offered, he would show himself the foremost captain of his time."

It is certain that Captain Lee came from this Mexican campaign crowned with honors and covered with brevets for gallant and meritorious conduct. In a brief six months campaign he had demonstrated in a wonderful manner his qualities as a soldier. He was then forty years old. Brevet major, brevet lieutenant colonel, and brevet colonel followed each other in rapid succession. An examination of his career in Mexico will show that the flanks of the hostile army were his favorite points of reconnoissance. If they could be successfully turned, victory would save human life; a reference to his campaigns, when he afterward became an army commander, will show that the flanks of his enemy were still objects of his greatest attention.

The Mexican campaign was finished, and the Peace Treaty occupied the front rank of importance. In a letter to his wife, dated City of Mexico, February 8, 1848, Captain Lee says: "You will doubtless hear many speculations about peace. The boundary is said to be the Rio Grande, giving us Texas, New Mexico, California, for which we pay twenty million dollars — five millions to be reserved for liquidation of claims of her citizens. These are certainly not hard terms for Mexico, considering how the fortune of war has been against her. For myself, I would not exact now more than I would have taken before the commencement of hostilities, as I should wish nothing but what was just, and that I would have sooner or later. I can readily see that the terms said to be offered on the part of Mexico may not prove satisfactory to a large part of our country, who would think it right to exact everything that power and might could require. Some would sacrifice everything under the hope that the proposition of Messrs. Clay, Calhoun, etc., would be acted upon, and save what they term the national honor. Believing that peace would be for the advantage of both countries, I hope that some terms, just to one and not dishonorable to the other, may be agreed on, and that speedily."

And again, five days later: "If any early session of the Mexican Congress can be obtained, I have still hopes that the treaty will be ratified, though I think the speeches and resolutions of some of our leading men, and probably by this time some action of Congress, may so confuse the Mexican mind in reference to her future course as to encourage the recusant members to absent themselves so as to defeat it. I think it is late on our part to stop now to demonstrate who are the first aggressors. It is certain we are the conquerors in a regular war, and by the laws of nations are entitled to dictate the terms of peace. We have fought well and fought fairly. We hold and can continue to hold their country, and have a right to exact compensation for the expenses of a war continued, if not provoked, by ignorance and vanity on the part of Mexico. It is true we bullied her. For that I am ashamed, for she was the weaker party, but we have since, by way of set-off, drubbed her handsomely and in a manner no man might be ashamed of. They begin to be aware how entirely they are beaten, and are willing to acknowledge it. The treaty gives us all the land we want; the amount we pay is a trifle, and is the cheapest way of ending the war. How it will all end I cannot say, but will trust to a kind Providence, who will, I believe, order all things for the best."

The brighter the deeds of the soldier and statesman, the greater the opportunity for the shaft of the critic. General Scott's behavior to a subordinate drew upon him a court of inquiry. In a letter to his wife, dated City of Mexico, March 15, 1848, he says: "The members of the court to sit on General Scott have arrived, and begin proceedings to-day. I fear nothing for General Scott, if the whole truth be known, though the whole country will have suffered by his suspension. The prospects of peace seem to be brightening, and all may yet be well."

Naturally, when the objective point in a campaign has been reached, and the swords go to the scabbards and the guns are stacked, the distribution of the rewards for meritorious services are of much interest to the friends of those who perform them. Mr. Custis, of Arlington, was properly concerned about the claims to honorable official mention of his son-in-law, and wrote to him on the subject, and the reply he received was eminently characteristic of that modest officer:

City of Mexico, April 8, 1848.

I hope my friends will give themselves no annoyance on my account, or any concern about the distribution of favors. I know how those things are awarded at Washington, and how the President will be besieged by clamorous claimants. I do not wish to be numbered among them. Such as he can conscientiously bestow, I shall gratefully receive, and have no doubt that those will exceed my deserts. It is a singular coincidence that in 1836 Santa Anna, as he passed through Fredericktown, Md., should have found General Scott before the court of inquiry clapped upon him by General Jackson. Our present President thought perhaps he ought to afford the gratification to the same individual to see Scott before another court in presence of the troops he commanded. I hope, however, all will terminate in good. The discontent in the army at this state of things is great.

Captain Lee was a great observer of Nature: he loved the country, the bright foliage of trees, the running waters, and flowery grasses. His beautiful mare carried him to all points outside of the city. To Mrs. Lee he writes:

City of Mexico, April 12, 1848.

I rode out a few days since for the first time to the "Church of our Lady of Remedies." It is situated on a hill at the termination of the mountains west of the city, and is said to be the spot to which Cortez retreated after being driven from the city on the memorable "noche triste." I saw the cedar tree at Popotla, some miles nearer the city, in which it is said he passed a portion of that night. The trees of the "noche triste" — so called from their blooming about the period of that event — were in full bloom. The flower is a round ellipsoid, and of the most magnificent scarlet color. The Holy Image was standing on a large silver maguey plant, with a rich crown on her head. There were no votaries at her shrine, which was truly magnificent, but near the entrance of the church, on either side, were the offerings of those whom she had relieved. They consisted of representations in wax of those parts of the human body that she cured of the diseases with which they had been afflicted.

The inactive life was growing burdensome. The strains of "Home, sweet home" were falling on the ears of the Americans, and their hearts were beating in anticipation of meeting once more relatives and friends. In a letter, dated City of Mexico, May 21, 1848, he writes to his naval brother, Sydney Smith Lee:

My dear rose (he calls him by a pet name): I have a little good news to tell you this evening and as little time to tell it in. The mail from Quereton last night brought letters from reliable persons, one of whom I saw, stating that on the evening of the 15th inst. a vote was taken in the Chamber of Deputies on the general passage of the Treaty of Peace and carried in the affirmative by forty-eight votes to thirty-six. That it would come up on the 19th on its final passage, and, after being passed, be sent to the Senate, where it would undoubtedly pass by an unusual majority and probably by the 24th. So certain was its passage through the Senate considered, that the President, Pena y Pena, had determined, as soon as it had finally passed the Deputies, to write our Commissioners to Quereton to be ready to make the interchange, etc. This morning at 10 A. M. a special express arrived from Quereton with the intelligence of the final passage by the Chamber of Deputies of the Treaty, with all the modifications of our Senate, by a vote of fifty-one to thirty-five. It therefore only wants the confirmation of the Senate, of which those who ought to know, say there is no doubt. We all feel quite exhilarated at the prospect of getting home, when I shall again see you and my dear Sis Nannie. Where will you be this summer? I have heard that the Commissioners start for Quereton to-morrow. I know not whether it is true. General Smith will probably leave here for Vera Cruz on the 24th or 25th to make arrangements for the embarkation of troops. As soon as it is certain that we march out, and I make the necessary arrangements for the engineer transportation, etc., I shall endeavor to be off. I shall therefore leave everything till I see you. Several of your naval boys are here who will be obliged to "cut out." Love to Sis Nannie and the boys. Rhett Buchanan and all friends are well.

Very truly and affectionately, R. E. Lee.

Again: "Mr. Gardner and Mr. Trist depart to-morrow. I had hoped that after the President had adopted Mr. Trist's treaty, and the Senate confirmed it, they would have paid him the poor compliment of allowing him to finish it, as some compensation for all the abuse they had heaped upon him; but, I presume, it is perfectly fair, having made use of his labors and taken from him all he had earned, that he should be kicked off as General Scott has been, whose skill and science, having crushed the enemy and conquered a peace, can now be dismissed and turned out as an old horse to die."

In Scott's army in Mexico at that time were many subordinate officers fighting under a common flag, who were destined to become familiar to the public fourteen years afterward by the skill and courage with which they fought each other. Their swords, then drawn for victory against a common foe, were to be pointed against each other's breasts, and those who had slept beneath the same blanket, drank from the same canteen, and formed those ties of steel which are strongest when pledged amid common dangers around a common mess table, were to be marshaled under the banners of opposing armies. Ulysses S. Grant was then twenty-five years old, a lieutenant of the Fourth Infantry, self-reliant, brave, and fertile in resources. He fought with old "Zach" at Palo Alto, Resaca de la Palma, and at Monterey; was at Vera Cruz, and in all the battles which followed until the Mexican capital was entered. George Gordon Meade was an officer of topographical engineers, first on the staff of General Taylor and afterward on the staff of General Patterson at Vera Cruz. There too was George B. McClellan, twenty-one years old, as an engineer officer, who received brevets as first lieutenant and captain for his bravery in battle. Irvin McDowell, who afterward became first commander of the Army of the Potomac, was aid-de-camp to General John E. Wool. George H. Thomas was second lieutenant, Third Artillery, and was brevetted three times for gallantry; Joseph Hooker was assistant adjutant general on the staff of General Persifor F. Smith; Gideon J. Pillow was brevetted three times. Ambrose E. Burnside joined the army on its march, with some recruits. Winfield Scott Hancock was there as second lieutenant, Sixth Infantry, twenty-three years of age, and was brevetted for his conduct at Contreras and Churubusco. There too was Albert Sidney Johnston of the First (Texas) Rifles and afterward inspector general of Butler's division; so also Joseph E. Johnston, lieutenant colonel of voltigeurs, wounded twice and brevetted three times. Braxton Bragg was present as a captain of a light battery in the Third Artillery, the first man to plant the regimental colors on the rampart of Chapultepec; and there too was Thomas Jonathan Jackson, twenty-three years old, second lieutenant of Magruder's light battery of artillery. Young in years and rank, he gave early evidence of those qualities of a soldier for which he became distinguished under the name of Stonewall Jackson. Magruder, his captain, commended him highly in his report, writing that "if devotion, industry, talent, and gallantry are the highest qualities of a soldier, then Lieutenant Jackson is entitled to the distinction which their possession confers." In the army also was Longstreet, lieutenant of infantry, twenty-six years old, brevetted twice and wounded at Chapultepec; and Magruder, known among his comrades as "Prince John," from courtly manners, distinguished appearance, and fine conversational powers, who commanded a light battery in Pillow's division, was twice brevetted and wounded at Chapultepec. John Sedgwick was with the army, first lieutenant of artillery, a classmate of Bragg and Early and Hooker, twice brevetted; and so was Richard S. Ewell, a typical dragoon; Ambrose P. Hill, only twenty-one years old, second lieutenant of the First Artillery; and Daniel H. Hill, Jubal Early, and many others who afterward became famous. Little did these young fellows, who marched, bivouacked, fought, and bled side by side on the burning sands of old Mexico, imagine that in less than two decades McDowell would be training his guns on Johnston and Beauregard at first Manassas, while McClellan, Pope, Burnside, Hooker, Meade, and Grant would each in turn test the prowess of Lee; nor did their old commander, Scott, dream he was training these young men in practical strategy, grand tactics, and the science of war, in order that they might direct the information thus acquired against each other.

The memory of Winfield Scott has not been securely embalmed in the hearts of the people of the Southern States, because he was a Virginian who did not resign his commission in the United States Army and tender his sword to his native State in 1861. It should be remembered, however, that for over half a century he had fought for the flag and worn the uniform of the army of the United States, and had been permanently partially disabled by wounds. Before his Mexican campaign he had served with distinction from where the Northern lakes are bound in icy fetters, to Florida, the land of sun and flowers, in a great degree losing touch with the citizens of States. In fifty-three years of continuous army service he had developed into a sort of national military machine, and when war began between the States of the North and those of the South he was seventy-five years old. Neither the Indian "Black Hawk," with his Sacs and Foxes, the Seminoles, the Mexicans, nor the unhappy condition of his own land, greatly disturbed him, for already his vision was fixed "across the river," and his tent was being erected upon the eternal camping ground. Naturally, he wanted to go to his grave wrapped in the folds of the starry flag he had so long defended. In the North his decision was highly applauded; in the South opinion was divided. In the estimation of some, he should have returned to his mother Commonwealth, for, under their construction of our forms of Government, his first allegiance was due to her. Others, however, heartily concurred in his decision to remain in the North, because "he might have been in the way." The solemn game of war can only be played by active participants, and when a soldier becomes inactive his place is in the rear rank. The aged warrior was consigned to a back seat by the Federal War Department, and quietly waited the summons of the trumpet of the Angel of Death. It is true Scott was pompous and vain of a splendid physical appearance, and had a full appreciation of the high and distinguished position he had attained, but he was a soldier of undoubted military capacity. The people nicknamed him "Fuss and feathers," because, in gaudy uniform, he sometimes made the atmosphere blue around him and imparted to it a smell of sulphur when things did not go exactly to suit him. He was a disciple of the doctrine of Epicurus so far as it related to the organ of taste. When he indulged in "a hasty plate of soup" it was unavoidable, and he has been known to raise a storm because the guest at his table would cut lettuce instead of rolling the leaf around his fork so as not to bruise it. The old soldier is resting quietly now where the "Hudson's silvery sands roll 'mid the hills afar," and if he lacked to some degree personal popularity, was without magnetic influence, and did not possess that power which Carnot calls the "Glory of the soldier and the strength of armies," he is remembered by the whole country as a courteous and chivalric gentleman and as a great commander of true military genius.

His unswerving friendship for Robert E. Lee and his never-failing belief in his military ability was demonstrated by his recommendation that he should be his successor, and which doubtless prompted the United States government to offer to Brevet-Colonel Lee the position of commander in chief of their armies in 1861.

"Peace hath her victories no less than war." A treaty was ratified between the United States and Mexico which was received with joy by the inhabitants of both countries, and was most heartily welcomed by the Americans in Mexico. Captain Lee was once more at home, bearing with him the plaudits of the army and the high appreciation of its commander. He wrote from Arlington, June 30, 1848, to his brother of the navy:

Here I am once again, my dear Smith, perfectly surrounded by Mary and her precious children, who seem to devote themselves to staring at the furrows in my face and the white hairs in my head. It is not surprising that I am hardly recognizable to some of the young eyes around me and perfectly unknown to the youngest, but some of the older ones gaze with astonishment and wonder at me, and seem at a loss to reconcile what they see and what was pictured in their imaginations. I find them too much grown, and all well, and I have much cause for thankfulness and gratitude to that good God who has once more united us. I was greeted on my arrival by your kind letter, which was the next thing to seeing you in person. I wish I could say when I shall be able to visit you, but I as yet know nothing of the intention of the Department concerning me, and cannot now tell what my movements will be. Mary has recently returned from a visit to poor Anne, and gives a pitiable account of her distress. You may have heard of her having hurt her left hand; she is now consequently without the use of either, and cannot even feed herself. She has suffered so much that it is not wonderful her spirits should be depressed. She sent many injunctions that I must come to her before even unpacking my trunk, and I think of running over there for a day after the Fourth of July, if practicable. You say I must let you know when I am ready to receive visits. Now! Have you any desire to see the celebration, etc., of the Fourth of July? Bring Sis Nannie and the little ones; I long to see you all; I only arrived yesterday, after a long journey up the Mississippi, which route I was induced to take for the better accommodation of my horse, as I wished to spare her as much annoyance and fatigue as possible, she already having undergone so much suffering in my service. I landed her at Wheeling and left her to come over with Jim. I have seen but few of our friends as yet, but hear they are all well. Cousin Anna is at Ravensworth. I met Mrs. John Mason yesterday as I passed through W. All her people are well. I hear that that pretty Rhett, hearing of my arrival, ran off yesterday evening to take refuge with you. Never mind, there is another person coming from Mexico from whom she cannot hide herself. Tell her with my regrets that I brought muchas cosas from her young rifleman, who is as bright and handsome as ever. No, Sis Nannie, your sister was not here when I arrived. Are you satisfied? She had gone to Alexandria to learn the news and do a little shopping, but I have laid violent hands on her now. An opportunity has just offered to the Post-office and I have scribbled off this to assure you of my love and remembrance. With much love to Sis Nannie and the children, and kind regards to Mrs. R. and Misses V. and C., I remain,

Affectionately your brother, R. E. Lee.

After the Treaty of Peace with Mexico, Lee was assigned to the important duty of constructing works for the defense of the harbor of Baltimore, and was so occupied until 1852, when he was made Superintendent of the United States Military Academy, from whose walls he had emerged as a cadet twenty-three years before. At West Point he was employed for three years in watching over the drill, discipline, and studies of cadets, who were one day to become officers of the army. The detail was a complimentary one, and the office of superintendent at that time, by law, could only be filled by engineer officers. His accustomed ability was displayed in these new duties, and the Academy received great benefit from a sagacious administration of its affairs. While so engaged, Mrs. Lee's mother — Mrs. Custis died. She was a perfect type of the Christian woman: soft in manner, kind in heart, affectionate in nature, and refined and ladylike in everything. From West Point, April 27, 1853, Captain Lee writes to his wife: "May God give you strength to enable you to bear and say, 'His will be done.' She has gone from all trouble, care, and sorrow, to a holy immortality, there to rejoice and praise forever the God and Saviour she so long and truly served. Let that be our comfort and that our consolation. May our death be like hers, and may we meet in happiness in heaven." And later, on the 10th of May, he says: "She was to me all that a mother could be, and I yield to none in admiration for her character, love for her virtues, and veneration for her memory."

CHAPTER 3

A CAVALRY OFFICER OF THE ARMY OF THE UNITED STATES.

His term of office at West Point terminated by his assignment to cavalry. The great civilizing arms of the United States had been extended so as to embrace large extents of territory, and more cavalry was required. An expenditure of one hundred and sixty millions of dollars, thirty victories in Mexico, and the capture of ten fortified places, including the capital city of the enemy, resulted in adding to the Republic New Mexico, Arizona, Utah, Nevada, and California. The increase in population made it necessary to increase the army in order to give full protection to all citizens within the new boundary lines. After the United States had secured independence, cavalry was not at first recognized as a component part of the regular army. The first mounted regiment, called the First Dragoons, was not organized until 1833. Then followed the Second Dragoons in 1836, and in 1846 another regiment was added, designated as "Mounted Riflemen." With a vast extent of territory and a population of whites numbering about twenty millions in 1855, the cavalry arm of the service consisted of but three regiments. General Scott, in his report of the operations of the army for 1853, first urged that the army be increased by two regiments of dragoons and two regiments of infantry. The following year Hon. Jefferson Davis, then Secretary of War, renewed the commander in chief's recommendation, and President Pierce asked its favorable consideration by Congress, stating that the army was of "inestimable importance as the nucleus around which the volunteer force of the nation can promptly gather in the hour of danger." And that he thought it "wise to maintain a military peace establishment." Mr. R. M. T. Hunter, at that time a distinguished senator in Congress from the State of Virginia, offered an amendment to the Army Appropriation Bill which had passed the House in 1854, authorizing the increase of the army by two regiments of cavalry and five hundred mounted volunteers, who were to serve for twelve months. James Shields, an Irishman by birth, who had served conspicuously in the Mexican War as a brigadier general, and who was then a senator from the State of Illinois, offered a substitute to Hunter's amendment, embodying the views of his former commander in chief, Scott. A protracted debate resulted. Sam Houston, of Texas, and Thomas H. Benton, of Missouri, led the opposition to the measure, the former saying that in the Texas Republic, before its annexation to the United States, the expenses of the Indian War had not exceeded ten thousand dollars a year, and that the settlers had better protection against hostile tribes of Indians than they had received from regiments of the regular army, while the latter indulged in a tirade of abuse against the army generally, calling them "schoolhouse officers and pothouse soldiers"; that he did not believe the aim of the Administration was to relieve the frontier settlements, but to furnish places for graduates of West Point and the friends of the Secretary of War, stating that the object of Mr. Pierce and Jefferson Davis was the ultimate conquest of the island of Cuba.

These views seem to have made an impression upon some sections of the country. The Comte de Paris adopted them in his History of the Civil War in America. He says: "In 1855 Congress passed a law authorizing the formation of two new regiments of cavalry, and Mr. Jefferson Davis, then Secretary of War, took advantage of the fact that they had not been designated by the title of dragoons to treat them as a different arm, and to fill them with his creatures, to the exclusion of regular officers, whom he disliked." It is hardly necessary to say that the comte was writing with limited knowledge. His epithet was applied to such officers as Sumner, Sedgwick, McClellan, Emory, Thomas, Stoneman, Stanley, Carr, etc., who served with much distinction on the Union side of the war from 1861 to 1865; as well as to Albert Sidney

Johnston, Joseph E. Johnston, Lee, Hardee, Kirby Smith, Field, Hood, J. E. B. Stuart, and a number of others who espoused the cause of the South in the late war — "names the world will not willingly let die." Edwin Sumner was promoted by Mr. Davis from major of Second Dragoons to colonel of First Cavalry, and Joseph E. Johnston, a captain in the Topographical Engineers, was made its lieutenant colonel. The colonelcy of the Second Cavalry was tendered to Albert Sidney Johnston, then a major in the Paymaster's Department of the army. This officer, who afterward became so distinguished, graduated at West Point in 1826, and was assigned as a lieutenant to the Second Infantry. His subsequent career in Texas and in the Mexican campaign is well known to the whole country. Zachary Taylor said of him that "he was the best soldier he had ever commanded," while Scott remarked that his appointment as colonel of the Second Cavalry "was a Godsend to the army and country."

Captain and Brevet-Colonel R. E. Lee, of the engineers, was promoted to be lieutenant colonel of this regiment, and William J. Hardee and William H. Emory to be its majors. The latter was soon transferred to the First Cavalry, and the vacancy offered to Braxton Bragg, of the artillery, who declined it because he did not want to remain in the service, and recommended George H. Thomas, of the Third Artillery, who was appointed. Van Dorn, Kirby Smith, James Oakes, Innis Palmer, Stoneman, O'Hara, Bradfute, Travis, Brackett, and Whiting were its captains, and Nathan G. Evans, Richard W. Johnson, Charles Field, and John B. Hood were among its first lieutenants.

Secretary of War Davis graduated at West Point in 1828, two years after Albert Sidney Johnston and one year before Robert E. Lee. He possessed an accurate knowledge of the individual merits of army officers, and time and history have indorsed his selection of officers for these new regiments; for on their respective sides in the late war nearly every one became celebrated. Mr. Davis said to the writer that when he carried the list to the President, the latter remarked that he thought too many of the officers were from the Southern States, and that for the first time his attention was directed to the section from which many of these officers came. In their appointment he had only considered that past services richly entitled them to promotion. At the date of the organization of the two new cavalry regiments seventy officers were appointed by Secretary Davis, but only twenty-nine of them came from States which seceded from the Union in 1861. It is, however, a "historical fact that the officers thus selected were superb soldiers, and that they were from the best to be found in the army and in civil life."

Brevet-Colonel Lee left the Engineer Corps with great regret; he had thoroughly mastered its scientific details, and, with a national reputation, stood in the front rank of military engineers. At West Point he had been instructed in cavalry, artillery, and infantry tactics, and, like all cadets at the date of graduation, was supposed to be equally well informed as to the drill and duties of each arm of service; but twenty-six years had rolled around since graduation, during which his attention had been entirely absorbed in the profession of engineer, and it was necessary that he should again study cavalry tactics. Promotion was slow in the United States Army, and in a long official life he had only reached the lineal rank of captain. By sudden transition, in a single bound he had been promoted to a lieutenant colonelcy, a position he possibly would not have reached in the ordinary course of promotion for many years; his duty to all concerned demanded that he should accept the position. It was an unwritten law in the army that if promotion was offered and declined, the reputation of the officer suffered; it was regarded as a confession on his part that he had not capacity to perform the duties of a higher grade.

Next to the engineer, the cavalry service was the most agreeable to Lee. He was fond of horses, and liked to see them cleaned, fed, and well taken care of; he had a firm seat in the saddle, and rode gracefully and well. He might never become, in the language of the cavalry song,

A bold dragoon, who scorns all care

As he stalks around with his uncropped hair.

And indeed it is difficult to picture him in short jacket, long boots coming above his knees, jingling spurs, clanking saber, and slouched hat, upon whose looped — up side gay feathers danced. Or can we imagine him with the devil-may-care look and jaunty bearing generally ascribed as attributes of the "rough rider"? We cannot fancy him charging the French columns with the fury of a Ponsonby at

Waterloo; or riding boot to boot with dashing Cardigan and his "death or glory" squadrons "into the jaws of death, into the mouth of hell" at Balaklava; or side by side with fearless Murat and his twelve thousand cavalry at Jena; or as fast and furious as Stuart, or Sheridan, Forrest, or Custer. And yet it is safe to say, had the opportunity offered, this new cavalry officer would have been found equal to the emergency. The cavalry genius of Cromwell is readily admitted, in spite of the fact that he was forty-four years of age when he first drew his sword, and Lee was now forty-six. General Foy, in his history of the Peninsular War, writes: "Apres les qualities necessaire[s]? au commandant en chef, le talent de guerre plus sublime est celui du general de cavalrie." Lee was endowed with youth, health, strength, and "talent for war"; he had been shaken well into the saddle by his Mexican campaign, and was buoyant and brave. A fearless and graceful rider, he could have manoeuvred squadrons, and when the bugle sounded the charge, reins loosened, and sabers flashed in the air, lead them to victory.

The headquarters of the Second Cavalry were established at Louisville, Ky., where Lieutenant-Colonel Lee assumed command on the 20th of April, 1855. Afterward he was transferred to Jefferson Barracks, Missouri, where the companies were to be organized and instructed, and which was then the temporary regimental headquarters. He writes Mrs. Lee from that post, July 1, 1855: "The chaplain of the post, a Mr. Fish, is now absent; he is an Episcopal clergyman and well spoken of; we have therefore not had service since I have been here. The church stands out in the trees, grotesque in its form and ancient in its appearance. I have not been in it, but am content to read the Bible and prayers alone, and draw much comfort from their holy precepts and merciful promises. Though feeling unable to follow the one, and truly unworthy of the other, I must still pray to that glorious God without whom there is no help, and with whom there is no danger. That he may guard and protect you all, and more than supply to you my absence, is my daily and constant prayer. I have been busy all the week superintending and drilling recruits. Not a stitch of clothing has as yet arrived for them, though I made the necessary requisition for it to be sent here more than two months ago in Louisville. Yesterday, at muster, I found one of the late arrivals in a dirty, tattered shirt and pants, with a white hat and shoes, with other garments to match. I asked him why he did not put on clean clothes. He said he had none. I asked him if he could not wash and mend those. He said he had nothing else to put on. I then told him immediately after muster to go down to the river, wash his clothes, and sit on the bank and watch the passing steamboats till they dried, and then mend them. This morning at inspection he looked as proud as possible, stood in the position of a soldier with his little fingers on the seams of his pants, his beaver cocked back, and his toes sticking through his shoes, but his skin and solitary two garments clean. He grinned very happily at my compliments. I have got a fine puss, which was left me by Colonel Sumner. He was educated by his daughter, Mrs. Jenkins, but is too fond of getting up on my lap and on my bed; he follows me all about the house and stands at the door in an attitude of defiance at all passing dogs."

In the November following he was in Kansas, having been temporarily detached from his regiment and detailed to serve as a member of a court-martial ordered to convene to try an assistant surgeon of the army for leaving his station in the midst of a fatal epidemic, and wrote Mrs. Lee, from Fort Riley, November 5, 1855: "The court progresses slowly. A good deal was told in the evidence of Saturday; Mrs. Woods, wife of Brevet-Major Woods, Sixth Infantry, whose husband had left on the Sioux expedition, was taken ill at 9 P. M. on the 2d of August. Her youngest child, a boy of three years, was taken that night at twelve, and about six next morning her eldest, a girl of five years. The mother, when told that her end was approaching, asked her only attendant, a niece of the chaplain, to take down the last request to her children and absent husband. The sickness of her children had kindly been concealed from her by this young lady, who managed, by the aid of a soldier, to attend to them all. They all died that morning, the 3d of August. The boy preceded, and the girl followed the mother by about an hour. Their bodies rest in the same grave. I pray their spirits may be united in heaven. The husband, stripped of all he loved, is still absent; and the same day Major Ogden, Mrs. Woods's nurse, a soldier and his wife, died — making seven corpses in the house in one day. Major Ogden was a valuable soldier and much beloved by his men. They have erected to his memory, on an adjacent hill overlooking the fort and the beautiful valley of the Kansas and its branches, a stone monument, their own design and workmanship. The epitaph on it relates in touching simplicity his services and death. He died as he had lived — a soldier and a Christian, and repeated the Lord's Prayer with his last breath. There were fifty-nine deaths during the epidemic. Mrs. Armistead, wife of Major Armistead (General Lewis Armistead, killed at Gettysburg), died in six hours after she was taken. Her husband had marched with his company, but only proceeded thirty miles when overtaken by an express. He returned in the night, found his wife dead, and after her funeral in the morning — this same fatal 3d of August — started for his camp, carrying his two little children with him. A soldier has a hard life and but little consideration."

The Second Cavalry, under the command of Colonel Johnston, on the 27th of October following began its long march from Jefferson Barracks to western Texas. It numbered seven hundred and fifty men and eight hundred horses. It marched under the command of its colonel, Major Hardee being the only other field officer who accompanied it, Lee and Thomas being on court-martial detail. The regiment was destined for the next few years to be stationed at the various posts of western Texas, and its duty was to protect the scalp of the settler from the tomahawk of the savage. Texas has an area of two hundred and seventy-four thousand square miles, or one hundred and fifty million acres of land, and is two and a half times the area of Great Britain and Ireland. In order to watch over such a stretch of frontier it was necessary to divide the regiment up so that only a few companies occupied the same post.

Lieutenant-Colonel Lee arrived in Texas in March, 1856: To Mrs. Lee he writes from San Antonio on March 20, 1856: "To-morrow I leave for Fort Mason, where Colonel Johnston and six companies of the regiment are stationed. Major Hardee and four companies are in camp on the Clear Fork of the Brazos, about forty miles from Belknap. I presume I shall go there. I have left it with Mr. Radiminski (a native of Poland and a lieutenant in the Second Cavalry) to make provision for the journey, and have merely indicated that I should be content with a boiled ham, hard bread, a bottle of molasses, and one of extract of coffee — all of which have been provided." Lee was afterward stationed at Camp Cooper, on the Clear Fork of the Brazos, so named in honor of Samuel Cooper, then adjutant general of the army; and from that point in June, 1856, he was dispatched with four companies of his regiment on an expedition against the Comanches, but was unsuccessful in finding them. It is mentioned because it was his first service of this nature, and the largest command he had ever exercised in the field up to that period. The Indians of western Texas in those days roved over the prairies in small bodies, and would descend suddenly upon the frontier settlements, scalping and killing the settlers and driving off their horses and cattle. They were fine specimens of irregular cavalry, were splendid riders, and when compelled to fight, used the open or individual method of warfare, after the manner of the Cossacks.

From Camp Cooper, Texas, August 4, 1856, remembering that Mr. Custis always celebrated his country's birth by a patriotic speech of welcome to the many who visited him on such occasions, he says to Mrs. Lee: "I hope your father continued well and enjoyed his usual celebration of the Fourth of July; mine was spent, after a march of thirty miles on one of the branches of the Brazos, under my blanket, elevated on four sticks driven in the ground, as a sunshade. The sun was fiery hot, the atmosphere like the blast from a hot-air furnace, the water salt, still my feelings for my country were as ardent, my faith in her future as true, and my hopes for her advancement as unabated as they would have been under better circumstances."

A week later, having received intelligence of the death of his youngest sister, Mildred, who, having married a Mr. Childe, had removed to and was a resident of Paris, France, he writes: "The news came to me very unexpectedly, and in the course of nature I might never have anticipated it, as indeed I had never realized that she could have preceded me on the unexplored journey upon which we are all hastening. Though parted from her for years, with little expectation but of a transient reunion in this life, this terrible and sudden separation has not been the less distressing because it was distant and unlooked for. It has put an end to all hope of our meeting in this world. It has cut short my early wishes and daily yearnings, and so vividly does she live in my imagination and affection that I cannot realize she only exists in my memory. I pray that her life has but just begun, and I trust that our merciful God only so suddenly and early snatched her away because he then saw that it was the fittest moment to take her to himself. May a pure and eternal life now be hers, and may we all live so that when we die it may be open to us." On the 25th of the same month he tells Mrs. Lee: "I shall leave here on the 1st proximo for the Rio Grande, and shall be absent from two and a half to three months; will go from here to Fort Mason and pick up Major Thomas and take him on with me, and thus have him as a traveling companion all the way, which will be a great comfort to me." And then mentioning the Comanche raids on the settlers of Texas, he says: "These people give a world of trouble to man and horse, and, poor creatures, they are not worth it."

Whenever a vacancy occurred in the army in a grade above lieutenant colonel, his chances for promotion were always discussed. His reply to a letter from his wife, informing him that his name was frequently mentioned for a brigadier generalcy, was written the day he set out for Ringgold Barracks to serve as a member of the court-martial ordered to try Major Giles Porter, of the rifles, and is very characteristic:

Camp Cooper, Texas, September 1, 1856.

We are all in the hands of a kind God, who will do for us what is best, and more than we deserve, and we have only to endeavor to deserve more, and to do our duty to him and ourselves. May we all deserve his mercy, his care, and protection. Do not give yourself any anxiety about the appointment of the brigadier. If it is on my account that you feel an interest in it, I beg you will discard it from your thoughts. You will be sure to be disappointed; nor is it right to indulge improper and useless hopes. It besides looks like presumption to expect it.

The journey to the Rio Grande is best told in his own words:

Ringgold Barracks, Texas, October 3, 1856.

I arrived here on the 28th, after twenty-seven consecutive days of travel. The distance was greater than I had anticipated, being seven hundred and thirty miles. I was detained one day on the road by high water — had to swim my mules and get the wagon over by hand. My mare took me very comfortably, but all my wardrobe, from my socks up to my plume, was immersed in the muddy water — epaulets, sash, etc. They are, however, all dry now. Major Thomas traveled with me from Fort Mason. We are in camp together. Captain Bradford, whom we knew at Old Point, is on the court. Colonel Chapman, of the infantry, from Georgetown, Captain Marsey, Colonels Bainbridge, Bumford, Ruggles, and Seawell, and Captain Sibley, an old classmate of mine. Colonel Waite is president of the court and Captain Samuel Jones, of the artillery, judge advocate. The latter brought his wife and child with him in a six-mule road wagon from Sinda, about one hundred and twenty miles up the river. All the court are present and yesterday we commenced the trial of our old friend, Giles Porter. I hope he will clear himself of the charges against him. I am writing with much inconvenience from a stiff finger, caused by a puncture from a Spanish bayonet, while pitching my tent on the road, which struck the joint. Every branch and leaf in this country nearly are armed with a point, and some seem to poison the flesh. What a blessed thing the children are not here! They would be ruined.

The discomforts of army travel and army life were very great in those days. Officers would scarcely get within their assigned quarters at one post before they would be ordered to another, and as transportation was limited to a few Government wagons, the transfer would always result in loss to the officers. Lieutenant-Colonel Lee gives as a glimpse of this in a letter to Mrs. Lee, dated:

Ringgold Barracks, Texas, October 24, 1856.

Major Porter had for his counsel two Texan lawyers, a Judge Bigelow and a Colonel Bowers, very shrewd men, accustomed to the tricks and stratagems of special pleadings, which, of no other avail, absorb time and stave off the question. The movement of troops to Florida will not take place, I presume, until the beginning of November. They are packing up and getting ready. The officers are selling their surplus beds and chairs, cows, goats, and chickens. I am sorry to see their little comforts going, for it is difficult on the frontier to collect them again. Mrs. Sibley told me her chairs and cow had gone, and Mrs. Waite her goats. The pigeons and chickens are disposed of on the table. General Vidaun, in his attack on Camargo, seems to progress pari passu with the court. I am more interested in the state of health of my man Johnson, who has fever. I hope it will prove a slight case for his sake and my own, for, though he is a poor cook, he is all I have, and neither the major [George H. Thomas] nor I can stand these long and interesting sessions of the court without eating. I have read in a stray number of the New York Times, that reached here somehow, a violent attack upon Secretary Davis [Jefferson Davis, then Secretary of War] for the removal of Professor Sprole [West Point]. It makes out a severe charge against the Secretary, the merits of which, though I am sorry for the professor, I am too dull to see. The Secretary and President have surely the right to appoint whom they think best to fill the station. I sincerely hope he will not suffer on account of his losing his place. He has some strong friends in the city of New York. At any rate you had better write to Miss Becky [his daughter] to stay with you till her father is located. In the same paper there are ill-natured strictures upon our regiment. The writer is opposed to the new regiments, particularly the First and Second Cavalry and the Ninth and Tenth Infantry, and calls for their early disbandment. They may suit themselves in everything relating to my services, and whenever they tell me they are no longer required they will not be obtruded on them.

Two months later Lieutenant-Colonel Lee was at Fort Brown, Texas, with thoughts filled with the approaching Christmas and his family's happiness. He Writes in December, 1856: "The time is approaching when I trust many of you will be assembled around the family hearth at dear Arlington another Christmas. Though absent, my heart will be in the midst of you, and I shall enjoy in imagination and memory all that is going on. May nothing occur to mar or cloud the family fireside, and may each be able to look back with pride and pleasure at their deeds of the past year, and with confidence and hope to that in prospect. I can do nothing but hope and pray for you all. Last Saturday I visited Matamoras, Mexico, for the first time. The town looked neat, though much out at the elbow, and nothing apparently going on of interest. The plaza or square was inclosed and the trees and grass flourishing, for which I am told the city is indebted to Major William Chapman, of the Quartermaster's Department, who made the improvement while it was in the occupation of the American army. The most attractive thing to me in town were the orange trees loaded with unripe fruit. The oleander was in full bloom, and there were some large date, fig, and palm trees."

Two days after the great festival the following letter to Mrs. Lee, giving in graphic words his views on slavery, a sly slap at the Pilgrim Fathers, and his personal Christmas doings, was written:

Fort Brown, Texas, December 27, 1856.

The steamer has arrived from New Orleans, bringing full files of papers and general intelligence from the "States." I have enjoyed the former very much, and, in the absence of particular intelligence, have perused with much interest the series of the Alexandria Gazette from the 20th of November to the 8th of December inclusive. Besides the usual good reading matter, I was interested in the relation of local affairs, and inferred, from the quiet and ordinary course of events, that all in the neighborhood was going on well. I trust it may be so, and that you and particularly all at Arlington and our friends elsewhere are well. The steamer brought the President's message to Congress, and the reports of the various heads of the departments, so that we are now assured that the Government is in operation and the Union in existence. Not that I had any fears to the contrary, but it is satisfactory always to have facts to go on; they restrain supposition and conjecture, confirm faith, and bring contentment. I was much pleased with the President's message and the report of the Secretary of War. The views of the President on the domestic institutions of the South are truthfully and faithfully expressed. In this enlightened age there are few, I believe, but will acknowledge that slavery as an institution is a moral and political evil in any country. It is useless to expatiate on its disadvantages. I think it, however, a greater evil to the white than to the black race, and while my feelings are strongly interested in behalf of the latter, my sympathies are stronger for the former. The blacks are immeasurably better off here than in Africa, morally, socially, and physically. The painful discipline they are undergoing is necessary for their instruction as a race, and, I hope, will prepare and lead them to better things. How long their subjection may be necessary is known and ordered by a wise and merciful Providence. Their emancipation will sooner result from a mild and melting influence than the storms and contests of fiery controversy. This influence, though slow, is sure. The doctrines and miracles of our Saviour have required nearly two thousand years to convert but a small part of the human race, and even among Christian nations what gross errors still exist! While we see the course of the final abolition of slavery is onward, and we give it the aid of our prayers and all justifiable means in our power, we must leave the progress as well as the result in his hands, who sees the end and who chooses to work by slow things, and with whom a thousand years are but as a single day; although the abolitionist must know this, and must see that he has neither the right nor the power of operating except by moral means and suasion; and if he means well to the slave, he must not create angry feelings in the master. That although he may not approve the mode by which it pleases Providence to accomplish its purposes, the result will never be the same; that the reasons he gives for interference in what he has no concern holds good for every kind of interference with our neighbors when we disapprove their conduct. Is it not strange that the descendants of those Pilgrim Fathers who crossed the Atlantic to preserve the freedom of their opinion have always proved themselves intolerant of the spiritual liberty of others? I hope you had a joyous Christmas at Arlington, and that it may be long and often repeated. I thought of you all and wished to be with you. Mine was gratefully but silently passed. I endeavored to find some little presents for the children in the garrison to add to their amusement, and succeeded better than I had anticipated. The stores are very barren of such things here, but by taking the week beforehand in my daily walks I picked up little by little something for all. Tell Mildred I got a beautiful Dutch doll for little Emma Jones — one of those crying babies that can open and shut their eyes, turn their head, etc. For the two other little girls, Puss Shirley and Mary Sewell, I found handsome French teapots to match cups given to them by Mrs. Waite; then by means of knives and books I satisfied the boys. After dispensing my presents I went to church; the discourse was on the birth of our Saviour. It was not as simply or touchingly told as it is in the Bible. By previous invitation I dined with Major Thomas at 2 P. M. on roast turkey and plum pudding. He and his wife were alone. I had provided a pretty singing bird for the little girl, and passed the afternoon in my room. God bless you all.

From the same place — Fort Brown, Texas, January 7, 1857 — writing to Mrs. Lee, whom he hears has been sick, he says: "Systematically pursue the best course to recover your lost health. I pray and trust your efforts and the prayers of those who love you may be favorably answered. Do not worry yourself about things you cannot help, but be content to do what you can for the well-being of what belongs properly to you. Commit the rest to those who are responsible, and though it is the part of benevolence to aid all we can and sympathize with all who are in need, it is the part of wisdom to attend to our own affairs. Lay nothing too much to heart. Desire nothing too eagerly, nor think that all things can be perfectly accomplished according to our own notions."

Mr. Custis, of Arlington, was very fond of cats, and his large yellow "Tom" was his constant attendant. Some of his household naturally grew fond of these animals, his son-in-law being among them. Lieutenant-Colonel Lee would not cut the skirt of his robe, as did Mohammed, to prevent disturbing his cat, which was sleeping on it, nor, like Cardinal Wolsey, give audience with a cat seated beside him, nor let his cat rest among his papers and books, as did Richelieu, nor wish a statue with his right hand resting on his cat, as did Whittington, the famous Lord Mayor of London, but he liked to see a well-fed puss, such as Gray described in his ode "On the death of a favorite cat":

> *Her conscious tail her joy disclosed,*
> *The fair round face, the snowy beard,*
> *The relish of her paws;*
> *Her coat that with the tortoise vies,*
> *Her ears of jet and emerald eyes,*
> *She saw and purr'd applause.*

From Fort Brown, Texas, February 16, 1857, he tells Mrs. Lee: "Tell your father Mrs. Colonel Waite has a fine large cat which she takes with her everywhere. He is her companion by day, and sleeps on her bed at night. In public conveyances she leads him in the leash, and carries along a bottle of milk for his use. In her own carriage he sits on her lap. I have been trying to persuade her to let me take him up to Camp Cooper, but she says she can't part from him. He must go to Florida. I have seen some fine cats in Brownsville in the stores kept by Frenchmen, but no yellow ones; the dark brindle is the favorite color on the frontier. In my walk the other evening I met a Mexican with a wild kitten in his arms enveloped in his blanket; it was a noble specimen of the Rio Grande wildcat, spotted all over with large spots like the leopard. I tried very hard to buy him, but he said he was already sold. I should prefer one of those at Camp Cooper. I fear, though, I should have to keep him chained, for they are very wild and savage."

And again from Indianola, Texas, March 27, 1857, he writes to his youngest daughter: "It has been said that our letters are good representatives of our minds. They certainly present a good criterion for judging of the character of the individual. You must be careful that yours make as favorable an impression of you as I hope you will deserve. I am truly sorry for the destruction of the Long Bridge. [Spans the Potomac between Arlington and Washington.] It will be an injury to the business of many and an inconvenience to you in taking your music lessons. You must be a great personage now — sixty pounds! I wish I had you here in all your ponderosity. I want to see you so much. Can you not pack up and come to the Comanche country? I would get you such a fine cat you would never look at 'Tom' again. Did I tell you Jim Nooks, Mrs. Waite's cat, was dead? He died of apoplexy. I foretold his end. Coffee and cream for breakfast, pound cake for lunch, turtle and oysters for dinner, buttered toast for tea, and Mexican rats, taken raw, for supper. He grew enormously and ended in a spasm. His beauty could not save him. I saw in San Antonio a cat dressed up for company: He had two holes bored in each ear, and in each were two bows of pink and blue ribbon. His round face, set in pink and blue, looked like a big owl in a full blooming ivy bush. He was snow white, and wore the golden fetters of his inamorata around his neck in the form of a collar. His tail and feet were tipped with black, and his eyes of green were truly catlike. But I 'saw cats as is cats' in Sarassa, while the stage was changing mules. I stepped around to see Mr. Monod and Mrs. Monod, a French couple with whom I had passed the night when I landed in Texas, in 1846, to join General Wool's army. Mr. Monod received me with all the shrugs of his nation, and the entrance of madame was foreshadowed by the coming in of her stately cats, with visages grave and tails erect, who preceded, surrounded, and followed her. Her present favorite, Sodoiska, a large mottled gray, was a magnificent creature, and in her train she pointed out Aglai, her favorite eleven years ago when I first visited her. They are of French breed and education, and when the claret and water was poured out for my refreshment they jumped on the table for a sit-to. If I can persuade the mail stage to give a place to one of that distinguished family, I will take it to Camp Cooper, provided madame can trust her pet into such a barbarous country and Indian society. I left the wildcat on the Rio Grande; he was too savage; had grown as large as a small-sized dog, had to be caged, and would strike at anything that came within his reach. His cage had to be strong, and consequently heavy, so I could not bring it. He would pounce upon a kid as Tom Tita [the cat at Arlington] would on a mouse, and would whistle like a tiger when you approached him. Be a good child and think always of your devoted father."

From the same place on the next day he lets his wife know how difficult it was for army officers to retain their servants:

Indianola, Texas, March 28, 1857.

Major Thomas, anticipating a long sojourn, brought down Mrs. Thomas with him, who told me last evening of her troubles in relation to her women-kind. She brought two sisters from New Orleans under obligation to remain in her service two years. One of them has become enamored of a soldier at Fort Mason, and has engaged herself to marry him. Colonel Taylor informs me that his two women servants married soldiers at Fort Brown without his knowledge about a fortnight after his arrival. It seems we have our troubles wherever we are and cannot escape them.

The court-martials being over, Colonel Lee started for his post, and at Fort Mason, en route, on the 4th of April, 1857, writes: "I write to inform you of my progress thus far on my journey. I arrived here yesterday in a cold norther, and though I pitched my tent in the most sheltered place I could find, I was surprised to see this morning, when getting up, my bucket of water, which was sitting close by my bed, so hard frozen that I had to break the ice before I could pour the water into the basin. On visiting the horses in the night they seemed to suffer much with cold, notwithstanding I had stretched their picket line under the lee of a dense thicket to protect them from the wind. This post has the advantage of Camp Cooper in providing habitable though homely quarters for officers and men. This is Easter Sunday. I hope you have been able to attend the services at Church. My own have been performed alone in my tent, I hope with a humble, grateful, and penitent heart, and will be acceptable to our Heavenly Father. May he continue his mercies to us both and all our children, relatives and friends, and in his own good time unite us in his worship, if not on earth, forever in heaven."

And on his arrival writes:

Camp Cooper, Texas, April 19, 1857.

After an absence of over seven months I have returned to my Texas home. I heard of Indians on the way but met none. I feel always as safe in the wilderness as in the crowded city. I know in whose powerful hands I am, and on Him I rely and feel that in all our life we are upheld and sustained by Divine Providence, and that Providence requires us to use the means he has put under our control. He designs no blessing to idle and inactive wishes, and the only miracle he now exhibits to us is the power he gives to Truth and Justice to work their way in this wicked world. After so long an absence I found my valuables in a better condition than I had anticipated. My tent had frequently been prostrated by storms but always rose again. It was, of course, attended by a natural crash not worth considering, could you replace your crockery, buckets, etc., which is impossible.

The change of the weather in Texas is the subject of a letter dated April 26, 1857: "The changes of the weather here are very rapid. Yesterday, for instance, I was in my white linen coat and shirt all the afternoon, and the thermometer in my tent, with the walls raised and a fine breeze blowing through it, stood at eighty-nine degrees. I could not bear the blanket at night, but about twelve o'clock a 'norther' came roaring down the valley of the Clear Fork and made all my blankets necessary. This morning fires and overcoats are in fashion again. A general court-martial has been convened here for the trial of Lieutenant Eagle, Second Cavalry. I am president of the court, I am sorry to say. Colonel Bainbridge, Major Thomas, Major Van Horn, Major Paul, Captain King, and others are members. I have pitched a couple of tents by the side of mine for the Major and Mrs. Thomas, for she has accompanied him again, and they are to take their meals with me. The major can fare as I do, but I fear she will fare badly, for my man Kumer is both awkward and unskilled. I can, however, give them plenty of bread and beef, but, with the exception of preserved vegetables, fruits, etc., I can give very little else. I sent yesterday to the settlements below and got a few eggs, some butter, and one old hen. I shall not reflect upon her. The game is poor now and out of season, and we are getting none of it. In my next I shall be better able to tell you how I got on with my entertainments."

In a letter dated Camp Cooper, June 9, 1857, he mentions the sickness of the troops: "The great heat has produced much sickness among the men. The little children, too, have suffered. A bright little boy died a few days since from it. He was the only child, and his parents were much affected by his loss. They expressed a great desire to have him buried with Christian rites, and asked me to perform the ceremony; so for the first time in my life I read the beautiful funeral service of our Church over the grave to a large and attentive audience of soldiers."

And on the 25th of June, 1857, Lieutenant-Colonel Lee, in advising his wife and one of his daughters to go to the Springs, suggested that they be escorted by his youngest son, saying: "A young gentleman who has read Virgil must surely be competent to take care of two ladies, for before I had advanced that far I was my mother's outdoor agent and confidential messenger. Your father [G. W. P. Custis] must have a pleasant time at Jamestown, judging from the newspaper report of the celebration. Tell him I at last have a prospect of getting a puss. I have heard of a batch of kittens at a settler's town on the river, and have the promise of one. I have stipulated if not entirely yellow, it must at least have some yellow in the composition of the color of its coat; but how I shall place it — when I get it — and my mouse on amicable terms I do not know."

In a letter dated Camp Cooper, June 22, 1857, he tells his wife again of the sickness of the troops and of the death of a little boy, the son of a sergeant, about one year old. "His father came to me," he writes, "with the tears flowing down his cheeks, and asked me to read the funeral services over his body, which I did at the grave for the second time in my life. I hope I will not be asked again; for, though I must believe it is far better for the child to be called by its heavenly Creator into his presence in its purity and innocence, unpolluted by sin and uncontaminated by the vices of the world, still, it so wrings a parent's heart with anguish that it is painful to see. Yet I know it was done in mercy to both. The child has been saved from all misery and sin here. The father has been given a touching appeal and powerful inducement to prepare for hereafter."

In the summer of 1857, Colonel Johnston being ordered to report to Washington for the purpose of taking charge of the Utah expedition, Lieutenant-Colonel Lee assumed command of his regiment. The death of his father-in-law, Mr. Custis, recalled him to Arlington in the fall of that year; but he returned as soon as possible to his regimental headquarters in Texas. The death of the "adopted son of Washington," October 10, 1857, in his seventy-sixth year, was greatly deplored. His unbounded hospitality was as broad as his acres, and his vivid recollections of the Father of his Country, though only eighteen when he died, and whose memory he venerated, were most charmingly narrated. His father, John Parke Custis, the son of Mrs. Washington by her first husband, was Washington's aid-de-camp at the siege of Yorktown, and died at the early age of twenty-eight.

G. W. P. Custis, the grandson of Mrs. Washington, was educated at Princeton. His early life was passed at Mount Vernon, but after the death of his grandmother, in 1802, he built Arlington House, opposite the city of Washington, on an estate left him by his father. In his will he decreed that all of his slaves should be set free after the expiration of five years. The time of manumission came in 1863, when the flames of war were fiercely raging; but amid the exacting duties incident to the position of army commander, Robert E. Lee, his executor, summoned them together within his lines and gave them their free papers, as well as passes through the Confederate lines to go whither they would.

Mr. Custis in his will says: "I give and bequeath to my dearly beloved daughter, Mary Custis Lee, my Arlington House estate, containing seven hundred acres, more or less, and my mill on Four Mile Run, in the County of Alexandria, and the lands of mine adjacent to said mill in the counties of Alexandria and Fairfax, in the State of Virginia, the use and benefit of all just mentioned during the term of her natural life… My daughter, Mary Custis Lee, has the privilege by this will of dividing my family plate among my grandchildren; but the Mount Vernon plate, together with every article I possess relating to Washington, and that came from Mount Vernon, is to remain with my daughter at Arlington House during said daughter's life, and at her death to go to my eldest grandson, George Washington Custis Lee, and to descend from him entire and unchanged to my latest posterity." These articles were taken from Arlington, General McClellan writes, and put into the Patent Office in Washington for safe-keeping until such times as they should be restored to their rightful owner, and that he [McClellan] would be willing to testify to that fact in a court of justice, if it were necessary. They were removed afterward from the Patent Office and placed in the National Museum, where they are now, and all applications for their restoration have been refused. A decision of the Supreme Court restored to General Custis Lee Arlington, and Congress should return these articles of Washington, which had been taken from his grandfather's house during the war.

Petty frontier war with savages was not congenial to the tastes or in accord with the genius of such a soldier as Lee. Army life there was not pleasant to officers of his rank; the forts were surrounded on all sides by long strips of dreary, uninhabited territory, and in order to better protect this vast section of western Texas, the ten companies constituting his regiment of cavalry were divided up into garrisons of one or two companies to each post. Prairie scouting was done principally by subalterns with small detachments, a lieutenant and twenty troopers being frequently detailed for that purpose. The duties of a department or regimental commander were for the most part supervisory.

No great continental lines of railroad bound in those days ocean to ocean with bands of steel. No telegraphs bore on electric wings communication from fort to fort; the United States mail was carried by armed soldiers on small mules, whose habitual gait was the gallop, while officers and their families were transported in ambulances drawn by mules, and accompanied by armed escorts. At the end of each day's journey the night was spent in tents. Sibley, of the Second Dragoons, when traveling in this way with his wife and daughter over Texas prairies, first conceived the idea of the famous tent called after him; he was caught in a "norther," and made a fire in his wall tent during the night, hoping the smoke would go out of the opening in front; it did not do so, and the next day he worked at the model of the tent, in shape similar to the Indian tepee; the present Army Sibley tent is the result. Officers stationed at frontier posts in those days could not communicate with the headquarters of the Department at San Antonio for many days, or hear from their homes in the States for many weeks.

The Indians, too, were not foemen worthy of Lee's steel; the Comanches were then the largest and fiercest tribe in Texas. Attached to Lee's first station, Camp Cooper, was an "Indian reserve." The Government was making its — first experiment toward civilizing the savage. The Indians were induced to come to such reservation, where they were fed and taken care of at Government expense; the great majority of them did not deign to associate so familiarly with the pale faces; some, however, came, especially in the winter months; but when the grass grew high in the spring, and the game fat, they resumed their wandering life, and with bent bow and a quiver full of arrows, lay in ambush to kill those who had fed them. Catumseh, one of the Comanche chiefs, was at the reserve when Lee was at Camp Cooper. With true official courtesy the lieutenant colonel, as the commandant of the fort and the representative of the Great Father at Washington, decided to visit him, and told the interpreter to say to the chief that he would treat him as a friend so long as his conduct and that of the tribe deserved it, but would meet him as an enemy the moment he failed to keep his word. Catumseh was not much pleased with Lee's views, receiving them with an emphatic grunt, relying principally upon producing a profound impression upon his visitor by the information that he was a "big Indian" and had six wives, and would have more respect for Lee if he had followed his example. The visit was not productive of results, and failed to establish the desired entente cordiale between the two chiefs. They separated, mutually convinced that the other was a cunning specimen who had to be watched. During the interview Catumseh was in all probability taking the measure of Lee's scalp, while Lee was in turn disgusted with the paint and ornaments of the Indian, for we find him writing word that he "was rendered more hideous than Nature made him." These Indians were treacherous in disposition and filthy in habit; a nomadic life made them active, vigilant, and a foe not to be despised. Their strength, however, was inferior to that of the soldier, because their food, clothing, and exposure were not conducive to its development. For breakfast, dinner, and supper, they had the raw meat of the antelope, deer, and buffalo. It was their habit to cut it into long strips, put it over the backs of their ponies, ride on it to keep it in place, and whenever hungry on the march, cut off a piece and eat it. They were matchless horsemen, and could crawl under or over the side of a horse with the ease a squirrel could circumscribe a tree. The bow and arrow was their principal weapon, and the precision of their aim was wonderful. They would draw rings a few feet in diameter on the ground, and shooting an arrow to a surprising height in the air, cause it to return and stick in a previously designated circle. The green turf was the couch of the red man, the blue sky his coverlet; stoicism and courage were the characteristics of the race, but combined with murder, theft, and perfidy. Colonel Lee was doubtless glad to get away from them. On that Sunday afternoon, October 16, 1859, when John Brown with a small force marched into Harper's Ferry with the avowed purpose of liberating slaves and inaugurating war between the whites and blacks, Colonel Lee was enjoying the hospitality of his Arlington home; having asked for the second furlough, in a long career, to settle up the estate of Mr. Custis, being his sole executor, he was within range of the Secretary of War when that officer decided to take prompt measures to regain the United States Arsenal which Brown had captured. No one then knew the limits of this aggressive action of Brown. An officer well equipped by experience, courage, and balanced judgment was required to represent the Government. The needle in the Secretary of War's office turned by mere force of instinct to Lee, and he promptly responded to the summons. A battalion of marines from the navy yard at Washington was ordered to be put at his service, and the troops of the regular army, at Fort Monroe. The "John Brown raid," as it was termed, was the natural outgrowth of the agitation by the abolitionists of the slavery question on the mind of a wild fanatic. The mad actor in the Harper's Ferry tragedy was born in the State of Kentucky, and for the greater part of fifty-nine years had been a monomaniac on the subject of freedom for the negro. His mind had become overexcited, and in his frenzy he had already performed deeds which placed him close to the dangling rope. At Springfield, Mass., where he once resided, he formed an order called the "League of Gileadites," pledged to rescue fugitive slaves. To this order he delivered addresses in manuscript, saying in one of them: "Stand by one another and by your friends while a drop of blood remains and by hanging, if you must." Nine years afterward in Virginia the rope was placed in uncomfortable proximity to his own neck.

Kansas when a Territory, and an applicant for admission to the American Union, was made the abolition battlefield; John Brown went there, of course, for agitation was the business of his life. Acts of violence were frequent. Excitement in the Territory grew, and finally culminated in the Pottawattamie massacre, where five unoffending citizens were called from their beds and assassinated by Brown and his companions. The commotion created by the carnage increased the notoriety of the butcher, and he was an abolition hero. Eastern agitators placed on his head the crown of heroism, and offers of arms and money were freely tendered. His fanaticism grew, and his zeal knew no proper bounds. Virginia was selected as the best point to carry out his plans. There he would incite the negroes to rebellion and furnish them with arms from the United States Arsenal. In his madness he pictured a great and growing army of black recruits from all portions of the Southern States.

War for the extermination of slavery should begin in the State where the Dutch first landed the negro. The choice was approved by New England supporters who lost their money while Brown lost his life. Lee went to Harper's Ferry. The marines, under their gallant officers, battered down the door of the engine-house into which he had fled with a portion of his men for refuge from the aroused citizens. Brown was captured, tried, convicted, and hung on the 2d of December, 1859.

Lieutenant-Colonel Lee, from Harper's Ferry, December 1, 1859, says in a letter to his wife: "I arrived here yesterday, about noon, with four companies from Fort Monroe, and was busy all the evening getting accommodations for the men and posting pickets to insure timely notice of the approach of the enemy. The feelings of the community seem to have calmed down, and I have been received with every kindness. I presume we are fixed here until after the 16th. To-morrow will probably see the last of Captain Brown (Old John Brown). There will be less interest for the others, but still I think the troops will not be withdrawn till they are similarly disposed of. This morning I was introduced to Mrs. Brown, who with a Mr. Tyndale and Mrs. McKim, all from Philadelphia, has come on to have a last interview with her husband. As it is a matter over which I have no control, and wish to take none, I referred them to General William B. Taliaferro. Tell Smith [his brother in the navy] that no charming women have insisted on taking charge of me, as they are always doing of him. I am left to my own resources."

A committee of Congress was appointed to investigate the matter, who reported that the invasion was an act of lawless ruffians under the sanction of no public or political authority, distinguished from ordinary violence only by the ulterior ends in contemplation by them and by the fact that the money to maintain the expedition, and the large amounts they had brought with them, had been contributed by other States of the Union.

Virginia, not knowing the extent of the insurrection, was preparing for war. Henry A. Wise, then Governor, promptly took active measures to preserve the peace of his State, and everywhere volunteers tendered their service. When Colonel Lee was ordered to Harper's Ferry, J. E. B. Stuart, a young lieutenant of the First Cavalry, was in Washington on leave of absence, and happened to be at Arlington on that day. Fond of enterprise and indifferent to danger, he at once volunteered as aid-de-camp to Lee, asked and received permission to accompany him, and was the first to recognize Brown, having seen him in Kansas. Afterward he became the great cavalry chieftain of the Army Lee commanded. The prisoners at Harper's Ferry were at once turned over to the United States District Attorney, Mr. Robert Ould, and Lee returned to Washington and Arlington, and in a short time was again on his way to resume his official duties in Texas. We find him writing from San Antonio, Texas, June 25, 1860, to Mrs. Lee, his impressions of one of the holidays there: "Yesterday," he says, "was St. John's Day, and the principal, or at least visible, means of adoration or worship seemed to consist in riding horses. So every Mexican, and indeed others, who could procure a quadruped were cavorting through the streets, with the thermometer over a hundred degrees in the shade, a scorching sun, and dust several inches thick. You can imagine the state of the atmosphere and suffering of the horses, if not the pleasure of the riders. As everything of the horse tribe had to be brought into requisition to accommodate the bipeds, unbroken colts and worn-out hacks were saddled for the occasion. The plunging and kicking of the former procured excitement for, and the distress of the latter merriment to the crowd. I did not know before that St. John set so high a value upon equitation."

There he remained until summoned to Washington in February, 1861, reaching that city on the 1st of March. Once more, and for the last time, he was with his family under the roof of stately old Arlington.

CHAPTER 4

WAR.

Robert E. Lee was now fifty-four years old, and the wheel of time had recorded thirty-two years of honorable service in the army of the United States. During that time his country had grown in population and increased in wealth and territory far exceeding the expectations and hopes of her people. His profession had absorbed his attention to such an extent that he had scarcely noticed a gathering war cloud destined to discharge death and destruction upon the American Republic, as well as mark a most important epoch in his own life and career. The Constitution adopted by the Convention at Philadelphia in 1787 was the result of a compromise of the opinions of its members. The scope and extent of the powers to be conferred on a government to be created by the representatives of the States, the line marking those powers, and the rights reserved by the States, was a most difficult problem to solve. On the one hand, if too little power were conferred on the legislative, executive, and judicial departments of the Federal Government, its organization might at any moment be broken to pieces, because not strong enough to enforce its legal decrees. On the other hand, should too much power be delegated, a strong central government might result, and the creators — the States — might be crushed out of existence by an instrument of their own creation. The people would in that case be returned to a form of government they abhorred, and from whose tyrannical methods their forefathers had breasted the waves of the Atlantic, and incurred all dangers in settling a newly discovered country. The safety of the States was the safety of the people, and only limited and defined powers must be conferred upon the Government of the United States. The Constitution, the supreme law of the land, must state in writing exactly the rights delegated by the States for their common government. The powers not so delegated were reserved by the States to themselves. They possessed them because they had never parted with them. An attempt in the Philadelphia Convention to insert a clause in the Constitution prohibiting a State's withdrawal from the Union then being formed could not have succeeded, while an express provision authorizing such secession would have been regarded as unwise and suggestive of disunion of States which were then trying to form "a more perfect union." If the framers of the Constitution, when at work in the Quaker City, said nothing upon this very important point, the States to be bound, if they ratified it, said much. They did not purpose to be blindly gagged and bound to the wheels of the Federal chariot, for they possessed sovereign power.

In the Declaration of Independence the colonies were not declared independent of Great Britain in a collective capacity, but each separate colony was transformed thereby into an independent State; and so his Britannic Majesty treats them by name in a provisional agreement in 1782. When George III withdrew the scepter of his power from the Virginia colony it was an empire in territory, and became absolutely a free, independent, and sovereign State. The allegiance of her citizens to her was undisputed and admitted. Before the life-blood could circulate in the veins of the new Government it must be stamped with the approbation of the States; it had no power to act unless ratified by nine of these States. If the other four did not ratify the Constitution, the government so formed was not binding on them. The State conventions called for this purpose were for the most part cautious and exceedingly slow of action.

To the State of Lee's nativity the independence of the colonies and their union afterward as States was largely due. One of her sons held the sword and another the pen that accomplished this great work. The superb oratory of another kept the camp fires of the Revolution burning brightly, while in ringing tones still another of her citizens moved "That these united colonies are, and of right ought to be, free and independent States, and that all political connection between these States and the State of Great Britain is, and ought to be, totally dissolved." Nine States, a requisite number, had approved the Constitution before Virginia acted. The debates in her convention on this subject have no equal in intellectual vigor. Mental giants, full-armed with wisdom, fought on either side. In one rank — opposed to the adoption of the Constitution as it came from the hands of its framers — was Patrick Henry, George Mason, Richard Henry Lee, James Monroe, Benjamin Harrison, and William Grayson. In the other were James Madison, John Marshall, Edmund Randolph, Edmund Pendleton, and General Henry Lee, and behind them, as a powerful reserve, was the great influence of Washington. On the final vote friends of the measure secured a majority of only ten votes. The next State to adopt it after Virginia was New York, and she did so by only three votes. North Carolina did not join the Union immediately, and Rhode Island for fifteen months, after the new Constitution had gone into operation. The delay in the action of these States, and the close votes in so many others, was the result of an undefined fear in the public mind that as years rolled on the government they were then creating might in turn destroy the autonomy of the various States.

Massachusetts, South Carolina, and New York had made, as the price of their ratifying the Constitution, amendments to guard as far as possible against consolidated powers. Robert Lee knew all this; he knew also that his own State had been remarkably careful upon this important point, for she had declared, upon consenting to go into the Union then formed by the action of nine States, "that the powers granted under the Constitution, being truly derived from the people of the United States, may be resumed by them whenever the same shall be perverted to their injury or oppression." Without any act of his, face to face he was confronted with the great question — loyalty to the General Government or loyalty to Virginia. Would it be treason to substitute for the E Pluribus Unum written upon the scroll of the beak of the eagle Virginia's Sic Semper Tyrannis? He had been taught when a boy that his first duty was to his mother Commonwealth. How, then, could he be a traitor if he placed his hand in hers and knelt at her feet when she called him lovingly to her side? His elevated character and conscientiousness of purpose appealed to him to decide in an honorable way this question. During those anxious moments how his thoughts must have marched and countermarched upon constitutional questions! At that very time he might have heard a distinguished senator, who afterward became Vice-President and President of the United States, declare from his seat that the Federal Government possessed no sovereign power; that it could not coerce a State; that under the Constitution you cannot apprehend any of the States as a party; and that all the powers of the General Government were derived, and that it had no single primitive power. The study of the early history of his country convinced Lee that while the secession of a State from the Union might not be a remedy, it was not a violation of the Constitution so far as the original thirteen States were concerned. He probably found also, in the anxious study he was then making to arrive at a proper solution of the question, that this theory of constitutional government was recognized by most of the States when the Union was formed.

For instance, Massachusetts had declared in 1809, when the Embargo Act was passed by Congress, that it was not binding upon her citizens; and in December, 1810, one of her members of Congress declared that if Louisiana were admitted into the Union it would lead to its dissolution; the New England States would secede, "amicably if they might, forcibly if they must." And he found similar instances in the history of Pennsylvania and Kentucky. In Pennsylvania he found that that State had placed herself on record by an act of her Legislature, as well as by her Governor, to prevent a decree of a United States judge from being executed, boldly asserting that it was her duty to protect her citizens, and to her their allegiance must first be given. In his examination of this perplexing subject he might have noticed that the Constitution of the United States at that time made it mandatory on the Governor of a State to give up a fugitive from justice to the Governor of the State he had fled from, in order that he might be tried by the laws of that State; but that, notwithstanding the Constitution, governors of sovereign States did not give up offenders unless they chose to do so. Indeed, in a rendition contest between the States of Ohio and Kentucky, Mr. Taney, then Chief Justice of the United States, delivering a decision of the Court, said:

"While admitting that the Constitution was mandatory on the governors, there was not a line in it which gave power to the General Government to compel a State to do anything."

Lee had probably read, too, that a convention composed of the representatives of the New England States had assembled in Hartford, Conn., in 1814, to protest against the war with England because of the great damage it was inflicting on the shipping interests of that section. He might have seen that secession was advocated as the remedy, while the declaration was made that "if the Union be destined to dissolution," some new form of confederacy should be substituted among those States which shall not need to maintain a federal relation with each other. Fortunately, peace was declared with Great Britain, or at that time there might have been a secession of the New England States. It was an interesting question to this lieutenant colonel of cavalry, that if this action had been taken by the New England States, and the States remaining in the Union had invaded their territory for the purpose of coercion, upon what side would the large majority of the citizens of the New England States have been found fighting?

The more Robert E. Lee thought upon the subject the more he became convinced, first, that Virginia in seceding from the Union was exercising the right she had reserved when she entered it. Second, that if war must follow, his sword should be drawn in her defense, and not be pointed against her. In the soil of old Virginia were buried those nearest and dearest to him. His ancestors had first settled within her limits. She was to be invaded because she exercised a right not denied her by the Constitution, and her course had been determined by a convention of the representatives of her people duly called to consider the question; and a convention voiced the highest authority of a State. He may have deplored her action, but he could not oppose his judgment to the collective wisdom of her representatives whose action had been solemnly indorsed by her people at the polls. The irrepressible conflict had to be met in his own person. He had seen, but could not prevent the sections from drifting apart. If the interests of the manufacturing and shipping States of the North and the agricultural States of the South were not in entire harmony, he had hoped that a possible remedy might be found. Mr. Lincoln received only 1,857,000 of the popular vote, while Breckinridge, Douglas, and Bell received 2,800,000; but that was not a sufficient reason in his opinion to declare war. If he had much to do with John Brown's body lying moldering in the ground, the fact that his spirit was marching on down the abolition ranks did not disturb him. His State when a colony was opposed to slavery. The first speech his eloquent relative, Richard Henry Lee, ever made was in favor of the motion to lay so heavy a duty on the importation of slaves as effectually to put an end to the iniquitous and disgraceful traffic in the colony of Virginia.

Lee had read, too, Jefferson's indictment of Great Britain for allowing the slave trade when he penned the Declaration of Independence. He knew that slavery existed in the Northern States so long as it was profitable, and was abolished when it was not, and that the Mayflower which landed the Pilgrim Fathers on Plymouth Rock sailed on its very next voyage with a cargo of slaves. He had found the negroes shucking corn and hoeing potatoes. They had always been kindly treated by him; and no more happy, contented, well-clothed and well-fed negroes ever existed than those at Arlington. He would not have fought to preserve slavery; he disapproved of it and had years before freed his own, and Mr. Custis had freed by will all of his. He regretted war, but did not regret as one of its results the probable freedom of the slave, although he knew that slavery had called a race of savages from superstition and idolatry and imparted to them a general knowledge of the precepts of religion. Indeed, he is recorded as saying at that time that if he owned all the negroes of the South he would gladly yield them up for the preservation of the Union. In 1861 Lee hoped and prayed that the Temple of American Liberty might still stand in the majesty of its vast proportions, complete in all of its parts, each pillar representing with equal strength an American State. He sincerely hoped each State would pursue the path designated for it by the Constitution, as the planets revolve in well-defined orbits around the great central sun. He wrote from Texas in 1861 that he could not anticipate a greater calamity for the country than the dissolution of the Union, and that he was willing to sacrifice anything but honor for its preservation. And in another letter from Fort Mason, Texas, January, 1861, to Mrs. Lee, he says: "You see by a former letter that I received from Major Nicholl, Everett's Life of Washington you sent me, and enjoyed its perusal very much. How his spirit would be grieved could he see the wreck of his mighty labors! I will not, however, permit myself to believe, till all ground for hope is gone, that the work of his noble deeds will be destroyed, and that his precious advice and virtuous example will soon be forgotten by his countrymen. As far as I can judge from the papers, we are between a state of anarchy and civil war. May God avert from us both. I fear mankind for years will not be sufficiently Christianized to bear the absence of restraint and force. I see that four States have declared themselves out of the Union. Four more apparently will follow their example. Then if the border States are dragged into the gulf of revolution, one half of the country will be arrayed against the other, and I must try and be patient and wait the end, for I can do nothing to hasten or retard it."

It was hard for Lee to give up his position in the army and separate himself from his army comrades and associations. He wrote in 1849, from Mobile, Ala.: "I have met many officers of the garrison who were with me in Mexico. You have often heard me say the cordiality and friendship in the army was the great attraction of the service. It is that, I believe, that has kept me in it so long, and it is that which now makes me fear to leave it. I do not know where I should meet with so much friendship out of it."

While he was wrestling with this disturbing question at Arlington his old commander, Scott, just across the river, was pleading for him to remain in the service of the United States. The veteran general had impressed the President with the distinguished services of Colonel Lee, and urged that every effort should be, made to keep him on the side of the Union, going so far as to say that he would be worth fifty thousand men to their cause. Probably it was due to Scott that Mr. Lincoln requested Mr. Francis Preston Blair to have an interview with Lee, and secure him by the tempting offer of the command of the active army of the United States. Neither the President nor his officers knew the man. Three years after the war, in a letter to the Honorable Reverdy Johnson, of Maryland, dated February 25, 1868, is found for the first time his account of this interview: "After listening to Blair's remarks," writes Lee, "I declined the offer he made me to take command of the army that was to be brought into the field, stating, as candidly and courteously as I could, that, though opposed to secession and deprecating war, I could take no part in an invasion of the Southern States."

"I went directly from the interview with Mr. Blair to the office of General Scott, told him of the proposition that had been made me, and my decision. After reflection upon returning home, I concluded that I ought no longer to retain any commission I held in the United States Army, and on the second morning thereafter I forwarded my resignation to General Scott. At the time I hoped that peace would have been preserved; that some way would be found to save the country from the calamities of war; and I then had no other intention than to pass the remainder of my life as a private citizen. Two days afterward, on the invitation of the Governor of Virginia, I repaired to Richmond, found that the convention then in session had passed an ordinance withdrawing the State from the Union, and accepted the commission of commander of its forces, which was tendered me."

"Since the Son of Man stood on the mount," said an orator, "and saw all the kingdoms of the earth and the glory thereof stretching before him, and turned away from them to the agony and bloody sweat of Gethsemane, and to the Cross of Calvary beyond, no follower of the meek and lowly Saviour can have undergone a more trying ordeal, or met it with a more heroic spirit of sacrifice."

Two and a half months before Colonel Lee's resignation the conventions of South Carolina, Mississippi, Florida, Alabama, Georgia, Louisiana, and Texas had respectively passed ordinances taking these States out of the Union; and their delegates had assembled at Montgomery, Ala., and formed a new government, under the name of the Confederate States of America. On February 4th, the date of the birth of the new government, at Virginia's request, a peace conference, composed of delegates from twenty-one States, met in Washington. The Congress of the United States rejected all terms of settlement proposed by it, and the rising tide of sectional strife passed the high-water mark.

If the seven Southern States which first formed the Confederacy were terribly in earnest, so equally were the Northern and Eastern States in opposition to the new government. The border States, upon whose breast the storm of war must break, were still hoping for a peaceable solution of the trouble; the problem

50

was soon solved for them. In Charleston Harbor, South Carolina, out of the waters rises a fortress of the United States called Sumter. It is situated in the middle of the harbor, and was erected on an artificial island built on the shoals. Its walls were eight feet thick and forty feet high. It was five-sided, inclosing a space of about three hundred and fifty feet. On its ramparts and in its casements one hundred and forty guns could be mounted, and its full garrison was six hundred men. This fort was originally occupied only by an engineer, who was employing some workmen in its repairs; but at Fort Moultrie, on a narrow neck of land extending into the harbor, was a garrison of sixty-nine soldiers and nine officers under the command of Major Robert Anderson. This officer, having every reason to apprehend an attack upon his position, decided to abandon Moultrie and take possession of Sumter, which he did on the night of December 26th. Robert Anderson was a Kentuckian, and a West Point graduate of the class of 1827, whose sympathies at the beginning of the war were rather on the side of the South. He continued to occupy with his little force this island fort, while Beauregard, who had resigned from the United States Army and was already commissioned by the seceding States, was building hostile batteries on every side. A crisis in this harbor was fast approaching. The Government of the United States decided to make an attempt to throw men and provisions into the fort, and when this became known, orders were issued from Montgomery for Beauregard to open his batteries. In the gray of the morning at half-past 4 on a certain Friday, April 12, 1861, a single shot fired from the Confederate batteries at Fort Johnson announced that the bombardment of a fort over whose grim walls floated the Stars and Stripes was about to begin. The report of the bursting of this shell startled the country from center to circumference. The Angel of Peace which for months had been hovering over the republic plumed his wings for flight and the Demon of War reigned supreme. President Lincoln followed this act of war by issuing a proclamation calling for seventy-five thousand troops. A prompt response was given to him by the governors of the Northern States; but those of Arkansas, Tennessee, Kentucky, North Carolina, Virginia, and Missouri declined in terms more or less emphatic. The secession of all these States from the Union followed, except Kentucky and Missouri, whose sympathies were divided, and their union with the Government formed at Montgomery, Ala., was speedily made. On April 17, 1861, the Ordinance of Secession was passed by the Virginia Convention, and the day following, Lee had a long interview with his old commander, General Scott. On the 20th the die was cast; his Rubicon was crossed, for the resignation of his commission in the army of the United States was respectfully tendered to the War Department. His letter explanatory of his position at that time, though familiar to the public, is given here as the best expression of his feelings upon so momentous a subject:

Arlington, Va., April 20, 1861.

General: Since my interview with you on the 18th inst. I have felt that I ought no longer to retain my commission in the army. I therefore tender my resignation, which I request you will recommend for acceptance. It would have been presented at once but for the struggle it has cost me to separate myself from a service to which I have devoted the best years of my life and all the ability I possessed. During the whole of that time more than a quarter of a century — I have experienced nothing but kindness from my superiors and a most cordial friendship from my comrades. To no one, General, have I been as much indebted as to yourself for uniform kindness and consideration, and it has always been my ardent desire to merit your approbation. I shall carry to the grave the most grateful recollections of your kind consideration, and your name and fame shall always be dear to me. Save in the defense of my native State I never desire again to draw my sword. Be pleased to accept my most earnest wishes for the continuance of your happiness and prosperity, and believe me, most truly yours,

(Signed) R. E. Lee.

To his sister in Baltimore, whose husband was a strong Union man, Colonel Lee wrote the same day, telling her that he had resigned; that he had decided the question whether he should take part for or against his native State, saying: "With all my devotion to the Union and the feeling of loyalty and duty of an American citizen, I have not been able to make up my mind to raise my hand against my relatives, my children, my home. I know you will blame me, but you must think as kindly of me as you can, and believe

I have endeavored to do what I thought right. May God guard and protect you and yours, and pour upon you every blessing, is the prayer of your devoted brother."

He wrote still a third letter, upon this eventful day, to his brother, Sydney Smith Lee, at that time a commander in the United States Navy:

Arlington, Va., April 20, 1861.

My dear brother Smith:

The question which was the subject of my earnest consultation with you on the 18th inst. has in my own mind been decided. After the most anxious inquiry as to the correct course for me to pursue, I concluded to resign, and sent in my resignation this morning. I wished to wait till the Ordinance of Secession should be acted on by the people of Virginia; but war seems to have commenced, and I am liable at any time to be ordered on duty, which I could not conscientiously perform. To save me from such a position, and to prevent the necessity of resigning under orders, I had to act at once, and before I could see you again on the subject, as I had wished. I am now a private citizen, and have no other ambition than to remain at home. Save in the defense of my native State, I have no desire ever again to draw my sword. I send you my warmest love.

Your affectionate brother,

(Signed) R. E. Lee.

It was necessary now to bid farewell to old Arlington, where so many happy memories of the past had clustered. He must say good-by to his army comrades, and his sword must soon be crossed with many of them on the bloody field of battle. With conflicting emotions he departed from what had been the capital of his country so long, and went immediately to Richmond, the capital of his State. His coming had been anxiously looked for, and his mother Commonwealth opened wide her arms to embrace her distinguished son. He was at once nominated by the Governor to the Virginia Convention still in session there, to be a major general and commander in chief of the Virginia forces. When the question of his nomination was put to that body, there was an immediate and ardent response, which attested the cordial and unbounded confidence in the man to whom Virginia committed her fortunes. The next day Major-General Lee was invited to appear before the convention. The invitation greatly disturbed him; he was so modest, so opposed to display, so little accustomed to be gazed at by the public, and certainly never before had been placed in such a trying position. But what could he do? The ceremony had been prepared; he had accepted the command of the troops of Virginia after having declined the command of the United States Army. Virginia, through her convention, wanted to see him. A committee had been appointed to transmit its invitation and conduct him to its presence. "The hall was crowded," said the historian, "with an eager audience." All the members of the convention stood as a mark of respect. On the right of the presiding officer were Governor Letcher, of Virginia, and Mr. Stevens, the Vice-President of the Confederacy, and on the left members of the Advisory Council of Virginia. Leaning on the arm of Mr. Marmaduke Johnson, of Richmond, chairman of the committee, General Lee entered the hall. Every spectator admired the personal appearance of the man, his dignified figure, his air of self-composure, his strength of feature, in which shone the steady animation of a consciousness of power, purpose, and decision. He was in the full and hardy flush of ripe years and vigorous health. His form was tall, its constituents well knit together; his head, well-shaped and squarely built, gave indication of a powerful intellect. The face, not yet interlined by age, still remarkable for its personal beauty, was lighted up by eyes black in the shade, but brown in the full light, clear, benignant, but with a deep recess of light, a curtained fire in them that blazed in moments of excitement; the countenance and natural expression were gentle and benevolent, yet striking the beholder as masking an iron will. His manners were at once grave and kindly without gayety or abandon. He was also without any affectation of dignity. Such is the man whose stately figure in the capital at Richmond brought to mind the old race of Virginians, and who was thereafter to win a reputation not only as the first commander, but also as a perfect and beautiful model of manhood.

When about half-way up the main aisle Mr. Johnson stopped, and in ponderous tones said: "Mr. President, I have the honor to present to you and to the convention Major-General Lee." The general's retreat was cut off by the crowd of people who pressed up the hall in his rear. The president of the convention, Mr. Janney, of the County of Loudoun, was to voice the sentiments of the body over which he had ably presided, and Lee must face the music of Janney's eloquence, so he stood calmly while the president of the convention said:

Major-General Lee, in the name of the people of our native State here represented, I bid you a cordial and heartfelt welcome to this hall in which we may yet almost hear the echo of the voices of the statesmen and soldiers and sages of bygone days who have borne your name, whose blood now flows in your veins. When the necessity became apparent of having a leader for our forces, all hearts and all eyes, with an instinct which is a surer guide than reason itself, turned to the old county of Westmoreland. We know how prolific she had been in other days of heroes and statesmen. We know she had given birth to the Father of his Country, to Richard Henry Lee, to Monroe, and last, though not least, to your own gallant father; and we knew well by your deeds that her productive power was not yet exhausted. We watched with the most profound and intense interest the triumphal march of the army led by General Scott, to which you were attached, from Vera Cruz to the capital of Mexico. We read of the sanguinary conflicts and blood-stained fields, in all of which victory perched upon our banners. We know of the unfading luster that was shed on the American armies by that campaign, and we know also what your modesty has always disclaimed — that no small share of the glory of these achievements was due to your valor and military genius. Sir, we have by this unanimous vote expressed our convictions that you are at this time among the living citizens of Virginia, 'first in war.' We pray to God most fervently that you may conduct the operations committed to your charge, that it will soon be said of you that you are the 'first in peace,' and when that time comes you will have earned the still prouder distinction of being 'first in the hearts of your countrymen.' When the Father of his Country made his last will and testament he gave his swords to his favorite nephews with the injunction that they should never be drawn from their scabbards except in self-defense, or in defense of the rights and principles of their country, and that if drawn for the latter purpose, they should fall with them in their hands rather than relinquish them. Yesterday your mother Virginia placed her sword in your hand upon the implied condition that in all things you will keep it to the letter and spirit, that you will draw it only in defense, and that you will fall with it in your hand rather than that the object for which it is placed there should fail.

The reply of General Lee was simple and short, Washington-like in modesty and touching in language. His heart was filled with emotion as he heard the very language his father had used in reference to the great Washington, applied so many years afterward to himself. The scene was solemn as well as new to the soldier.

"Mr. President and gentlemen of the Convention," said he in reply, "profoundly impressed with the solemnity of the occasion, for which I must say I was not prepared, I accept the position assigned me by your partiality. I would have much preferred had the choice fallen upon an abler man. Trusting in Almighty God, an approving conscience, and the aid of my fellow-citizens, I devote myself to the service of my native State, in whose behalf alone will I ever again draw my sword." It was his first and last speech, and under all the circumstances he could safely rest his oratorical reputation upon this, single effort. It is possible, had he selected a public profession after the war, we could have said of him as Pope said of Argyll:

The State's thunder born to wield,

And shake at once the Senate and the field.

He had now entered upon the discharge of new duties and assumed new responsibilities. The bridge over which he had crossed from Colonel Lee, of the United States Army, to Major-General Lee, of the Virginia forces, had been burned behind him. He was enlisted for the war, In the prime of manhood and physical vigor he held what he considered the greatest honor — his State's highest commission. He had sacrificed exalted rank, home, and fortune, and had followed only the conscientious voice of duty. The words of his own father were ringing in his ears as he once exclaimed, "No consideration on earth could induce me to act a part, however gratifying, which could be construed into a disregard or forgetfulness of this Commonwealth." Therefore he would not join the confederacy of States, but was waiting for the endorsation by the people of Virginia of the action of her representatives duly assembled in convention. One hundred and twenty thousand votes were cast for the ratification of the Ordinance of Secession, some twenty thousand against it. Before this popular decision was reached, the convention gave to the Confederate Government the control of the military operations within her border, and the Secretary of War, Mr. L. P. Walker, had, by an order dated Montgomery, Ala., in May, 1861, placed under General Lee's command all troops of the Confederate States as soon as they arrived in Virginia. Previous to this, his command was limited to the Virginia forces. Virginia having united her fortune with her Southern sister States, the Confederate Congress in session at Montgomery ten days afterward adjourned to meet in Richmond, Va. A letter from General Lee to his wife, who was still at Arlington, April 30, 1861, tells her that he is "glad to hear all is well and as yet peaceful. I fear the latter state will not continue long. I think, therefore, you had better prepare all things for removal from Arlington — that is, plate, pictures, etc., and be prepared at any moment. Where to go is the difficulty. When the war commences no place will be exempt; in my opinion, indeed, all the avenues into the State will be the scene of military operations. I wrote to Robert [his son] that I could not consent to take boys from their schools and young men from their colleges and put them in the ranks at the beginning of the war when they are not needed. The war may last ten years. Where are our ranks to be filled from then?"

And again he writes: "I am very anxious about you. You have to move, and make arrangements to go to some point of safety which you must select. The Mount Vernon plate and pictures ought to be secured. War is inevitable, and there is no telling when it will burst around you. Virginia yesterday, I understand, joined the Confederate States. What policy they may adopt I cannot conjecture." And Mrs. Lee, from Arlington, May 5, 1861, sent the following note to General Scott in Washington:

My dear General:

Hearing that you desire to see the account of my husband's reception in Richmond, I have sent it to you. No honors can reconcile us to this fratricidal war which we would have laid down our lives freely to avert. Whatever may happen, I feel that I may expect from your kindness all the protection you can in honor afford. Nothing can ever make me forget your kind appreciation of Mr. Lee. If you knew all you would not think so hardly of me. Were it not that I would not add one feather to his load of care, nothing would induce me to abandon my home. Oh, that you could command peace to our distracted country!

Yours in sadness and sorrow, M. C. Lee.

Occasionally this wife and mother's heart would beat with happiness at the stories of successful compromise between the sections and then sink in despair at the continued prospects of war. From Richmond, May 13, 1861, her husband wrote her: "Do not put faith in rumors of adjustment. I see no prospect for it. It cannot be while passions on both sides are so infuriated. Make your plans for several years of war. If Virginia is invaded, which appears to be designed, the main routes through the country will, in all probability, be infested and passage interrupted. I agree with you in thinking that the inflammatory articles in the papers do us much harm. I object particularly to those in the Southern papers, as I wish them to take a firm, dignified course, free from bravado and boasting. The times are indeed calamitous. The brightness of God's countenance seems turned from us, and its mercy stopped in its blissful current. It may not always be so dark, and he may in time pardon our sins and take us under his protection. Tell Custis he must consult his own judgment, reason, and conscience as to the course he may take. I do not wish him to be guided by my wishes or example. If I have done wrong, let him do better. The present is a momentous question which every man must settle for himself and upon principle. Our good Bishop Meade has just come in to see me. He opens the convention tomorrow, and, I understood him to say, would preach his fiftieth anniversary sermon. God bless and guard you." A few days before he had written:

Richmond, May 8, 1861.

I received yesterday your letter of the 5th. I grieve at the anxiety that drives you from your home. I can appreciate your feelings on the occasion, and pray that you may receive comfort and strength in the difficulties that surround you. When I reflect upon the calamity pending over the country my own sorrows sink into insignificance.

On the 2d of the same month he told her: "I have just received Custis's letter of the 30th, inclosing the acceptance of my resignation. It is stated it will take effect on the 25th of April. I resigned on the 20th, and wished it to take effect on that day. I cannot consent to its running on further, and he must receive no pay if they tender it beyond that day, but return the whole if need be." And again, in a letter May 16, 1861, he writes: "I witnessed the opening of the convention yesterday, and heard the good bishop's sermon for the fiftieth anniversary of his ministry. It was most impressive, and more than once I felt the tears coursing down my cheeks. It was from the text: 'And Pharaoh said unto Jacob, How old art thou?' It was full of humility and self-reproach."

Mr. Jefferson Davis, the provisional President of the new Government, reached Richmond on the 29th of May. Virginia's capital then became the capital of the Confederacy. The journey from Alabama by the Southern President was a triumphal march. At every station crowds of people met and cheered him, and on his arrival in Richmond he received an ovation. He had graduated at West Point the year before General Lee, but was one year and a half his junior in age. He had served in the infantry, and later in the dragoons in the United States Army, and then resigned his commission. When the Mexican War broke out his soldierly instincts could not be repressed. His services were greatly demanded, and he entered Mexico as the colonel of a Mississippi regiment. He had also held the highest positions in civil life, as a member of the United States House of Representatives, as a Senator of the United States, and Secretary of War in Mr. Pierce's Cabinet. Distinguished in war and in peace, a statesman and a soldier, he combined in his person the qualities necessary for the head of a new government born amid the throes of war, whose cradle had been lighted by the rifle's flash. No stain had ever been found on the polished armor of his career during a long term of public service. His courage could not be assailed, his honor questioned, or his ability denied. He had been made on the secession of Mississippi commander in chief of her forces, just as General Lee had been commissioned in the Virginia forces. Had he consulted his own wishes he would have respectfully declined the position of President, and upon the pages of history, from 1861 to 1865, might have been found the record of his deeds as an army commander.

The role assigned to him in the tragedy of war was a most difficult one to discharge, and in the eyes of his opponents he was "the villain of the play." When the red curtain of war rolled up from the American stage, to the world were revealed two presidential chairs. In one was seated Mr. Abraham Lincoln, in the other Mr. Jefferson Davis. These two chief magistrates were both born in Kentucky. One, when a small child, was carried by his parents to Mississippi; the other, when about eight years old, was taken to Indiana, and afterward to Illinois. Each absorbed the political theories of their respective States. Had Davis been carried to Illinois and Lincoln to Mississippi, in the war between the States Lincoln might have been carrying a Mississippi rifle, while Davis held aloft the star-spangled banner. Each represented, as powerful exponents, the constructions of the Constitution, referred to the sword for decision, there being no common arbiter in such case. Mr. Davis's office had none of the elements of popularity. Upon it was showered the criticisms of the South, while at the North every finger, every pen, every gun was pointed at its occupant. Davis used every possible effort to make two republics grow on this continent where only one grew before; and so likewise did Lee.

The former, as President, could not have written success on the standards of the Confederacy; it was not so ordained — the contest was too unequal in men, money, and means of war. The people of the whole South, who stood behind their guns, or were left at their hearthstones, numbered only six million whites, while the population in the Northern States amounted to eighteen million. The former were animated by the tie which binds the heart to home, and which it is said "stretches from the cradle to the grave, spans the heavens, and is riveted through eternity to the throne of God on high." On the other hand, the Northern people desired to see the great republic stretch from the waves of the Atlantic to the golden sands of the Pacific, and from the Northern lakes to where the Father of Waters rolls his tribute to the Gulf as an undivided country. The North was thickly populated, and the whole machinery of its Government was in running order. It had its regular army around which the volunteer regiments could rally. Its navy rode undisputed the adjoining seas; its arsenals and forts were crammed with weapons, and its Treasury filled with precious metals, out of which could be manufactured all the sinews of war. In a long struggle, under these circumstances, victory was to the strong. The deeds of a brave soldier, even if unsuccessful, excite the admiration of mankind. The civil ruler of the vanquished is not so fortunate when the power to sustain his government departs. Mr. Davis was not the demon of hate his enemies have painted. He did not thirst for the blood of his countrymen. His whole character has been misunderstood by the mass of the people who opposed his public views. His heart was tender as a woman's; he was brave as a lion, and true as the needle to the pole to his convictions; in disposition generous, in character courteous and chivalric.

When his voice was heard for the last time in the Senate Chamber of the United States it did not breathe hatred to sections of the country other than his own, but he spoke in affectionate terms of those with whom he had to conscientiously differ upon great questions. "I am sure," said he, "that I feel no hostility to you Senators from the North. I am sure there is not one of you, whatever sharp discussion there may have been between us, to whom I cannot say in the presence of my God, I wish you well, and such is the feeling, I am sure, of the people whom I represent and those whom you represent. For whatever offense I have given, I have, Senators, in this hour of our parting, to offer you my apology."

General Lee found himself surrounded on all sides by war. From Richmond, June 9, 1861, he wrote his wife: "You may be aware that the Confederate Government is established here. Yesterday I turned over to it the command of the military and naval forces of the State, in accordance with the proclamation of the Governor, under an agreement between the State and the Confederate States. I do not know what my position will be. I should like to retire to private life, so that I could be with you and the children, but if I can be of service to the State or her cause, I must continue. Mr. Davis and all his Cabinet are here." And two days afterward he tells her: "I am sorry to learn that you are anxious and uneasy about passing events. We cannot change or hinder them, and it is not the part of wisdom to be annoyed by them. In this time of great suffering to the State and country, our private distresses we must bear with resignation, and not aggravate them by repining, trusting to a kind and merciful God to overrule them for our good."

Preparations were now being rapidly made for war, which could be no longer prevented or postponed. The firing upon and capture of Fort Sumter, the hostile reception given the Massachusetts troops in Baltimore on April 19th, the great excitement all through the country, caused everyone to speedily join the side he desired to unite with. In the North every arsenal was put to work on the manufacture of arms for their troops. It was the first duty of the Federal Government to make Washington, the capital, secure. Then an army of invasion must be organized and a plan of campaign mapped out, whose objective point was the capture of Richmond, the capital of the Southern Confederacy.

CHAPTER 5

INVASION OF VIRGINIA.

On the 24th of May the advance guard of the Federal army occupied the heights of Washington, with Arlington, the former home of General Lee, as headquarters, as well as all the country stretching down the Potomac eight miles below to Alexandria. Only a few persons understood the magnitude of the impending contest. The "Rebellion" many thought was to be crushed in ninety days, and most of the volunteer troops were enlisted by the North for that period.

One hundred and fifteen miles away, at Richmond, great activity prevailed also. The sagacity, skill, and experience of Lee were taxed to the uttermost equipping and sending to threatened points the troops rapidly arriving from the South. There was no regular army to serve as a nucleus, or navy, commissary, quartermaster's, or ordnance departments. Everything had to be provided. General Gorgas, the Chief of Ordnance of the Confederate States, reported that he found in all the arsenals of the Confederate States but fifteen thousand rifles and one hundred and twenty thousand inferior muskets. In addition there were a few old flint muskets at Richmond, and some Hall's rifles and carbines at Baton Rouge. There was no powder, except some which had been left over from the Mexican War and had been stored at Baton Rouge Arsenal and at Mount Vernon, Ala. There was but little artillery, and no cavalry, arms, or equipments. Raw recruits had to be drilled and disciplined, companies assigned to regiments, regiments to brigades, brigades to divisions. With the map of Virginia before him, Lee studied to make a successful defensive campaign. He knew that the object of the greatest importance to his enemy was the capture of Richmond, and that the fall of that city early in the contest might terminate the war. His genius for grand tactics and strategy taught him at once that the most natural advance to Richmond from Washington would be along the Orange and Alexandria Railroad, as it was called then. It was the only railway running into the State at that time from Washington, and troops moving along its line could be so directed as not to uncover their capital, while prompt facilities could be obtained for transportation of supplies from the base established at Alexandria or Washington. Another route lay up the peninsula lying between the James and York Rivers, with Fort Monroe and its vicinity as a base for operations. Another way to enter the State was by crossing the upper Potomac at Harper's Ferry and Williamsport, and then on through the great valley of Virginia between the Blue Ridge and Shenandoah Mountains; and still another entrance might be effected through the mountain ranges of West Virginia. Norfolk, too, by the sea, had to be watched and protected. Troops, therefore, as fast as they arrived in Richmond and could be prepared for the campaign, were sent principally to these points. It was necessary that organized forces should be in such position as to check any forward movements by any of these routes. General Lee early had predicted the march of the Army of the Potomac, as the Washington army was called, and pointed out what would in all probability be the battlefield. He ordered the largest number of troops to Manassas Junction, that being the point of union of the railroad coming into Virginia from Washington with a branch road leading into the Valley of Virginia. It was a strategic point, because an army in position there would be able to resist the further progress of the opposing hosts, and could, if necessary, re-enforce the troops in the valley. Competent and experienced officers were at an early date placed in command of the important stations. For Manassas, General P. G. T. Beauregard was selected. This officer, having been the first employed in active operations, and having compelled the surrender of Fort Sumter, was the military hero of the hour. He was a graduate of West Point, and had served in the Engineer Corps with marked distinction. His skill in that branch of the service was admirably displayed in the selection of positions for the batteries erected to defend Charleston Harbor, and his vigilance, activity, and military knowledge were rewarded by the prompt reduction of the fort. He assumed command of the troops at and in the vicinity of Manassas about the 1st of June, and possessed the entire confidence of his army.

Harper's Ferry received also the prompt attention of the Confederate authorities. To this important post General Joseph E. Johnston was ordered, superseding in the command there Colonel T. J. Jackson. General Johnston assumed command of the Army of the Shenandoah on May 23, 1861. He was a classmate of Lee's at West Point. On being graduated he was assigned to the artillery, and then to the topographical engineers. He became distinguished before his beard grew. In the Indian wars in Florida and in Mexico his coolness, address, soldierly bearing, daring deeds, and his many wounds made him famous. General Scott is reported to have said "Johnston is a great soldier, but was unfortunate enough to get shot in nearly every engagement." In 1861 he was at the head of the Quartermaster's Department of the United States Army, with the rank of brigadier general. Upon the resignation of his commission he was commissioned a general officer in the Virginia service by Governor Letcher. Later he was given a brigadier general's commission in the Confederate service in the regular army, then the highest grade in it. The resignation of his commission and his decision to fight under the flag of the South was hailed with delight by the Southern people, who felt they were securing the services of an army commander of undoubted merit. General Benjamin Huger, another distinguished officer of the army of the United States, who had also resigned, was charged with watching over Norfolk. General John Bankhead Magruder, who had acquired distinction in the Federal army but had joined his fortunes to the South, was ordered to Yorktown to defend the peninsular route. General Holmes, who had rendered conspicuous service in the army of the United States, was sent to command at Acquia Creek, some twelve miles east of Fredericksburg. Robert Garnett, also an officer of the United States Army, of tested ability, was ordered to West Virginia to take charge of the department and of the forces assembling in that region. All of these officers had been selected with great care, and had been more or less distinguished in the army, but not one of them had ever before been in command of large numbers of men.

The regular army of the United States previous to 1861 was a small organization of fifteen thousand soldiers. Including the quartermaster general, there were only five general officers in it — Scott, Wool, Harney, Twiggs, and Joe Johnston. A few only of the officers, to whom was assigned on either side the command of armies, corps, and divisions, had ever previous to the war commanded a regiment, the great majority of them not more than one company.

In these operations of defense General Lee's whole time was employed. The larger number of troops were sent to Beauregard and Johnston, it being evident that one or both of the points occupied by their armies would be the scene of the earliest conflicts. His services were great and indispensable, but it can be readily seen that after supplying the threatened points with troops, and after providing commanding officers for the different armies when the battles of the war began, there would be no place for him in the field, but that the active operations there would be intrusted to others at first.

To Mrs. Lee, from Richmond, June 24, 1861, he wrote: "My movements are very uncertain, and I wish to take the field as soon as certain arrangements can be made. I may go at any moment to any point where it may be necessary. Custis is engaged on the works around this city, and many of our old friends are dropping in. E. P. Alexander is here. Jimmy Hill, Alston, Jenifer, etc., and I hear that my old colonel, A. S. Johnston, is crossing the plains from California."

Preparations for the advance of the Federal army of the Potomac on Manassas were rapidly nearing completion. Everything needed was bountifully provided from an overflowing Treasury. General Scott was still Commander in Chief of the United States Army, and still the possessor of the entire confidence of his country. Mr. Simon Cameron, Mr. Lincoln's Secretary of War, wrote to Mr. John Sherman, then in the field as a volunteer aid-de-camp to General Patterson, that the whole administration has but one safe course in this emergency, and that is to be guided by the counsels of the general in chief in all that relates to the plans, movements, and commands of the campaign. He has superior knowledge, wisdom, and patriotism over any other member of the administration, said Cameron, and enjoys the unlimited confidence of the people, as well as that of the President and his advisers.

The day after General Scott's last interview with General Lee he published General Order No. 3, which created the Department of Washington, embracing Pennsylvania, Delaware, Maryland, and the District of Columbia, and Major-General Robert Patterson, of Pennsylvania, was placed in command. On June 3, 1861, the headquarters of this officer were at Chambersburg, Pa., where he was busy organizing and equipping the army whose objective point was Harper's Ferry, at that time occupied by a small number of the Southern troops. It was General Scott's original plan to make Patterson fight the first great battle in the war, giving him all the troops he could possibly spare from the defense of Washington. It was his first purpose to make a feint on Beauregard at Manassas, while making a real attack upon Joe Johnston in the Valley of Virginia. With the defeat of Johnston the victorious army could march on Beauregard at Manassas, re-enforced by the troops around the Federal capital. Soldiers of high reputation and great merit were ordered to report to Patterson. Fitz John Porter was his adjutant general, Amos Beckwith commissary of subsistence, Crosman quartermaster, Sampson topographical engineer, Newton engineer; while such men as A. E. Burnside, George H. Thomas, Miles, Abercrombie, Cadwalader, Stone, and Negley commanded troops; and then, the laws being silent in the midst of arms, Senator John Sherman, of Ohio, was his aid-de-camp. From Patterson's position two routes led to the Valley of Virginia, one via Frederick, Md., across the Potomac at Harper's Ferry, the other by Hagerstown, Md., crossing at Williamsport and thence to Martinsburg. Patterson wisely selected the latter route, because it was a flank movement on his enemy at Harper's Ferry, who could present no obstacle to a successful passage to the Potomac. He therefore marched his army to Hagerstown, where, on the 15th of June, he had ten thousand men. On that day General Johnston evacuated Harper's Ferry, and two days later, with a force of sixty-five hundred men, was at Bunker Hill, a point twelve miles from Winchester and between that city and Martinsburg.

This was wise on the part of Johnston. His intention to do so was accelerated from a well-authenticated rumor that had reached him of the advance of the Federal forces in the direction of Winchester from Romney, some forty-three miles west of that place. Indeed, he had detached two regiments under Colonels A. P. Hill and Gibbons, and sent them to Winchester with orders to proceed out on the road toward Romney for the purpose of checking any march of hostile troops from that direction. These troops were thought to be the advance of a force under General McClellan, which had been organized in that section of western Virginia. When Patterson crossed the Potomac Johnston very properly moved to Bunker Hill, so as to be in position to prevent the junction of McClellan and Patterson, by fighting a battle with Patterson before McClellan could reach Winchester, if indeed the force reported to be advancing from the direction of Romney were McClellan's troops. He soon became convinced that no considerable body of United States troops was approaching Winchester from the direction of Romney, and so the two regiments sent there were recalled to Winchester. If the action of Johnston had not been guided by the reports received, he would have evacuated Harper's Ferry at once upon the passage of the Potomac by Patterson. Harper's Ferry was not a defensible point. It was a cul-de-sac commanded thoroughly by Maryland Heights. Later in the war a large force of Federal troops was easily forced to capitulate by a portion of the Confederate army approaching from the direction of Maryland.

Patterson commenced to cross the Potomac with the avowed purpose of fighting a battle with the army under Johnston, but when about two thirds of his troops had crossed he received a telegram from General Scott ordering him to send to Washington at once all the regular troops he had, horse and foot, as well as the Rhode Island regiment under Burnside, which was a very fine one. If this telegram had not been received, and Patterson had continued the march of his troops into Virginia, he would have reached Martinsburg on the 17th of June, and on the 18th could have attacked the Confederate troops then in line of battle awaiting him at Bunker Hill, eleven miles distant, and there might have been on the pages of American history a second battle of that name. The explanation of General Scott's telegram is to be found in the fact that he had changed his plan of offensive operations. He had reversed his former purposes and now proposed to fight the first battle with the army around Washington, while the army of Patterson should make the feint, to prevent a junction of Johnston's army with that of Beauregard's at Manassas. General Sanford, who commanded the State troops of New York, was the senior officer at that time on duty in Washington; and at two o'clock on the morning of May 21, 1861, with eleven thousand men first invaded Virginia and took possession of Arlington Heights and the adjacent section as far as Alexandria. The Department of Virginia was created, and General Irvin McDowell was selected by the Washington Cabinet to command it.

Up to that time it is said General Scott did not want anything done on the Virginia side of the Potomac except to fortify Arlington Heights. He was "piqued and irritated" that the Cabinet should have sent McDowell into Virginia, and sent him two messages by his aid-de-camp asking him to make a personal request not to be sent on the other side of the river, and took occasion to say to the Cabinet that he was never in favor of going over into Virginia. He did not believe in a little war by piecemeal, but he believed in a war of large bodies. He was in favor of moving down the Mississippi River with eighty thousand men, fight all the battles that were necessary, take all the positions he could find and garrison them, fight a battle at New Orleans, win it, and thus end the war. His marvelous plan met with serious objections from the powers at Washington. Could it have been submitted to those in Richmond it would have been unanimously adopted.

Irvin McDowell, the commander selected to lead the Federal army against its opponent at Manassas, was a native of Ohio, and graduated at the Military Academy at West Point in 1838. He was assigned to the First Artillery, served in the Mexican War, and was brevetted major for gallant and meritorious conduct at Buena Vista. He was afterward transferred to the Adjutant General's Department, and served there till he was promoted brigadier general in 1861. At this period McDowell was about forty-three years of age, a capable soldier, and a gallant and courteous gentleman. He was kind-hearted, considerate, and tender of the feelings of others. His letter to Mrs. Lee, in reply to one received from her, addressed to the commander of the Federal forces at Arlington, has the ring of the pure metal, and is as follows:

Headquarters, Departments Northeastern Virginia, Arlington, May 30, 1861.

Mrs. R. E. Lee.

Madam: Having been ordered by the Government to relieve Major-General Sanford in command of this Department, I had the honor to receive this morning your letter of to-day addressed to him at this place. With respect to the occupation of Arlington by the United States troops I beg to say it has been done by my predecessor with every regard for the preservation of the place, I am here temporarily in camp on the grounds, preferring this to sleeping in the house under the circumstances which the painful state of the country places me with respect to these properties. I assure you it will be my earnest endeavor to have all things so ordered that on your return you will find things as little disturbed as possible. In this I have the hearty concurrence of the courteous, kind-hearted gentleman in the immediate command of the troops quartered here, and who lives in the lower part of the house to insure its being respected. Everything has been done as you desire with respect to your servants, and your wishes, so far as they have been known or could have been understood, have been complied with. When you desire to return every facility will be given you for doing so. I trust, Madam, you will not consider it an intrusion when I say I have the most sincere sympathy for your distress, and, so far as compatible with my duty, I shall always be ready to do whatever may alleviate it. I have the honor to be, very respectfully,

Your most obedient servant, I. Mcdowell.

P. S. I am informed it was the order of the general in chief if the troops on coming here should have found the family in the house, that no one should enter it, but that a guard should be placed for its protection.

Generals Scott and Lee were organizing their respective armies with the same celerity apparently, for on the 24th of June McDowell had twenty regiments of infantry, aggregating less than fourteen thousand men, two hundred and fifty cavalry, two batteries of light artillery, and three other batteries in the earthworks. His field return, dated June 26th, makes his aggregate forces sixteen thousand six hundred and eleven. At that time the Confederate army, under Beauregard, had nineteen regiments of infantry. The Federal commander estimated Beauregard's force at twenty thousand, and a statement upon which he said he relied, told him that the South Carolina regiments were the best armed and equipped, had negroes with them as servants, were in high spirits, and though the month was June, were freezing for a fight.

It was fully determined now that the Federal army should move against Manassas, and General McDowell was requested to submit a plan of operations and an estimate of the force necessary to carry it out. He did so, and the plan was approved by General Scott, the Cabinet, and Generals Sanford, Tyler, Mansfield, and Meigs, who were present. It was then given to the engineer officers to discuss, and finally was fully adopted. The Federal army was to move out from the vicinity of Washington and Alexandria in four columns and give battle to the enemy by turning their right flank. McDowell exacted two conditions: One that he should be provided with thirty thousand troops; the other that he should not be required to fight any of the Confederate forces then opposed to General Patterson in the Valley of Virginia. The first condition was pledged, and he was told by General Scott that if Johnston joined Beauregard he should have Patterson at his heels.

General Lee had worked incessantly, leaving no stone unturned to give Beauregard a sufficient force to cope successfully with McDowell. He put away personal ambition, and had no thought except to do all in his power to enable others to win victories. From Richmond, July 12, 1861, he wrote Mrs. Lee: "You know that Rob has been made captain of Company A of the University. He has written for a sword and sash, which I have not yet been able to get for him. I shall send him a sword of mine, but cannot procure him a sash. I am very anxious to get into the field, but am detained by matters beyond my control. I have never heard of the assignment to which you allude — of commander in chief of the Southern army — nor have I any expectation or wish for it. President Davis holds that position. I have been laboring to prepare and get into the field the Virginia troops to strengthen those from other States, and the threatened commands of Johnston, Beauregard, Huger, Garnett, etc. Where I shall go I do not know, as that will depend upon President Davis."

The press on both sides, North and South alike, excited by the probability of a battle, began to severely criticize the delay in decisive movements. They did not understand that armies composed almost exclusively of citizen soldiers had to be organized with great care. Regiments had to be placed in brigades, and they in turn formed into divisions; ammunition, the means of subsistence, and the requisite amount of transportation had to be provided. General Lee resisted public clamor in his usual calm and dignified way. McDowell too, like a seasoned soldier, stood the pressure against him as long as he could, but at last it became so great he could wait no longer. So he issued General Order No. 17, dated Arlington Heights, July 16th, which started from camp and put on the march thousands of armed men, as a vast engine is put in motion by pressure on a button. Some thirty miles away, behind a small stream called Bull Run, Beauregard waited the arrival of McDowell. The two army commanders were classmates at West Point, and had studied and marched side by side for four years. It was a strange sight to see them now manoeuvring hostile armies.

The capture of Washington should have been the legitimate military result of the Southern victory at Manassas. A great part of Beauregard's army had not fired a gun on the 21st; the brigades of Ewell, D. R. Jones, Longstreet, Bonham, and Holmes had been quietly resting all day, if we except a small skirmish by Jones. Ewell moved to the battlefield in the afternoon, but was not engaged. If these fresh troops had been led direct on Centreville by the roads crossing the fords they were guarding, they could easily have reached that point, four or five miles distant, before the fugitives of the Federal army, who for the most part were returning by the circuitous route over which they marched in the morning, and which was the only road they knew. The six thousand Federal reserve at Centreville, under Miles, certainly, in view of the demoralization of the rest of the army, could not have made a successful resistance. Bonham and Longstreet crossed Bull Run in pursuit, but were stopped by three regiments of General Blenker's brigade. Three hours and a half of daylight still remained.

The Confederates had nineteen companies of cavalry, McDowell seventeen. In neither army at that time was the employment of cavalry understood. It was not massed, but distributed around among the various infantry brigades where the troopers were principally used for couriers. If the whole of the Southern cavalry had been ordered forward under an enterprising soldier like Stuart, supported by the troops that had not been engaged, Centreville might have easily been reached that night. The next day, while Stuart was moving in the direction of Alexandria and Washington, with some of the freshest infantry as supports, the head of the Confederate army might have been turned toward White's Ford, on the upper Potomac, some twenty-five or thirty miles away. Patterson's army was disintegrating by the expiration of enlistments; Banks, his successor, had at Harper's Ferry about six thousand men and was fearing an attack. Dix, at Fort McHenry and Baltimore, with a small force, was uncomfortable; and Butler, at Fort Monroe, was protesting against Scott's order to send to Washington his Illinois volunteers. All conditions were favorable to a march through Maryland by the Southern army, and either capture the Federal capital or occupy the strategic point at the junction of the Baltimore and Ohio Railroad with the Washington and Baltimore Railroad at the Relay House. Thousands of Marylanders whose sympathies were with the South would have increased the numbers of the Confederate army. Fairfax and Loudoun counties in Virginia, and Howard and Montgomery counties in Maryland, were teeming with food for men and horses. Half a million rounds of ammunition for small arms had been captured. Gorgas, chief of ordnance, had many rounds also in Richmond, for on July 14th General Lee ordered him to send a full supply to General Wise in West Virginia. Besides ammunition, large quantities of muskets, pistols, knapsacks, swords, cannons, blankets, wagons, ambulances, hospital and subsistence stores, and camp and garrison equipment were captured.

On July 22, 1861, there were no troops in Baltimore with which any defense of that city could have been made. There were a few regiments for provost duty, but no available fighting force. Banks was ninety-five miles from Baltimore by the nearest road. White's Ford, on the Potomac, where Johnston and Beauregard could have crossed, is about forty-five miles from Baltimore. The occupation of the Relay House might have produced the immediate evacuation of Washington by the Federals, the transfer of the seat of war to Pennsylvania, the accession of Maryland to the Confederacy, and fifty thousand more men as recruits as fast as they could have been armed, for Baltimore would have clothed and equipped them. Next year, when the second battle of Manassas was fought, General Lee crossed the Potomac and entered Maryland without difficulty under much less favorable conditions. His inferiority of numbers to those of his antagonists were greater, and his ammunition, supplies, and transportation less in proportion to the strength of his army.

The extent of the Southern victory was not known on that hot afternoon of July 21, 1861, because the pursuit had been feeble. Later in the evening, when the Federals were in full retreat, the report reached the Confederate commanders that a strong body of Union troops was advancing via Union Mills on Manassas, and orders were issued in consequence for the rapid march of some troops back to this position, infantry being mounted behind cavalry in order to get there at the earliest possible moment, and Beauregard started in that direction in person with the understanding that Johnston should send him re-enforcements.

The defeat of McDowell's army not being fully utilized by the Confederates caused the victory to be regarded by some at the South as unfortunate, for it was followed by a period of fancied security, while the opposite effect was produced at the North. So great was the confidence in the power to establish another republic on this continent that politicians at the South already began to plot for the Presidential succession. Beauregard was one of those named for office, and he wrote a letter to the public press, dated "within the hearing of the enemy's guns," declaring that he was not a candidate. On the other hand, the day that Washington was crowded with fugitives from the Federal army the House of Representatives passed a resolution pledging to the country and to the world "the employment of every resource, national and individual, for the suppression and punishment of armed rebels." While the South rested on the laurels of Manassas the North went vigorously to work to repair its fortunes. Congress authorized an army of half a million of men to be enlisted for three years, an increase of the navy, and a large loan.

CHAPTER 6

THE CAMPAIGN IN WEST VIRGINIA.

General Lee was in Richmond during the operations at Manassas, and contributed his humble part by the organization and equipment of the army, as well as in the selection of the battlefields. He was not dazzled by the blaze of victory which glistened from the tips of the Southern bayonets, or filled with undue elation. He was one among the very few in the South who always felt the contest would be obstinate and prolonged. No one knew better than he the great resources of one of the combatants, as well as the determination and courage of both. Six days after the battle he writes Mrs. Lee from Richmond, July 27, 1861: "That, indeed, was a glorious victory, and has lightened the pressure upon us amazingly. Do not grieve for the brave dead, but sorrow for those they left behind — friends, relatives, and families. The former are at rest; the latter must suffer. The battle will be repeated there in greater force. I hope God will again smile on us and strengthen our hearts and arms. I wished to partake in the former struggle, and am mortified at my absence. But the President thought it more important that I should be here. I could not have done as well as has been done, but I could have helped and taken part in a struggle for my home and neighborhood. So the work is done, I care not by whom it is done. I leave to-morrow for the army in western Virginia."

As no immediate hostile advance now threatened the Federal or Confederate capitals, other sections began to receive attention. Northwest Virginia lies between the Alleghany Mountains and the Ohio River. It is a rough, mountainous district, with only a few passable roads connecting it with the remainder of the State. The iron horse had never penetrated its soil or watered in its mountain streams. There was not that touch and feeling of interest that is derived from personal contact between the citizens of northwest Virginia and other portions of the Old Dominion. On the question of secession the majority of them differed widely from the great mass of Virginians. It was doubtful territory, and both the Governments at Washington and at Richmond recognized the importance at an early date of sending troops there, the one to protect and nourish the Union sentiment, the other to aid and encourage those who sympathized with the South. Henry A. Wise, once their governor, was made a brigadier general and assembled a force with which he advanced to Charleston, on the Kanawha River, but afterward returned to Lewisburg, on the Greenbrier. It was thought by his presence and eloquence that the resident population might be made confederate in feeling and his army largely recruited. General John B. Floyd, who had been President Buchanan's Secretary of War, had been commissioned at Richmond as brigadier general, and had recruited and organized a brigade in southwest Virginia, and in July led it over to the region of the Kanawha. This was the first field assigned to George B. McClellan by the Federal War Department, an officer of great promise, who, graduating at West Point in 1846, had for his classmates, among others, Burnside and Stonewall Jackson. He served first in the Engineer Corps, and in 1855 was appointed a captain in the First Cavalry. His previous military experience had been much the same as Lee's. In 1857 he resigned, to take up railroad work, and when war commenced he was made a major general of Ohio volunteers. He crossed into northwest Virginia on the 26th of May, he says, of his own volition and without orders. A portion of his command was under General Cox on the Kanawha. In McClellan's immediate front was a Confederate force under General Robert S. Garnett, who had been ordered to defend that portion of northwest Virginia.

Garnett was a Virginian, who had graduated at the Military Academy five years before McClellan. He had won his laurels in the Mexican campaign and afterward against the Indians. Upon resigning from the United States Army his first service in the South was as adjutant general of the Virginia forces. He was considered an excellent officer, a rigid disciplinarian, and, in consequence of many soldierly traits, had at one time been appointed commandant of the Cadet Corps at West Point. In June this officer occupied, with a force of about five thousand men, Laurel Hill, thirteen miles south of Philippi, on the turnpike leading to Beverly, in Randolph County. McClellan reached Grafton on the 23d of the same month, and on the same day issued a proclamation to the inhabitants of West Virginia, and on the following day another to the "soldiers of the Army of the West," both in the bombastic, inflated style followed by officers on each side in the early days of the war. He called his enemies hard names and charged them with grave offenses, and in many ways differed from the same McClellan who afterward commanded the Army of the Potomac. "Soldiers," said he, "I have heard there was danger here. I have come to place myself at your head and share it with you. I fear now but one thing — that you will not find foemen worthy of your steel." He had evidently been reading some of the proclamations of a "great master of war," and attempted to follow his style. The attention of the public was drawn to this Napoleonic imitation, for about that time he received the appellation of the "Young Napoleon," and was so called after he had been brought from West Virginia to the command of the Army of the Potomac. The headquarters of the Department of the Ohio were established at Buckhannon, and from this point McClellan determined to attack the force on Rich Mountain, and advanced and deployed in front of the opposing army, which he found strongly intrenched. He promptly resorted to the only method left in military operations in the mountains, and decided to turn their flank and rear, which General Rosecrans successfully did with four regiments. The troops at this point were a portion of Garnett's force under Lieutenant-Colonel John Pegram. Beverly was occupied by the Federal troops the next day, and General Garnett with the remainder of his army, finding that retreat had been cut off in that direction, abandoned his intrenchments on Laurel Hill and made a hasty retreat in the night over a rough country road in the direction of St. George, in Tucker County. He was rapidly followed and his rear overtaken at Carrick's Ford, on the Shafer Fork of the main branch of Cheat River. In the engagement which followed Garnett was killed.

Lieutenant-Colonel Pegram, who had escaped with a force of some five hundred men from Laurel Hill, not being able to join General Garnett in consequence of the latter's retreat, determined to surrender his little force, which had been without food for two days, as prisoners of war, and on July 12th surrendered to General McClellan five hundred and sixty men and thirty-three commissioned officers. Four days afterward McClellan issued another address to his troops: "Soldiers of the army of the West," said he, "I am more than satisfied with you; you have annihilated two armies commanded by educated and experienced soldiers." The two armies here referred to were the four thousand men under Garnett, and Pegram's small force. In his dispatch of July 12th to the adjutant general at Washington he estimated Garnett's force at ten thousand, beginning at this time a habit of multiplying the number of his enemy by two, which he never afterward abandoned. The success of the campaign, however, had a marked effect upon his future. General Scott telegraphed: "The General in Chief, the Cabinet, the President, are charmed with your activity and valor. We do not doubt that you will in due time sweep the rebels from western Virginia, but we do not mean to precipitate you, as you are fast enough." After McDowell's defeat at Manassas, McClellan was selected to command the defenses at Washington, and the day after that battle, while at Beverly, was informed by Adjutant-General Thomas, at Washington, that his presence there without delay was necessary. General William S. Rosecrans succeeded him.

On July 28th McClellan assumed command of the Department of Northeastern Virginia and of Washington. Being necessary to select another commanding officer for the Southern troops in Northwest Virginia, General Lee designated Brigadier-General Loring, who had been a distinguished officer in the United States service, to be Garnett's successor. Loring left Richmond July 22d and proceeded at once to Monterey, in Highland County, and thence to Huntersville, where a force was being organized for the purpose of securing the Cheat Mountain pass, a strategic point of great value over which the Staunton and

Parkersburg turnpike crossed. The Confederate authorities — having been informed of the advance of the Federal General Cox in the Kanawha Valley and that there would probably be two armies operating in northwest Virginia, and also being disappointed in what had been accomplished in that section — determined to send out there an officer of high rank and reputation. Mr. Davis offered the command of that department, therefore, to General Joseph E. Johnston first, as there was no necessity for Johnston and Beauregard both to remain at Manassas. General Johnston declined the offer, because he thought the most important battles would be fought between Washington and Richmond. It was then determined that General Lee should assume command in person of that department, for his duties of organizing and assigning troops to the different sections had nearly terminated. The Secretary of War and the adjutant general, under the direction of the President, were the proper persons to direct army movements now. General Lee proceeded at once to West Virginia, and for the first time assumed active command of the troops in the field. He went at first to Huntersville, where he found Loring, then to Valley Mountain, where Colonel Gilliam had been stationed. From the former point he wrote to his wife, August 4, 1861:

I reached here yesterday to visit this portion of the army. The points from which we can be attacked are numerous, and the enemy's means unlimited, so we must always be on the alert; it is so difficult to get our people, unaccustomed to the necessities of war, to comprehend and promptly execute the measures required for the occasion. General Johnson, of Georgia, commands on the Monterey line, General Loring on this line, and General Wise, supported by General Floyd, on the Kanawha line. The soldiers everywhere are sick. The measles are prevalent throughout the whole army. You know that disease leaves unpleasant results and attacks the lungs, etc., especially in camp, where the accommodations for the sick are poor. I traveled from Staunton on horseback. A part of the road I traveled over in the summer of 1840 on my return to St. Louis after bringing you home. If anyone had told me that the next time I traveled that road would have been my present errand, I should have supposed him insane. I enjoyed the mountains as I rode along. The views were magnificent. The valleys so peaceful, the scenery so beautiful! What a glorious world Almighty God has given us! How thankless and ungrateful we are!

And from Valley Mountain, August 9, 1861, he writes: "I have been three days coming from Monterey to Huntersville. The mountains are beautiful, fertile to the tops, covered with the richest sward and blue grass and white clover. The inclosed fields wave with a natural growth of timothy. This is a magnificent grazing country, and all it wants is labor to clear the mountainsides of timber. It has rained, I believe, some portion of every day since I left Staunton. Now it is pouring. Colonel Washington, Captain Taliaferro, and myself are in one tent, which as yet protects us. I have enjoyed the company of our son while I have been here. He is very well and very active, and as yet the war has not reduced him much. He dined with me yesterday and preserves his fine appetite. To-day he is out reconnoitering, and has the full benefit of this fine rain. I fear he is without his overcoat, as I do not recollect seeing it on his saddle. I told you he had been promoted to a major in the cavalry, and he is the commanding cavalry officer on this line at present. He is sanguine, cheerful, and hearty as ever. I sent him some corn meal this morning, and he sent me some butter — a mutual exchange of good things. The men are suffering from measles and so on, as elsewhere, but are cheerful and light-hearted. The nights are cool and the water delicious. Send word to Miss Lou Washington that her father is sitting on his blanket sewing a strap on his haversack. I think she ought to be here to do it."

And on September 1st, from the same place, he tells her: "We have had a great deal of sickness among the soldiers, and those now on the sick list would form an army. The measles is still among them, but I hope is dying out. The constant cold rains, mud, etc., with no shelter or tents, have aggravated it. All these drawbacks, with impassable roads, have paralyzed our efforts."

It was Loring's purpose to attempt a movement on Reynolds's rear. This officer occupied, with two thousand men, Cheat Mountain pass, through which the Staunton and Parkersburg pike passed, and had three thousand men in Tygart's Valley on the road to Huttonsville, with a reserve at Huttonsville, so he could re-enforce his troops on the Staunton road, or on the Valley Mountain road, as necessary. Loring, with thirty-five hundred effective troops, was in front of him on the latter, while General H. R. Jackson, with twenty-five hundred men, opposed him on the Staunton road. The natural topographical features, supplemented by artificial means, rendered his position very strong on both. General Lee promptly took the offensive by threatening his front, while a column should proceed, if possible, around one of his flanks and assault his rear — a plan similar to that adopted by McClellan at Rich Mountain.

The greatest difficulty in a campaign of this description is to discover suitable routes or paths over the rocks and precipitous mountain sides for the troops of the turning column. General Lee's experience as an engineer in Mexico had taught him the duties of a reconnoitering officer. He therefore not only availed himself of the information derived from others, but would personally proceed daily long distances for that purpose.

At this time Rosecrans was in the Kanawha Valley with Cox's column, and was opposed by the troops of the Confederate Generals Floyd and Wise, and was not with the force in General Lee's front. He and Lee commanded the whole department on their respective sides. The army whose movements General Lee was about to superintend in person consisted, as stated, of about six thousand men, including a few companies of cavalry, as well as a fine battalion of the same arm under General Lee's son, Major W. H. F. Lee. Reynolds's force was estimated at about ten thousand.

After Floyd's clever defeat of Tyler at Cross Lane, on the 26th of August, he and General Wise seem to have kept on different sides of the Gauley River, and there did not seem to be that concert of action between them necessary to win success. General Rosecrans, an able and sagacious officer, was not slow to recognize the detached positions of these commands, and determined to re-enforce Cox and attempt the defeat of one or both of them. He advanced rapidly and assaulted Floyd's position, but was repulsed. Floyd then crossed the Gauley, followed by Rosecrans, and with Wise fell back to Sewell Mountain, the latter remaining on its eastern front, while the former fell still farther back to Meadow Bluff, eighteen miles west of Lewisburg.

Leaving the operations in this section for the present to the immediate commanders of the troops, General Lee proposed first to win a victory, if possible, over Reynolds. He was combative, anxious to strike, but many difficulties confronted him. He fully realized he had been sent to West Virginia to retrieve Confederate disasters, and that he had a most difficult task to perform. The Federal commander held the center summit of Cheat Mountain pass, the mountain having three well-defined summits. The center one was selected by the Federals as the best one to defend, and there a block fort was constructed with flanking outworks consisting of intrenchments of earth and logs, the whole line of defense being protected by dense abatis. The position chosen was inaccessible in many directions by the steep, rugged walls of the mountain. It was necessary first to carry this well-selected position of the Federal troops. A citizen surveyor, in sympathy with the South and familiar with the mountain paths, had made a trip to an elevated point where he could clearly see the Federal position, and reported his observations to General Lee. Afterward he made a second reconnoissance, accompanied by Colonel Albert Rust, of the Third Arkansas Regiment, who was anxious to see the nature of the ground and the strength of the position for himself. They reported to General Lee that in their opinion the enemy's position could be assailed with success with troops which could be guided to the point they had reached. General Lee decided to make the attack, and gave to Rust a column of twelve hundred infantry, with such capable officers as Taliaferro and Fulkerson. General Jackson was to advance via the turnpike to confront the enemy from that direction, while another column, under Brigadier-General Anderson, was to advance to the third or west top of Cheat Mountain, where they could secure possession of the turnpike and be in the rear of the enemy. The rest of the army was to move down the Tygart's River valley upon the forces of the enemy stationed there. The attack on these troops, however, was to depend on the successful assault of the fortified position on Cheat Mountain. It was an admirably conceived plan. The key point was first to be carried; the report of the guns of the troops engaged there was the signal for an assault in front, while a force was thrown in the rear of both positions to cut off retreat. General Loring issued his order of attack on September 8, 1861. General Lee issued an order approving it on the same date, telling his troops that the safety of their lives and the lives of all they held dear depended upon their courage and exertions. "Let each man," said he, "resolve to be victorious, and that the right of self-government, liberty, and peace shall in him find a defender." The movement was to begin at night, which happened to be a very rainy one. All the troops, however, got in the positions assigned to them without the knowledge of the enemy, where they waited, every moment expecting to hear the rattle of Rust's muskets, who had been charged with the capture of the pass on Cheat Mountain; but hour after hour passed, and no sounds were heard. After a delay of many hours, and the enemy had divined the nature of the attack, the troops were ordered back to their former position. There had been only a small conflict between cavalry, in which Colonel John A. Washington, General Lee's aid-de-camp, who had been sent with Major W. H. F. Lee to reconnoiter the enemy, was killed from an ambuscade. Colonel Rust did not report to General Lee until the next day — September 13, 1861; he admits that he got to the designated place at the appointed time, notwithstanding the rain; that he seized a number of pickets and scouts, and learned from them that the enemy in front of him was between four and five thousand strong and was strongly fortified. He made a reconnoissance and found these representations were fully corroborated. Rust claims in his reports that spies had communicated the movements of the Confederate troops to the enemy. This officer evidently did not attack, because he found, on getting close to the Federal position, that it was much stronger than he thought it was from the preliminary reconnoissances he had made. As the attack of the whole depended on the assault of this force, the failure to attack caused a corresponding failure of the whole movement. The plan of operations was well devised, and, under ordinary circumstances, might have proved successful.

Military operations are often like a vast piece of machinery: with one part out of gear, the successful operation of the whole machine is not possible. In a letter to Mrs. Lee, dated Valley Mountain, September 17, 1861, the general writes: "I had hoped to have surprised the enemy's works on the morning of the 12th, both at Cheat Mountain and on Valley River. All the attacking parties with great labor had reached their destination over mountains considered impassable to bodies of troops, notwithstanding the heavy storm that had set in the day before and raged all night, in which they had to stand till daylight; their arms were then unserviceable, and they in poor condition for a fierce assault. After waiting till ten o'clock for the assault on Cheat Mountain, which did not take place, and which was to be the signal for the rest, they were withdrawn, and after waiting three days in front of the enemy, hoping he would come out of his trenches, we returned to our position at this place. I cannot tell you my regret and mortification at the untoward events that caused the failure of the plan. I had taken every precaution to 'insure success, and counted on it; but the Ruler of the Universe willed otherwise, and sent a storm to disconcert the well-laid plan. We are no worse off now than before, except the disclosure of our plan, against which they will guard. We met with one heavy loss which grieves me deeply: Colonel Washington, accompanied Fitzhugh [his son] on a reconnoitering expedition. I fear they were carried away by their zeal and approached within the enemy's pickets. The first they knew there was a volley from a concealed party within a few yards of them. Three balls passed through the colonel's body, three struck his horse, and the horse of one of the men was killed. Fitzhugh mounted the colonel's horse and brought him off. I am much grieved. He was always anxious to go on these expeditions. This was the first day I assented. Since I had been thrown in such immediate relations with him, I had learned to appreciate him very highly. Morning and evening have I seen him on his knees praying to his Maker.' The righteous perisheth, and no man layeth it to heart; the merciful men are taken away, none considering that the righteous are taken away from the evil to come. 'May God have mercy on us all!'"

And on the 26th of the same month he writes from his camp on Sewell Mountain: "I told you of the death of Colonel Washington. I grieve for his loss, though I trust him to the mercy of our heavenly Father. It is raining heavily. The men are all exposed on the mountains, with the enemy opposite to us. We are without tents, and for two nights I have lain buttoned up in my overcoat. To-day my tent came up and I am in it, yet I fear I shall not sleep for thinking of the poor men. I have no doubt the socks you mentioned will be very acceptable to the men here and elsewhere. If you can send them here I will distribute to the most needy."

This movement having failed, and knowing that the enemy would be prepared for any second attempt which, from the nature of the country, would have to be similar to the one already tried, General Lee decided to turn his attention to the commands of Wise and Floyd in front of Rosecrans, leaving General H. R. Jackson in Reynolds's front. He proceeded at once to Floyd's command, which he reached on September 20th, and then to Wise's camp, closely inspecting both. He at once perceived that Wise's position was the strongest and offered the best means for successful defense, and promptly concentrated his forces at that point.

General Lee expressed regret at not finding the commands of Floyd and Wise united, and said it would be the height of imprudence to submit them separately to the attack of Rosecrans. He desired the troops to be massed at once, so that "We conquer or die together," a most extravagant and unusual form of speech for him to adopt. "You have spoken," said he to Wise, "of want of consultation and concert. Let that pass till the enemy is driven back. I expect this of your magnanimity. Consult that and the interest of your cause, and all will go well." "Just say, then," replied Wise, "where we are to 'unite and conquer or die together,' and I will delight to obey you."

Rosecrans had advanced to the top of Big Sewell Mountain and had placed his army in a strong position. General Lee, with the troops of Wise, Floyd, and Loring — about eight thousand men — occupied a position on a parallel range. The two armies were now in close proximity to each other, both occupying strong defensive positions. Lee and Rosecrans, having been officers of the engineers, were fully aware of the great disadvantage an attacking army would have, and each waited, hoping the other would attack. After occupying these positions for twelve days, Rosecrans, on the night of October 6th, retreated. The condition of the roads, the mud, the swollen streams, the large numbers of men with typhoid fever and measles, the condition of the horses, of the artillery, and transportation, were such that Lee decided not to pursue. It is possible that had he known Rosecrans would not attack he would have given battle himself, notwithstanding the great advantage Rosecrans would have possessed by accepting it in his strong defensive position. The rapid approach of winter and the rainy season terminated the campaign in this section.

In a letter dated Sewell Mountain, October 7, 1861, General Lee tells Mrs. Lee that at the time of the reception of her letter "the enemy was threatening an attack, which was continued till Saturday night, when, under cover of darkness and our usual mountain mist, he suddenly withdrew. Your letter, with the socks, was handed to me when I was preparing to follow. I could not at the time attend to either, but I have since; and as I found Perry [his colored servant from Arlington] in desperate need, I bestowed a couple of pairs on him as a present from you; the others I have put in my trunk, and suppose they will fall to the lot of Meredith [a colored servant from the White House], into the state of whose hose I have not yet inquired. Should any sick man require them first he shall have them, but Meredith will have no one near to supply him but me, and will naturally expect that attention. The water is almost as bad here as in the mountains I left. There was a drenching rain yesterday, and as I left my overcoat in camp, I was thoroughly wet from head to foot. It has been raining ever since, and is now coming down with a will; but I have my clothes out on the bushes, and they will be well washed. The force of the enemy, estimated by prisoners captured, is put down at from seventeen to twenty thousand — General Floyd thinks eighteen thousand. I do not think it exceeds nine or ten thousand, but it exceeds ours. I wish he had attacked, as I believe he would have been repulsed with great loss. The rumbling of his wheels, etc., were heard by our pickets; but as that was customary at night in moving and placing his cannon, the officer of the day, to whom it was reported, paid no particular attention to it, supposing it to be a preparation for an attack in the morning. When day appeared the bird had flown, and the misfortune was that the reduced condition of our horses for want of provender, exposure to cold rains in these mountains, and want of provisions for the men, prevented the vigorous pursuit of following up that had been prepared. We can only get up provisions from day to day, which paralyzes our operations. I am sorry, as you say, that the movements of the armies cannot keep pace with the expectations of the editors of papers. I know they can regulate matters satisfactory to themselves on paper. I wish they could do so in the field. No one wishes them more success than I do, and would be happy to see them have full swing. General Floyd has three editors on his staff. I hope something will be done to please them."

It is true West Virginia, as it is called, would have been a desirable accession to either side. Both Governments were actuated in its occupation by a desire to protect the citizens who adhered respectively to their cause. The country abounded in vast forests, coal, and iron, presenting fields of wealth and enterprise. The advantage, however, in a campaign there was in favor of the Federals. The proximity of their railroads on the one side made it easier for them to concentrate troops rapidly and furnish them with supplies, while on the other hand the Southern lines of communication from Staunton and other portions of eastern Virginia were necessarily long and difficult.

At the termination of this campaign of General Lee's the Confederate Government did not bestow much attention upon this section. The majority of the people seemed inclined to support the Federal side; indeed, most of the counties sent representatives to a convention which passed an ordinance creating them into a new State, which the Government at Washington recognized as the State of Virginia.

It must be admitted that General Lee retired from West Virginia with diminished military reputation. Great results had been expected from his presence there. Garnett's defeat and death were to be avenged, and the whole of that portion of Virginia speedily wrested from the Federal arms. The public did not understand the difficulties of the situation, or comprehend why he did not defeat Reynolds, or the failure to attack Rosecrans. The news of the expected great victories did not reach Richmond. Men apparently wise shook their heads and said he had been overrated as a soldier; that he relied upon a "showy presence" and a "historic name," and that he was "too tender of blood" and leaned too much to the engineer side of a military question, preferring rather to dig intrenchments than to fight. There were two men, however, who stood by him faithfully in this doubtful period of his career. One of them was the President of the Confederate States, the other the Governor of Virginia. They knew him well, and that the failure of the West Virginia campaign could not be fairly attributed to him. General Lee remained quiet under the occasional attacks of the public press. He knew that his duty had been discharged conscientiously. He was not aware that he had a "showy presence." On the contrary, he was modest, unassuming and simple. He conducted the campaign in the most unostentatious manner. He had only two aid-de-camps, Colonels Washington and Taylor. The former was killed; the remaining aid-de-camp shared the same tent with him. The mess furniture was of the plainest kind — tin cups, tin plates, tin dishes, which Colonel Taylor says were carried all through the war. In the full zenith of his fame as a great army commander, anyone who accepted his hospitality would be obliged to eat from this same old tinware with which he commenced the war in West Virginia. It is not known that General Lee ever attempted in any way to make explanation or defense of these attacks. In a private letter to Governor Letcher, dated September 17, 1861, he simply states that "he was sanguine of success in attacking the enemy's works on Rich Mountain"; that "the troops intended for the surprise had reached their destination, having traversed twenty miles of steep and rugged mountain paths, and the last day through a terrible storm, which had lasted all night, in which they had to stand, drenched to the skin, in a cold rain"; that he "waited for an attack on Cheat Mountain, which was to be the signal, till 10 A. M., but the signal did not come. The chance for surprise was gone. The provisions of the men had been destroyed the preceding day by the storm. They had nothing to eat that morning and could not hold out another day, and were obliged to be withdrawn. This, Governor," he writes, "is for your own eye. Please do not speak of it; we must try again. Our greatest loss is the death of my dear friend, Colonel Washington. He and my son were reconnoitering the front of the enemy. They came afterward upon a concealed party who fired upon them within twenty yards, and the colonel fell, pierced by three balls. My son's horse received three shots, but he escaped on the colonel's horse. His zeal for the cause to which he had devoted himself carried him too far."

General Lee, in obedience to instructions, returned to Richmond, but not amid the shouts of the populace. The bands did not play, "See the conquering hero come"; the chaplet of victory was missing from his brow, the scalps of Rosecrans and Reynolds from his belt. The public looked at the cold facts, and were interested in actual results. The difference between war in the mountains and war amid the hills and valleys and green fields was never for a moment considered. Four hundred and eighty-four years before the birth of our Saviour, history tells us that Xerxes marched with over one million men and twelve hundred war ships to invade Greece. And that Leonidas, with three hundred Spartans and about four thousand men from the other parts of Greece, defied the King of Persia and for two days held the defile in the mountains known as the Pass of Thermopylae.

In 1861 there were still passes among the mountains, and a few men could hold them against an army, and could only be dislodged by flank and rear attacks over long, steep, circuitous paths. Lee made the attempt when in front of Reynolds. Had his well-laid plans been carried out, possibly he might have defeated the Federal general. In an offensive movement against Rosecrans the elements of success were against him. The naturally strong, elevated position on Sewell Mountain, made still stronger by the methods of an engineer of such great ability as Rosecrans, could not have been easily carried. When it was abandoned, the Federal rear guard, every few miles, could have found other strong positions where Lee's army could have been detained for days had the condition of his troops and the roads permitted pursuit. On General Lee's return to Richmond his duties as military adviser at the side of the chief executive officer of the Confederacy were resumed. No response was ever made to public criticisms. His vision swept the future, his vindication would come if opportunity offered.

CHAPTER 7

ATLANTIC COAST DEFENSES. — ASSIGNED TO DUTY IN RICHMOND AS COMMANDER IN CHIEF UNDER THE DIRECTION OF THE SOUTHERN PRESIDENT.

The defenseless condition of the States south of Virginia bordering on the Atlantic coast was an object of solicitude to the Confederate War Department. Important seaports and the sections adjoining them were at the mercy of combined Federal fleets and armies. Their proper defense was most difficult, the means most inadequate. It was a good field for a capable engineer. Lee was available, and the emergency demanded his services. Reluctantly he was ordered from Richmond, cheerfully he obeyed, and on November 6th proceeded to South Carolina, where he at once commenced to erect a line of defense along the Atlantic coasts of that State, Georgia, and Florida.

His four months labors in this department brought prominently into view his skill. Exposed points were no longer in danger. Well-conceived defensive works rose rapidly. Public confidence in that department was permanently restored, and with it came to Lee a new accession of popularity and esteem. His headquarters was wisely established at Coosawhatchie on the railroad, a point midway between Charleston, S. C., and Savannah, Ga., and from which he could give close supervision to the defenses of these important cities. From this point, referring to the union of his family on Christmas day, he writes:

Coosawhatchie, S. C., December 22, 1861.

I shall think of you on that holy day more intensely than usual, and shall pray to the great God of heaven to shower his blessings upon you in this world and to unite you all in his courts in the world to come. With a grateful heart I thank him for his preservation of you thus far, and trust to his mercy and kindness for the future. Oh, that I were more worthy and more thankful for all that he has done and continues to do for me!

And again on Christmas day he wrote:

I cannot let this day of grateful rejoicing pass without some communion with you. I am thankful for the many among the past that I have passed with you, and the remembrance of them fills me with pleasure. As to our old home, if not destroyed it will be difficult ever to be recognized. Even if the enemy had wished to preserve it, it would almost have been impossible. With the number of troops encamped around it, the change of officers, the want of fuel, shelter, etc., and all the dire necessities of war, it is vain to think of its being in a habitable condition. I fear, too, the books, furniture, and relics of Mount Vernon will be gone. It is better to make up our minds to a general loss. They cannot take away the remembrances of the spot, and the memories of those that to us rendered it sacred. That will remain to us as long as life will last and that we can preserve. In the absence of a home I wish I could purchase Stratford. It is the only other place I could go to now acceptable to us, that would inspire me with pleasure and local love. You and the girls could remain there in quiet. It is a poor place, but we could make enough corn-bread and bacon for our support, and the girls could weave us clothes. You must not build your hopes on peace on account of the United States going to war with England. Our rulers are not entirely mad, and if they find England is in earnest, and that war or a restitution of the captives must be the consequence, they will adopt the latter. We must make up our minds to fight our battles and win our independence alone. No one will help us.

In still another letter from the same place the general writes Mrs. Lee:

71

I am truly grateful for all the mercies we enjoy, notwithstanding the miseries of war, and join heartily in the wish that the next year may find us in peace with all the world. I am delighted to hear that our little grandson is improving so fast and is becoming such a perfect gentleman. May his path be strewn with flowers and his life with happiness. I am very glad to hear also that his dear papa is promoted. It will be gratifying to him, I hope, and increase his means of usefulness. While at Fernandina I went over to Cumberland Island and walked up to Dungeness, the former residence of General Greene. It was my first visit to the house, and I had the gratification at length of visiting my father's grave. He died there, you may recollect, on his way from the West Indies, and was interred in one corner of the family cemetery. The spot is marked by a plain marble slab, with his name, age, and date of his death. Mrs. Greene is also buried there, and her daughter, Mrs. Shaw, and her husband. The place is at present owned by Mr. Nightingale, nephew of Mrs. Shaw, who married a daughter of Mrs. James King. The family have moved into the interior of Georgia, leaving only a few servants and a white gardener on the place. The garden was beautifully inclosed by the finest hedge of wild olive I have ever seen.

The harbor of Charleston, S. C., was now greatly strengthened. Floating batteries were constructed and earthworks at proper places erected. At Savannah forts were built opposite Hilton Head, and at the best points to cover the river approaches. Lee watched every detail, and his eye, with a soldier's glance, overlooked the whole Department. His lines were admirably located, and his dispositions for the general defense of the department were so skillfully planned that it was not until near the close of the four years war that his enemy could surmount the difficulties they presented. These cities were the cherished objective points of the administration at Washington, and large numbers of soldiers and sailors were at various times during the war employed to secure their capture. Their safety for so long a period from impending dangers upon every side was due to the military skill of Lee, as well as to the efforts of the accomplished officers who were in immediate command — General Ripley at Charleston and General Lawton at Savannah. Well might a prophetic tongue utter at this period that the "time would come when Lee's superior abilities would be vindicated, both to his own renown and the glory of his country."

On February 8, 1862, he writes his wife from Savannah: "I wrote you the day I left Coosawhatchie. I have been here ever since endeavoring to push forward the works for the defense of the city. Guns are scarce as well as ammunition. I shall have to bring up batteries from the coast, I fear, to provide for this city. Our enemies are trying to work their way through the creeks and soft marshes along the interior of the coast, which communicate with the sounds and sea, through which the Savannah flows, and thus avoid the entrance to the river, commanded by Fort Pulaski. Their boats require only seven feet of water to float them, and the tide rises seven feet, so that at high water they can work their way and rest on the mud at low. I hope, however, we shall be able to stop them, and my daily prayer to the Giver of all victory is to enable us to do so. We must make up our minds to meet with reverses and overcome them. But the contest must be long, and the whole country has to go through much suffering. It is necessary we should be humble and taught to be less boastful, less selfish, and more devoted to right and justice to all the world."

And again from the same place, he says on February 23d: "The news from Tennessee and North Carolina is not at all cheering. Disasters seem to be thickening around us. It calls for renewed energies and redoubled strength on our part. I fear our soldiers have not realized the necessity of endurance and labor, and that it is better to sacrifice themselves for our cause. God, I hope, will shield us and give us success. I hear the enemy is progressing slowly in his designs. His gunboats are pushing up all the creeks and marshes to the Savannah, and have obtained a position so near the river as to shell the steamers navigating it. I am engaged in constructing a line of defense at Fort Jackson, which, if time permits and guns can be obtained, I hope will keep them out."

Spring was now rapidly approaching, and active military operations would soon be resumed in many quarters. Richmond, the dual capital city, was menaced by an army from the North large in numbers and splendidly equipped. Forts Henry and Donelson had fallen in February before the combined attacks by land and water of the Federals, opening the Cumberland and Tennessee Rivers, and resulting in the capitulation of Nashville, the capital of Tennessee. The outlook was a serious one from a Southern standpoint, and demanded the counsel of the wisest, coolest, and most courageous leaders. The great interests at stake induced the President to summon General Lee from the Southern Department to Richmond, and on March 13th he was assigned to the position of commander of the armies of the Confederacy and charged with the duty of conducting all the military operations of the Southern armies under the direction of the President. A few months previous to this his name had been mentioned in connection with the position of Secretary of War. The appointment, however, was not made, possibly because it was considered unwise to confine such great military talent within the bureau of a cabinet officer.

General Lee's youngest son, Robert, eighteen years old at this time, made up his mind to leave the University of Virginia and go into the army. His father gave him permission, saying in a letter to his wife:

Richmond, March 16, 1862.

I went with him to get his overcoat, blankets, etc. There is great difficulty in getting what is good. They have all to be made, and he has gone to the adjutant general's office of Virginia to engage in the service. God grant it may be for his good. I told him of the exemption granted by the Secretary of War to the professors and students of the University, but he expressed no desire to take advantage of it. As I have done all in the matter that seems proper, I must now leave the rest in the hands of our merciful God. I hope our son will make a good soldier.

During that month the Federal commanders displayed great activity. McClellan's large and well-organized army was being transferred to the Peninsula. General Lee wrote to his wife from Richmond, March 22, 1862: "Our enemies are pressing us everywhere and our army is in the fermentation of reorganization. I pray that the great God may aid us, and am endeavoring by every means in my power to bring out the troops and hasten them to their destination."

Much had happened during his absence from Virginia. The campaign was subjected to new conditions, and the location of the two principal armies in that State had been changed. The next battlefield was to be much closer to Richmond. Johnston and Beauregard after the battle of Manassas continued to occupy that section, extending their outposts, however, closer to Washington, while partially blockading the Potomac River by some heavy guns at a point near the mouth of Quantico Creek, where the channel runs on the Virginia side.

The inactivity of this army during the remainder of the summer and the fall months convinced the Federal authorities that no offensive campaign would be undertaken by it. About the latter part of September the Southern President visited the army and held a conference with Generals Johnston, Beauregard, and G. W. Smith in reference to active operations. These officers proposed, General Johnston states, a plan to cross the upper Potomac and place their army in the rear of Washington and fight the battle there. They demanded that the army should be increased for that purpose by troops drawn from all parts of the Confederacy, so as to number sixty thousand effectives. These conditions the President was unable to comply with, so all hope of any advance was abandoned, and the army prepared to go into winter quarters. Mr. Davis frankly told them that the whole country was applying for arms and troops, and that he could do no more to increase the strength of the army at that point than to send it as many recruits as there were arms in the ordnance stores at Richmond — namely, twenty-five hundred. Many advantageous changes were now made in the organization of the army. Brigades were put into divisions and placed under such commanding officers as Van Dorn, G. W. Smith, Longstreet, T. J. Jackson, and Holmes. The northern frontier of Virginia was formed into a new military department, and General Johnston's command was extended to the Alleghany Mountains on one side, Chesapeake Bay on the other, and divided into three districts: the Valley, to be commanded by T. J. Jackson; the District of the Potomac, under the immediate charge of Beauregard; and that section lying around the mouth of Acquia Creek was placed under the immediate charge of Major-General Holmes. On August 31st the President nominated to the Senate five persons to be generals in the Confederate army: First, Samuel Cooper, from May 15, 1861; second, A. S. Johnston, May 28th; third, R. E. Lee, June 14th; fourth, J. E. Johnston, July 4th; fifth, G. T. Beauregard, July 21st. Officers who resigned from the United States Army had been promised by the Confederate Government when it was first established at Montgomery, Ala., that they should hold the same relative rank to each other when commissioned in the army of the Confederate States. Cooper, who had been the adjutant general of the United States Army, was the senior colonel. Albert Sidney Johnston resigned a colonelcy, General Lee a colonelcy, which he had only held a short time, and Beauregard a captaincy. General Joseph E. Johnston but a short time previous to the outbreak of the war had been a lieutenant colonel of the First Cavalry, United States Army, and was ranked in that army by all the officers named except Beauregard. Upon the death of General Jesup, the quartermaster general shortly before the war, General Scott was asked to recommend an officer to fill the vacancy, and he is reported to have said that if the Secretary of War would put into a hat the names of A. S. Johnston, R. E. Lee, and J. E. Johnston, and one of said names be taken out, a good quartermaster general would be secured. Mr. John B. Floyd, who was the Secretary of War at the time, naturally threw his influence in favor of J. E. Johnston, as he came from his section of Virginia and was a relative, and he received the appointment. In those days the quartermaster general had the rank of brigadier general. When the writer once asked Mr. Davis if J. E. Johnston was not entitled to be the ranking senior general in the Southern army, he replied, "No, because the quartermaster general was not considered in the line of promotion or eligible to active work in the field. It was a staff position, and by law he could not command troops except by special assignment, and that therefore I went back to General Johnston's old rank in determining the relative rank of the five generals."

As the Confederate army showed no disposition to enter upon an offensive campaign, it soon became an interesting problem to the Washington authorities how to defeat Johnston's army and capture Richmond. This indisposition to attack gave McClellan ample time to arrange his plans, and he took it. His deliberate methods were very provoking to his own Government, and a matter of much suspense to the one opposed to him. He leisurely organized and equipped his army. The North liberally and rapidly responded to the demand for more men. For the three months succeeding the battle of Manassas troops were poured into the Department at Washington at the rate of 40,000 per month, so that at the end of that period McClellan officially reported that he had 147,695 men present for duty. In December following, his report shows 175,854 present for duty, and in March, 1862, 171,602, while the army of his opponent in February had only 47,306 present for duty, including the force under Jackson in the valley and a small number under Holmes at Acquia Creek, and in March about 50,000.

It is difficult to conceive why, with these immense odds in his favor, McClellan did not advance in the early spring against Johnston's position. This plan was discussed as well as two or three others. McClellan at last, it seems, told the Federal President in positive language that he did not approve the movement on Johnston's position at Centreville, but preferred to take his army down the Potomac River into Chesapeake Bay, up the Rappahannock River, and form a base of operations at a place called Urbana; or, better still, continue down Chesapeake Bay and around to Fort Monroe, using that formidable fort as a base, and advance on Richmond from that direction up the Peninsula formed by the James and York Rivers, upon whose surfaces the gunboats of his navy could be floated, and thus a thorough protection be given to his flanks. A solemn conclave of twelve general officers of the Federal army considered these various propositions, and, by a vote of eight to four, agreed to approve McClellan's plan of the peninsular route as opposed to Mr. Lincoln's proposition for a movement similar to the one made by McDowell. The difficulties in the way at the time for a change of base to the lower Peninsula were the fact that the proximity of Johnston's army to Washington seriously threatened the safety of that city. In March, however, General Johnston solved the problem by a retrograde movement to the line of the Rappahannock, trebling his distance from the Federal capital. While this retreat gave up a great deal of valuable country and raised the blockade of the Potomac, its strategic advantages were great. His army could then be in a position to better receive a direct advance from the Federal troops, or could by a rapid march prevent any army which should be transported by water and landed at points closer to Richmond from reaching that city before he could.

As soon as Johnston had retreated McClellan advanced his troops to the position Johnston had occupied during the winter. They were then countermarched and brought back to Alexandria, a Virginia city a few miles below Washington, where arrangements were made as rapidly as possible to transport them to the Peninsula, Mr. Lincoln stipulating that at least fifty thousand men should be left in and around Washington for its immediate defense. He did not propose to "exchange queens," because the capture of Washington by Johnston would be attended with much greater results than the capture of Richmond by McClellan.

At that time the Southern forces on the Peninsula were under the command of Major-General J. Bankhead Magruder, an accomplished and well-known officer, who had formerly distinguished himself in the service of the United States. "Prince John," as he was called, occupied a strong position from river to river. The embarkation of McClellan's troops began on March 17th, and he left in person on April 1st, reaching Fortress Monroe on the afternoon of the 2d. When he arrived fifty-eight thousand men and one hundred guns had preceded him. Magruder was a short distance in his front with eleven thousand men. His left was at Yorktown, on York River, and his line of battle extended along the Warwick River to Mulberry Island, on the James, where his right rested. Gloucester Point, opposite Yorktown, projects well out into the river. Fortifications had been constructed there, and it was expected that the guns at that point as well as those at Yorktown by crossfire could prevent the passage of the Federals up York River in any attempt to reach the Confederate rear.

It will be remembered that when the British held Yorktown over a century ago they also fortified and held Gloucester Point, and to it, at one time, Cornwallis attempted to retreat when the troops of Washington were closing around him. Magruder's front was twelve miles long and in many respects strong. In a portion of it the ground was swampy, while dams had been constructed by which the water could be backed up, rendering the passage of the stream impracticable for artillery and infantry nearly three fourths of its distance. McClellan stopped in front of this line on April 5th, having left Fort Monroe the day before. Until he reached it he was ignorant of its existence. In addition to the large army which McClellan proposed should accompany him up the Peninsula, was a separate or detached corps under McDowell, over forty thousand strong, which was intended to operate upon either bank of York River in order to turn the Confederate position, should much resistance be offered to McClellan's advance on Richmond. After McClellan left Washington, the military governor, General Wadsworth, reported to President Lincoln that he had left only twenty thousand troops for its defense. This report, and General Jackson's movements in the Valley of Virginia, alarmed the Federal authorities, and they immediately ordered McDowell's corps to return to Washington. With the corps of McDowell's added to McClellan's great army the fall of Richmond might have been accomplished.

These movements of the Federal troops were of course speedily communicated to General Johnston on the Rappahannock, and D. H. Hill's, D. R. Jones's, and Early's divisions were put in march to re-enforce Magruder. General Beauregard had been detached from Johnston and sent to Kentucky. When later it was evident the Peninsula would be the route selected for the Federal advance, Johnston at once proceeded to that point with the remainder of his army, except General Ewell's division, which with a regiment of cavalry was left on the line of the Rappahannock, and Jackson's division, in the Valley of Virginia. Had McClellan assailed Magruder's lines at once his largely superior numbers would have won a victory in all probability, though the defensive line was a strong one. General Johnston arrived in person April 14th, and assumed command on the 17th. His advance did not arrive at Yorktown till the 10th, the other divisions following a few days later. For six days McClellan was in front of Magruder before Johnston's arrival, but instead of assaulting, he commenced arrangements for a dilatory siege. Johnston, upon the arrival of all of his troops, had, together with Magruder's forces, fifty-three thousand men; McClellan one hundred and thirty-three thousand, including twelve thousand of Franklin's division on board of transports in readiness to move up York River. He sat down in front of Magruder's position to await the arrival of his siege trains, and began the construction of scaling ladders, which might be useful to assault permanent works, and the erection of batteries for his heavy guns, much to the annoyance of the Washington authorities, for the falling back of his opponents to new intrenched lines in rear would render useless his great guns and his great labor in getting them in position.

On Johnston's arrival in the Peninsula he closely examined the defensive lines of Magruder, but did not like them, and returned at once to Richmond to lay his views before his President. "McClellan's army," said he, "should be encountered in front of Richmond by uniting there all the available forces of the Confederacy; the grand army thus formed, surprising that of the United States by an attack, when it was expecting to besiege Richmond, would be almost certain to win." Mr. Davis declined to decide so important a question hastily, and asked General Johnston to call upon him at a stated hour, when he would have Randolph, his Secretary of War, and General Lee both present. Johnston suggested that he invite Generals G. W. Smith and Longstreet also, and the conference was duly held. The Secretary of War objected to Johnston's plan because it involved the evacuation of Norfolk and the destruction of the famous Merrimac, or Virginia, as she was last named. General Lee could not vote in favor of General Johnston's proposition because the withdrawal of troops from South Carolina and Georgia would expose the important seaports of Charleston and Savannah to danger and capture. He thought that the Peninsula had excellent battlefields for a small army contending with a great one, and for that reason argued that the contest with McClellan's army should be made there. General G. W. Smith agreed with General Johnston's views, while Longstreet took but little part, which Johnston attributed to his deafness. Mr. Davis announced his decision in favor of the opinion of General Lee, and ordered Johnston to concentrate his army on the Peninsula as soon as possible, giving him in addition the command of the Department of Norfolk. McClellan threw up an immense amount of earth in front of the Confederate position. Batteries were erected for one hundred of the heaviest Parrott guns and thirty mortars, the range of some of the former being over four miles. His big gun batteries were out of the reach of any guns in Johnston's army, and therefore would be unmolested while delivering their fire. Ascertaining that these batteries would be ready for action in a few days, General Johnston gave orders to General Huger, in command at Norfolk, and to General Lee's brother, Captain Sydney Smith Lee, of the navy, who was in command of the Gosport navy yard, to evacuate these places and to remove to a safe place as much of the valuable public property as possible.

On May 3d General Johnston issued his orders for the withdrawal of his army from the Yorktown lines. He had delayed McClellan's advance for a month, which gave time to greatly strengthen the works around Richmond, as well as to advance the preparations for the great battle which now was inevitable. The Confederate army marched out of its lines at midnight. The rear guard of cavalry followed at daylight.

This retreat of Johnston's was a surprise to McClellan. He did not anticipate a retrograde movement on the part of the Confederates till they should have been hammered out of their lines by his big guns. His pursuit was not commenced for six hours after the departure of the Southern rear guard. At noon on the 4th Johnston's army had only reached Williamsburg and its vicinity. At this point the Federal advance encountered his rear guard. Some fighting took place in the afternoon, and on the next day a heavy conflict ensued between portions of the two armies, resulting in the loss to the Federals of twenty-two hundred and twenty-eight men, and to the Confederates of twelve hundred. Johnston then leisurely continued his retreat. A force under Franklin was sent up York River by McClellan to make an attempt to get on his flank and rear. When they landed they were attacked and driven back to their boats, and held in that position till the whole of Johnston's force had passed the threatened point. His army was now composed of four divisions under G. W. Smith, Magruder, D. H. Hill, and Longstreet. Jackson was in the Shenandoah Valley, while Ewell, who had been left on the Rappahannock, had retired to Gordonsville. He could not depend, therefore, upon these two commands for immediate re-enforcement.

It cannot be denied that a battle fought at Richmond would liberate troops from other points and thus give additional re-enforcements to Johnston; but the evacuation of Norfolk and the destruction of the Virginia — which had been such a protection to James River — as well as the moral effect of a retreat which allowed a vast hostile army to knock at the very gates of Richmond, were undesirable.

McClellan, with his five corps under Sumner, Franklin, Porter, Heintzelman, and Keyes, slowly followed the Confederate army as it fell back on Richmond. As he arrived in its immediate vicinity he began to deploy his legions, taking care to extend well his right so that it might reach out for McDowell's junction. This officer, with an army nearly equal to Johnston's whole force, was directly charged with the protection of Washington, and was specially instructed in any manoeuvres he should attempt, that the safety of the Federal capital must be steadily kept in view. From the vicinity of Washington he moved out on the line of railroad beyond Manassas to Culpeper Court House. Ewell, who had been on the Rappahannock with his division, was then at Gordonsville, and later went over into the Shenandoah Valley to join Jackson. There being no enemy directly threatening Washington then, McDowell wisely marched to Fredericksburg. He was well located there, being about fifty miles from his capital and about the same distance from McClellan's right flank. He could therefore easily return to Washington, if necessary, or re-enforce McClellan in his attack on Richmond.

In order to watch this movement of McDowell's, General Joseph R. Anderson, with nine thousand men, had taken up a position between Fredericksburg and Richmond, with the object of holding McDowell in check as well as he could with such an inferior force, while General Johnston attacked McClellan's army. Both commanders knew well that if these forty-one thousand men could be added to the Federal army, the capture of Richmond would follow. McClellan at last succeeded in getting orders issued from Washington for McDowell to advance to his support. General Johnston promptly decided, upon this information reaching him, to try at once the fortunes of battle; but was greatly relieved, when he received word from Stuart's cavalry that McDowell, after starting from Fredericksburg, had countermarched and was proceeding in the direction of Washington. A Confederate commander in the Valley of Virginia was responsible for McDowell's change of direction.

Thomas Jonathan Jackson was born at Clarksburg, Harrison County, then in Virginia, now West Virginia. Thirty-seven years afterward he was born again on the field of Manassas, and, amid the rifle's flash and cannon's roar, christened "Stonewall." Neither of the two Governments lost sight of the great importance of the Valley District — one, because Washington could be easily reached by hostile troops from that section; the other, because the force there was a part of General Johnston's army, and might enter into future military combinations as an important factor. It was most fortunate for the South that Stonewall Jackson was selected to command this department. He was combative; his facial characteristics, "including a massive iron-bound jaw," have been compared to those of Julius Caesar and William of Normandy. Activity, vigilance, and restlessness were marked traits of his character. His thoughts were with God and his cause. In camp he organized prayer meetings among his soldiers, and when the meeting began, the hymn raised, and the proceedings evidently a success, he often went to sleep. "If silence be golden, he was a bonanza." It was said of him at that time that he sucked lemons, ate hardtack and drank water — and praying and fighting appeared to him to be the whole duty of man. General Ewell, it is related, once said he admired Jackson's genius, but he never "saw one of his couriers approach him without expecting an order to assault the North Pole."

From a humble professor in the Virginia Military Institute he rapidly grew into a giant of war. He believed in a short, sharp, decisive contest. When first appointed a professor he occupied a room on one of the upper floors of barracks. Some of the cadets, in a mischievous spirit, took away a portion of the steps below his room during the night. The next morning, having an appointment to fill, he came out at an early hour, and, seeing what had been done, without a moment's hesitation seized one of the supporting posts and lowered himself hand over hand. "In civil war," said he, in 1860, "when the swords are drawn the scabbards should be thrown away"; and he would have fought under the "black flag" with as pleasant a smile as his countenance could assume. Earnestly and conscientiously believing the South was right, in the spring of 1861 he was strongly inclined to war.

In some respects he resembled Blucher; like him he was bold, bluff, and energetic, and, as with Blucher, his loyalty to the cause he adopted was a passion. The grim old soldier whom Wellington welcomed at Waterloo smoked, swore, and drank at seventy, and just there the resemblance ceased.

Above others, on either side, Jackson understood the great value of celerity in military movements, and his infantry was termed "foot cavalry." To be under heavy fire, he said, filled him with a "delicious excitement." His death afterward, at Chancellorsville, lost the South Gettysburg; for General Lee has said, "Had I Stonewall Jackson at Gettysburg I would have won a great victory."

He was a blazing meteor of battle; his enterprising and aggressive spirit sought relief in motion — always motion. To such a commander the defense of the beautiful Valley of Virginia was intrusted.

After his return from Romney he was at Winchester, then Woodstock, some forty miles below, then following Shields from Strasburg, and on March 23d attacked him at Kernstown and was repulsed; Banks, who was on his way from the Valley to Manassas, was ordered back to destroy this bold soldier; and Blenker, with ten thousand men on his way to Fremont, was instructed to report to him as he followed Jackson up the Valley, where later the latter took up position at Swift Run Gap in the Blue Ridge Mountains, the Shenandoah River being in his front, his flanks protected by the mountain sides, while Ewell was not far away across the mountains in his rear at Gordonsville. "Stonewall" did not like to be cooped up in the mountains, and wrote General Lee at Richmond, asking him to re-enforce him with five thousand men, intimating that he would then be glad to get reports from him. On April 29th Lee replied that his request could not be complied with, but suggested his union with General Edward Johnson, who had some thirty-five hundred men near Staunton. Lee was anxious to gain success in the Valley, because it would retard the offensive campaign against Richmond, and informed Jackson that if he was strong enough to hold Banks in check, Ewell might, by uniting with Anderson's force between Fredericksburg and Richmond, attack and possibly destroy McDowell, then at Fredericksburg. Banks had some twenty thousand men at Harrisonburg watching General Edward Johnson, and six thousand men, under Milroy and Schenck, had moved west of the mountains, and were in front of Johnson, while Fremont was marching with ten thousand men to join them.

Evading Banks at Harrisonburg, Jackson moved to Staunton, joined his force with Johnson's, and defeated Milroy and Schenck; Ewell marched then from Gordonsville to the Valley, and Banks fell back to Strasburg. Jackson, having disposed of the two Federal commanders, returned with great swiftness, united with Ewell, defeated the Federal forces at Front Royal, and then pushed on with great rapidity to attack Banks, who, hearing of his approach, fell back to Winchester, where he was defeated and followed to the Potomac River. The defeat of the Federal troops in the Valley, and Jackson's presence on the Potomac, produced consternation at the Federal capital. General McDowell, who had commenced his march from Fredericksburg to join McClellan, was turned back toward Washington, being directed to send twenty thousand men of his command at once to the Shenandoah Valley to reinforce Fremont, who had moved down the Valley to get in Jackson's rear and capture him. McClellan wanted McDowell badly, and McDowell desired to go to his support, and both generals practically intimated to the Washington authorities that they were scared; that they did not think Washington was in danger of capture by Jackson, and that moving a part of McDowell's troops to the Shenandoah Valley would not succeed in destroying Jackson's forces.

Jackson in the meantime, having disposed of Banks, determined to prevent the union of Shields (who had arrived from McDowell's army) with Fremont, and by a series of brilliant manoeuvres fought the battles of Cross Keys and Port Republic, holding one commander at arm's length while he hammered the other. By this admirable campaign, in which his great military genius was displayed, McClellan was deprived of the co-operation of McDowell's army, while Jackson contributed largely to the success of the battles around Richmond.

His splendid work in the Valley is summed up by one of his biographers: "In three months he had marched six hundred miles, fought four pitched battles, seven minor engagements, daily skirmishes, defeated four armies, captured seven pieces of artillery, ten thousand stand of arms, four thousand prisoners, and a very great amount of stores." His movements produced a panic at the Federal capital. The Secretary of War issued a call to the governors of the loyal States for militia to defend the city. On May 25th, to the Governor of Massachusetts he declared that "intelligence from various quarters leaves no doubt that the enemy in great force are marching on Washington. You will please organize and forward immediately all the militia and volunteer forces in your State." John A. Andrew, the Governor of Massachusetts, issued a proclamation: "Men of Massachusetts, the wily and barbarous horde of traitors menaces again the national capital." Todd, Ohio's Governor, following suit, said: "To the gallant men of Ohio: I have the astounding intelligence that the city of our beloved Government is threatened with invasion, and am called upon by the Secretary of War for troops to repel the overwhelming and ruthless invaders."

Richmond was probably saved at that period by Jackson. McClellan determined to clear the way for McDowell's march by attacking a brigade of North Carolinians under Branch, which was then at Hanover Court House, some fourteen miles from Richmond, guarding and watching the country in front of Johnston's left. To make this attack certain, General Fitz John Porter was given twelve thousand men, and partially accomplished the object of the expedition by defeating Branch and destroying the bridges and railroads in the vicinity of Ashland. Slowly but surely McClellan was diminishing the distance between the lines of his army and the Southern capital, and his big Parrott guns were now nearly in a position to throw shot within the walls of the city. On May 23d the Fourth Corps, under Keyes, crossed the Chickahominy at Bottom's Bridge and took position at a place called Seven Pines, some five miles from the city; the Third Corps, under Heintzelman, followed. The Chickahominy now divided McClellan's army into two parts. Two of his corps were on the south, and three — Sumner's, Franklin's, and Porter's — on the north side, McClellan's headquarters being at Gaines Mill. The Chickahominy River rises some twelve miles northwest of Richmond, flows in an easterly direction at first, and then takes a southeasterly course, till it empties into the James, some thirty miles below Richmond. It was directly interposed between McClellan and Richmond, being in some places not more than four or five miles from the city, and the numerous roads leading out from Richmond to the Peninsula and adjacent sections of country cross it on bridges. North of Richmond was Meadow Bridge; a little farther down, and opposite to Gaines Mill, New Bridge; still farther down, where the Williamsburg road crosses the Chickahominy, Bottom's Bridge; while lower down still is Long Bridge.

McClellan spent two weeks in traversing the forty miles from Williamsburg to the Chickahominy at Bottom's and New Bridges. His base of supplies was established at West Point; his stores could be safely transported by water, and from West Point the railroad running to Richmond had been put in good order in his rear, so that his supplies could be easily brought within reach for distribution. The Chickahominy proper afforded no greater obstacle to the advance of an army than an ordinary small river, the obstruction being the swamps and bottom lands. The stream flowed through a belt of heavy timbered swamp, which averaged three hundred or four hundred yards wide, sometimes in a single channel and sometimes in two or three, and the water when high overflowed the land.

The Federal army having large pontoon trains, as well as facilities for making trestle bridges, surmounted these difficulties. After two of McClellan's corps crossed this stream and took position nearer to Richmond, it was evident the battle could be no longer postponed. General Johnston therefore decided to attack these advance corps, and if possible overwhelm them before they could be re-enforced by any portion of the three corps upon the other side of the Chickahominy. The heavy rains had swept away the communicating bridges between the two wings of McClellan's army, but the railroad bridge, which had been repaired, was not affected by the swollen condition of the stream. On it planks were laid, and in that way the left wing supplied.

The battle of Seven Pines, or Fair Oaks, was well planned, and had the Southern attack been made in the forenoon instead of the afternoon, Johnston would have had greater success. "It can never be too often repeated that war, however adorned by splendid strokes of skill, is commonly a series of errors and accidents." Sumner succeeded in crossing his corps over the bridges trembling with the current's rush, and over causeways on each side covered with mud and water. His guns had to be unlimbered and prolonges used, while the men who were tugging at the ropes were nearly waist deep in some places in the water. It cannot be said that this battle was a complete success for the Southern arms. Sumner's arrival enabled the other two Federal corps to maintain their ground until the curtain of night lowered on the scene. Ten pieces of artillery, sixty-seven hundred rifles and muskets, and quantities of stores and tents were, however, secured by the Confederates. The two corps of the Federals numbered thirty-eight thousand, and after Sumner's re-enforcements arrived, fifty-six thousand. The former lost some six thousand men, the latter fifty-seven hundred and thirty-nine; and McClellan had received a check to his "On to Richmond!"

Johnston, after giving orders to his troops to sleep on the ground they occupied when the contest for the night ceased, and to renew the battle at dawn the next morning, was wounded, at first slightly in the shoulder by a musket ball, and a few moments afterward was struck on the breast by a heavy fragment of shell, knocked from his horse, and had to be carried from the field in an ambulance. General Gustavus W. Smith, the next officer in rank, immediately assumed command of the army. He determined to carry out Johnston's plans and continue the attack on the next day, and so informed General Lee, asking for all the assistance he could give him. In a note dated Richmond, June 1st, 5 A. M., General Lee replies:

Ripley will be ordered, and such forces from General Holmes as can be got up will be sent; your determination to strike the enemy is right. Try and ascertain his position and how best he can be hit. It will be a glorious thing if you can gain a complete victory. Our success on the whole, yesterday, was good, but not complete.

Truly, R. E. Lee, General. To General G. W. Smith, Commander of the Army of Northern Virginia.

When that note was penned, General Lee knew he had been directed to take command of the army on that day; he did not reach Smith's headquarters until 2 P. M., and was magnanimous enough to wish that Smith should gain and get the credit for a great victory.

The attack on June 1st was not made as contemplated by General Johnston first and Smith afterward, because it was apparent that the destruction of a portion of McClellan's army before it could be succored was no longer a possibility. There was no demoralization in the Confederate ranks anywhere, and the assertion that the Federal army could have gone into Richmond on the second day — June 1st — cannot be maintained. General G. W. Smith, commanding, sums up the fighting on that day by saying: "The Federals, in position, were attacked on the first day of June by but two Confederate brigades. That attack was repulsed. Four Federal regiments then advanced and attacked the position held by one Confederate brigade. These four regiments were withdrawn from the front of that brigade." Only small portions of either army were engaged on the first of June.

The battle on the Williamsburg road on the day before was fought by D. H. Hill with four of his brigades and one of General Longstreet's. The other five of Longstreet's and the whole of Huger's division, which General Longstreet was expected to employ, were not put into the fight, while the troops charged with the duty of attacking the Federal right were advanced too late to be of service. Napier has well said that "he who wars walks in a mist through which the keenest eye cannot always discern the right path." If the incomplete battle of Seven Pines or Fair Oaks did not add to the military fame of the Union commander or to that of the officer charged with the details of the attack on the Confederate side, it was nevertheless of benefit to the Southern commander, for it kept McClellan quiet for a month, and enabled him to complete his preparations to beat him.

CHAPTER 8

COMMANDS THE ARMY DEFENDING RICHMOND, AND SEVEN DAYS BATTLES.

General Lee and Mr. Davis were on the field on May 31st, and the latter was at once informed of General Johnston's being wounded. Riding back with General Lee to Richmond that night, Mr. Davis told him he proposed to assign him at once to the command of the Confederate army defending Richmond, and would make out the order as soon as he reached the city. Accordingly, very early the next morning General Lee received the following:

Richmond, Va., June 1, 1862.

General R. E. Lee.

Sir: The unfortunate casualty which has deprived the army in front of Richmond of its immediate commander, General Johnston, renders it necessary to interfere temporarily with the duties to which you were assigned in connection with the general service, but only so far as to make you available for command in the field of a particular army. You will assume command of the army in eastern Virginia and in North Carolina, and give such orders as may be needful and proper.

Very respectfully, Jefferson Davis.

On the reception of this note, General Lee published

Special orders no. 22.

Headquarters, Richmond, Va., June 1, 1862.

In pursuance of the orders of the President, General R. E. Lee assumes command of the armies of eastern Virginia and North Carolina. The unfortunate casualty that has deprived the army in front of Richmond of the valuable services of its able general is not more deeply deplored by any member of the command than by its present commander. He hopes his absence will be but temporary, and while he will endeavor to the best of his ability to perform his duties, he feels he will be totally inadequate to the task unless he shall receive the cordial support of every officer and man.

By order of General Lee. W. H. Taylor, Assistant Adjutant General.

On June 2d Special Orders No. 126 were issued from the Adjutant and Inspector General's office.

Special orders no. 126.

Richmond, Va., June 2, 1862.

By direction of the President, General Robert E. Lee, Confederate States army, will assume the immediate command of the armies in eastern Virginia and North Carolina.

By command of the Secretary of War.

John Withers, Assistant Adjutant General

At an early hour on June 1st the Southern President rode to the front to direct, in person, General Smith to transfer the command of the army to General Lee, in order to relieve the latter from the embarrassment of first announcing this change. Later General Lee rode out, reaching the field about two o'clock, and formally assumed command of the Army of Northern Virginia, which he was thereafter destined to lead against the Army of the Potomac on many hard-fought fields. Eighteen hours afterward General G. W. Smith, whose health had not been strong, was taken ill, and had to be relieved of all military duty.

At last, one year after the commencement of the war, Robert E. Lee was in active command of a large army in the field. His task was difficult, his responsibility great. The opposing hosts were thundering at the city's gates. Inch by inch they had crept so close that spectators on the housetops could see their fire-fringed lines and hear the angry roar of their cannon. Upon his shoulders rested the safety of his capital. With quiet dignity he assumed his duties. The troops were immediately ordered back to their former stations, and the battle of Seven Pines was confided to the Muse of History. The next move on the military chessboard absorbed his immediate attention. The strongly constructed battle lines of his powerful enemy were uncomfortably close. McClellan had already commenced to strengthen his front at Seven Pines. Franklin's corps was brought from the north to the south side of the Chickahominy and posted on the right of that portion of his line. On the left was Sumner, and to his left Heintzelman extended as far as the White Oak swamp. In their rear Keyes was in reserve. On the north or left bank of the Chickahominy Fitz John Porter's corps was still stationed, near Gaines Mill, with McCall's division of Pennsylvania reserves at Mechanicsville and on Beaver Dam Creek — eleven divisions in all. Richmond, McClellan's coveted prize, was but five miles away. To reach it he had to pass over the lines of the Army of Northern Virginia. These lines were held by five divisions — A. P. Hill's on the left: at Meadow Bridge, Huger's and Magruder's next, supported by Longstreet's and D. H. Hill's. Lee at once considered the best manner to attack. The intrenchments in his front were too strong for a direct assault, so the only alternative left was to turn one or both of his enemy's flanks. The Federal left was "defended by a line of strong works, access to which, except by a few narrow roads, was obstructed by felling the dense forests in front." These roads were commanded to a great distance by heavy guns in the fortifications. The difficulties here were as great as would be encountered in a direct attack. The only way to get at McClellan was by assaulting his right, and the Confederate commander was not long in finding it out. In order to do this successfully he must fortify his lines, particularly his center and right, so that they could successfully resist any attack made upon them, while his left wing was withdrawn to be thrown on the Federal right and rear.

In Lee, as with McClellan, the military engineer was combined with the army commander. Earthworks were rapidly constructed. The topographical features of the country were scientifically made available; and ere many days had passed the Southern troops were everywhere behind strong intrenchments, while between them and the city was a line of more permanent works, which had been constructed some time before as a precautionary measure, and behind which the troops could be rallied if the first lines were successfully assailed. Almost every day now a soldierly looking man, clad in a neat but simple gray uniform, conspicuous by the absence of the wreath, gold braids and stars usually found on the uniforms of general officers, sitting his horse like a dragoon, might be seen riding along the lines. No long column of staff or couriers followed him, no display, no ostentation, none of the pomp of war. His enemy's right was the place to attack, but where was it located and how was it defended? Were the roads leading to it obstructed, and were the woods "slashed," or would the attacking column have to assault lunettes, redans, irregular pentagons, and inclosed redoubts? How was he to ascertain all this? Fortunately he had the very officer in his army who could obtain replies to these important questions, and he was the commander of his cavalry, James Ewell Brown Stuart, commonly called Jeb Stuart from the three first initial letters of his name. This distinguished cavalryman was a native of Patrick County, Va., a graduate at West Point of the class of 1854, and a soldier from the feathers in his hat to the rowels of his spurs. He was twenty-nine years old when Lee ordered him to locate McClellan's right flank and in the full vigor of a robust manhood. His brilliant courage, great activity, immense endurance, and devotion to his profession had already marked him as a cavalry commander of unquestioned merit. He had the fire, zeal, and capacity of Prince Rupert, but, like him, lacked caution; the dash of Murat, but was sometimes rash and imprudent; was as skillful and vigorous as Frederick the Great's celebrated cavalry leader, and, like Seidlitz, was willing to break the necks of some of his men by charging over rough ground if he made bold horsemen of the rest and gained his object. He would have gone as far as Cardigan, with "cannon to right of him, cannon to left of him, cannon in front of him." He was a Christian dragoon — an unusual combination. His Bible and tactics were his text-books. He never drank liquor, having given a promise to his mother to that effect when a small boy, but when wet from the storm and wearied from the march he would drink, without cream or sugar, the contents of a tin quart cup of strong coffee. Duty was his guiding star. Once when on the eve of an expected battle he was telegraphed that his child was dying and urged to go to her, he replied: "I shall have to leave my child in the hands of God; my duty requires me here." Lee knew him well. He had been a classmate at the United States Military Academy of his eldest son, and was his aid-de-camp when John Brown was captured. Such was the man who stood before his commander on June 11, 1862, to receive his instructions. The next morning, at an early hour, Stuart was in the saddle, and, with twelve hundred cavalry and a section of artillery, started to blaze the way for Stonewall Jackson's descent on the right rear of the Federal army, and for an assault on the Federal right by the left wing of the Confederate army. That night he went into camp twenty-two miles north of Richmond. His line of march conveyed the impression that he had been sent to re-enforce Jackson in the Valley, but the next day the head of his column was turned eastward toward Hanover Court House, which he reached about nine o'clock, driving out a body of the enemy's cavalry. Between that point and Old Church his advance squadron, under Captain Latane, met and charged a squadron of regular cavalry under Captain Royall. Latane was killed, and Royall severely wounded by a saber cut and his squadron put to flight. The Southern cavalry now followed rapidly to Old Church, where the Federal cavalry made another stand, but was soon driven from its position. Stuart was now far enough on the right flank of the Federal army to get all the information he desired. He could return only by the way he had marched, which would be attended with much danger, as the troops on that flank were thoroughly roused, or make the entire circuit of the Federal army. He determined upon the latter course, and, in defiance of many dangers and difficulties, succeeded in moving his whole command not only around the right of McClellan's line of battle, but along his rear and around his left, bringing it in safety to the Richmond lines. It was hazardous, because any prolongation of McClellan's left from White Oak swamp to James River would have cut him off from his own army.

This celebrated raid brought the Southern cavalry leader prominently before the public, and his rapid and successful march received favorable comment. From the left of his own army he had marched for Hanover Court House, Old Church, Tunstall's Station, on the York River Railroad, and Talleysville, to the lower Chickahominy, where the road from Providence Forge to Charles City Court House crosses it thirty-five miles from Richmond. Finding that the bridge had been carried away by the swollen stream, he tore down an old barn in the vicinity, and, as rapidly as his men could work, threw over another bridge, upon which he crossed men and guns, returning to his quarters near Richmond, having been continuously in the saddle for thirty-six hours. The whole distance was traversed in forty-eight hours, with but a single halt after reaching the south bank of the Chickahominy. He was enjoined by Lee to "remember that one of the chief objects of the expedition is to gain intelligence for the guidance of future movements."

The news of this expedition amazed the North. It did not understand how twelve hundred troopers could ride so close to the right, rear, and left of one hundred and fifteen thousand men in line of battle without being killed or captured. In his march he had crossed all roads leading to McClellan's right, and located his lines of communication. General Lee's General Orders No. 74 in part read:

Headquarters, Army of Northern Virginia.

The commanding general announces with great satisfaction to the army the brilliant exploit of Brigadier-General J. E. B. Stuart with part of the troops under his command. This gallant officer, with portions of the First, Fourth, and Ninth Virginia Cavalry, and part of the Jeff Davis Legion, with the Boykin Rangers and a section of the Stuart Horse Artillery, on June 13th, 14th, and 15th, made a reconnoissance between the Pamunkey and Chickahominy Rivers and succeeded in passing around the rear of the whole of the Union army, routing the enemy in a series of skirmishes, taking a number of prisoners, destroying and capturing stores to a large amount. Having most successfully accomplished its object, the expedition recrossed the Chickahominy, almost in the presence of the enemy, with the same coolness and address that marked every step of his progress, and with the loss of but one man, the lamented Captain Latane, of the Ninth Virginia Cavalry, who fell bravely leading a successful charge against a force of the enemy. In announcing the signal success to the army, the general commanding takes great pleasure in expressing his admiration of the courage and skill so conspicuously exhibited throughout by the general and the officers and men under his command.

General Lee had secured, by this brilliant exploit of Stuart's, the information he desired. As early as June 8th he had suggested to the Secretary of War that "Jackson be prepared to unite with the army near Richmond, if called on." The next day he announced to the Secretary of War "a glorious victory by the gallant Jackson and his troops," and writes to him that reenforcements should be sent to Jackson to enable him to take the offensive again. The 11th of June was a busy day. Lee first prepared the instructions to start Stuart on his expedition, and then wrote Jackson as follows:

Headquarters near Richmond, June 11, 1862.

Brigadier-General Thomas J. Jackson, Commanding the Valley District.

General: Your recent successes have been the cause of the liveliest joy to this army, as well as to the country. The admiration caused by your skill and boldness has been constantly mingled with solicitude for your situation. The practicability of reenforcing you has been the subject of earnest consideration. It has been determined to do so at the expense of weakening this army. Brigadier-General Lawton, with six regiments from Georgia, is on the way to you, and Brigadier-General Whiting, with eight veteran regiments, leaves here to-day. The object is to enable you to crush the forces opposed to you, then leave your unavailable troops to watch the country and guard the passes covered by your cavalry and artillery and with your main body, including Ewell's division and Lawton's and Whiting's command, move rapidly to Ashland by rail or otherwise, as you may find most advantageous, and sweep down between the Chickahominy and Pamunkey, cutting up the enemy's communications, while this army attacks General McClellan in front. He will thus, I think, be forced to come out of his intrenchments, where he is strongly posted on the Chickahominy, and apparently prepared to move by gradual approaches on Richmond. Keep me advised of your movements, and, if practicable, precede your troops, that we may confer and arrange for simultaneous attack. I am, with great respect, your obedient servant,

(Signed) R. E. Lee, General.

On the same day, Lee writes to Randolph, the Secretary of War at Richmond:

Headquarters, Dobb's House, June 11, 1862.

Honorable George W. Randolph, Secretary of War, Richmond, Va.

Sir: It is very desirable and important that the acquisition of troops to the command of Major-General T. J. Jackson should be kept secret. With this view I have the honor to request that you will use your influence with the Richmond newspapers to prevent any mention of the same in the public prints. I am, most respectfully, your obedient servant,

(Signed) R. E. Lee.

The Southern commander desired to give Jackson a sufficient force to enable him to fight a decisive battle in the Valley, and then, before his enemy could recover, watch him with a picket line while he reported at Richmond with the greater part of his effective forces. Lee wished the first information of the arrival of Whiting and Lawton to Jackson to be given to his enemy by a victory in the Valley. On this day, too, he published Special Orders No. 130, Headquarters, Northern Virginia, June 11, 1862, directing Brigadier-General W. H. C. Whiting, with two brigades of Smith's division to be selected by himself, to report to General T. J. Jackson, commanding the Army of the Valley. He directed that this command be detached for temporary special service, and that it should move in light marching order. Three days after these various instructions were issued, General Lee decided that it would not do to wait for Jackson to fight before he should bring him to the army in front of Richmond, and told him to form a junction at once, and "to be efficacious, the movement must be secret." This detachment of troops from Lee's army, then in front of his powerful antagonist, did not produce in the Southern mind a feeling of uneasiness; so great was the confidence in the Southern leader that the movement, without knowing for what intended, was considered proper, timely, and judicious! Lee's object was to render the diversion of McDowell from McClellan's army more decided by re-enforcing the commander whose victories had already directed the attention of the Federal authorities from the capture of Richmond to their own security at Washington. Mr.

Lincoln telegraphed McClellan on June 20th that Jackson is being heavily re-enforced from Richmond, and that he did not think he could send him more troops. Two days previous McClellan had informed Lincoln that some ten thousand troops from Lee's army had been sent to Jackson, to which the Union President replied that if the report were true, it would be as good as a re-enforcement to him of an equal force, and that he would be glad to be informed what day he would attack Richmond. While these telegrams were being exchanged Jackson was rapidly moving to the support of Lee. The main portion of his army left the Valley on June 18th, marching by Charlottesville and Gordonsville, which latter place was reached on the 21st. Jackson, leaving his army to follow, took an express car accompanied only by his chief of staff, who, strange to say, was not a military man, but a Presbyterian minister and a professor in a theological seminary. When Sunday morning, June 22d, dawned, Jackson, with his ministerial aid, had reached Frederickshall, a point on the Central Railroad, now called the Chesapeake and Ohio, some fifty-two miles from Richmond. Being the Sabbath, and against his religious convictions to travel on Sunday, he left his car and went to a gentleman's house and remained quiet that day, except that he attended camp services of some of the troops stationed near there in the afternoon. Not desiring to be transported to Richmond in a car, as he might be recognized, he determined to proceed the rest of his journey on horseback; and accordingly at one o'clock Monday morning he mounted a horse and started with a single borrowed courier for General Lee's headquarters near Richmond, fifty-two miles away. He had requested Major Dabney to get from the senior officer an order to impress horses on the way, and also a pass, in case he should get into the pickets of General Lee's army. At 3 P. M. on Monday, the 23d, he had covered the whole distance, and, travel-stained, dusty, and weary from riding all night, he participated in a conference called that afternoon by General Lee, of the commanding officers of the divisions he proposed should attack McClellan's right and rear, namely, Longstreet, D. H. Hill, and A. P. Hill. These officers, with Jackson, having received the instructions of the army commander, rejoined their respective commands. Perhaps if "Old Stonewall" had traveled to Richmond on his car, and been spared the loss of sleep and the all-night ride on the eve of a great battle, he would have swept around on A. P. Hill's left in time to have saved the lives of many brave men at Mechanicsville and Beaver Dam Creek.

Jackson's troops had been rapidly approaching Richmond since his departure. The night of the 25th his command was encamped in the vicinity of Ashland, on the Richmond and Fredericksburg Railroad, some sixteen miles from Richmond. Early on the morning of the 26th he moved easterly, crossing the Central Railroad below Hanover Court House about ten o'clock, and, taking the Mechanicsville road, camped for the night south of the Totopatomoy Creek at a place called Hundley's Corner, some seven or eight miles northeast of Mechanicsville. He was thus getting well in the rear of the right of the Federal army. Lee's preparations for assault had been completed. His battle order was as follows:

General orders no. 75.

Headquarters, Army of Northern Virginia, June 24, 1862.

1. General Jackson's command will proceed to-morrow from Ashland toward the Slash Church and encamp at some convenient point west of the Central Railroad. Branch's brigade, of A. P. Hill's division, will also to-morrow evening take position on the Chickahominy near Half-Sink. At three o'clock Thursday morning, 26th inst., General Jackson will advance on the road leading to Pole Green Church, communicating his march to General Branch, who will immediately cross the Chickahominy and take the road leading to Mechanicsville. As soon as the movements of these columns are discovered, General A. P. Hill, with the rest of his division, will cross the Chickahominy near Meadow Bridge and move direct upon Mechanicsville. To aid his advance the heavy batteries on the Chickahominy will at the proper time open upon the batteries at Mechanicsville. The enemy being driven from Mechanicsville and the passage across the bridge opened, General Longstreet, with his division and that of General D. H. Hill, will cross the Chickahominy at or near that point, General D. H. Hill moving to the support of Jackson, and General Longstreet supporting General A. P. Hill. The four divisions — keeping in communication with each other and moving en echelon on separate roads, if practicable, the left division in advance, with skirmishers and sharpshooters extending their front — will sweep down the Chickahominy and endeavor to drive the

enemy from his position above New Bridge, General Jackson bearing well to his left, turning Beaver Dam Creek and taking the direction toward Cold Harbor. They will then press forward toward the York River Railroad, closing upon the enemy's rear and forcing him down the Chickahominy. Any advance of the enemy toward Richmond will be prevented by vigorously following his rear and crippling and arresting his progress.

2. The divisions under Generals Huger and Magruder will hold their positions in front of the enemy against attack, and make such demonstrations on Thursday as to discover his operations. Should opportunity offer, the feint will be converted into a real attack, and should an abandonment of his intrenchments by the enemy be discovered, he will be closely pursued.

3. The Third Virginia Cavalry will observe the Charles City road. The Fifth Virginia, the First North Carolina, and the Hampton Legion (cavalry) will observe the Darbytown, Varina, and Osborne roads. Should a movement of the enemy down the Chickahominy be discovered, they will close upon his flank and endeavor to arrest his march.

4. General Stuart with the First, Fourth, and Ninth Virginia Cavalry, the cavalry of Cobb's Legion and the Jeff Davis Legion, will cross the Chickahominy to-morrow and take position to the left of General Jackson's line of march. The main body will be held in reserve, with scouts well extended to the front and left. General Stuart will keep General Jackson informed of the movements of the enemy on his left and will co-operate with him in his advance. The Tenth Virginia Cavalry, Colonel Davis, will remain on the Nine-mile road.

5. General Ransom's brigade, of General Holmes's command, will be placed in reserve on the Williamsburg road by General Huger, to whom he will report for orders.

6. Commanders of divisions will cause their commands to be provided with three days cooked rations. The necessary ambulances and ordnance trains will be ready to accompany the divisions and receive orders from their respective commanders. Officers in charge of all trains will invariably remain with them. Batteries and wagons will keep on the right of the road. The Chief Engineer, Major Stevens, will assign engineer officers to each division, whose duty it will be to make provision for overcoming all difficulties to the progress of the troops. The staff departments will give the necessary instructions to facilitate the movements herein directed.

By command of General Lee. (Signed) R. H. Chilton, Assistant Adjutant General.

Lee designed that Jackson should progress sufficiently far on the 26th to relieve A. P. Hill from any difficulty in capturing Mechanicsville. This being done, it would unmask the bridge at that point, and Longstreet and D. H. Hill could cross. The four commands, being thus united, with Jackson in advance and on the left, would flank the very strong position of the Federals on the left bank of Beaver Dam Creek, which emptied into the Chickahominy about one mile below Mechanicsville. But Jackson was one day behind time. He did not proceed from Ashland on the 25th, as ordered, because he arrived there only that night, and did not leave till the next morning. A. P. Hill, after waiting the greater part of the 26th for Jackson, grew impatient, and, fearing there might be a failure of the offensive plan, crossed the Chickahominy at Meadow Bridge at 3 P. M. and moved direct on Mechanicsville, hoping that as soon as he became engaged at that point Jackson would appear on his left and they would open the way for a union with D. H. Hill and Longstreet; and then these troops could all, as directed in General Lee's order, "sweep down the north side of the Chickahominy." They were to advance in two lines: Jackson on the left and A. P. Hill on the right of the first line, the former being supported by D. H. Hill and the latter by Longstreet. This movement rapidly and successfully executed would unmask the "new bridge" on the Chickahominy below, by means of which General Lee could reunite the left wing of his army with Huger's and Magruder's divisions on its right bank. The strategy was a repetition of that adopted by McDowell at the first Manassas, and afterward by Lee at Chancellorsville. After A. P. Hill drove the Federals out of Mechanicsville he found himself in front of the strongly intrenched lines on Beaver Dam, and the remainder of the afternoon of the 26th was occupied in attempting to carry them, assisted by Ripley's brigade, of D. H. Hill's division. The approach to the Federal position being over an open plain and exposed to a murderous fire of all arms, was not successful that night. Had Jackson been up he would have crossed the Beaver Dam Creek above the right of the Federal line that evening, as he did the next day, and thus prevented a great loss of life.

It has been said we were lavish of blood in those days, and it was thought to be a great thing to charge a battery of artillery or line of earthworks with infantry. On the morning of the 27th the attack was renewed at dawn. While it was in progress Jackson crossed the creek above, and the enemy at once abandoned his intrenchments, retiring rapidly down the river, destroying a great deal of property and leaving much in his deserted camps. As soon as the bridges could be repaired across the Beaver Dam, Lee's left wing resumed its march. About noon the Federal troops were found in position behind Powhite Creek. This second line taken by Fitz John Porter was a strong one, and made more so by breastworks of trees and rifle trenches, while the crests of the position were crowned with artillery. General Lee says the approach to this position was over an open plain about a quarter of a mile wide commanded by a triple line of fire and swept by the heavy batteries south of the Chickahominy. Hill, still in advance, first encountered the enemy, was soon hotly engaged, and met the large force with the "impetuous courage for which that officer and his troops are distinguished." The battle raged fiercely and with varying fortune for more than two hours. The attack on the Federal right being delayed by the length of Jackson's march and the obstacles he encountered, Longstreet was directed to make a feint on the enemy's left, which he soon converted into a real attack. Jackson arrived about this time, and, after a short and bloody conflict, his troops forced their way through the morass and obstructions and drove the Federals from the woods on the opposite side. Lee now ordered a general advance from right to left. The enemy's breastworks were quickly stormed, and he was forced back with great slaughter toward the banks of the Chickahominy till night put an end to the pursuit. On the morning of the 28th there were no Federal troops in Lee's front north of the Chickahominy. McClellan had united what was left of Porter's corps with the rest of his army on the south side of that stream.

What would McClellan do now? Would he attempt to open communication with his base of supplies at the White House, or would he retreat down the Peninsula in the direction of Fort Monroe, skirting the James River, where he could be in communication with the Federal gunboats on that stream, or would he seek shelter at the nearest point on James River? If he attempted to go down the Peninsula or to fight for his line of communication on York River, Lee was on the proper side of the Chickahominy to meet such movements. Should he retreat in a direct line across the White Oak Swamp for James River it would be necessary for the Southern troops to get on the south bank of the Chickahominy as soon as possible in order to pursue. The seizure of the York River Railroad by Ewell's division and a portion of the cavalry under Stuart convinced the Southern commander that McClellan had abandoned his York River base, and shortly afterward it was ascertained that there were no indications of a retreat down the James River. Lee then knew McClellan had determined to get to the James by the nearest practicable route. The Federal right had been so pounded to pieces that Lee did not fear an advance on Huger and Magruder, because in that case the victorious Southern legions would have been in his rear, and such an attempt would have resulted in the sacrifice of his army. The battle of Gaines Mill having been won and the future purpose of his enemy discovered, early on the 29th Longstreet and A. P. Hill were directed to recross the Chickahominy at New Bridge, while Jackson and D. H. Hill crossed at Grape Vine Bridge.

General Lee had now united his whole army south of the Chickahominy. That afternoon Magruder attacked the enemy near Savage Station, being the rear guard of a retreating army. The lateness of the hour and the small force employed did not produce a decisive result. On the next day, the 30th, at 4 P. M., the Union troops were again overtaken, and the battle of Frazier's Farm, sometimes called Glendale, or Nelson's, Farm, was fought by Longstreet and A. P. Hill. Huger did not get up, and Jackson was unable to force a passage through the White Oak Swamp. The battle raged from 4 till 9 P. M. By that time, General Lee says, his enemy had been driven with great slaughter from every position but one, which he maintained till he was enabled to withdraw under cover of darkness. Jackson reached the battlefield on July 1st, having succeeded in crossing the swamp, and was directed to continue the pursuit down the Willis Church road, and soon came upon the enemy, who occupied the high range extending obliquely across the road in front of Malvern Hill, a position of great natural strength. There McClellan had concentrated his artillery, supported by large masses of infantry, protected by earthworks. Immediately in the Federal front the ground was open, varying in width from a quarter to a half mile, sloping gradually from the crest, and completely swept by the fire of his infantry and artillery. General Lee in his report says: "To reach this open ground our troops had to advance through a broken and thickly wooded country, traversed nearly throughout its whole extent by a swamp passable at but few places, difficult at those. The whole was in range of the batteries on the heights and the gunboats on the river, under whose incessant fire our movements had to be executed." Here the Federals were assaulted by portions of Jackson's, D. H. Hill's, Magruder's, and Huger's divisions, but from want of concert among the attacking columns, General Lee reports, their assaults were too weak to break the Federal line, and, after struggling gallantly and inflicting great loss, they were compelled successively to retire. Night was approaching when the attack began, and it soon became difficult to distinguish friend from foe. "The firing continued," General Lee reports, "till after 9 P. M., but no decided result was gained. The lateness of the hour at which the attack necessarily began gave the enemy the full advantage of his superior position and augmented the natural difficulties of our own." In these offensive movements the Southern cavalry under Stuart were directed to move to the left of Jackson, breaking the Federal lines of communication and giving notice of any attempt to get down the Peninsula. The greater part of McClellan's cavalry, under Stoneman, which had been picketing on Porter's right flank, was cut off from his army by the march of Jackson and Stuart, and, not being able to reach their troops, proceeded rapidly down the Peninsula. Stuart reached McClellan's base at the White House on the 29th, to find it abandoned. On Stuart's approach the greater part of the enemy's stores were destroyed, but a large amount of property was rescued, including ten thousand stand of small arms, partially burned. Stuart took up his march to again place himself on Jackson's left, reaching the rear of the Federals at Malvern Hill at the close of the engagement on the night of July 1st. The next day the Federals, having again retreated, were pursued by Lee, with his cavalry in front, in the midst of a violent storm, which somewhat retarded their progress. The Union troops, having retired during the night, succeeded in reaching the protection of their gunboats. At Westover on the James River, the approach to their front was commanded. by the heavy guns of the shipping in addition to those mounted in intrenchments. In view of these facts General Lee deemed it inexpedient to attack him. His troops had been marching and fighting for seven days, and after remaining in close vicinity to McClellan's army, on July 8th they were returned to their former position. In concluding his report of these engagements, General Lee says that "under ordinary circumstances the Federal army should have been destroyed. Its escape was due to the causes already stated. Prominent among these is the want of correct and timely information. This fact, attributable chiefly to the nature of the country, enabled General McClellan skillfully to conceal his retreat and to add much to the obstructions with which Nature had beset the way of our pursuing columns, but regret that more was not accomplished gives way to gratitude to the Sovereign Ruler of the Universe for the results achieved. The siege of Richmond was raised, and the object of a campaign which had been prosecuted after months of preparation at an enormous expenditure of men and money completely frustrated. More than ten thousand prisoners (including officers of rank), fifty-two pieces of artillery, and upward of thirty-five thousand stand of small arms were captured. The stores and supplies of every description which fell into our hands were great in amount and value, but small in comparison with those destroyed by the enemy."

When McClellan's army, worn with conflict and broken by defeat, reached, on July 2d, the plains of the James River, above Westover, had the Southern infantry moved along the route taken by the cavalry of Stuart, he might have been attacked again with every element of decisive success. During the night of the 1st Stuart's celebrated horse artillery commander, Pelham, informed his chief that the Federal troops, after leaving Malvern Hill, had reached this position in a disorderly state, and that their position on the James River flats was completely commanded by a ridge parallel to the river called Evelington Heights. These heights commanded the enemy's encampment, and, crowned with artillery and taken possession of by infantry, would have compelled, in all probability, McClellan's surrender. Stuart forwarded Pelham's report at once to the commanding general, and proceeded to gain these heights. A squadron of the Federal cavalry vacated them without much hesitation on his approach. Upon getting in sight of the enemy Stuart determined to send back for one of his howitzers to fire upon their camp below. It was ascertained that the main body of the enemy were there much reduced and demoralized. These facts were promptly furnished to the commanding general, who in turn informed him that Longstreet and Jackson were en route to his support. Stuart held this ground from 9 A. M. till 2 P. M., when he was finally driven off by bodies of the enemy's infantry, after the exhaustion of his howitzer ammunition. He held the heights as long as it was possible, till he learned that Longstreet had taken the wrong road, and was then at Nance Shop, six or seven miles off, and could not possibly reach him in time to secure them. It was suggested to Stuart by one of his officers not to occupy the heights in force, nor to fire cannon from them, because it would call the attention of McClellan to the great importance of securing and fortifying them (before Lee's army could arrive), as necessary to his own protection. The cavalry commander disregarded this suggestion, and was driven from them. It seems absolutely certain that had Longstreet followed Stuart's march, Jackson Longstreet's, and the remainder of the army followed them, on July 2d, these heights could have been occupied by Lee's army and McClellan's command attacked and destroyed. The guns of the gunboats had to be so greatly elevated to fire over the banks of the river that the projectiles passed over the heights, so that the Southern army would not be much exposed to that fire, while a plunging fire from Lee's batteries on the Federal troops in the plains below must have resulted most disastrously.

McClellan, in a dispatch to Mr. Lincoln on the 4th, two days afterward, says: "We now occupy Evelington Heights, about two miles from the James, a plain extending from there to the river. Our front is about three miles long; these heights command our whole position, and must be maintained."

The total losses to the Army of the Potomac in these seven days of conflict are put down at fifteen thousand eight hundred and forty-nine, and the list of casualties in the Army of Northern Virginia in the fights before Richmond, commencing June 22d and ending July 1, 1862, is placed at sixteen thousand seven hundred and eighty-two. The Southern losses were the greater because during the battles they invariably formed the attacking column, while the Federal troops fought more or less behind intrenchments.

It cannot be denied that the retreat of McClellan from his position in front of Richmond to the James River was cleverly executed. After his right was rolled up the various positions selected to keep the Southern troops from destroying his army were well selected and ably defended. The Federal commander got unduly excited over what he supposed was the great preponderance of the Southerners in numbers, as well as over the re-enforcements which they were supposed to be receiving. On the night Stonewall Jackson encamped at Ashland McClellan told the Secretary of War by telegraph that he had received information from various sources that Beauregard and his troops had arrived in Richmond; and a half hour later he telegraphed Casey in command of his depot supplies at the White House that "it was said Jackson is coming from Fredericksburg with the intention of attacking the right flank soon." Six and a half hours later, on the morning of the 26th, at three o'clock, he informed Mr. Stanton that his "impression was confirmed that Jackson would soon attack our right rear," and added if he "had another good division he would laugh at Jackson." At 9 A. M. on the morning of the 26th a negro servant who had been in the employ of some of the officers of the Twentieth Georgia was brought before him, and, after questioning him, he telegraphed Stanton, "There is no doubt that Jackson is coming upon us." At midnight on June 24th he had informed Stanton that a "peculiar case of desertion had just occurred from the enemy." The deserter stated that he had left Jackson, Whiting, and Ewell, and fifteen brigades at Gordonsville on the 21st, and that it was intended to attack his [McClellan's] rear on the 28th, and asked for the latest information about Jackson. Mr. Stanton replied to him on June 25th, Jackson then being at Ashland, that he had no definite information as to the number or position of Jackson's forces; that it was reported as numbering forty thousand men. He had also heard that "Jackson was at Gordonsville with ten thousand rebels. Other reports placed Jackson at Port Republic, Harrisonburg, and Luray, and that neither McDowell, who was at Manassas, nor Banks and Fremont, who were at Middletown, appear to have any knowledge of Jackson's whereabouts." On the day Jackson arrived at Ashland McClellan was engaged in pushing Heintzelman's corps closer to the Richmond lines in prosecution of his general plan of advance. The night of the 25th, when Jackson was sleeping at Ashland, McClellan again telegraphed to the Secretary of War that he was inclined to think that Jackson would attack his right and rear, and that the rebel force was at least two hundred thousand; that he regretted his inferiority of numbers, but felt he was not responsible for it, and that if his army was destroyed by overwhelming numbers he could at least die with it and share its fate; that he felt there was no use in his again asking for re-enforcements. It seems that McClellan was deceived to some extent by the report of his chief of Secret-Service Corps. This was a corps one of whose objects was to question prisoners and deserters and ascertain in every other possible way the numbers of Lee's army. He was fully convinced he had to fight two hundred thousand troops. Lee's army numbered at the beginning of these combats eighty-one thousand. It was composed of thirty-nine brigades of infantry (twelve more, including those under Jackson, than General Johnston had when he relinquished the command at Seven Pines), six regiments and three battalions of cavalry, and sixteen batteries of reserve artillery (exclusive of those with the various infantry divisions). Fifty-three thousand Southern troops were massed on McClellan's right, and constituted the force which attacked Porter's command, numbering of all arms of service about thirty-six thousand men; while twenty-eight thousand Confederate troops stood between some seventy thousand of McClellan's army on the south bank of the Chickahominy and Richmond. The certified morning reports of the Federal Army of the Potomac, dated June 20, 1862, gives 115,102 as the aggregate present for duty. Six days later, when the battles commenced, the force probably did not exceed one hundred and five thousand. If in round numbers we put it at one hundred thousand, Lee was outnumbered nineteen thousand. When McClellan discovered that his opponent had on the left bank of the Chickahominy two thirds of his army, but three courses were left to him: One, to re-enforce the three divisions of Porter. Another, to strengthen and fortify the position along Beaver Dam Creek, and, relying on Porter to hold at bay as long as possible Jackson, Longstreet, and the two Hills, boldly set in motion his four corps on the right bank of the Chickahominy for the coveted prize, his enemy's capital. By destroying Huger and Magruder or crippling them, a portion of his troops could have kept them quiet, and then, facing about with the remainder, he might have marched to Porter's assistance and possibly defeated Lee. It was hazardous, however. Richmond was not Austerlitz, nor McClellan Napoleon. Third, to rescue Porter from his enemy, get him safely across to the south side of the Chickahominy, and unite him with the rest of his army.

This plan, if it had been adopted before the Confederate attack, might have forced the Southern commander to attack his united army on the right bank. He decided to receive the attack in the position then occupied by Porter, and only withdrew him to the Richmond side of the Chickahominy after he had been badly hammered and had lost some six thousand men.

Perhaps if McClellan had known that he was fighting eighty-one thousand men, and not two hundred thousand, he might have acted with more confidence. Mr. Lincoln telegraphed June 26th that his suggestion of, the probability of his being overwhelmed by two hundred thousand men, and talking about where the responsibility would belong, pained him very much. On June 27th McClellan began to realize that he was going to have some very serious work, and begged the Secretary that he would put someone general in command of the Shenandoah Valley and of all troops in front of Washington for the sake of the country. On the same day he complimented Porter for his fine efforts at Gaines Mill, says he looks upon the day as decisive of the war, and tells him to "try and drive the rascals, and take some prisoners and guns." This was an hour or two before Porter's defeat. General Hooker did not seem to be so confident, for about the same time he reported that he had just returned from the front, where "we have nothing but a stampede, owing to the behavior of the troops occupying the picket line. The first shot from a rebel was sufficient to start regiments." Later that day Admiral Goldsborough, the flag officer of the Federal squadron on the James, was notified by McClellan that he had met with a severe repulse, and asked him to send gunboats up the James River to cover the left flank of his army.

The Washington War Secretary was confident of Federal success as late as the evening of June 29th, for he telegraphed Hon. William H. Seward, at New York, that his inference is, from what has taken place around Richmond, that McClellan will be in the city within two days; and the day after, to General Wool, at Fort Monroe, that McClellan had a favorable position near Richmond, and that it looked more like occupying that city than any time before. At 11.30 on the night of June 30th the Union army commander had begun to realize that his "change of base," as he termed it, would not be attended with favorable results, and telegraphed Mr. Stanton that he feared he would be forced to abandon his material in order to save his men, under cover of the gunboats, and that if none of them escaped, they would at least have done honor to the country.

On July 1st his army was at Haxall's plantation, on the James, and McClellan says he dreaded the result if he was attacked; that if possible he would retire that night to Harrison's Bar, where the gunboats could aid in covering his position. "I now pray for time. We have failed to win only because overpowered by superior numbers." On July 2d McClellan's army had succeeded in reaching Harrison's Landing. He told Mr. Lincoln that if he were not attacked during that day his men would be ready to repulse the enemy on the morrow. On the same day he received a dispatch from President Lincoln in that vein of humor for which he was remarkable. "If you think you are not strong enough to take Richmond just now, I do not ask you to. Try just now to save the army material and personnel, and I will strengthen it for the offensive again as fast as I can. The governments of eighteen States offered me a new levy of three hundred thousand, which I accepted." And in a letter of the same date, in reference to sending him re-enforcements, Mr. Lincoln adds a postscript: "If at any time you feel able to take the offensive, you are not restrained from doing so."

The respective commanders of the two armies decided to rest and recruit their forces. McClellan resumed the habit he contracted in West Virginia of issuing proclamations. On July 4th the following was read to his army from the headquarters of the Army of the Potomac, camped near Harrison's Landing.

Soldiers of the Army of the Potomac:

Your achievements of the last ten days have illustrated the ability and endurance of the American soldier. Attacked by vastly superior forces, and without hope of re-enforcements, you have succeeded in changing your base of operations by a flank movement, regarded as the most hazardous of military expedients. You have saved all your material, all your trains, and all your guns, except a few lost in battle. Upon your march you have been assailed day after day with desperate fury by men of the same race and nation, skillfully massed and led, and under every disadvantage of numbers, and necessarily of position also. You have in every conflict beaten back your foes with enormous slaughter.

(Signed) Geo. B. McClellan, Major General Commanding.

By a series of brilliant movements General Lee had driven an army superior to him in numbers from the gates of his capital, and had fully restored himself in the confidence of his people by the exercise of military genius and by his personal conduct and supervision of the troops on the battlefield. It might be said of him, as Addison wrote of the great Marlborough, that

His mighty soul inspired repulsed battalions to engage,

And taught a doubtful battle where to rage.

Or, as was written of Wellington, "no responsibility proved too heavy for his calm, assured, and fertile intellect. If he made a mistake, he repaired it before the enemy could profit by it. If his adversaries made one, he took advantage of it with immediate decision. Always cool, sagacious, resolute, reliant, he was never at a loss for expedients, never disturbed by any unforeseen accidents, never without a clear conception of the object to be achieved, and the best way of achieving it."

The character of Lee is most apparent from his own words, only written for the eyes of the members of his family. When by his skill his brave soldiers had removed from the front of his capital McClellan's army, in a letter to his wife he disposes of the matter in a few lines by saying, on July 9, 1862, from Dobb's Farm, on the Nine Mile Road: "I have returned to my old quarters, and am filled with gratitude to our Heavenly Father for all the mercies he has extended to us. Our success has not been as great or complete as we could have desired, but God knows what is best for us. Our enemy has met with a heavy loss, from which it must take him some time to recover before he can recommence his operations."

General Henry Fitz had been wounded and was a prisoner in Richmond. General Lee answered a letter in reference to him and other wounded prisoners:

Headquarters, July 15, 1862.

My dear Fitz:

I have just received your letter of the 13th. I am very sorry to hear of the sufferings of the wounded prisoners, and wish I could relieve them. I proposed to General McClellan on Tuesday, before the battle of that day, to parole and send to him all his wounded if he would receive them. Since that the arrangement has been made, and the sick and wounded are now being conveyed to him. This will relieve them very much, and enable us to devote our attention to those retained. In addition, the enemy has at last agreed to a general exchange of all prisoners of war, and Generals Dix and D. H. Hill are to meet to-morrow to commence the negotiations. I hope in this way much relief will be afforded; at first the hospitals were overtaxed, men could not be had to bury the dead, and the sufferings of all were increased. Friend Clitz ought to recollect that this is a matter of his own seeking, and he has only to blame himself. I will still be happy to do for him all I can, and will refer your letter to the director of the hospital if I can find him.

Your loving uncle, R. E. Lee. General Fitz Lee.

The offensive tactics of the Confederate commander raised the siege of Richmond and the hopes of the South. From the various churches prayers ascended to the throne of the God of Battles, and humble supplications were offered for the cessation of hostilities.

The removal of McClellan's army from the walls of Richmond brought great relief to its inhabitants; the blood of the bravest had been poured at their feet, the moans of the wounded had fallen upon their ears, and the dead lay silent and cold before their eyes. The war had been brought to their hearthstones.

General Lee now proposed to transfer its horrors to fields at a greater distance from the Southern capital, for the proximity of a large hostile army still menaced its safety. McClellan had been driven from its gates, but Richmond was still his objective point. But two marches away there were encamped on James River ninety thousand men; twenty days after the battle of Malvern Hill it numbered 101,697 — a grand army, well equipped with all the sinews of war, whose principal officers were men of undoubted courage and military ability.

Lee had three alternatives: First, to attack; second, to await an attack; third, manoeuvre so as to threaten Washington and draw McClellan's army from the vicinity of Richmond. The Army of the Potomac was now behind too much dirt, and had too many big guns in position on land and water to admit of an attack with reasonable hopes of success; and time was too precious to wait for it to get in condition to assume the offensive again, so Lee promptly decided to move it to a safe distance. Mr. Lincoln was naturally solicitous about the security of the Federal capital. After McClellan's defeat he determined to do two things: One, to concentrate the commands which Jackson had scattered and put them under one officer, who should be charged with the guardianship of Washington; the other, to buckle to his side by day and night a military adviser in whose abilities he had confidence, and who should be commander in chief of all the Federal armies.

He was singularly unfortunate in the selection of the officers to fill these two important places. The forces of Fremont, Banks, and McDowell were united into what was termed the Army of Virginia, and its command was assigned to Major-General John Pope. This officer, a Kentuckian by birth and a West Point graduate, was then forty years old. When a captain of engineers in the United States Army he had been detailed as one of the army officers to escort Mr. Lincoln to Washington where he was to assume the duties of the presidency, and, it is presumed, did not fail to impress upon the President his qualifications for command. Pope had met with some success in the campaigns in the West, and was looked upon as a rising officer whose military capacity would be productive of great results, and ultimately seat him in McClellan's saddle. On assuming his new command, it must be confessed he made a bad beginning, which was not attended with the usual good ending. He was evidently deeply impressed with the idea that the war in Virginia had not been conducted properly, and that he had been brought from the West — where, as he said, he had only seen the backs of his enemies — to destroy the human race at the South generally, whether they were armed soldiers or unarmed citizens. There was a striking contrast between McClellan and Pope. The former had announced that private property and unarmed citizens should be protected, and that neither confiscation of property, political execution of persons, nor forcible abolition of slavery should be contemplated for a moment; the latter had ordered the arrest of all disloyal male citizens, and their banishment from their homes unless they took the oaths of allegiance, threatening them if they should ever return that they would be visited with the extreme rigor of military law, and should their oaths be violated, the offenders would be shot and their property confiscated. He also directed that prominent citizens, however inoffensive they might be, should be seized on every side and held as hostages for Union soldiers captured by "roving bands." The intimation to his soldiers that they were free to enter upon a campaign of robbery and murder against unarmed citizens and peaceful tillers of the soil produced a sensation in the army of Lee, which had been accustomed to encounter troops under leaders of a different type, and also a desire to get at Pope at the earliest moment. The North was not prepared at that date for such extreme measures. Men who at home would have shuddered at the suggestion of taking another's property now appropriated remorselessly whatever came within their reach. The Southern President directed General Lee to say to the authorities at Washington that a cartel for the exchange of prisoners between the belligerents had just been signed by Generals Dix and D. H. Hill, representing their respective governments, stipulating that all prisoners hereafter taken will be discharged on parole till exchanged, and that Pope had violated it, because his orders contemplated the murder of peaceful inhabitants as spies; that innocent people had been seized, to be murdered in cold blood if any of his soldiers should be killed by unknown persons; and that, in consequence, neither Pope nor his commissioned officers, if captured, should be considered as prisoners of war. To this communication President Lincoln's new military adviser replied that the communication of Mr. Davis, inclosed to him by General Lee, was couched in language exceedingly insulting to the Government of the United States, and that he [Halleck] must respectfully decline to receive it. Later it was stated that the Government disavowed these measures of the commander of the Army of Virginia. Pope was more or less ridiculed by soldiers on both sides for his bombastic declamations. He did not want to hear, he told his troops, of taking strong positions and holding them, of lines of retreat and bases of supply. His "headquarters" were reported "in the saddle," and his army was to be launched upon a sea of strife without a compass. The safety of Washington, with which he was particularly charged, was to be secured by marvelous methods. He proposed to keep his army on the flank of any hostile force that approached it, because he thought that no commander would have the temerity to pass him, in the first place; and, in the second, if he should seek to attack him, he could lead him off in another direction, and was satisfied that if he had McClellan's numbers he could march to New Orleans and dictate the terms of peace in the Crescent City.

General Lee early measured Pope, and when it became necessary to transact military business with him paralyzed him with movements as brilliant as they were bold, but which it is safe to say he would never have attempted against an army commander for whose military genius he had profound respect. In a letter from near Richmond, July 28, 1862, after telling Mrs. Lee: "In the prospect before me I cannot see a single ray of pleasure during this war; but so long as I can perform any service to the country I am content," he could not resist giving Pope a slight slap, and adds: "When you write to Rob again" (his youngest son, who was a private in the Rockbridge Battery) "tell him to catch Pope for me, and also to bring in his cousin Louis Marshall, who, I am told, is on his staff. I could forgive the latter fighting against us, but not his joining Pope."

Out in the West, too, President Lincoln found his commander in chief, and on July 11th ordered that Major-General Henry W. Halleck be assigned to command the whole land force of the United States as general in chief, and that he repair to the capital. The Confederates were re-enforced by these appointments of Halleck and Pope. If the latter was, as Swinton, the historian of the Army of the Potomac, puts it, "the most disbelieved man in the army," the former was a perpetual stumbling-stone in the path of

93

the field commanders of the Federal army. His position was a most difficult one to fill. Mr. Lincoln's attention was drawn to him by his past record. Halleck graduated at the United States Military Academy in the class of 1849, and was forty-seven years old when summoned to Washington. Like Lee, McClellan, and Pope, he was an engineer officer, but resigned in 1854 to practice law, and was so engaged in San Francisco, Cal., when the war began. General Scott had a high opinion of his ability. A lawyer, a soldier, and an author, he had written on both military and legal topics. He had many of the qualifications necessary for his trying office. This appointment was made by Mr. Lincoln immediately after a personal inspection of McClellan's army on the James River. On that visit, July 8th, the Northern President ascertained that the Army of the Potomac numbered 86,500 men present and 73,500 absent to be accounted for. The tri-monthly return for July 10th fixed the number of men present equipped for duty at 98,631. "To make this army march to Richmond with any hope of success it must be re-enforced by at least 100,000 good troops; any officer here whose opinion is worth one penny will not recommend a less number," wrote one of his corps commanders on the day of this return, and strongly advised the removal of the army to Washington. Whether to re-enforce McClellan or Pope was the question. The former could not well be attacked in his fortified camp, nor could he assault with much prospect of success Lee's lines, as they were much stronger now than when he was last in front of them. Burnside, who had been ordered from the South to re-enforce McClellan, was halted at Newport News, ready, as Mr. Lincoln informed McClellan on July 14th, "to move on short notice one way or the other when ordered." By which he meant up the Potomac to Washington, or up the James to McClellan, and a week afterward he wrote McClellan that he would decide what he should do with Burnside in the next two or three days.

General Lee decided the question for him. With watchful eye he had noticed the concentration of Pope's army and its gradual extension into Virginia. He saw that it had passed McDowell's battlefield, crossed the Rappahannock, and was getting too near to the important town of Gordonsville, where the railroad from Richmond met the one from Washington. He resolved to stop Pope, and, if possible, overwhelm him before he could be largely re-enforced by McClellan, for a victory over him would remove McClellan's army to Washington. On July 10th Lee had 65,419 men, exclusive of the Department of North Carolina, which was under his command, or some 23,000 less than the army opposed to him. This fact did not deter him three days afterward from making the disparity of numbers still greater by sending a detachment of 8,000 men to Pope's front. For the commander of this force Lee wisely selected Jackson, who was so aggressive and so swift in his movements that he would create a disturbance in the guardian army of Washington before his departure from Richmond would be known. Stonewall Jackson left Lee on July 13th with his old division and that of Ewell's, both having been much weakened by hard marches and severe fighting. One week afterward Mr. Lincoln was informed by McClellan that he had heard Jackson had left Richmond by rail, going either toward Gordonsville or Fredericksburg, that the movement continued three days, and that he might be going against Buell in the West via Gordonsville, so as to leave the Petersburg and Danville roads free for the transportation to Lee of recruits and supplies. On the same day Pope reported to Lincoln that Ewell was at Gordonsville with six thousand men, and Jackson at Louisa Court House, but a few miles distant, with twenty-five thousand, and that his [Pope's] advanced posts were at Culpeper and Madison Court House. Jackson, the bête noir of the Federal capital, was on the war path, and again produced consternation. Halleck hurried to McClellan, and had a personal interview on July 25th, urging upon him to attack Richmond at once, or he would have to withdraw him to reenforce Pope. McClellan finally agreed to attack if Halleck would send him twenty thousand more troops, all that Halleck could promise. McClellan would not say, says Halleck, that "the probabilities of success were in his favor, but there was a chance, and he was willing to try it; that the force of the enemy was two hundred thousand; and that in this estimate most of his officers agreed." His own effective force was ninety thousand, which, with twenty thousand re-enforcements, would make one hundred and ten thousand; and his officers were about equally divided in opinion in regard to the policy of withdrawing or risking an attack on Richmond.

Five days before Halleck's visit General Lee's army numbered 57,328. Estimating it at 60,000 when McClellan and Halleck were in conference, it is seen the former overestimated Lee's strength only about 140,000. The interview between these two officers highest in rank in the Federal army was productive of temporary respect, confidence, and friendship. Halleck writes McClellan a few days afterward that "there was no one in the army under whom I could serve with greater pleasure." McClellan replies: "Had I been consulted as to who was to take my place, I would have advised your appointment; and that if we are permitted to do so, I believe that together we can save this unhappy country and bring this war to a comparatively easy termination. The doubt in my mind is whether the selfish politicians will allow us to do so." The next few days saw changes not only in the relations between these two officers, but in the plans and purposes of the contending forces. Jackson arrived at Gordonsville on July 19th, and at once began to consider the best way to strike Pope. Finding that his antagonist had practically concentrated the corps of Sigel (formerly Fremont's), Banks's, and McDowell's, and had nearly six times his numbers, he wisely decided to apply to General Lee for more troops before he assumed the offensive. On July 27th Lee sent A. P. Hill's division, which gave him an army of 18,623. While he could not hope to beat the whole of Pope's army, numbering on July 31st, according to Pope, 40,358, or, if we accept the reports of the various corp commanders, 47,000 men, the disposition of these forces gave him an opportunity to strike a part of it. Banks was in advance at Culpeper Court House, with his cavalry picketing the line of the Rapidan. Jackson always availed himself of such opportunities, and promptly moved forward and crossed the Rapidan on August 8th. Pope, on learning of Jackson's advance, ordered Banks to move in his direction from Culpeper Court House; so Jackson encountered him on the 9th about eight miles in front of that place, a short distance west and north of Slaughter Mountain near Cedar Run. A well-tested battle was fought, resulting in a victory for the Southern troops, their pursuit being stopped by night. Banks fell back to his old position north of Cedar Run, while Jackson remained in the field next day, and then, hearing that Banks had been heavily re-enforced, returned to the vicinity of Gordonsville. The Confederates sustained a loss of thirteen hundred officers and men, including General Charles Winder, of Maryland, one of the most promising and gallant soldiers of the South. Jackson mourned him as one of his most accomplished officers. "Richly endowed," he wrote, "with those qualities of mind and person which fit an officer for commanding, and which attract the admiration and excite the enthusiasm of the troops, he was rapidly rising to the front rank of his profession. His loss has been severely felt." By this movement Jackson, as usual, had rendered great service. The question whether to re-enforce Pope or McClellan was decided. Stonewall Jackson was in front of the army covering Washington. Halleck's orders for the evacuation of the Peninsula by McClellan's army must be carried out. Burnside, hanging for so long a time between McClellan and Pope, must go to Pope.

The anticipations of General Lee had been realized; it was now a race who should get to Pope first — the Army of Northern Virginia or the Army of the Potomac. The movements of the Southern general had been delayed because he did not desire to risk the detachment of too many troops from Richmond lines until he had a reasonable confidence that McClellan's offensive operations were at an end. Four days after Jackson's fight he determined to transfer the theater of action to Pope's front, and accordingly ordered Major-General Longstreet, with ten brigades, commanded by Kemper, Jenkins, Wilcox, Pryor, Featherstone, D. R. Jones, Toombs, Drayton, and Evans, to Gordonsville, and on the same day Hood, with his own and Whiting's brigades, was sent to the same place. Two days afterward — namely, August 15th — General Lee proceeded in person to join Longstreet and Jackson. He was distressed at being deprived of the services of Richmond, his cheval de bataille, in the approaching campaign. His favorite riding mare was a sorrel called Grace Darling. When the war began he had her sent down from Arlington to the White House. He writes that he heard of Grace. She was seen bestridden by some of the Federal soldiers, with her colt by her side, and adds that he could have been better resigned to many things than that. "I have also lost my horse Richmond." (Presented to him by some citizens of Richmond.) "He died Thursday. I had ridden him the day before. He seemed in the morning as well as ever; but I discovered in the evening he was not well. I thought he was merely distressed by the heat, and brought him along very slowly.

Finding at bedtime he had not recovered, I had him bled, which seemed to relieve him. In the morning he was pronounced better; at noon he was reported dead. His labors are over and he is at rest. He carried me very faithfully, and I shall never have so beautiful an animal again. His fate is different from Grace's, and to his loss I can easily be resigned. I shall want but few horses more, and have as many as I require."

Three days after Longstreet, and one day after Lee left, McClellan telegraphed (August 16th) Halleck: "Movement has commenced by land and water. All sick will be away to-morrow night. Everything being done to carry out your orders. I do not like Jackson's movements. He will suddenly appear when least expected." It is apparent that General Lee was confident of McClellan's withdrawal, or he would hardly have left in person or detached Longstreet from Richmond. On Lee's departure, General G. W. Smith, who had returned to duty, was left in command with his own division and that of D. H. Hill (at Petersburg commanding the Department of North Carolina), as well as McLaw's and R. H. Anderson's divisions and Hampton's cavalry brigade; but on the 15th Lee telegraphed to Mr. Davis requesting him to order R. H. Anderson's division to him, and on the 17th General G. W. Smith was ordered to join him also. The great value of time was appreciated by the Southern leader. It was his plain duty to force Pope to accept battle before he was joined by the whole of McClellan's army. When Pope discovered that Lee was marching to fight him he fell back behind the line of the Rappahannock, though he thought that river was too far to the front, because, he said, "the movements of Lee were too rapid and those of McClellan too slow to make it possible with his force to hold that line, or to keep communication with Fredericksburg without being turned on my right flank by Lee's whole army and cut off altogether from Washington." He was told that in two days more he would be largely re-enforced by the Army of the Potomac, and would not only be secure, but strong enough to assume the offensive. He was instructed, he reports, to hold on there, "and fight like the devil." Lee therefore found Pope on the Rappahannock, with his right at the Waterloo Bridge and his left at Kelly's Ford. He had stretched down the river as far as he well could so as to keep his communication open with Fredericksburg, from which point Burnside and Fitz John Porter's corps of the Army of the Potomac were coming. Lee was anxious to get at Pope at once, but there was a river rolling between them. From "Camp near Orange Court House," August 17, 1862, he wrote: "Here I am in a tent instead of my comfortable quarters at Dobbs's" (his headquarters in front of Richmond). "The tent, however, is very comfortable, and of that I have nothing to complain. General Pope says he is very strong, and seems to feel so, for he is moving apparently up to the Rapidan. I hope he will not prove stronger than we are. I learn since I have left that General McClellan has moved down the James River with his whole army. I suppose he is coming here, too, so we shall have a busy time. Burnside and King from Fredericksburg have joined Pope, which, from their own report, has swelled Pope to ninety-two thousand. I do not believe it, though I believe he is very big. Johnny Lee saw Louis Marshall after Jackson's last battle, who asked him kindly after his old uncle, and said his mother was well. Johnny said Louis looked wretchedly himself. I am sorry he is in such bad company, but I suppose he could not help it."

Lee promptly decided to destroy the railroad in Pope's rear so as to capture re-enforcements and supplies from the direction of Washington and Alexandria, for he knew that the portion of McClellan's army which should be transferred by water would take that route to join Pope. This duty he intrusted to his chief of cavalry, J. E. B. Stuart, who had been commissioned as a major general on July 25th. Three days thereafter his cavalry was organized into a division consisting of two brigades under Wade Hampton and Fitz Lee: Hampton's, the First North Carolina Cavalry, Cobb Legion Cavalry, Jeff Davis Legion, Hampton Legion, and the Tenth Virginia, while Fitz Lee's brigade consisted of the First, Third, Fourth, Fifth, and Ninth Virginia Cavalry. When these new operations commenced, Stuart, leaving Hampton on the Richmond lines, moved Fitz Lee's brigade to the Rapidan, while he went by rail to join General Lee at Orange Court House for consultation. After his consultation with General Lee, Stuart proceeded to Verdierville, on the road from Orange Court House to Fredericksburg, where he had expected to find Lee's brigade on the evening of the 17th, a proceeding which came very near resulting in the capture of himself and staff. Not finding the brigade as contemplated, he sent one of his staff officers in the direction he expected to meet it to conduct it to his headquarters. A body of the enemy's cavalry, which had started on a reconnoissance the day before, was marching in that direction, and into their ranks in the darkness of the night Major Fitzhugh, of his staff, rode, and was captured. On his person was found an autograph letter from General Lee to Stuart, disclosing the design of turning his left flank. Stuart and his staff proceeded to pass the night on the porch of an old house. He was awakened at dawn by the sounds of approaching horsemen; sent two of his aids off in that direction to find out who was coming, and walked out to the front gate, bareheaded, to greet, as he supposed, his brigade commander; but in another instant he heard pistol shots and saw Mosby and Gibson rapidly returning, pursued by a party of the enemy. He and the rest of his staff then rushed back, jumped over the fence, and made across the fields to the nearest woods. They were pursued only a short distance. When the pursuit stopped, Stuart returned to a point where he could observe the house, and saw the enemy departing with his cloak and hat, which he had been compelled to leave on the porch where he had slept. Stuart's hat was generally a conspicuous one, having a broad brim looped up on one side, over which always floated large black feathers, and for many days thereafter he was subject to the constant inquiry of "Where's your hat?" The brigade commander he had expected did not understand from any instructions he received that it was necessary to be at this point on that particular afternoon, and had marched a little out of his direct road in order to reach his wagons and get from them a full supply of rations and ammunition. After Stuart reached the army, to the brigade he brought from Richmond was added another which had previously served in the Valley, and was commanded by General Beverley Robertson, which consisted of the Second, Sixth, Seventh, Twelfth, and Seventeenth Battalions of Virginia cavalry. Having detached a regiment under Munford to operate on the left of the army, Stuart crossed the Rapidan on the 20th with Fitz Lee's brigade and the remainder of Robertson's, and proceeded at once to drive the Federal cavalry from out of the section between the Rapidan and Rappahannock Rivers, across the latter stream. Lee now began to extend his left, and on the 22d and 23d Jackson moved up the Rappahannock River to the Warrenton Springs ford. Stuart started on his mission, crossing at Waterloo Bridge, a point above Warrenton Springs, and, moving by way of Warrenton, reached the vicinity of Catlett's Station, twelve miles in Pope's rear, after dark. The rain fell in such torrents and the night was so dark that it was not possible for him to damage the road to any great extent. At that point was encamped the whole reserve, baggage, and ammunition train of Pope's army as well as his headquarters tent and personal effects. Stuart captured a number of officers and men, a large sum of money in a safe in one of the tents, dispatches and other papers of Pope's office, and his personal baggage. Had it not been raining so hard the destruction of the railroad bridges and of the track itself, as well as an immense number of wagons, would have seriously crippled Pope, and the object of the expedition would have been accomplished. He was obliged to withdraw before daylight, and returned to his army at Warrenton Springs the next day, bringing back with him over three hundred prisoners. Pope now ascertaining that Lee was turning his attention to a flank movement on his right, began extending his lines up the river. The Southern commander was not content with what had been done by Stuart, and determined to execute the same movement on a larger scale, which would have the effect of severing Pope's communications with his base of supplies and compel him to leave the lines of the Rappahannock.

CHAPTER 9

SECOND BATTLE OF MANASSAS.

The strategy of Lee was daring and dangerous, the conception brilliant and bold. Self-reliant, he decided to separate his army into two parts. On August 24, 1862, he had fifty thousand troops, while Pope, including his own army, had, with Reno's corps of Burnside's army and Reynolds's division of Pennsylvania reserves, about the same number, which two days later was increased to seventy thousand by the arrival of the corps of Fitz John Porter and Heintzelman. Lee proposed to hold the line of the Rappahannock and occupy Pope's attention with thirty thousand troops under the immediate command of Longstreet, while he rapidly transferred Jackson by a circuitous march of fifty-six miles to a point twenty-four miles exactly in rear of Pope's line of battle. On August 25th Jackson, with three divisions of infantry, under Ewell, A. P. Hill, and W. B. Taliaferro, preceded by Munford's Second Virginia Cavalry, crossed the upper Rappahannock, there called the Hedgman River, at Hinson Mills, four miles above Waterloo Bridge, where the left and right of the two opposing armies respectively rested. The "Foot cavalry" were in light marching order, and were accompanied only by a limited ordnance train and a few ambulances. Three days cooked rations were issued and duly deposited in haversacks, much of which was thrown away in the first few hours' march, the men preferring green corn, seasoned by rubbing the meat rations upon the ears, and the turnips and apples found contiguous to their route. After the sun sank to rest on that hot August day, Jackson went into bivouac at Salem, a small village on the Manassas Gap Railroad, having marched in the heat and dust twenty-six miles. But one man among twenty thousand knew where they were going. The troops knew an important movement was on hand, which involved contact with the enemy, and possibly a reissue of supplies. At early dawn the next day the march was resumed at right angles to the course of the day before, following the Manassas Gap Railroad and passing through Bull Run Mountains at Thoroughfare Gap. At Gainesville, Stuart, with Robertson and Fitz Lee's brigades of cavalry, overtook Jackson, whose subsequent movements were "greatly aided and influenced by the admirable manner in which the cavalry was employed and managed by Stuart." On reaching the vicinity of Manassas Junction, his objective point, Jackson inclined to the right and intersected the main railroad in Pope's rear at Bristoe Station, four miles closer to Pope, where he halted for the night, having marched nearly thirty miles. That night he sent General Trimble, who had volunteered for the occasion, with five hundred men, and Stuart, with his cavalry, to capture Manassas, which was handsomely done. Pope claims that Jackson's movement was known, and that he reported it to Halleck, but on the day Jackson marched Pope was disposing his army along the Rappahannock from Waterloo to Kelly's Ford. On the night of the 26th, when Jackson began to tear up the railroad at Bristoe, the nearest hostile troops were the corps of Heintzelman and Reno at Warrenton Junction, ten miles away. The next day, leaving General Ewell's division at Bristoe to watch and retard Pope's march to open his communications, Jackson, with the remainder of his troops, proceeded to Manassas. He found that Stuart and Trimble had captured eight guns, three hundred prisoners, and an immense quantity of stores. The vastness and variety of the supplies was a most refreshing sight to his tired and hungry veterans. All of the 27th his troops, transformed from poverty to affluence, reveled in these enormous stores, consisting of car loads of provisions, boxes of clothing, sutler's stores containing everything from French mustard to cavalry boots. Early that morning Taylor's New Jersey brigade, of Slocum's division of Franklin's corps, which had been transported by rail from Alexandria to Bull Run for the purpose of attacking what was presumed to be a small cavalry raid, got off the cars and marched in line of battle across the open plain to Manassas. Fitz Lee, who with his cavalry brigade had crossed Bull Run to make a reconnoissance in the direction of Alexandria, ascertained that Taylor was not supported by other troops and sent information of this fact to Jackson, suggesting that Taylor be allowed to march to Manassas, where he and his whole command would be most certainly captured. The artillery, however, opened on the brigade, giving them notice that a large force was present, which resulted in the killing of many men, including the gallant brigade commander, and capturing many others. The remainder beat a hasty retreat. That afternoon Ewell was attacked by Hooker's division of Heintzelman's corps, who had been ordered to re-open the Federal communications, and retired, as he had been directed, to join Jackson. This enterprising officer, having executed General Lee's instructions and having torn up the railroad and burned the bridges in that vicinity, now determined to move in such a manner as to avoid disaster to his own troops, while he united them at the earliest possible moment with those under Longstreet en route to his assistance. He had successfully thrown his fourteen brigades of infantry, two of cavalry, and eighteen light batteries in Pope's rear; but his position was perilous.

Two plans were open to Pope after he had ascertained that Jackson was on the line of his communication and between him and his capital — one to throw his whole force on Longstreet and, if possible, destroy him, and then move with his victorious legions on Jackson; the other to hold Longstreet apart from Jackson with a portion of his force, in which he would be greatly assisted by the topographical features of the country, while moving with the remainder of his command on the Confederate forces in his rear. He decided to adopt the latter, and might have succeeded had he so manoeuvred as to prevent the junction of the two wings of Lee's army. There can be no fault found with the skillful directions issued for the movements of Pope's army on Jackson on the 27th. At sunset of that day Jackson's command was still eating, sleeping, and resting at Manassas. McDowell, with his own, Sigel's corps, and Reynolds's division of Pope's army, was at Gainesville, fifteen miles from Manassas and five from Thoroughfare Gap, through which Lee's route to Jackson lay, being directly between Jackson and Lee, while Reno's corps and Kearny's division of Heintzelman's corps were at Greenwich, in easy supporting distance. Hooker at Bristoe Station was four miles from Manassas, and Banks and Fitz John Porter at Warrenton Junction ten miles. On the night of the 27th everything was favorable to Pope, and it seemed his various corps would only have to be put in motion on the morning of the 28th to crush Jackson. McDowell was told by Pope if he would move early with his forty thousand on Manassas he would, as Pope expressed it, with the assistance of troops coming in other directions, "bag Jackson and his whole crowd."

But Pope made two great mistakes — one in not holding, with a large force, at all hazards, Thoroughfare Gap, five miles from McDowell's position at Gainesville, and thus shut the door of the battlefield in Longstreet's face. The other, in supposing Jackson was going to remain at Manassas in order that he might carry out his plans to beat him; for while Pope was arranging that night to his own satisfaction his tactical bagging details for the next day, the three divisions of that wide-awake officer were marching away from Manassas: A. P. Hill to Centreville, Ewell to the crossing of Bull Run at Blackburn Ford, and up the left bank of that stream to Stone Bridge, where the Warrenton turnpike crosses, and Taliaferro, whose march Jackson in person accompanied, to the vicinity of Sudley Mills, north of Warrenton turnpike and west of Bull Run, at which point Jackson designed to concentrate his command. The movements of the two divisions across Bull Run were made to mislead Pope, and did so. When he reached Manassas the next day Jackson was not there. He thought from the passage of Bull Run he had gone to Centreville, and so the march of his converging troops was directed upon that point. Jackson had exercised his usual skill in the selection of his position. He could attack any of Pope's troops marching down the Warrenton turnpike in the direction of Centreville, where they hoped to find him, and at the same time by prolonging his right he would be in a position to communicate at the earliest possible moment with General Lee as he came through Thoroughfare Gap with Longstreet. After Jackson had arrived at his new position a courier of the enemy was captured by the cavalry, who was conveying a dispatch from McDowell to Sigel and Reynolds, which disclosed Pope's intention to concentrate on

Manassas. One of Jackson's division commanders writes that the messenger bearing the captured orders "found the Confederate headquarters established on the shady side of an old-fashioned fence, in the corners of which General Jackson and the commanders of his divisions were profoundly sleeping after the fatigue of the preceding night, and there was not as much as an ambulance at his headquarters." The headquarters train was back beyond the Rappahannock, with servants, camp equipage, and all the arrangements for cooking and serving food. The property of the general, of the staff, and of the headquarters bureau was strapped to the pommels and cantles of the saddles, which formed pillows for their weary owners. The captured dispatch roused Jackson like an electric shock; he was essentially a man of action, and never asked advice or called council. "Move your division to attack the enemy," said he to Taliaferro; and to Ewell, "Support the attack." The slumbering soldiers sprang from the earth. They were sleeping almost in ranks, and by the time the horses of the officers were saddled, lines of infantry were moving to the anticipated battlefield. It was Stonewall's intention to attack the Federals who were on the Warrenton road moving on his supposed position, but after marching some distance north of the turnpike in the direction of Thoroughfare Gap no enemy was found. McDowell, after sending Rickett's division to the gap to retard the advance of Longstreet, moved it direct to Manassas and not down the Warrenton pike; so finding this pike clear of his enemy, he halted, and, keeping his flanks guarded by cavalry, watched it, while ever and anon he turned a wistful eye in the direction of the gap in the mountain to his right.

Pope now seemed to have lost his military head. It did not occur to him that his success lay wholly in keeping Longstreet and Jackson apart. Jackson alone was a subject of concern to him. He reached in person Manassas about midday on the 28th, and found that Jackson had left the night before after burning five thousand pounds of bacon, a thousand barrels of corned beef, two thousand barrels of salt pork, two thousand barrels of flour, together with large supplies of every sort. While Pope was following his supposed route to Centreville, Jackson in his war paint was in line beyond the Warrenton turnpike waiting for Longstreet. He had evidently determined to attack any and every one who dared to occupy the pike he was keeping open for Longstreet. It so happened that King's division of McDowell's corps, which on the night of the 27th was near Buckland, in getting the order to march to Centreville had to pass without knowing it in front of Jackson, by whom he was promptly and furiously attacked, and a most stubborn contest followed. King's troops fought with determined courage, and his artillery was admirably served. In addition to the four brigades of his division, he had two regiments of Doubleday's, and fought two of Ewell's and three of Taliaferro's brigades of Jackson's command. A. P. Hill's division was not engaged. It was an exhibition of superb courage and excellent discipline on both sides, and a fight face to face. "Out in the sunlight, in the dying daylight, and under the stars they stood," neither side yielding an inch, while brave men in blue and gray fell dead almost in each other's arms. Jackson's loss was heavy. Ewell and Taliaferro were both wounded, the former losing a leg, while King lost over a third of his command. The Federal commander held his ground till 1 A. M., when, being without support or orders, he marched to Manassas Junction. Jackson, who was not at Manassas or Centreville on the days Pope desired him to be, informed that officer by this fight exactly where he was; so on the 29th Pope once more changed the march of his columns, still hoping he would be able to defeat him before being re-enforced by General Lee. General Lee, with Longstreet's command, left the Rapidan on the 26th and followed Jackson's route. A little before dark on the 28th he reached and occupied the western side of Thoroughfare Gap with one brigade. At the same time Ricketts came up from Gainesville with his division and occupied the eastern side of the same pass. Longstreet describes this pass as rough and at some points not more than one hundred yards wide. A turbid stream rushes over its rugged bottom, on both sides of which the mountain rises several hundred feet. On the north the face of the gap is almost perpendicular. The south face is less precipitous, but is covered with tangled mountain ivy and projecting bowlders, forming a position unassailable when occupied by a small infantry and artillery force. This gap and the Hopewell Gap, three miles north, if seriously disputed by the Federals would have embarrassed Lee. Prompt measures were taken to prevent it. Hopewell was occupied, and through it three brigades under Wilcox were passed during the night, while Hood climbed over the mountain near Thoroughfare Gap by a trail. At dawn on the 29th, much to General Lee's relief, Ricketts had marched away to join McDowell. At 9 A. M. the head of Longstreet's column reached Gainesville on the Warrenton pike. The troops passed through the town and down the turnpike and were deployed on Jackson's right, and ready for battle at twelve o'clock on the 29th. At daylight on that day, to Sigel, supported by Reynolds, was delegated the duty of attacking Jackson and bringing him to a stand, as Pope expressed it, until he could get up Heintzelman and Reno from Centreville, and Porter, with King's division, from Bristoe and Manassas. Pope reached in person the battlefield about noon, and found nearly his whole army in Jackson's front. Longstreet had connected with Jackson's right, which Pope did not know, but rode along his lines and encouraged his men by stating that McDowell and Fitz John Porter were marching so as to get in Jackson's right and rear. The Federal attack had been principally made with the center and right against Jackson. The left, under Fitz John Porter some ten thousand men — was stationary, McDowell having gone to the support of the rest of the army. Lee's line had been advanced in the fierce contests of the day, but during the night was retired to its first position.

Porter's inaction in front of Longstreet has been the subject of much comment, and did not please either Longstreet or Pope. Both wanted him to attack — Pope, because he was under the impression it would be a flank and rear attack on Jackson's position; Longstreet, because, having nearly three men to Porter's one, he could easily defeat him. It is certain that when Pope ordered Porter at half past 4 o'clock in the afternoon to attack, Longstreet's whole force had been in front of him for four hours and a half. Porter reported the enemy were in great force in front of him. "They had gathered artillery, cavalry, and infantry, and the advancing masses of dust showed the enemy coming in great force," said he. The "indefatigable Stuart" had ridden out in the direction of Thoroughfare Gap to meet General Lee and inform him of the exact position of Jackson and the general disposition of the troops on both sides. He then passed the cavalry he had on that flank through Longstreet's column so as to get on his right, and directed Rosser to have brush dragged up and down the road by the cavalry from the direction of Gainesville so as to deceive the enemy, and according to Porter's dispatch, it had the desired effect. Stuart found an elevated ridge in front of Porter, and sent back and got three brigades of infantry and some artillery, which, in addition to his cavalry and the effect produced by dragging the brush and making a great dust, gave the impression that he had a large force in Fitz John Porter's front. The next day — the 30th — Pope, desiring to delay as long as possible General Lee's further advance on Washington, renewed the engagement. He advanced Porter, whom he had called to him during the night, supported by King's gallant division, to attack the Confederates along the Warrenton pike, while he assaulted with his right wing Jackson's left. His first impression in the morning was that General Lee was retreating, and he so telegraphed to Washington, having derived the impression from the retirement of Lee the night before to his original lines. Jackson was still Pope's objective point. It was evident Lee must re-enforce Jackson or attack with Longstreet. He did the latter after first pounding the flanks of Pope's assaulting columns with artillery, under Stephen D. Lee, splendidly massed and served. Pope and Lee were of the same mind that day from their respective standpoints, for as the former was moving on Lee's center and left, the latter was marching to attack the Federal left. A bloody and hard-fought battle resulted, in which the Federal troops were everywhere driven back, and when night put an end to the contest, Pope's line of communication was threatened by the Southern troops occupying the Sudley Springs road close to the stone bridge on Bull Run. He could stay in Lee's front no longer, for he had been badly defeated, and that night withdrew to Centreville, having lost, since he left the Rappahannock, in killed, wounded, and missing, nearly fifteen thousand men. On the 31st his army was posted on the heights of Centreville. Halleck telegraphed him on that day from Washington: "You have done nobly. All reserves are being sent forward. Do not yield another inch if you can avoid it. I am doing all I can for you and your noble army."

Pope now occupied a strong and commanding position along the Centreville heights. He had been reenforced by the corps of Franklin, which arrived on the 30th, and Sumner on the 31st, and the divisions of Cox and Sturgis. These two latter amounted to seventeen thousand men, and the infantry of Sumner's and Franklin's corps to twenty-five thousand. The march of these troops and their junction with Pope had been reported to General Lee by the cavalry, under Fitz Lee, which, having left Manassas the day of Jackson's arrival there, had penetrated the country as far as Fairfax Court House. Near that point the cavalry commander captured a squadron of the Second Regular Cavalry, which was sent out reconnoitering by General Sumner, having surrounded it while halting to feed their horses. The officers were captured in the house just as they were going to dinner. The cavalry commander did not know whether they would be considered as belonging to McClellan's or Pope's army; and as orders had been received not to parole any of Pope's officers, he kept the Federal officers with him, having simply exacted from them their pledged word that they would not attempt to escape. These officers rode with his staff during the battle of the 30th, and one of them bore a dispatch for the Confederate commander, who had sent off all his staff officers on the ground that he had been kindly and courteously treated. After the battles were over they were duly paroled and permitted to ride their horses to the Federal lines near Washington. McClellan reports this capture in a dispatch to Halleck on December 31st, and adds that he had no confidence in the dispositions made by Pope; that there appeared to be a total absence of brains, and he feared the total destruction of the army; while Halleck, in a dispatch from Washington on August 29th, telegraphs McClellan, then in Alexandria, that he had been told on good authority that Fitzhugh Lee had been in that town the Sunday preceding for three hours.

The great strength of the Federal position with the large re-enforcements Pope had received decided General Lee to turn Centreville by moving to Pope's right and striking his rear in the vicinity of Fairfax Court House. Jackson was again employed for this purpose. He crossed Bull Run at Sudley, and marched to the Little River turnpike, pursuing that road in the direction of Fairfax Court House. As soon as this movement was perceived Pope abandoned Centreville. Hooker was immediately ordered to Fairfax Court House to take up a line on the Little River pike to prevent Lee's troops getting in his rear at the point where it joins the Warrenton pike, the movement to be supported by the rest of his army. As his troops reached the vicinity of Fairfax Court House, Jackson determined to attack them, and moved at once upon the force which had been posted on a ridge near Germantown for the purpose of driving them before him, so he could be in a position to command the pike from Centreville to Alexandria, down which Pope's troops must pass on their retreat. A sanguinary battle ensued just before sunset, terminated by darkness. The battle of Oxhill, as it was called, was fought in the midst of a thunderstorm. Longstreet's troops came on the field toward its conclusion. The loss on both sides was heavy, the Federals losing two of their best generals, Kearny and Stevens. The former was a dashing officer of undoubted courage and great merit. Had he lived he might have been an army commander. He rode into the Confederate lines, thinking they were occupied by a portion of his troops. It was nearly dark and raining. Seeing his mistake, he whirled his horse around, threw himself forward in the saddle, Indian fashion, and attempted to escape. A few men close to him fired, and he fell from his horse. General Lee had his body returned to the Federal lines the next day, accompanied with a courteous note to Pope.

On September 2d Pope's army, by Halleck's direction, was withdrawn to the intrenchments around Washington. While Pope was undoubtedly overmatched in generalship, an analysis of his tactics on the battlefield will show that they are of a higher order of merit than he is credited with, and many of his troops fought with stubbornness and courage. It is true he did not at times seem to appreciate his situation, and his orders were the subject of rapid and radical change. He telegraphed after the battle of the 30th: "We have fought a terrific battle here which lasted with continuous effort from daylight till dark, by which time the enemy was driven from the field, which we now occupy." Whereas the facts of the case were that the Confederate lines were advanced and were only retired after the fighting was over, during the night, to their former positions. The very next day, however, at Centreville, he wires Halleck that his troops were in position there, "though much used up and worn out," but that he could rely upon his giving his enemy as desperate a fight as he could force his men to stand up to, and adds that he should "like to know if you feel secure about Washington should this army be destroyed." He had still an army much greater than Lee's, but there was more or less demoralization in the ranks.

General Franklin, who arrived at Centreville on the 30th with his corps, threw out Slocum's division across the road between that point and Bull Run at Cub Run, to stop, as he says, "an indiscriminate mass of men, horses, guns, and wagons all going pell-mell to the rear. Officers of all grades, from brigadier general down, were in the throng." McClellan estimated the number of stragglers he saw two days later at twenty thousand; and Assistant-Adjutant-General Kelton, who had been sent out by Halleck, puts the number at thirty thousand. Much uneasiness prevailed in the Federal capital, disorder reigned, and confusion was everywhere. As a precautionary measure, it was said, the money in the Treasury and in the banks was shipped to New York, and a gunboat with steam up lay in the river off the White House, and yet there was in and around Washington one hundred and twenty thousand men. On the 1st of September McClellan was again assigned to the command of the defenses around Washington. He had been much mortified in listening to the distant sound of the firing of his men, and asked General Halleck on the night of the 30th of August for permission to go to the scene of battle, telling him his men would fight none the worse for his presence; and that if it was deemed best not to intrust him with the command of even his own army, he simply desired permission to share their fate on the field of battle. Kelton had reported that General Pope was entirely defeated and was falling back to Washington in confusion, and McClellan reports that Mr. Lincoln told him he regarded Washington as lost, and asked him to consent to accept command of all the forces, to which McClellan replied that he would stake his life to save the city, but that Halleck and the President said it would, in their judgment, be impossible to do that.

General McClellan having accepted command, on September 2d rode out in the direction of Upton's Hill to meet Pope's army and direct them to their respective positions in the line of the Washington defenses. He met Pope and McDowell riding toward Washington, escorted by cavalry, when the former asked if he had any objection to McDowell and himself going to Washington; to which McClellan replied: "No, but. I am going in the direction of the firing."

Lee's military plans had been wisely conceived, and the tactical details splendidly executed by his officers and men. Only three months had elapsed since he had been in command of the army, and in that brief period he had transferred a hostile army superior in numbers from the lines in front of his capital to the redoubts of the capital of his enemy. Richmond had been relieved; Washington was threatened. He could not hope with prospect of success to attack the combined armies of Pope and McClellan in their intrenchments on the Virginia side of the Potomac, for behind them they could fight two soldiers where he could bring only one in front of them. Apart from these difficulties a wide and unfordable river rolled between Virginia and Washington. His residence at Arlington had made him familiar with the topography of that section. He had but two alternatives: One, to withdraw his army and take up a line farther back in Virginia, rest and recruit his army, and patiently wait, as was done after the first battle of Manassas, till his antagonist should again assume the offensive. The other, to continue the active prosecution of the campaign and fight another battle while he had the prestige of victory and his enemy the discomfiture of defeat. He determined to adopt the latter method, and decided to cross the Potomac at the fords near Leesburg, some forty miles above Washington, and march into western Maryland.

Having received the approval of the Southern President to this plan, he immediately proceeded to put it into execution. First, because he believed if he could win a decisive victory the fall of Washington and Baltimore would follow, with far-reaching results. Second, because it would relieve Virginia and the Confederate quartermasters and commissary departments at Richmond of the support of his army for a time. Third, because it was hoped that large accessions to his decimated ranks would be obtained from those who sympathized with his cause in Maryland. Accordingly, the heads of his columns were turned toward the Potomac, and on September 5th successfully crossed that river and advanced to Frederick, where he established himself behind the Monocacy. He had been joined by the divisions of McLaws and D. H. Hill, which had been left at Richmond, but many of his men were obliged to be left on the Virginia side on account of their condition — long marches in bare feet had incapacitated them for further service. His army had been so constantly engaged in marching and fighting during the past few months that its condition was not favorable to further active work. The soldier was still there with his gun and his ammunition, but his clothes — from the hat on his head to his shoeless feet — were tattered and torn. The army was not presentable to the inhabitants of a State who had been accustomed to the sight of Federal troops well clothed and well fed. It was with difficulty they could understand that these troops had gained fame. The Southern feeling had been overawed and kept down in Maryland for so long a time by Federal occupation that recruits from that State did not care to join the Southern army till it was demonstrated that it could seize and hold their territory. They were not prepared to leave their homes and accompany the army back to Virginia.

Near Frederick, on September 8th, General Lee issued a proclamation to the people of Maryland in accordance with the suggestion of President Davis, who wrote him that it was usual on the occupation by an army of another's territory. General Lee told them that the people of the Confederate States had seen with profound indignation their sister State deprived of every right and reduced to the condition of a conquered province. That his army was there to enable them again to enjoy the inalienable rights of freemen, and restore independence and sovereignty to their State. That no constraint upon their free — will was intended, and no intimidation would be allowed. That it was for them to decide their destiny freely and without restraint, and that his army would respect their choice, whatever it might be; for, "while the Southern people will rejoice to welcome you to your natural position among them, they will only welcome you when you come of your own free-will."

Lee's crossing the Potomac and marching to Frederick relieved the Federal authorities from their immediate anxiety about the safety of their capital. As he had supposed, they determined to send an army after him, marching in such a way as not to uncover the capital, because it was feared that, after drawing their troops away from Washington, Lee might suddenly cross the Potomac and, with the rapidity of march for which he was noted, seize Washington, which attempt would be facilitated by its lines being weakened by troops taking the field. The time had arrived for the Federal army to advance, but no commander had been assigned to take the field with it. Halleck had intimated that McClellan would not be allowed to have it. The latter has stated that he was expressly told that no commander had been selected, but that he determined to solve the question for himself, so left his "cards at the White House and War Department with 'P. P. C.' written upon them, and then went to the field." That he "fought the battles of Antietam and South Mountain with a halter around his neck." If he had been defeated and had survived, he "would have been tried for assuming authority without orders, and probably been condemned to death." There is no doubt that at that time much dissatisfaction existed in the Federal councils with McClellan. His great personal popularity with his troops, the threatened safety of Washington, and the difficulty of finding a suitable successor, all combined to produce a negative acquiescence in his assuming command of the army for offensive operations. McClellan pushed slowly and cautiously his march in Lee's direction; for he said he knew Lee well, had served with him in Mexico, and had the "highest respect for his ability as a commander, and knew that he was a general not to be trifled with or carelessly tendered an opportunity of striking a fatal blow." General McClellan was deceived, too, as usual, in reference to his opponent's numbers, which he estimated to be one hundred and twenty thousand men — about three times the actual strength of Lee's army.

The determination of the boundary line between Maryland and Virginia has been attended with much expense and discussion. It never has been satisfactorily ascertained, because, as a talented son of Maryland put it, "there is no real division between them." The acquisition of Maryland would have added a bright star to the Southern constellation; but for many reasons there was no rushing to arms or many recruits added to Lee's army. The sons of Maryland in the Confederate army were splendid soldiers, enthusiastic in the cause, and brave in battle; and they knew, as the Southern commander did, that a battle fought and won in western Maryland, followed by a rapid march in the direction of Baltimore and Washington, would be attended with immense results, and that nothing would be accomplished, so far as Maryland was concerned, till then. Much curiosity existed in that State to see the victors of the first Manassas, the Seven Days Battles around Richmond, and the three days combats on the plains of the second Manassas. Inquisitive crowds hung around the commanding officers. Jackson was especially an object of much interest. The magic name of "Stonewall" had been heard at the hearthstones of the people, and they wanted to see him. He was described by one of them as wearing a coarse homespun, over which flapped an old soft hat that any Northern beggar would have considered an insult to have offered him. It was reported that he was continually praying, and that angelic spirits were his companions and counselors, and a desire was expressed to see him at his "incantations." His dress and deportment disappointed many who expected to see a great display of gold lace and feathers; and when he ordered his guards, said a writer, to clear his headquarters of idle crowds, many went away muttering, "Oh, he's no great shakes after all!"

Lee did not move on Washington after crossing the Potomac, because his numbers were too small to encounter the fortifications and large force assembled for their defense. His line of march was so directed as to draw a portion of the force at Washington after him and then defeat it. Frederick, in Maryland, was his first objective point, and then, it was said, Harrisburg, Pa. The Monocacy River, flowing from north to south, empties into the Potomac about twenty miles below Harper's Ferry. Behind the line of that river he determined to halt and be governed by the movements of his enemy. From that point he could open his communications with the Valley of Virginia by Shepherdstown and Martinsburg; resupply his ammunition; gather in detachments of his men left behind in Virginia, from bare feet and other causes, and fill up his supply trains. He knew his enemy occupied Harper's Ferry in large force, and Martinsburg in his rear, and that his proposed line of communication could not be opened so long as these places were garrisoned, and that sound military principles required that they should be evacuated when his army passed beyond them. So did McClellan, and urged it more than once. Halleck, the strategist of the Federal administration, differed from both Generals Lee and McClellan. Harper's Ferry was in his opinion the key to the upper door of the Federal capital, and should be held till the wings of the Peace Angel were spread over the republic. General Lee promptly planned to show that McClellan was right and Halleck wrong, though it involved a change of his original designs. His cavalry, under the vigilant Stuart, was at Urbana and Hyattstown, and well advanced on the road from Frederick to Washington, and every mile of McClellan's march was duly recorded and reported. The progress of this officer was so slow, his movements so cautious, that Lee determined to detach sufficient troops from his army to capture Harper's Ferry and Martinsburg, and bring them back in time to present a united front to McClellan. Daring, skill, celerity, and confidence were the qualifications of an officer to execute the movement. In Jackson they were all combined. He moved on September 10th from Frederick with three divisions; crossed the Potomac into Virginia; marched on Martinsburg, which was evacuated on his approach; and then to Harper's Ferry, which he reached on the 13th. McLaws, with his own and Anderson's division, was directed to seize the Maryland heights overlooking Harper's Ferry, while Brigadier-General Walker was instructed to cross the Potomac below Harper's Ferry and seize the Loudoun heights in Virginia. These movements were successfully accomplished, and on the 14th Harper's Ferry was closely invested. The heights were crowned with artillery ready to open at command on the doomed garrison. The little village of Harper's Ferry lies in an angle formed by the Shenandoah and Potomac where their united waters break through the Blue Ridge Mountains. It is a troop trap unless defended by the adjacent heights. Colonel Miles had strongly fortified the ridge in Virginia called Bolivar Heights, lying between the rivers; but Maryland heights, the key to the situation, was only feebly garrisoned. At dawn on the 15th, in response to Jackson's order, a line of fire leaped from the mountain-crowned heights and told Colonel Miles, the Federal commander, in no uncertain tones, that his surrender was demanded. For two hours this plunging fire was maintained, and at the moment A. P. Hill advanced to storm the town from the Virginia side a white flag was displayed. The firing ceased, and Hill entered the village to receive the surrender of its garrison. Jackson's work was well done. Twelve thousand men stacked their arms. Seventy-three pieces of artillery, thirteen thousand stand of small arms, large numbers of horses and wagons, and immense supplies were the results of his expedition. The cavalry, skillfully conducted by Colonel B. F. Davis, alone escaped on the Sharpsburg road.

When Jackson left Lee, five days before, McClellan was less than five marches from him. It was necessary that he should return as soon as possible, so leaving A. P. Hill to manage the details of surrender with his other two divisions, he marched day and night, recrossing the Potomac and reaching Sharpsburg on the 16th, followed by Walker. For the purpose of facilitating this reunion, Lee had retraced his steps from Frederick, directing the only two divisions Longstreet had left under Hood and Jones to move to Hagerstown, west of the mountains, while D. H. Hill with his division should halt at Boonsboroa, where were parked most of his wagons, and where he would be only three miles west of Turner's Pass on the Frederick road. Two days after Lee left Frederick, McClellan occupied it, and at eleven o'clock on the night of the 13th informed Halleck that an order of General Lee's, addressed to D. H. Hill, had accidentally fallen into his hands, the authenticity of which he thought was unquestionable. "It discloses," said he, "some of the plans of the enemy, and shows most conclusively that the main rebel army is now before us. It may therefore be regarded as certain that this rebel army, which I have good reason for believing amounts to one hundred and twenty thousand men or more, and known to be commanded by Lee in person, intended to penetrate Pennsylvania." Lee was fortunate in having the Federal commander overestimate his strength by eighty-five thousand; for confidence, a great attribute in war, is much more easily instilled into troops attacking an army of thirty-five thousand than one of one hundred and twenty thousand. But he was unfortunate in having a confidential order to one of his commanders find its way to the headquarters of the enemy. General D. H. Hill was under Jackson's command. When the latter received Special Orders No. 191 he had a copy of it made and sent to Hill before starting for Harper's Ferry, which Hill produced after the termination of the war, and his adjutant general made affidavit that no other order was received at his office from General Lee. As Hill was to remain with Lee and not march with Jackson, another copy of this order was addressed to him, but how transmitted from Lee's headquarters to Hill's camp, and who was guilty of gross carelessness in losing it, has never been ascertained. The Twelfth Federal Army Corps stacked arms when they arrived at Frederick on the 13th, on the ground that had been previously occupied by General D. H. Hill's division; and Private B. W. Mitchell, of Company F, Twenty-seventh Indiana Volunteers, Third Brigade, First Division, found it on the ground wrapped around three cigars. Little did he think how his discovery would affect a great campaign! The knowledge of its contents had a marvelous effect upon McClellan. Lee had been informed by his cavalry of McClellan's reaching Frederick. He did not know that his designs had been disclosed to him, and therefore did not understand the sudden life infused into the legs of the Federal soldiers; but learning at Hagerstown that McClellan was advancing more rapidly than he had anticipated, he determined to return with Longstreet's command to the Blue Ridge, to strengthen D. H. Hill's and Stuart's divisions, engaged in holding the passes of the mountains, lest the enemy should fall upon McLaws's rear, drive him from Maryland Heights, and thus relieve the garrison at Harper's Ferry. Stuart, who had occupied Turner's Gap with Hampton's brigade of cavalry this gallant officer having rejoined his army — moved to Crampton's Gap, five miles south of Turner's, to reenforce his cavalry under Munford there, thinking, as General Lee did, that should have been the object of McClellan's main attack, as it was on the direct route to Maryland Heights and Harper's Ferry. When D. H. Hill, at dawn on the 14th, re-enforced his two advance brigades in Turner's Gap, Stuart had gone, leaving one regiment of cavalry and some artillery under Rosser to guard Fox's Gap, a small one to the south of Turner's. As Hill reached the top of the mountain on that September morning a magnificent spectacle was presented. Far as the eye could reach flashed the bayonets of the advancing columns of McClellan's army. It was a sight not often vouchsafed to any one, and was both grand and sublime. Hill must have felt helpless with his five small brigades numbering less than five thousand men, and must have been impressed vividly with "how terrible was an army with banners!" It was his duty to retard the march of this immense host, to give Lee time to get his trains at Boonsboroa out of the way, to bring Longstreet from Hagerstown to his support, and to give Jackson time for his work at Harper's Ferry. The resistance of Hill's troops — from nine in the morning till half-past 3 in the afternoon — to the attack of Reno's corps reflected great credit upon the capacity of the commander and the courage of his men. The combat later in the afternoon between

Longstreet and Hill on the one side, and Burnside with the two corps of Reno and Hooker on the other, was marked by great gallantry on the part of both. Of the nine brigades Longstreet had with him, whose strength he estimated at thirteen thousand men (three of his brigades were with Jackson), Hill says only four were seriously engaged. So the struggle on the part of the Confederates was made with nine thousand men, one third less in numbers than their antagonists. The Southern lines were generally held, but when night put an end to the contest the advantage of the position was with the Federals.

In a consultation that night between Generals Lee, Longstreet, and Hill, it was decided to withdraw the troops from that point, and form a line of battle at Sharpsburg, where he would be in a position to unite with Jackson, when he should recross the Potomac at Shepherdstown. Fitz Lee, who had been with his cavalry brigade in the rear of the Federal army at Frederick, arrived at Boonsboroa during the night, and was directed by General Lee to remain there and retard as much as possible the Federal advance the next day. On the morning of the 15th, when the Federal army debouched from the mountains, the cavalry brigade was alone between the Federals and Lee at Sharpsburg to dispute with their advance every foot of ground between the base of the mountains and Boonsboroa. This was done with artillery, dismounted cavalry, and charges of mounted squadrons. The object having been accomplished, the brigade was slowly withdrawn and placed on the left of the line of battle at Sharpsburg.

While McClellan was attempting the passage of Turner's Gap with his main army, Franklin with the Sixth Corps, supported by Couch's division, was struggling to get through Crampton's Gap, where McLaws had left a brigade and regiment of his division, and a brigade of Anderson's, to prevent the enemy from passing through the mountains at that point, and threatening his rear at Maryland Heights. The work of these brigades and a portion of Stuart's cavalry was well performed; and when the fighting, which had been going on from twelve o'clock, ceased at night, Franklin had made such progress that they were withdrawn also. On the morning of the 15th, as McClellan was passing through the mountains near Boonsboroa, Franklin was marching through Crampton Pass at about the same time, and occupying Pleasant Valley. Both were too late to relieve Miles at Harper's Ferry, who surrendered about half-past 7 that morning. Franklin declined to attack McLaws after reaching Pleasant Valley, remained there (the 16th) without receiving any orders, and on the morning of the 17th marched for the battlefield at Sharpsburg, arriving at ten o'clock.

McClellan did not anticipate Lee would offer battle on that side of the Potomac. When the head of his columns arrived west of the mountains he informed Halleck that his enemy was making for Shepherdstown in a perfect panic, and that General Lee had stated publicly the night before that he must admit he had been shockingly whipped, and that Lee was reported wounded. Mr. Lincoln was well pleased with this statement, and replied to McClellan: "God bless you and all with you. Destroy the rebel army if possible." A little later, when the Federal commander discovered Lee's army in line of battle waiting an attack, he declined to make it, stating that his troops had arrived in Lee's front in sufficient force too late in the day to attack. He remained quiet all the next day, because he said the fog had prevented him from developing the situation of the enemy. Both sides had lost heavily in the mountain passes, and the deaths of such capable officers as Reno on the Federal and Garland on the Confederate side were greatly deplored by their respective armies.

CHAPTER 10

SHARPSBURG AND FREDERICKSBURG.

The small town of Sharpsburg, lying amid surrounding hills, formed an attractive center to the beautiful landscape stretching away on every side. Here, in the embrace of the Potomac on the west and the Antietam Creek on the east, with rolling fields well cultivated and fenced, and fringed here and there with picturesque patches of woodland, it presented an inviting field for battle; but the rich fields were destined to be plowed by cannon balls and fertilized with blood; while against such desecration the peaks above the passes in the mountains loomed up in the distance, as if pointing to heaven in solemn protest.

The position was well selected by Lee to deliver a defensive battle; and while a big, though fordable, river a few miles in the rear was objectionable, its concave curve allowed each of his flanks to rest on the river, though the center of his line of battle was some three miles to the front. There could be no overlapping his flanks by the superior numbers of his opponent, who had to meet a line of battle at whatever point he might select for the attack. It is true the scattered Southern troops could have been more easily concentrated in Virginia and, if necessary, a battle avoided; but Lee had entered Maryland with the intention of fighting, and did not care to change his plans until he had appealed to the God of War.

The troops under Longstreet and D. H. Hill were leisurely marched the four or five miles from Boonsboroa to Sharpsburg. After crossing the Antietam Creek on the morning of September 15th, Lee formed his line of battle along the hills — Longstreet on the right and D. H. Hill on the left of the road facing the creek, which runs north and south. General Lee reported that the advance of the enemy was delayed by the brave opposition encountered from his cavalry, and did not appear on the opposite side of the Antietam until about 2 P. M., when the battalions began filing to the right and left of the road, taking up their position in his front and exchanging artillery salutations. The sluggish creek flowing between the two armies was spanned by four bridges at the various road crossings converging at Sharpsburg, and was fordable at other points.

McClellan, always deliberate, consumed the whole of the 16th in making his arrangements for approaching battle, much to General Lee's relief. At 4 P. M. in the afternoon Hooker from the Northern right crossed the Antietam with instructions to take position in front of the Southern left, and during the night Mansfield's Twelfth Corps also crossed. In anticipation of such a movement Lee had ordered Longstreet to send Hood with two brigades to prolong D. H. Hill's left, so that when Hooker, with three divisions under Meade, Ricketts, and Doubleday (an officer that Jackson in one of the few jokes of his life called "Forty-eight hours"), proceeded to execute his orders, he found General Hood across his path with a command equal in efficiency and courage to the best troops of either army, and each claimed the advantage in the engagement which followed.

Jackson reached Sharpsburg that morning from Harper's Ferry, and Walker later. At night Hood was relieved by Lawton's and Trimble's brigades of Ewell's division. Jackson's division, under General J. R. Jones, was placed on Lawton's left, supported by the remaining brigades of Ewell, while General Walker with his two brigades was placed on Longstreet's right. The cavalry were located on either flank.

These are all the troops McClellan would have encountered if he had attacked on the 16th. Anderson's six brigades, McLaws's four, and A. P. Hill's five — making fifteen brigades — did not reach Lee until the 17th. After they had arrived the total infantry amounted to 27,255 men, which, with eight thousand cavalry and artillery, would make Lee's army at Sharpsburg 35,255. McClellan reports he had in action, on the 17th, 87,164 troops of all arms. He had therefore present fifty-two thousand more men than Lee. When the inequality in numbers and the difference in quality of cannon, small arms and ammunition, food and raiment is considered, Sharpsburg, as it is called at the South, Antietam at the North, is a superb monument to the valor of the Confederate soldier and the tactical genius of a great commander.

The picture of the private soldier of Lee's army at Sharpsburg, as he stood in the iron hail with the old torn slouch hat, the bright eye glistening with excitement, powder-stained face, rent jacket and torn trousers, blanket in shreds, and the prints of his shoeless feet in the dust of the battle, should be framed in the hearts of all who love true courage wherever found. He was a veritable tatterdemalion, loading and firing his rifle with no hope of reward, no promise of promotion, no pay, and scanty rations. If he stopped one of the enemy's bullets he would be buried where the battle raged, in an unknown grave, and be forgotten, except by comrades, and possibly a poor old mother who was praying in her Southern home for the safe return of her soldier boy.

Six corps of Federal troops, under Hooker, Sumner, Burnside, Franklin, Mansfield, and Fitz John Porter, stood in battle array, while Pleasonton had forty-three hundred and twenty cavalry. McClellan's plan of battle was to envelop the Confederate flanks — first the left, and then the right — and could he have succeeded in breaking through either of them and gaining the Williamsport road in Lee's rear and cutting him off from the Potomac, his victory would have been decisive. Had General Lee not divined the main struggle would be on his left, McClellan informed him when he ordered Hooker over the Antietam the evening before?

The fighting at Sharpsburg on the Federal side was done by four corps, numbering fifty-seven thousand six hundred and fourteen men, with a loss of twenty per cent of their numbers. Porter's and Franklin's corps and the cavalry, numbering twenty-nine thousand five hundred and fifty troops, were not engaged. As all of General Lee's army fought except a portion of his cavalry, the actual difference between the active combatants was some twenty-six thousand.

On that memorable autumn morning, about the center of his long, slim, gray battle line, Lee stood on a large rock to the right of the Boonsboroa road, east of the town, calm, dignified, and confident, as his glance swept the country in front. "His fine form was sharply outlined against the sky," says a Confederate general, "and I thought I had never seen a nobler figure. He seemed quite unconscious that the enemy's shells were exploding around and beyond him."

Most of the time he was on foot, having both arms and hands injured before leaving Virginia from being thrown violently to the ground, his horse making a sudden jump when he was standing by his side with the bridle reins over his arm. Some of the bones in one hand were broken, and the other arm injured. He was obliged to ride in an ambulance or let a courier lead his horse. In the tumult of battle he could ride but little along his lines on his famous war horse Traveler. So McClellan on that day had the advantage of him as he galloped about on his black charger Daniel Webster.

Jackson, too, had been stunned by the rearing and falling back of a large gray mare which had been presented to him a few days before by an enthusiastic admirer, and was obliged to ride in an ambulance, but fortunately recovered in time for the battle. His horse at Sharpsburg seemed to be gentle enough, for during a lull in the firing Jackson was found under an apple tree, with one leg over the pommel of the saddle, eating apples. The fate of a battle with Generals Lee and Jackson both in ambulances would have been uncertain.

At dawn on the 17th the Federal artillery opened on Hood's front, being directed against the Confederate left, to mask and assist the advancing columns of attack on Jackson. "For several hours the conflict raged," says General Lee, "with great fury and alternate success." The troops advanced with great spirit and the enemy's lines were repeatedly broken and forced to retire. Fresh troops, however, replaced those that were beaten, and Jackson's men were in turn compelled to fall back. General J. R. Jones was obliged to leave the field, and "the brave General Starke" (as General Lee called him), who succeeded him, was killed. General Lawton was wounded, and was succeeded by Early, who had been supporting the cavalry and horse artillery in defending a most important hill, which if occupied by the enemy would have commanded and enfiladed Jackson's position, and who "got in" with his brigade, as he usually did, at the proper moment. Hood and Early, re-enforced by the brigades of Ripley, Colquitt, and Garland, under Colonel McRae, of Hill's division, and D. R. Jones, under Colonel G. T. Anderson, now took up the fighting; the Federals were again driven back, and again brought up fresh troops. General McLaws arrived just in time to meet them; General Walker brought from the right, together with Early's division, drove the Federals back in confusion, beyond the position occupied at the beginning of the engagement.

The long lines of blue which first recoiled from the walls of gray on the Southern left were Hooker's corps, fourteen thousand eight hundred and fifty-six men, which was to have formed, with the Ninth Corps, the left of McClellan's battle line, both to be commanded by Burnside. But Hooker was ambitious and enterprising and secured permission to lead the assault on Lee's left against Jackson, around the well-known Dunker Church, a mile to the north of Sharpsburg on the Hagerstown road, and over the historic cornfields and the "east and west woods," where raged all the morning, with varying fortunes, the bloody combat.

As early as 7 A. M. Hooker had given up the task assigned him, and Mansfield's corps, ten thousand one hundred and twenty-six in numbers, with flags flying, advanced to his support; but in the midst of deploying his columns this veteran general was killed, and in two hours "the corps seems to have about lost all aggressive force," said a Federal historian. Sumner's corps marched next into the battle — Sedgwick's division in advance. The Federal troops previously fighting had melted away, and the march of Sedgwick in close column of three brigades in the direction of the Dunker Church was unsupported, and it appeared as if he had been assigned to fight the remainder of the battle alone. The First Corps had been disposed of and Hooker wounded and carried to the rear, the Twelfth broken into fragments and Mansfield killed. Sedgwick was annihilated by the Confederate fire in front and on both flanks. The ground was strewn with the bodies of the dead and wounded, while the unwounded men moved rapidly away. "Nearly two thousand men were disabled in a moment."

The other divisions of the Second Corps under Richardson — who was mortally wounded — and French were ordered up to support Sedgwick, but too late, for R. H. Anderson's division, just from Harper's Ferry, had re-enforced D. H. Hill in his position on the famous Sunken road, which enabled the Confederates to vigorously assume the offensive, and the assaults of the remainder of Sumner's corps were repulsed.

The terrible carnage had progressed six hours. Franklin, with his Sixth Corps from Pleasant Valley, arrived about 10 A. M. — having sent Couch's division of the Fourth Corps to guard Maryland Heights. His leading division under Smith, whose advance brigade was commanded by Hancock, went to the support of Sumner; a forward movement of this division and that of Slocum, which had arrived about noon, was stopped by McClellan, who feared a counter attack on his vanquished right. The attack on the Confederate left being foiled, McClellan next threw a heavy force on the Southern center, which was repulsed by a part of Walker's division and the brigade of General G. B. Anderson, and Rodes of D. H. Hill's, assisted by a few pieces of artillery. R. H. Anderson came to the support of this line too, and formed in rear. The Fifth Alabama, on Rodes's right, was being enfiladed by battery fire, and Rodes gave directions to retire it, when the whole brigade, through a misapprehension of orders, moved back, making a gap which was immediately occupied by the Federals. G. B. Anderson's brigade was broken, its commander being mortally wounded, and Major-General R. H. Anderson and Brigadier-General Wright were also borne from the field wounded. General Lee says that "heavy masses of the enemy again moved forward, being opposed by only four pieces of artillery, supported by a few hundreds of men rallied by General D. H. Hill, being parts of Walker's and R. H. Anderson's commands. Colonel John R. Cook, with the Twenty-seventh North Carolina, stood boldly in line without a cartridge. The firm front presented by this small force, and the well-directed fire of the artillery under Captain Miller of the Washington Artillery, and Captain Boyce's South Carolina Battery, checked the progress of the enemy, and in about an hour and a half he retired." Longstreet states that the only troops there were Cook's regiment, and that as he rode along he saw two pieces of Washington Artillery, but that there were not enough men to man them, and that he put his staff officers to work the guns, while he held their horses.

During the battle McClellan held Fitz John Porter's corps, twelve thousand nine hundred and thirty men, with his cavalry, in reserve in the rear of his center. The "Little Napoleon," as he was then sometimes called, was reserving it to be used as the Great Napoleon employed the "Old guard," to win a battle at the opportune moment, or save an army from destruction should defeat ensue. Had they supported Burnside even as late as his attack was made, McClellan might still have gained a great victory.

"In the afternoon," General Lee says, "the enemy began to extend his line as if to cross the Antietam below, and at 4 P. M. Toombs retired from the position he had so bravely held. The enemy immediately crossed the bridge in large numbers, and advanced against General D. R. Jones, who held the crest with less than two thousand men. After a determined and brave resistance he was forced to give way and the enemy gained the summit. General A. P. Hill had now arrived from Harper's Ferry, having left that place at 7 A. M., and immediately attacked, while his batteries and those of D. R. Jones and D. H. Hill opened an enfilade fire north of the Boonsboroa road, and the Federal progress was arrested, seeing which, General Jones ordered Toombs to charge the flank, while Archer, supported by Branch and Gregg, moved upon the front of the Federal line. The enemy made a brave resistance, and then broke and retired in confusion toward the Antietam, pursued by the troops of Hill and Jones until he reached the protection of the batteries on the opposite side. In this attack the brave and lamented General L. O. B. Branch was killed, gallantly leading his brigade."

While this attack was going on, Lee ordered Jackson to turn the enemy's right, but found it extended nearly to the Potomac, and was so strongly defended with artillery that the attempt had to be abandoned. J. E. B. Stuart had been selected to command the advance in this movement. The Union attack on the Confederate right was made by Burnside's Ninth Corps of four divisions. It was on the eastern side or left bank of the Antietam Creek in front of a bridge, and he was ordered early in the morning to hold his men in readiness to assault.

At eight o'clock McClellan says he sent Burnside orders to cross the creek and take the heights beyond, and move so as to gain possession of them and cut Lee off from the Williamsport or Shepherdstown road, and Burnside immediately prepared to execute them. Toombs had only some four hundred Georgians at this bridge, but his defense of the passage was well executed. Burnside's thirteen thousand troops took three hours to cross, and lost five hundred men. It was now one o'clock, and two hours more were consumed in preparations to assault the ridge held by Jones. The opportune arrival of A. P. Hill, with his thirty-four hundred men, saved Lee's right. Had McClellan placed a portion of his large cavalry force on that flank, Hill's approach might have been retarded and the battle won before his arrival. It is difficult to explain, too, why Couch was not recalled from the vicinity of Maryland Heights after Harper's Ferry was abandoned by Hill.

The bloody battle of Sharpsburg, or Antietam, has passed into impartial history as a drawn combat. The next day neither side would renew the fighting — Lee says because he was too weak to renew the offensive; but that he awaited without apprehension the renewal of the attack. He had received reports that McClellan was expecting the arrival of re-enforcements, and as he could not look for a material increase of his strength, it was not thought prudent to wait until his adversary should be ready to again fight a battle. During the night of the 18th his army was passed to the south of the Potomac, near Shepherdstown. The enemy advanced next morning, but was held in check by cavalry, who covered his movements with success.

The Southern loss in the Maryland campaign was ten thousand two hundred and ninety-one — eight thousand at Sharpsburg. McClellan's loss in the battle was twelve thousand four hundred and ninety-six. He did not claim a victory until Lee had recrossed the Potomac. At 1.20 P. M., during the battle, he telegraphed Halleck: "We are in the midst of the most terrible battle of the war — perhaps of history. Thus far it looks well, but I have great odds against me." And at 8 A. M. on the 18th he telegraphed: "The battle of yesterday continued for fourteen hours, and until after dark. We hold all we gained, except a portion of the extreme left. Our loss was very heavy, especially in general officers. The battle will probably be renewed to-day." But it was only on the 19th — thirty-six hours after the fighting was over — that he informed Halleck that "we may safely claim a complete victory."

General Lee's Maryland campaign was a failure. He added but few recruits to his army, lost ten thousand men, and fought a drawn battle, which for an invading army is not a success. It was preferable, in his opinion, to consuming the substance of the Confederacy in Virginia after the second Manassas, and the result of a victory in Maryland was worth the attempt. McClellan threw two divisions of infantry across the river, but was driven back, the Confederates losing four guns — a part of their reserve artillery.

The Confederate army then moved back to the Opequan, near Martinsburg, and after a few days' rest to the vicinity of Bunker Hill and Winchester. McClellan occupied Harper's Ferry and the surrounding heights with two corps under Sumner, and encamped the remainder near the scenes of its late exploits, amid the picturesque hills and vales of southwestern Maryland. Rest with regular rations at regular times was most grateful to both armies, for both were more or less exhausted. General Lee's two weeks campaign in Maryland had demonstrated that his army, without re-enforcements, was too small for offensive operations.

His son Robert was at that time a private in the Rockbridge Battery, and was in the thickest of the fight. Just after the battle the general wrote to Mrs. Lee: "I have not laid eyes on Rob since I saw him in the battle of Sharpsburg going in with a single gun of his battery for the second time after his company had been withdrawn in consequence of three of its guns having been disabled. Custis has seen him, and says he is very well and apparently happy and content. My hands are improving slowly, and with my left hand I am able to dress and undress myself, which is a great comfort. My right is becoming of some assistance, too, though it is still swollen, and sometimes painful. The bandages have been removed. I am now able to sign my name. It has been six weeks to-day since I was injured, and I have at last discarded the sling."

In his tent near Winchester he heard of the death of his daughter Annie, who had always been the greatest favorite with her father, and on October 26, 1862, in a letter to Mrs. Lee, he said: "I cannot express the anguish I feel at the death of our sweet Annie. To know that I shall never see her again on earth, that her place in our circle, which I always hoped one day to enjoy, is forever vacant, is agonizing in the extreme. But God in this, as in all things, has mingled mercy with the blow in selecting that one best prepared to leave us. May you be able to join me in saying, 'His will be done!' When I reflect on all she will escape in life, brief and painful at the best, and all we may hope she will enjoy with her sainted grandmother, I cannot wish her back. I know how much you will grieve, and how much she will be mourned. I wish I could give you any comfort, but beyond our hope in the great mercy of God, and the belief that he takes her at the time and place when it is best for her to go, there is none. May that same mercy be extended to us all, and may we be prepared for his summons."

It was now McClellan's turn to assume the offensive. To cross the Potomac, having that river at his back, and to fight Lee, was too hazardous for a man of his prudence; but by crossing below Harper's Ferry and marching into Virginia he could keep interposed between his capital and the Confederate army, and at the same time move on interior lines toward Lee's capital, which would bring Lee from the Valley of Virginia to offer battle at a point where, if he could be defeated, Richmond might fall. Both armies had increased in numbers. Three days after the battle Lee had 40,000 men, and McClellan notwithstanding his loss in the two battles, had 80,930, exclusive of the two divisions of Couch and Humphreys, which reached him the day after the battle. The morning report, dated September 20th, sent by McClellan which included the troops at Washington under Banks and 3,500 men at Williamsport, Frederick, and Boonsboroa — showed an aggregate present for duty of 164,359, and an aggregate absent of 105,124, making a total present and absent of 293,798.

"General McClellan was never in a hurry, but wanted to reach the ideal of preparation before action." He was deliberate, his Government impatient. The chasm between the two was widening. The blood on the field of Sharpsburg was not dry before the Federal army commander was expressing his regret that every dispatch from his general in chief, Halleck, was fault-finding; he asked him to say something in commendation of his army; that it had been lately "badly cut up and scattered by the overwhelming numbers brought against them in the battle of the 17th, and it was only by very hard fighting that we gained the advantage we did. As it was, the result was at one period very doubtful, and we had all we could do to win the day." On the other side Halleck was, with Mr. Lincoln's assistance, putting hot coals on his back. "The country is becoming very impatient at the want of activity in your army, and we must push it on," the former writes, October 7, 1862. And again: "There is a decided want of celerity in our troops. They lie still in camp too long."

Three days after the withdrawal of the Southern army from Maryland the President of the United States issued his proclamation proclaiming freedom to the slaves. It was admitted to be a war measure, whose purpose, if necessary, was to kindle insurrectionary fires in the Southern States, which should assist the Federal arms in crushing the "Rebellion," as it was termed; but to McClellan and a large part of his army it was objectionable. In his General Order No. 163, of October 7th, in reference to it, he deprecated in the army heated political discussions, and reminded them that the remedy for political errors is at the polls, thus widening the growing gulf between him and his administration, which President Lincoln's visit to him on October 1st, and charging him with being overcautious, did not diminish.

As soon as Lincoln returned to Washington he directed Halleck to order McClellan to "cross the Potomac and give battle to the enemy and drive him South." But many suns were destined to rise and set before that order was executed. General Lee, as well as the Union President, was growing impatient, and wondering why McClellan did not promptly obey orders. So he directed his chief of cavalry, Stuart, on October 8th, to cross the Potomac above Williamsport with his cavalry and ascertain McClellan's positions and designs; to enter Pennsylvania, and to do all in his power to impede and embarrass the military operations of his enemy.

Stuart left the army next morning with detachments of six hundred men from each of the brigades of Hampton, Fitz Lee, and W. E. Jones, and four guns. He was considerate in his orders to his own troops, directing them to give receipts for everything that they were obliged to take in the way of subsistence for man and horse, and also that whenever his column met ladies in Maryland and Pennsylvania, it should turn out of the road to let them pass with their conveyances without molestation. He marched to Chambersburg, in Pennsylvania, passing the right flank of the Federal army, and made a complete circuit, returning by the left flank. He rode eighty miles in twenty-seven hours, and by his swiftness and boldness deceived and evaded every effort to intercept him. "His orders were executed," says General Lee, "with skill, address, and courage." He had destroyed a large amount of public property, reported McClellan's exact position to General Lee, and recrossed the Potomac without loss. "Not a man should be permitted to return to Virginia," telegraphed Halleck to McClellan in informing him that Stuart was at Chambersburg, Pa., and was answered that, in spite of all precautions, Stuart "went entirely around this army"; and calls attention to his deficiency in cavalry, and complained that "the horses of the army were fatigued and had sore tongues," which called forth an inquiry from Mr. Lincoln: "Will you pardon me for asking what the horses of your army have done since Antietam that fatigues anything?" And that "Stuart's cavalry had outmarched ours, having certainly done more marked service in the Peninsula and everywhere since." And yet McClellan had received seventeen thousand nine hundred and eighteen fresh horses since the Sharpsburg battle.

At last on October 26th, three weeks after he had received orders, he began crossing his army over the Potomac into Loudoun County, Va., at Berlin, below Harper's Ferry. This occupied nine days. A slow concentration of his army in the direction of Warrenton followed. Lee met this movement, and later, on November 3d, marched Longstreet's corps to Culpeper Court House to McClellan's front, and brought the corps of Jackson to the east side of the mountain. He had crossed swords, however, for the last time with his courteous adversary. The axe had fallen, and with it McClellan's official head into the basket already containing Pope's. General Order No. 182 from the War Department, dated November 5, 1862, announced, by direction of President Lincoln, that General McClellan be relieved from the command of the Army of the Potomac, and that Major-General Burnside take command of that army.

"Late at night," says McClellan, "I was sitting alone in my tent writing to my wife. All seemed to be asleep. Suddenly someone knocked upon the tent pole, and upon my invitation to enter, there appeared Generals Burnside and Buckingham, both looking very solemn. After a few moments Buckingham said to Burnside: 'Well, General, I think we had better tell General McClellan the object of our visit'; whereupon Buckingham handed me the order of which he was the bearer. I read the papers with a smile, and immediately turned to Burnside and said: 'Well, Burnside, I turn the command over to you.'" When General Lee heard of it he said he was sorry to part with McClellan; not that he anticipated his army would be defeated by a change of commanders, but it was a satisfaction to know that as long as McClellan was in command everything would be conducted by the rules of civilized warfare. The soldiers parted with McClellan with great grief, and tears stood in many an eye that had learned to look on war without a tremor.

Many circumstances directed Mr. Lincoln's course. The entente cordiale between his Secretary of War, Commander in Chief, and McClellan had been broken. The little value the latter placed upon time as an important element in military operations had been exasperating to them. It had been charged, too, that his different political faith from the party in power, his popularity with his troops, and the probability of his becoming the presidential candidate of his party in opposition to Mr. Lincoln, united to effect his removal. It is not thought that this last condition weighed with the Federal President, or tipped the scales, but rather McClellan's procrastination and his overcautiousness, added to an absurd overestimation of his opponent's strength, and the impatience of the Northern people for more battles. McClellan was always and everywhere a gentleman, who believed in conducting war in a Christian and humane manner. He had strategic, but no tactical ability. Risks have to be taken when battle is joined, but he never took them. Broken, wavering lines were not restored beneath the wave of his sword, and his personal presence was rarely felt when it might have been beneficial. He had none of the inspiration of war. Lee had a great respect for him as a soldier, though he counted on his being slow when manoeuvring in his front. The Federal general could organize with great ability and inspire confidence in his troops, and would have been a great commander had he been more rapid in his movements and adventurous in his plans.

His unwilling successor, Ambrose E. Burnside, was the soul of good-fellowship, an amiable officer, and a kind-hearted gentleman. He possessed these qualities as a cadet. The celebrated Benny Havens, who kept a saloon in the old days outside of West Point limits, had a special toast which he invariably repeated every time he indulged in a stimulant — and the repetition of the toast was very frequent during the day. He drank to the health of the two greatest men, in his opinion, who had ever lived — St. Paul and Andrew Jackson; but he took such a fancy to Burnside, when he was a cadet, that he added his name to his toast, and ever thereafter, to the day of his death, he drank to St. Paul, Andrew Jackson, and A. E. Burnside.

This officer conceived the idea of concentrating his army on the Rappahannock River opposite Fredericksburg. The position there would be about sixty miles from Richmond, and by a short railroad to his rear he could reach the Potomac near Acquia Creek, and then, by water some fifty miles, his Washington base. He divided his six corps into three grand divisions — the right, composed of the Second and Ninth, under Sumner; the Third and Fifth Corps, the center, under Hooker; and the left, under Franklin, consisting of the First and Sixth. Sumner, in advance, arrived opposite Fredericksburg on November 17th. Franklin was in supporting distance on the 18th, and Hooker on the 19th, but their pontoons did not arrive for eight days afterward. The vigilance of Stuart informed Lee of this movement on the 15th, and he ordered at once two divisions of infantry and a brigade of cavalry and a battery to proceed to Fredericksburg. A forced reconnaissance of Stuart to Warrenton told him that the whole of Burnside's army had gone to the Rappahannock opposite Fredericksburg. On the 19th Longstreet was ordered to Fredericksburg with the remainder of his corps, and Jackson, who had been moved to Orange Court House, was, about the 26th, ordered to Fredericksburg also. There was much deliberation in Lee's movements. His army was stretched out from the mountains to the river, and it was only after he was satisfied that the Federal army had gone to the Rappahannock that he moved Longstreet, and not for nine days afterward did he direct Jackson to unite with him. He knew a large army changing its line of communication with its base of supplies required time to assume the offensive.

When Sumner arrived at Falmouth, a little village on the left bank of the river a mile above Fredericksburg, with his thirty-three thousand men, across the river was only a regiment of cavalry, a battery, and four companies of infantry. Four days afterward Longstreet arrived, and his attempt to cross then would have been resisted. The surrender of the town had been demanded by Sumner just before the arrival of Longstreet. If not granted, the women, children, aged and infirm, could have sixteen hours to leave their homes, and then "I shall proceed," said Sumner, "to shell the town."

Fredericksburg, a typical Virginia town, is built on a plain every foot of which is commanded by the heights opposite in Stafford County. A plunging fire would destroy it, and Sumner's threat was a serious one to the inhabitants. The man of the house was in the Southern army, and it was a heart-rending experience for the women and children to have their homes and their household goods battered to pieces with cannon. Before the expiration of the time arranged, Longstreet arrived and told the authorities he would not occupy the town for military purposes, and that there was no reason why it should be shelled, and this being communicated to Sumner, he decided not to execute his threat.

It was not wholly Burnside's fault that he was sluggish in his preparations. The railroad to the Potomac had to be prepared, his pontoons were late getting up, and many unexpected matters had to be considered. The twenty-four days which elapsed before he delivered battle were greatly appreciated by Lee. It gave him time to concentrate his army and deploy and strengthen his line of battle on a most defensible position. He would have preferred fighting the battle at North Anna, a defensive point in his rear, because it would draw Burnside farther from his base, and if in the fortunes of battle he could assume the offensive, decisive results would follow, and so thought Jackson; but an unwillingness to give up more of the country, and a desire to draw supplies from the Rappahannock Valley, decided him to fight at Fredericksburg.

Picture a river about two hundred yards wide running east the short distance you see it, and then southeast, the little village of Falmouth, in Stafford County, being on its left, and the town of Fredericksburg, in Spottsylvania, a mile below on its right bank. Imagine a high line of hills from Falmouth down the river whose western slopes touch the water. These are Stafford Heights. On the Fredericksburg side a level plateau stretches out to a range of hills which, beginning at a point above the town, runs parallel to the river for a mile or two, then extends back in a curve for four miles, until at its southern extremity at Hamilton's Crossing they gradually sink to the level of the surrounding country. Along Stafford Heights was posted the army of Burnside — 104,903 infantry, 5,884 cavalry; and 5,896 artillery, making, by the report of December 10th, 116,683 men present for duty equipped. On the Spottsylvania hills, a cannon-shot away, lay Lee's legions 78,513 of all arms, which included the cavalry brigades of Hampton and W. E. Jones, both of whom were absent.

A river and a plain lay between the hostile forces, and the Northern troops had to cross both to reach the Southern position. The Federal batteries commanded the town of Fredericksburg and the contiguous plain, while the Confederate batteries everywhere swept the open plain nearest to the Southern lines. Burnside's army had to cross this open plain in full view of Lee, and he knew that it would be plowed by shot and shell, and any assault would have to be made amid the iron hail of small arms. Lee's position was strong by nature and made stronger by art. No troops could successfully assail it, and no commanding general should have ordered it to be done. Burnside's order for battle was fathomless; he could not carry Lee's position by surprise, as he told Franklin he expected to, or hope for success least of all by the tactics adopted and made known to his right and left grand division commanders on the morning of battle. Three weeks after Burnside arrived on the Rappahannock, public pressure pushed him across it. He did not cross some miles below Fredericksburg, as first contemplated, because he said Lee had divined his intention and prepared for it, but would cross directly in his front, because General Lee was not expecting it, and attack him before re-enforced by the troops detached to prevent his crossing at the lower point.

The night of December 10, 1862, was a long one for Burnside. One hundred and forty-seven rifled cannon, 20-pound Parrotts, and 4-inch siege guns were distributed along Stafford Heights by Hunt, Burnside's able chief of artillery. The pontoons were placed in position, and at three o'clock on the morning of the 11th the task of constructing four or five bridges opposite the town and two miles below began.

Scarcely had the work commenced before Lee's signal gun announced the news to his sleeping troops. He had never contemplated making a serious resistance at the river banks. To use his own words: "The plain of Fredericksburg is so completely commanded by the Stafford Heights that no effectual opposition could be made to the construction of bridges or the passage of the river. Our position was therefore selected with a view to resisting the enemy's advance after crossing, and the river was guarded only by a force sufficient to impede his movements until the army could be concentrated."

The Thirteenth, Seventeenth, Eighteenth, and Twenty-first Mississippi, of Barksdale's brigade of McLaws's division, and the Third Georgia and Eighth Florida of Anderson's division, guarded the points where pontoons were to be laid, and displayed such skill as marksmen and such courage as men, sheltered behind the houses at the river banks, that the Federal army was delayed at the river bank for sixteen hours, giving the Confederate commander ample time to prepare for battle. During the night of the 11th and succeeding day Sumner's two corps, with one hundred and four cannon, crossed at the upper, and Franklin's two corps, with one hundred and sixteen guns, crossed at the lower bridge, and by the night of the 12th Burnside's army was in readiness for the attack. His plans for the next day were ambiguous. A Federal general reports him as riding about on the evening of the 12th as if he had arrived at the conclusion to attempt to do something with his left, and, if successful, to do something with his right. The tremendous responsibility of having one hundred thousand men on the wrong side of the Rappahannock was having its full effect. He seemed to expect Franklin to get in somewhere on Lee's right and Sumner on his left, and these lodgments being made, the Confederate line between would have to retire or be crushed. He increased Sumner's troops to about sixty thousand, and added Butterfield's corps and Whipple's division to Franklin's command, giving him about forty thousand; At 5.55 A. M. on the 13th, the day of battle, he sent orders to Franklin — which he received two hours and a half afterward (it was said, because the staff officer who carried them stopped to get his breakfast) — to keep his command in readiness to move down the old Richmond road, and send out at once a division at least to seize the heights at Hamilton's Crossing, where Lee's right rested, taking care to keep it well supported. In an order dated 6 A. M., the same morning, he directs Sumner to "push a division or more along the streets and roads on the line from the town to Lee's left, with a view to seizing the heights in the rear of the town," but not to attack until he got additional orders.

Lee was quietly awaiting him. Earthworks had been constructed at points on the crests of the hills, skillfully designed by General Pendleton, chief of artillery, and the engineer officers. His army was divided into two corps, under Longstreet and Jackson, Longstreet being on the left. Anderson's division rested on the river, and then McLaws, Pickett, and Hood extended to the right in the order named. Ransom's division supported the batteries on Marye's and neighboring hills, at the foot of which Cobb's brigade, of McLaws's division, and the Twenty-fourth North Carolina, were stationed, protected by a stone wall. The Washington Artillery, under Colonel Walton, occupied the redoubts on the crest of Marye's Hill, and those on the heights to the right and left were held by a part of the reserve artillery. Colonel E. P. Alexander was in charge of the division batteries of Anderson, Ransom, and McLaws. A. P. Hill, of Jackson's corps, was posted between Hood's right and Hamilton's Crossing. Early's and Taliaferro's divisions composed Jackson's second line, while D. H. Hill's division was formed in reserve. Stuart, with two brigades of cavalry, under General Lee's son and nephew, was on Jackson's right. A dense fog overhung the plain and river until after 9 A. M., obscuring from view the movements of the Federals. Then, as the struggling rays of the sun lifted the mist, it unmasked to Lee and his army a picture unparalleled in surpassing splendor, unequaled in terrible sublimity.

From his lofty position on Telegraph Hill, in the center of his line, Lee saw the mass of Federals deploying in A. P. Hill's front. Franklin was about to assault with "one division at least," as ordered. As a matter of fact, his attack was afterward made with Reynolds's First Corps of three divisions, under Meade, Gibbon, and Doubleday. Meade, an excellent soldier, was sent in first; Gibbon to support him, and Doubleday to follow. Meade selected for his point of attack the place where the ridge on Lee's right terminated and where it gradually reached the level of the plain. It was a salient point, and at its southern end devoid of fortification. Stuart had placed his cavalry and horse artillery far out on the plain, and his guns enfiladed the march of this attacking column. The fire of his horse artillery, under his celebrated boy chief, Pelham, was very effective. The second ball from a Whitworth gun tore through the knapsack of a Federal infantryman, distributed his clothing to the winds, threw a pack of playing cards twenty feet in the air, and created consternation and death as it flew a long distance down the line. Doubleday's division was halted by Pelham's fire and the presence of cavalry on its flank, and Reynolds was deprived of its support, and with only two divisions and two regiments of Stoneman's Third Corps was attempting to overthrow Jackson, who lay in his front with thirty thousand men in a sheltered, and for a portion of the line, fortified position. Why Reynolds was not supported by Smith's Sixth Corps of twenty-four thousand men, which was a short distance behind him, is one of the mysteries of war. Franklin would still have had fourteen thousand men — namely, two divisions of the Third Corps and one of the Ninth — exclusive of thirty-five hundred cavalry, under the gallant Bayard, as a reserve. The Federal advance marched to destruction. Meade broke through a gap in Jackson's line between Thomas's and Archer's brigade, but fresh troops came up under Taliaferro and Early, amid cries of "Here comes old Jubal!" "Let Jubal straighten that fence!" and it was securely rebuilt.

The Union troops were broken and driven back with great slaughter. Meade lost in killed, wounded, and missing, 1,853, and Gibbon 1,266 men, in a short, fierce, furious and useless combat. Meade told Franklin he "found it quite hot," taking off his slouch hat and showing two bullet holes between which and the top of his head there must have been little space. To Lee — calm, self-contained and self-reliant as Wellington at Waterloo — from his position on Telegraph (since called Lee's) Hill, the movement appeared like an armed reconnoissance, and was only considered a precursor to something more serious. Jackson was much pleased at the result on his front. He appeared that day for the first and last time in a bright new uniform which replaced his former dingy suit, having actually exchanged his faded old cap for another which was resplendent in gold lace, a present from J. E. B. Stuart. It was a most remarkable metamorphosis of his former self, and his men did not like it, fearing, as some of them said, that "Old Jack would be afraid of his clothes and would not get down to his work."

Burnside's plans seem to have been to attack simultaneously on both of Lee's flanks, like Napoleon when he had the river and three bridges behind him at Dresden, and he may have reasoned, as did that great French soldier, that an assault on both flanks would demoralize the center, which he would overwhelm by concentrated attack. Sumner's right grand division held the town. Couch's Second Corps occupied it, and Wilcox's Ninth Corps stretched out from Couch's left toward Franklin's right. At 8.15 A. M. Couch received an order from Sumner, who was across the river at the Lacy House, "to form a column of a division for the purpose of seizing the heights in the rear of the town"; to advance in three lines, and be supported by another division to be formed in the same manner as the leading division; but the movement should not begin until further orders. French's division in column of three brigades, at two hundred yards' interval, was selected to lead, Hancock's in similar formation to follow. About eleven o'clock, the fog lifting, Couch signaled to Sumner that he was ready, and received orders to move. The troops debouched from the town, crossed with difficulty the bed of an old canal at right angles to their course, and deployed along the bank bordering the plain over which they were to charge. At this time Burnside, the army commander, was two miles away, across the river at his headquarters, the Phillips House. Sumner, the right grand commander, was at his headquarters also, on the other side of the Rappahannock. Couch, in command of the corps, and Howard, his remaining division commander, climbed the steeple of the courthouse in the town, and the battle began. It was not long before Couch exclaimed to Howard: "Oh, great God! See how our men, our brave fellows, are falling!" And so they were. They "could not make reply" or protest, and nothing was left but "to do and die." "I remember," said Couch, "that the whole plain was covered with men prostrate and dropping, the live men running here and there, and in front, closing upon each other, and the wounded coming back. The commands seemed to be mixed up. I had never before seen fighting like that, or anything approaching it in terrible uproar and destruction. There was no cheering on the part of the men, but a stubborn determination to obey orders and do their duty. As they charged, the artillery fire would break their formation and they would get mixed. Then they would close up together, everywhere receiving the withering infantry fire, and those who were able would run to the lines and fight as best they could; and then the next brigade coming up in succession would do its duty and melt like snow coming down on a warm morning." Hancock and French sent promptly for assistance. Two brigades of Wilcox's corps were sent to the slaughter pen, and one of Howard's, and then a division of Stoneman's, of Hooker's center grand division, as well as Gifford's division of Butterfield's corps. The other divisions of the same corps were also put in supporting distance, and it now began to look like a genuine attempt to crush Lee's left. At 3 P. M. Couch was told by a dispatch from Sumner that Hooker had been ordered to put in everything. "His coming to me," said Couch, "was like the breaking out of the sun in the storm." It had been demonstrated the storm was there, but what became of the sun? Hooker consulted Hancock, who had been in the leaden hail and had lost two thousand out of five thousand men composing his division in a very brief interval of time, after which, without obeying orders, he rode back at 2 P. M. across the river to Burnside, and did not return for two hours.

The battery of artillery on Marye's Hill was relieved in the meantime by fresh batteries, under Wolfolk and Moody, which produced the impression that the hill was being abandoned, so Couch directed Humphreys to attack with his two brigades and Getty's division of the Ninth Corps. This was bravely done, but with the same result. Humphreys lost seventeen hundred out of three thousand men. It was hardly possible for Hooker's whole army to have carried Marye's Hill by direct assault as long as Confederate ammunition lasted. It resisted the successive charges of the Federals as Gibraltar withstands the surging seas. It was defended by the famous battalion of Washington Artillery from New Orleans. The men and officers were full of fight, enthusiastic, vigilant, enterprising, and brave. No mistake had been made in committing this important post to that organization. Around and stretching on either side was the left wing of the army. Marye's Hill met the streets leading from the town, and offered the most inviting point of attack. The front sloped to a sunken road, on the town side of which was a stone wall some four feet high; the excavated dirt had been thrown on the other side of the wall, so that no part of the wall showed on the side of the Federal advance, and their troops were in ignorance of its existence. Behind this wall, four files deep, was the Georgia brigade of General Thomas R. Cobb, which was afterward re-enforced by portions of Kershaw's and Cook's brigades. To reach this wall the Union troops were obliged to march over a plain swept by artillery. General E. P. Alexander, Longstreet's accomplished artilleryman, remarked before the battle: "We cover that ground now so well that we will comb it as with a fine-toothed comb. A chicken could not live on that field when we open on it."

The dauntless courage displayed by the Federal officers and men availed nothing against the rapid plunging fire of well-served 12-pound howitzers, Napoleons, and rifle guns. The three-inch rifle balls of the Federals that fell near these batteries were hurled back at them out of Confederate guns. "On they came in beautiful array," wrote a Washington Artillery participant, "more determined to hold the plain than ever; but our fire was murderous, and no troops on earth could stand the feu a'enfer we were giving them. In the foremost line we distinguished the green flag with the golden harp of old Ireland, and we knew it to be Meagher's Irish brigade."

It was a picturesque field, the blue, the red breeches of the Zouaves, and the green of old Ireland were mingled in Death's cold embrace. Imagine troops, as soon as deployed, stormed at with shot and shell, and those who escaped, treated next to canister, and the brave survivors exposed to the severe fire of concealed infantry which scorched the ground beneath their feet! The battle on Lee's left was fought principally by the artillery and the few thousand infantry in the sunken road — troops whose courage, steadiness, and endurance has been honorably mentioned. Were it possible to have scaled Marye's Hill no hostile force could have lived there, for a concentrated, converging fire from the heights in the rear which commanded it, and of which it was simply an outpost, would have swept it from its face.

The battle of Fredericksburg was a grand sight as Lee witnessed it from Lee's Hill in the center of his lines, and Burnside through his field glass from a more secure position, two miles in the rear of the battlefield, with the river flowing between himself and his troops. The roar of over three hundred cannon — the Federals alone had three hundred and seventy-five in their army — formed an orchestra which had the city of Fredericksburg for audience, as well as both armies.

Earth shook, red meteors flashed along the sky, And conscious Nature shuddered at the cry. A hundred thousand men in line of battle, both flanks being visible, from whose bristling bayonets were reflected the rays of the morning sun as they penetrated the rising mists, was a gorgeous pageant viewed from the Confederate lines.

The battle of Fredericksburg was a farce which one could laugh at, except for the sacrifice of human life. A grand army seeks offensive battle, makes isolated attacks by fractional forces, remains in position two days, and secretly, in the midst of a violent storm, recrosses the river during the night, with a loss of twelve thousand six hundred and fifty-three. If Burnside had held fast with a small force in Fredericksburg, protected by the reserve artillery on Stafford Heights, while re-enforcing Franklin with the bulk of Sumner's and Hooker's forces so as to have threatened the Confederate line of communication, he would have drawn Lee from Marye's Hill and forced him to deliver battle on more equal terms.

The popular notion that General Jackson wanted to move on the Federals after their repulse and drive them into the river is disposed of by his own report, in which he says: "The enemy making no forward movement, I determined, if prudent, to do so myself; but the first gun had hardly moved from the woods a hundred yards when the enemy's artillery reopened and so completely swept our front as to satisfy me that the projected movement should be abandoned."

Lee had really fought a defensive battle to a finish without knowing it. Only one third of his army had been engaged, and in killed, wounded, and missing his losses were only five thousand three hundred and seventy-seven. The Washington Artillery, which for four hours and a half mowed down the charging columns until their canister, case, and solid shot had been exhausted, lost three killed and twenty-four wounded. Naturally the Southern commander waited in his advantageous position for the big battle, but he waited in vain. It would have been a mistake to have done otherwise; and "in war the crown of laurel is reserved for him who makes the fewest mistakes himself and most promptly profits by the mistakes of others."

Lee greatly regretted the loss of his brave men, the wounding of the gallant Cook and the death of such splendid soldiers as Cobb, and Maxey Gregg. Cobb fell mortally wounded at the foot of the stone wall he had so bravely defended, at the door of the house of Mrs. Martha Stevens, who must have been a sort of "Molly Pitcher," for it is related that she was very active all day in the Confederate cause, and after using all her materials for bandages for the wounded, actually tore from her person most of her garments, on that cold December morning, in her anxiety to minister to their necessities.

After one or two abortive attempts to assume the offensive were made later by Burnside, the two armies looked quietly at each other from their respective positions on either side of the Rappahannock for four months. A few wall and common tents, pitched half way between Fredericksburg and Hamilton's Crossing on the border of an old pine field, marked the headquarters of the Confederate commander, and here Lee labored to promote the efficiency of his troops and prepare them for the active operations which he knew must commence when spring succeeded winter.

It was at this time, Long tells us, that among a number of fowls presented to the general was a sprightly hen, who went into the egg business before her turn came to lose her head, and thus persuaded Bryan, General Lee's well-known steward, that her egg, which she each morning deposited in the general's tent, was better for the general's breakfast than herself. Lee, fond of domestic animals, appreciated her selection of his quarters, and would leave the tent door open for her and wait elsewhere until her cackle informed him that he could return to his canvas home. She roosted and rode in his wagon, was an eye-witness of the battle of Chancellorsville, and there it is said she refused to lay until victory perched upon her general's plume, when she at once recommenced. Many months she soldiered — participated, in her way, in the battle of Gettysburg, but when the orders were given to fall back, and the headquarters wagons had been loaded, the hen could not be found. General Lee joined others in a search for her, and finally she was found perched on top of the wagon seemingly anxious to return to her native State.

In the fall of 1864, when Lee's headquarters were near Orange Court House, the hen had become fat and lazy, and on one occasion when the general had a distinguished visitor to dine with him, Bryan, finding it difficult to procure suitable material, unknown to everyone, killed the hen. At dinner the general was surprised to see so fine a fowl, and all enjoyed it, not dreaming of the great sacrifice made upon the altar of hospitality.

Lee's forced inactivity brought homesickness. He longed to be reunited to his family. In his letters he tells them of the noble spirit displayed by the people of Fredericksburg; that the faces of the old and young were wreathed with smiles and glowed with happiness at their sacrifices for the good of their country. "Many have lost everything. What the fire and swords of the enemy spared, their pillagers destroyed; but God will shield them I know." That the only place he "can be found is in camp, and there I will have to be taken with the three stools, the sun, the rain and mud." That "Hooker, Burnside's successor, is obliged to do something, but what, I do not know." That "he plays the Chinese game, runs out his guns, starts his wagons and troops up and down the river, and creates an excitement generally. Our men look on in wonder, give a cheer, and immediately again subside." That "God is kind and gives me plenty to do in good weather and bad, and that I owe Mr. J. Hooker no thanks for keeping me here, for he ought to have made up his mind long ago what to do." Later he writes: "The cars have arrived from Richmond and brought me a young French officer, full of vivacity and ardor, for service with me. I think the appearance of things will cool him. If they do not the night will, for he brought no blankets."

In a letter to his daughter Mary, previous to Burnside's attack, dated Camp near Fredericksburg, November 24, 1862, he says: "I have just received your letter of the 17th, which has afforded me great gratification. I regretted not finding you in Richmond, and grieve over every opportunity at not seeing you that is lost, for I fear they will become less and less frequent. The death of my dear Annie was, indeed, to me a bitter pang, but 'the Lord gave and the Lord has taken away, blessed be the name of the Lord.' In the quiet hours of the night, when there is nothing to lighten the full weight of my grief, I feel as if I should be overwhelmed. I have always counted, if God should spare me a few days of peace, after this cruel war was ended, that I should have her with me, but year after year my hopes go out, and I must be resigned. General Burnside's whole army is apparently opposite Fredericksburg, and stretches from the Rappahannock to the Potomac. What his intentions are he has not yet disclosed. I am sorry he is in position to oppress our friends and citizens of the Northern Neck. He threatens to bombard Fredericksburg, and the noble spirit displayed by its citizens, particularly the women and children, has elicited my highest admiration. They have been abandoning their homes night and day during all this inclement weather cheerfully and uncomplainingly, with only such assistance as our wagons and ambulances could afford — women, girls, children, trudging through the mud and bivouacking in the open fields."

Again, in a letter to his wife from the same camp, on December 2, 1862, he writes: "I am glad you had the opportunity of visiting New Kent; but the sight of the White House must have brought particularly sad thoughts. It will all come right in the end, though we may not live to see it. That is Lieutenant Spangler who addressed me so familiarly. He was orderly sergeant of Captain Evans's company, Second Cavalry, United States Army, and was a good soldier. I tremble for my country when I hear of confidence expressed in me. I know too well my weakness, and that our only hope is in God."

On December 11th, at the commencement of the Federal operations, General Lee writes Mrs. Lee: "I return a bit sent up by Custis. It is not the one I wished, but I do not want the one I wrote for now, as I have one that will answer as well. The enemy, after bombarding the town of Fredericksburg, setting fire to many houses, and knocking down nearly all those along the river, crossed over a large force about dark, and now occupy the town. We hold the hills commanding it, and hope we shall be able to damage him yet. His positions and heavy guns command the town entirely."

On December 16th he thus writes of the recrossing of the Federals, and also of the liberation of the Arlington slaves: "I had supposed they were just preparing for battle, and was saving our men for the conflict. Their hosts crown the hill and plain beyond the river, and their numbers to me are unknown. Still, I felt a confidence we could stand the shock, and was anxious for the blow that is to fall on some point, and was prepared to meet it here. Yesterday evening I had my suspicions that they might return during the night, but could not believe they would relinquish their hopes after all their boasting and preparation, and when I say that the latter is equal to the former, you will have some idea of the magnitude. This morning they were all safe on the north side of the Rappahannock. They went as they came — in the night. They suffered heavily as far as the battle went, but it did not go far enough to satisfy me. Our loss was comparatively slight, and I think will not exceed two thousand. The contest will have now to be renewed, but on what field I cannot say. As regards the liberation of the people [slaves] I wish to progress in it as far as I can. Those hired in Richmond can still find employment there if they choose. Those in the country can do the same or remain on the farms. I hope they will all do well and behave themselves. I should like if I could to attend to their wants, and see them placed to the best advantage. But that is impossible. All that choose can leave the State before the war closes. The quartermaster informs me he has received the things you sent. The mitts will be very serviceable. Make as many as you can obtain good material for. I have everything I want." General Lee was the executor, and the date of the emancipation of the slaves under Mr. Custis's will had arrived.

From the same camp on Christmas day he writes Mrs. Lee: "I will commence this holy day by writing to you. My heart is filled with gratitude to Almighty God for the unspeakable mercies with which he has blessed us in this day, for those he has granted us from the beginning of life, and particularly for those he has vouchsafed us during the past year. What should have become of us without his crowning help and protection? Oh, if our people would only recognize it and cease from vain self-boasting and adulation, how strong would be my belief in final success and happiness to our country! But what a cruel thing is war; to separate and destroy families and friends, and mar the purest joys and happiness God has granted us in this world; to fill our hearts with hatred instead of love for our neighbors, and to devastate the fair face of this beautiful world! I pray that on this day, when only peace and good — will are preached to mankind, better thoughts may fill the hearts of our enemies and turn them to peace. Our army was never in such good health and condition since I have been attached to it. I believe they share with me my disappointment that the enemy did not renew the combat on the 13th. I was holding back all that day and husbanding our strength and ammunition for the great struggle for which I thought I was preparing. Had I divined what was to have been his only effort he would have had more of it. My heart bleeds at the death of every one of our gallant men." Again, from the same place he tells her: "We had quite a snow day before yesterday, and last night was very cold. It is thawing a little this morning, though the water was freezing as I washed. I fear it will bring much discomfort to those of our men who are barefooted and poorly clad. I can take but little pleasure in my comforts for thinking of them. A kind lady — Mrs. Sallie Braxton Slaughter — of Fredericksburg, sent me a mattress, some catsup, and preserves during the snowstorm. You must thank Miss Norvell [Caskie] for her nice cake, which I enjoyed very much. I had it set out under the pines the day after its arrival, and assembled all the young gentlemen [of his staff] around it; and though I told them it was a present from a beautiful young lady, they did not leave a crumb. I want a good servant badly. Perry [an old Arlington servant] is very willing, and I believe does as well as he can. You know he is very slow and inefficient, and moves very like his father Lawrence. He is also very fond of his blankets in the morning — the time I most require him. I hope he will do well when he leaves me, and get in the service of some good person who will take care of him."

On the 8th of January he again makes reference to the Arlington servants, and says: "I executed the deed of manumission sent me by Mr. Caskie, and returned it to him. I perceived that John Sawyer and James's names among the Arlington people had been omitted, and inserted them. I fear there are others among the White House lot which I did not discover. As to the attacks of the Northern papers, I do not mind them, and do not think it wise to make the publication you suggest. If all the names of the people at Arlington and on the Pamunkey are not embraced in the deed I have executed, I should like a supplementary deed to be drawn up containing all those omitted. They are all entitled to their freedom, and I wish to give it to them. Those that have been carried away I hope are free and happy. I cannot get their papers to them, and they do not require them. I will give them if they ever call for them. It would be useless to ask their restitution to manumit them. The enemy is still in large force opposite to us. There is no indication of his future movements." And on the 29th of January he writes: "The storm has culminated here in a deep snow, which does not improve our comfort. It came particularly hard on some of our troops whom I was obliged to send some eleven miles up the Rappahannock to meet a recent move of General Burnside. Their bivouac in the rain and snow was less comfortable than at their former stations, where they had constructed some shelter. General Burnside's designs have apparently been frustrated, either by the storm or by other causes, and on last Saturday he took a special steamer to Washington, to consult the military oracles at the Federal seat of Government. Sunday I heard of his being closeted with President Lincoln, Secretary Stanton, and General Halleck. I suppose we shall have a new programme next week. You had better finish all the gloves you intend making at once, and send them to the army. Next month they will be much needed. After that no use for this winter. Tell Mr. Haskins I am delighted the turkey was so good. I was that day up at United States Mine Ford, on the Rappahannock. Did not get back till late at night. After our nocturnal repast was over, having been on horseback from early breakfast, you can imagine how I would have enjoyed it. I was, however, thinking so much of General Burnside's playing us such a shabby trick, running off to Washington when we were waiting for him, that I did not then miss my dinner."

General Lee was surrounded by embarrassments during the winter — the troops were scantily clothed, rations for men and animals meager. The shelters were poor, and through them broke the sun, rains, and winds. He could not strike his enemy, but must watch and be patient, for he remembered the favorite maxim of Marlborough, "Patience will overcome all things, and the gods smile on those who can wait." He was obliged to send Longstreet with two of his four divisions to the section south of James River, nearly one hundred miles away, to relieve his commissary department and to collect supplies, and was thus deprived of their support when the campaign opened. Across the river his better sheltered, fed, and clothed opponent had his troubles too. Burnside had lost the confidence of many of his principal officers, and after a harmless attempt to reach Lee by Banks's Ford, six miles above Fredericksburg, further winter operations were suspended.

Then Burnside prepared a sweeping order, dismissing from the Army Generals Hooker, Brooks, Cochrane, and Newton, and relieving from their commands Generals Franklin, W. F. Smith, Sturgis, Ferrero, and Colonel Joseph Taylor, Sumner's adjutant general. To approve the order, or accept his resignation, was the alternative presented to the President. Mr. Lincoln accepted his resignation, and immediately placed the baton of the army commander in the hands of Joseph Hooker, the head and front of the caballed officers. Mr. Lincoln's letter of January 26, 1863, to Hooker, is characteristic. He tells him he has thwarted Burnside as much as he could, doing a great wrong to his country and to a most meritorious brother officer; that he had heard of his saying that both the army and country needed a dictator. "What I ask," he adds, "is military success. In that event I will risk the dictatorship"; and concludes by begging him to "Beware of rashness!"

Hooker, or "Fighting Joe," as he was sometimes called, had managed a corps well, possessed personal magnetism and a fine presence, but had not the ability to conduct great operations; and yet it must be admitted his preliminary steps toward reorganization and the promotion of the battle power of his army were well taken. He found his army amid the Stafford hills, on the left bank of the Rappahannock, and stretching back to the Potomac some twelve miles, which river gave him a splendid line of communication with his capital, secure from an enemy who had no boats. Much discontent prevailed in the ranks, and his men were deserting at the rate of two hundred per day. A majority of the officers, too, were hostile to the policy of the Government, and the number of absentees without leave amounted to 2,922 officers and 81,964 non-commissioned officers and privates, while the express trains to the army were filled with citizens' clothing, sent to assist soldiers to desert. Hooker, by judicious furloughs, stopped this in a measure, filled up his ranks, instilled discipline, gave leaves to the officers, consolidated his cavalry into a corps, and replaced the Corps d'armee or Grand Divisions by an army organization of seven corps, commanded by, First, Reynolds; Second, Couch; Third, Sickles; Fifth, Meade; Sixth, Sedgwick; Eleventh, Howard; and Twelfth, Slocum. Then he began to study strategy, for Mr. Lincoln had said, "Go forward and give us victories." Lee's army, his objective point, must be reached but how? The more the problem was considered the more he was convinced its solution involved reaching General Lee's left rear.

CHAPTER 11

CHANCELLORSVILLE.

Chancellorsville was the most wonderful of Lee's battles, and demanded the highest exercise of his military ability. The Army of Northern Virginia amounted to 53,303 present for duty at Chancellorsville, with one hundred and seventy pieces of artillery.

The Federals numbered, according to the return of April 30th, an aggregate of officers and men present of 138,378, and, under the head of "present for duty equipped," which embraces those actually available for the line of battle at the date of the report, the army numbered 133,708. Hooker had by these returns, therefore, a numerical superiority on the field of 80,000.

The Southern commander, penetrating the Federal plan of operations, placed one of the only two cavalry brigades with his army in the vicinity of Culpeper Court House, and had the Rappahannock picketed for twenty-five miles above the left of his infantry. Hooker determined to break up this observation cavalry, for they would be too near his flanking route, and on the 16th dispatched three thousand cavalry under Averell to attack them. The Southern brigade was small at the time. The cavalrymen owned their horses, and many of them had been detailed to go home to get fresh horses for the spring campaign. Owing to that fact, and the absence of many squadrons on detached service, only eight hundred men could be placed in the saddle. Butterfield, Hooker's chief of staff, reported the combat that followed as the best cavalry fight of the war, lasting five hours, charging and recharging on both sides, and that the Confederate cavalry were driven back three miles into cover of earthworks and heavy guns. Stanton, the Federal Secretary of War, congratulated Hooker on the success of the expedition. "You have drawn the first blood, and I hope now to see the boys up and at them." It was Sir Walter Raleigh who said that human testimony was so unreliable that no two men could see the same occurrence and give the same report of it. The Confederate official reports state that Averell was defeated and driven back across the river. Major John Pelham, who was accidentally present, being summoned to Culpeper Court House as a witness in a court-martial, borrowed a horse and rode out on the field, where he acted temporarily as aid-de-camp, and was killed. He was Stuart's chief of horse artillery, and a graduate of West Point of the class of 1861. The death of this blue-eyed Alabama boy was a great loss. His superb courage and dash had been immortalized by Jackson's expression, after seeing him handle his guns at Sharpsburg, that "an army should have a Pelham on each flank," while General Lee called him, at Fredericksburg, "the gallant Pelham"; and Stuart in General Orders wrote: "The memory of the gallant Pelham, his many virtues, his noble nature, his purity of character, is enshrined as a sacred legacy in the hearts of all who knew him."

On the arrival of spring the two armies were still in sight of each other occupying the old lines. Hooker must now assume the offensive. In addition to his twelve corps of infantry-three divisions to a corps, except Slocum's, who had two — he had a large, finely appointed cavalry corps under Stoneman, numbering thirteen thousand three hundred and ninety-eight sabers, and three hundred and seventy-five cannon. The Confederate force consisted of McLaws and Anderson's divisions of Longstreet's corps (Hood and Pickett's divisions of that corps being absent in the vicinity of Suffolk, south of James River), and Jackson's corps, composed of the divisions of A. P. Hill, Early, and D. H. Hill under Rodes, and Trimble under Colston.

The Federal general's designs were well conceived. He proposed to march three of his corps up the Rappahannock twenty-seven miles, cross them at Kelly's Ford, add to them one corps which should cross below at United States Ford, and with these four corps make a great turning column, which should move down on Lee's left rear, while the remaining three corps, constituting his left wing, should cross à la Burnside in Lee's front at Fredericksburg, hold him steady by the menace of a direct attack, and when he was manoeuvred out of his intrenchments, pursue him. In order to make the blow more effective, Stoneman was directed to make a wide detour well around the Southern left and rear, throw ten thousand sabers between Lee and Richmond, breaking up his communications, stopping his supplies, and be in a position to obstruct the Confederate retreat until Hooker could deliver a final blow.

The Union cavalry were put in motion as early as the 13th of April to cross the upper fords of the Rappahannock. Mr. Lincoln, who was alive to all that was going on, telegraphed Hooker: "The rain and mud were, of course, to be calculated upon. General Stoneman is not moving rapidly enough to make the expedition come to anything. He has now been out three days, two of which were unusually fair weather, and all free from hindrance by his enemy, and yet he is not twenty-five miles from where he started. To reach his point he has still sixty to go. By arithmetic how many days will it take him to do it?" The general impatience for a move was prevalent everywhere. Even the Union General Peck, at Suffolk, hoping to be relieved from Longstreet's presence, wired urging it, to which Hooker replied on April 21st: "You must be patient with me. I must play with these devils before I can spring."

On the 27th Hooker's turning column of the Eleventh, Twelfth, and Fifth Corps began its march, while two divisions of Couch's Second Corps were sent to United States Ford, between Kelly's and Fredericksburg. On the night of the 28th and the morning of the 29th the right wing crossed the Rappahannock River, marched under Hooker's immediate command in two columns for the Rapidan, crossing that stream at Germania and Ely's Fords. Having brought Couch to him, Hooker was concentrated on the night of the 30th at Chancellorsville, ten miles west of Fredericksburg, but had consumed four days in getting this far on Lee's left.

The day before Hooker moved, Sedgwick, proceeding to carry out his part of the plan, crossed the Rappahannock below Fredericksburg with the First, Third, and Sixth Corps, numbering fifty-two thousand four hundred and one. This imposing demonstration on Lee's front, it was expected, would make him arrange for another defensive battle, and while doing so, Hooker's right wing would overwhelm his left and attack in reverse his fortified lines. The next day Sickles's Third Corps, having assisted Sedgwick to demonstrate, went to Hooker at Chancellorsville to join in the contemplated crushing; but Sedgwick still had for his feint thirty-seven thousand six hundred and seventy-three troops.

Hooker was greatly elated at the situation on the night of the 30th. The next day he would advance with "the finest army on the planet," as he called it, uncover Banks's Ford six miles below, and thus have direct communication by a short route with Sedgwick. He congratulated in General Orders the right wing at the great success attending their operations, telling them that his enemy "must ingloriously fly, or come out from behind his defenses and give us battle on our own ground, where certain destruction awaits him." On May 1st Hooker started for Fredericksburg. The four corps with him, less Gibbon's division of the Second at Falmouth, and exclusive of a cavalry brigade, amounted to seventy-three thousand one hundred and twenty-four. What a grand army to hurl on an enemy's flank!

If the Union general's tactics had kept pace with his strategy, his numbers might have given him a great victory. His well-devised plans were divined by his alert antagonist. Stuart's cavalry pickets, which were driven away from Kelly's Ford on the 28th, reported infantry crossing there that night; their line of march was quickly ascertained next day and reported to General Lee by telegraph from Culpeper Court House. Stuart made a detour with one of his two brigades of cavalry, after throwing a regiment in front of the Federal advance, and reaching Todd's Tavern on the 30th, placed his cavalry across the routes leading to Lee's lines of communication. Jackson, whose right stretched fourteen miles below Fredericksburg, was brought up to Hamilton's Crossing the same day Hooker's right wing was crossing the river at Kelly's, and then Lee waited for his enemy's plans to be more fully developed, believing the war maxim, "When your enemy is making a mistake he must not be interrupted." He readily perceived that with Hooker at Chancellorsville and Sedgwick three miles below Fredericksburg, the two wings were thirteen miles apart, and that his army was directly between them. He understood the military problem drive the wedge in and keep them separate, hold one still by a feint or retard his march by fighting, concentrate on and overwhelm the other. Sedgwick lay quiet while Hooker was massing at Chancellorsville.

"Jackson at first," says Lee, "preferred to attack Sedgwick's force in the plain of Fredericksburg, but I told him I feared it was as impracticable as it was at the first battle of Fredericksburg. It was hard to get at the enemy, and harder to get away, if we drove him into the river, but if he thought it could be done, I would give orders for it." Jackson asked to be allowed to examine the ground, and did so during the afternoon, and at night came to Lee and said he thought he [Lee] was right. It would be inexpedient to attack there. "Move, then," said Lee, "up to Anderson," who had been previously ordered to proceed to Chancellorsville. "And the next time I saw Jackson," says General Lee, "was the next day — May 1st — when he was on our skirmish line, driving in the enemy's skirmishers around Chancellorsville."

McLaws reached Anderson's position before sunrise on the 1st, and Jackson at 8 A. M. It was determined to hammer Hooker while Sedgwick was held at arm's length. Lee wisely selected Early to keep, if possible, Sedgwick out of the difficulty he proposed to have with Hooker, and, in addition to his own division, gave him Barksdale's brigade of McLaws's division and the reserve artillery under General Pendleton. Jackson found Anderson some six miles from Chancellorsville, intrenching. He ordered the work discontinued, for, as usual, he wanted at once to find his enemy. At 11 A. M. the Confederates, in two columns under Anderson and McLaws, with Jackson closely following, moved on Chancellorsville.

The same morning Hooker put his troops in motion in three columns on the roads Lee was marching, thinking the latter was held at Fredericksburg by his demonstration there, and ordered his headquarters to be established at Tabernacle Church, half-way between Chancellorsville and Fredericksburg, at 2 P. M.; but the church was not destined to be so marked. As the head of his columns debouched from the forest a few miles from Chancellorsville, they encountered the Army of Northern Virginia advancing in line of battle, which so surprised Hooker that he lost for the first time his self-confidence. He had not dreamed that Lee would assume the offensive. It embarrassed him so much that he decided on defensive tactics — a decision fatal to him. Fearing he could not throw his troops through the forest fast enough, and apprehensive of being whipped in detail, he ordered his army to retire to their lines around Chancellorsville. Lee, with brilliant daring worthy of the hero of Malakoff, followed him and established a line of battle in front of him, at some points within a mile of Chancellorsville. "Here," says he, "the enemy had assumed a position of great natural strength, surrounded on all sides by a dense forest filled with tangled undergrowth, in the midst of which breastworks of logs had been constructed with trees felled in front so as to form an almost impenetrable abatis. His artillery swept the few narrow roads by which his position could be approached from the front, and commanded the adjacent works." The left of Hooker's line extended from Chancellorsville to the Rappahannock River, covering the United States Ford, while on the other side it reached west as far as Wilderness Church. His left flank was unassailable, as Lee found from a personal reconnoissance that afternoon, and his front impregnable. Of the five miles of battle line, his right alone could be considered. That night Stuart brought the Rev. Dr. B. T. Lacy to Lee, who told him a circuit could be made around by Wilderness Tavern, and General Lee directed Jackson to make his arrangements to move early next day around the Federal right flank. The sun rose on this eventful 2d of May unclouded and brilliant, gilding the hill tops and penetrating the vapors of the valley — as gorgeous as was the sun of Austerlitz, which produced such an impression upon the imagination of Napoleon. Its rays fell upon the last meeting in this world of Lee and Jackson. The Duke of Wellington is reported to have said: "A man of fine Christian sensibilities is totally unfit for the position of a soldier"; but here were two great soldiers who faithfully performed all their duties as Christians.

Lee, erect and soldierly, emerged from the little pine thicket where he had bivouacked during the night, and stood on its edge at sunrise to see Jackson's troops file by. When Jackson came along he stopped and the two conversed for a few moments, after which Jackson speedily rejoined his troops, now making their famous flank march. Bold, but dangerous, was Lee's strategy. He had decided to keep some 14,000 men, under Anderson and McLaws, in front of Hooker's 73,000, while Jackson marched by a wide circuit with less than 30,000, to gain the Union right rear. Reynolds's First Corps on that day was marching from Sedgwick to Hooker. It numbered 19,595, and reached Hooker at daylight on the 3d. General Hooker then had around Chancellorsville 92,719 men.

At Austerlitz, when the Russians made the flank movement around the French right, Napoleon moved at once upon the weakened line of the allies in his front and burst through it. Leaving some battalions to hold the right wing, he wheeled the remainder upon the left and destroyed it, and then, turning toward the right wing, he directed upon it a terrible onset, and it too was no more. In some places the men in Lee's thin gray line in front of Hooker were six feet apart. Jackson marched rapidly diagonally across the front of Hooker's line of battle, screened from view by the forest and by three regiments of cavalry which had been ordered to mask the movement as well as to precede it.

As early as 8 A. M. Birney, of Sickles's corps, reported a continuous column of infantry trains and ambulances passing his front. His division was on Howard's left, whose corps formed the right of the Union army. Sickles sent a battery forward to a commanding position on his front and fired at the moving column, and at 12 M. moved with two of his divisions and Barlow's brigade of Howard's corps and gained the road Jackson was moving on, capturing a few hundred of his men. Howard did not fear an attack on his right, for his brigade, in reserve at that point, was selected to assist in Sickles's pursuit.

At 9.30 A. M. Hooker notified Slocum and Howard that the right of their line did not appear to be strong enough. "We have good reason to suppose the enemy is moving to our right." Howard does not admit that he ever received the notification — Slocum says he read it; but at 10.50 A. M. Hooker received a dispatch from Howard that a column of infantry had been observed moving west, and that he had taken measures to resist an attack from the west. Later he became convinced it was a retreat, not an attack. At 2 P. M. Couch, next in command, was told by Hooker that Lee was in full retreat toward Gordonsville, and that he had sent out Sickles to capture his artillery; and at 4.10 P. M., the hour Jackson was forming his column of attack behind his right, Hooker sent a dispatch to Sedgwick: "We know the enemy is flying, trying to save his trains. Two of Sickles's divisions are among them."

About 3 P. M. Jackson's van reached the plank road, three miles west of Chancellorsville. The commander of the cavalry accompanying him had made a personal reconnoissance while waiting for Jackson to come up, and had located the exact position of the Union right. When Jackson arrived, at his request, he accompanied him through a concealed wooded road to a hill overlooking the rear of the Federal right. Below and but a few hundred yards' distant ran their line of battle, with abatis in front and long lines of stacked arms in the rear. Cannon in position were visible, and the soldiers were in groups, chatting, smoking, and playing cards, while others in the rear were driving up and butchering beeves. Stonewall's face bore an expression of intense interest during the five minutes he was on the hill, and the Federal position was pointed out to him. His eyes had a brilliant glow. The paint of approaching battle was coloring his cheeks, and he was radiant to find no preparation had been made to guard against a flank attack. He made no remarks to the officer with him; his lips were, however, moving, for, sitting on his horse in sight of and close to Howard's troops, he was engaged in an appeal to the God of Battles. He quickly perceived what had been suggested — that by moving to the old turnpike, a little farther to the rear, and not turning down the plank road as proposed, he would take Howard's line in reverse and not in front. "Tell General Rodes," said he, suddenly wheeling his horse to a courier, "to move across the plank road and halt when he gets to the old turnpike. I will join him there." And then he rode rapidly back.

The cavalry, supported by Paxton's brigade of infantry, was placed a short distance down the plank road to mask the march of the remaining troops across it. Jackson's troops reached the old turnpike at 4 P. M. Two hours were consumed in getting the command up and organizing for the attack. At this point Jackson wrote his last note to General Lee:

Near 3 P. M., May 2, 1863.

General: The enemy has made a stand at Chancellors, which is about two miles from Chancellorsville. I hope as soon as practicable to attack. I trust that an ever-kind Providence will bless us with great success. Respectfully,

T. J. Jackson, Lieutenant General.

The leading division is up, and the next two appear to be well closed.

T. J. J. General R. E. Lee.

As the different divisions arrived they were formed at right angles to the road, Rodes's in front, Trimble's division, under Colston, in the second line two hundred yards in the rear, and A. P. Hill's in supporting distance in column. At 6 P. M., all being ready, Jackson ordered the advance. His men burst with a cheer upon the startled enemy, and, like a disciplined thunderbolt, swept down the line and captured cannon before they could be reversed to fire on them. Howard had two regiments and two guns, under Von Gilsen, at right angles to his main line. The Confederate rush first struck him, and he called for re-enforcements. Howard told him he must "hold his post with the men he had and trust to God!" His command of fourteen hundred did not hold on long, as they only lost one hundred and thirty-three killed, wounded, and missing. Rabbits and squirrels ran and flocks of birds flew in front of the advance of these twenty-six thousand men who had dropped so suddenly into their forest haunts, giving in some instances the first notice of an unusual disturbance there.

The Union commander, whose surprised troops were about to be overwhelmed, was recalled to the period when, as a youth, he says, he watched the appearance of contending winds, when the clouds, black and blacker, swift and swifter, rose high and higher as they pushed forward their angry front. He heard the low rumbling from afar, and, as the storm came nearer, the woods bent forward and shook furiously their thick branches. The lightning zigzagged in flashes. The deep-bassed thunder echoed more loudly, till there was scarcely an interval between its ominous crashing discharges.

One half of the eleven thousand five hundred of Howard's corps were Germans, and occupied the exposed flank. Devens's, Steinwehrs's, Schurz's, Schimmelfennig's, and Kryzancerski's troops were rolled over and under by this rapid "rolling reconnoissance." Quickly there was a blind panic and great confusion. Sickles, who had moved to the front from his place in line to attack Jackson's marching flank, and to whom Howard had sent re-enforcements "to make a grand attack with brilliant results," was near the furnace, and came near being severed from his army. The air was filled with noise and smoke; the mighty current of panic-stricken men grew momentarily deeper and wider. Dickinson, one of Hooker's staff, implored Howard to fire on his own men to stop their flight. The surging, seething sea swept away all barriers. Many of the officers attempted to turn back the human tide, but as well might Pharaoh have tried to resist the walls of the Red Sea. Riderless horses and men without arms were everywhere, and guns, caissons, forges, ambulances, battery wagons rolled and tumbled like runaway wagons in a thronged city. Mules tied in couples (a device of Hooker's to carry ammunition) added unearthly brays to the uproar and scattered the ammunition. One pair of them entangled around a tree, was struck by a shell which exploded their load and blew them to pieces. Into all Jackson's ranks blazed a ceaseless fire. Lee's brilliant tactics had succeeded, and Hooker's right had been fairly turned and rolled in a sheet of flame upon his center.

Rodes, who led with so much spirit, says: "The enemy, taken in flank and rear, did not wait for an attack." Colston's division followed so rapidly that it went over the enemy's works at Dowdall's with Rodes's troops, and both divisions fought with mixed ranks until dark. In a piece of woods the line was then halted to reform. There was no apparent line of battle between them and Chancellorsville, and Crutchfield's guns were turned on Chancellorsville. They were immediately responded to by a terrific fire from twenty-two guns on the plank road, loaded with double canister. Jackson was most impatient to work to Hooker's rear and cut him off from the United States Ford, his line of retreat, and drive him on the lines of McLaws and Anderson, where Lee was. These lines, from the nature of the country, had been greatly strengthened with axe and spade. To "huddle" in confusion Hooker's army in the tangled wilderness and surround it seemed possible.

A. P. Hill was now ordered to the front to take charge of the pursuit. While he was engaged in forming his lines, Jackson, who was a little in advance, sent a staff officer to order Hill to move forward as soon as possible, and then, accompanied by Captain Wilbourn, of the Signal Corps, Captain Boswell, and some of his signal men and couriers, rode slowly along the road toward the enemy to reconnoiter for Hill's advance, thinking perhaps a skirmish line was in his front. He had not proceeded far before he came upon a line of Federal infantry lying on their arms. Fired at, he turned his horse, but unfortunately rode a little outside of the route toward the front of some of his own troops, who, ignorant that Jackson had passed out of the lines and mistaking his party for a squad of Union cavalry, fired upon it, killing his engineer officer, Captain Boswell, and Sergeant Cunliff, of the Signal Corps. Jackson immediately crossed the road to avoid the fire and enter his lines at another point, when, again mistaken by his troops, he received at a few paces another volley from the right company of Pender's North Carolina Brigade. Three balls penetrated him at the same time. A round ball from a smooth-bore Springfield musket passed through his right hand, and was cut out that night under the skin. Another entered the outside of his left forearm near the elbow, coming out near the wrist, while still another struck him three inches below the left shoulder joint, divided the artery, and fractured the bone. Reeling in his saddle and losing hold of his bridle rein, he was caught by Captain Wilbourn and placed on the ground. A. P. Hill was soon at his side, as well as his two aids, Smith and Morrison. The two latter placed him in a litter, and then in an ambulance he was carried from the field amid the shrieks of the shells, the whistling of the bullets, and the groans of the wounded and dying. His last order, after being so fearfully wounded, was to tell General Pender to hold his ground. "You must hold your ground, sir," said he.

The ambulance which carried to the field hospital at Wilderness Tavern this great soldier contained his chief of artillery, Crutchfield, also dangerously wounded, and each seemed more concerned about the other's injuries than his own. Here Jackson's left arm was amputated two inches below the shoulder, and three days afterward he was taken to the Chandler House, near Guinea Station, on the railroad from Fredericksburg to Richmond, where he died on the following Sunday. "Order A. P. Hill to prepare for action," he cried in the delirium just before death. "Pass the infantry to the front rapidly. Tell Major Hawkes —" He stopped, and then with a feeling of relief he said: "Let us cross over the river and rest under the shade of the trees." The sword which carved his name upon the shield of fame had returned forever to its scabbard. His wish was fulfilled. "I have always desired to die on Sunday," he had said. When Lee received a notification of his being wounded he wrote to Jackson that, could he have directed the course of events, he would have chosen for the good of his country to have been disabled in his stead. "I congratulate you," he added, "upon the victory which is due to your skill and energy." Howard thought his death was providential, "for in bold planning, in energy of execution, in indefatigable activity and moral ascendency, he was head and shoulders above his confreres."

During the flank march of his great lieutenant, Lee reminded the troops in his front of his position by frequent taps on different points of their lines, and when the sound of cannon gave notice of Jackson's attack, Lee ordered that Hooker's left be strongly pressed to prevent his sending re-enforcements to the point assailed. Sunday, May 3d, was an eventful day. Jackson's corps must complete its work; but who should lead it? A. P. Hill, the next in rank, had been disabled shortly after Jackson was struck down. Rodes, as modest as he was daring, was next in rank to Hill, but in a conference with Major Pendleton, Jackson's chief of staff, and some of the general officers, quickly acquiesced in a suggestion that General J. E. B. Stuart be sent for, because he was satisfied the good of the service demanded it. Stuart was at Ely's Ford with the cavalry and Sixteenth North Carolina Infantry, having gone there to watch Averell, who, having returned from his raid, was reported to be at that point. At 10.30 P. M. Captain Adams, of Hill's staff, summoned him to the command of Jackson's corps. Upon Stuart's arrival upon the battlefield, Jackson had been taken to the rear, but A. P. Hill, still there, turned over the command to him. With the assistance of Colonel E. P. Alexander, of the artillery, he was engaged all night in preparations for the morrow. At early dawn on the 3d Stuart pressed the corps forward — Hill's division in the first line, Trimble's in the second, and Rodes's in the rear.

As the sun lifted the mist, the hill to the right was found to be a commanding position for artillery. Quickly thirty pieces, under Colonels T. H. Carter and Hillary P. Jones, were firing from it, and their fire was very effective. Hooker was standing on the steps of the portico of the Chancellor House, giving directions about the battle, which was now raging with great fury, when a solid shot struck the pillar near him, splitting it in two, and throwing one half longitudinally against him. He says for a few moments he was senseless, and the report spread that he had been killed. To correct the impression, as soon as he revived he insisted on mounting his horse and riding back toward a white house, which subsequently became the center of his new position. Just before reaching it the pain from the wound became so intense that he was obliged to dismount, and was laid upon a blanket spread out upon the ground. He was revived by brandy and assisted to remount. He had hardly risen from the blanket when a solid shot struck in the very center of it, where a moment before he had been lying, and tore up the earth in a savage way. Pleasonton says, when he saw him, about 10 A. M., he was lying on the ground, usually in a doze, except when awakened to attend to some important dispatch. General Couch was temporarily called to the command of the army.

In the meanwhile Stuart was pressing the attack. At one time his left was so strongly resisted that his three lines were merged into one. To a notice sent him that the men were out of ammunition, he replied that they must hold their ground with the bayonet. About this time Stuart's right connected with Anderson's left, uniting thus the detached portions of General Lee's army. He then massed infantry on his left and stormed the Federal works. Twice he was repulsed, but the third time Stuart placed himself on horseback at the head of the troops, ordered the charge, carried the intrenchments, and held them, singing with ringing voice, "Old Joe Hooker, won't you come out of the wilderness?" An eye-witness says he could not get rid of the impression that Harry of Navarre led the charge, except that Stuart's plume was black, for everywhere the men followed his feather. Anderson at the same time moved rapidly upon Chancellorsville, while McLaws made a strong demonstration in his front. At 10 A. M. the position at Chancellorsville was won, and Hooker had withdrawn to another line nearer the Rappahannock. Preparations were at once made by Lee to attack again, when further operations were arrested by intelligence received from Fredericksburg.

Sedgwick, after the departure of the First and Third Corps from his position below Fredericksburg, was still left with twenty-nine thousand three hundred and forty-two troops, which included Gibbon's division of five thousand, but excluded his reserve artillery. On May 2d, at 9.55 A. M., Hooker telegraphed him: "You are all right. You have but Early's division in your front balance all up here." To oppose Sedgwick, Early had his division of seventy-five hundred officers and men, and Barksdale's brigade of fifteen hundred, making nine thousand. In addition, Early had Andrew's battalion of artillery of sixteen guns, Graham's four guns, a Whitworth gun posted below the Massaponax, and portions of Walton's, Cabell's, and Cutts's battalions of artillery, under General Pendleton, making in all some forty-five or fifty guns. At 9 P. M. on the 2d Hooker telegraphed Sedgwick to cross the Rappahannock at Fredericksburg and move toward Chancellorsville until he connected with him, destroying Early in his front. He tells him that he "will probably fall upon the rear of the troops commanded by General Lee, and between us Lee must be used up." This order was issued under the impression that Sedgwick was on the north side of the river, but it found him below Fredericksburg on the south side. He moved up during the night, and on the morning of the 3d, after three assaults, carried Marye's Hill, capturing eight pieces of artillery upon that and the adjacent heights. Wilcox, who was at Banks's Ford, threw himself in front of Sedgwick's advance up the plank road and gallantly disputed it, falling slowly back until he reached Salem Church, five miles from Fredericksburg. When Lee heard that Sedgwick, with thirty thousand men, was marching on his rear, he stopped his projected attack on Hooker and dispatched McLaws with his division and one of Anderson's brigades to re-enforce Wilcox, that Sedgwick might be kept back. McLaws arrived in time to assist Wilcox to repulse Sedgwick's further advance. On the morning of the 4th Early advanced along the telegraph road and regained Marye's and the adjacent hills.

General Lee now determined to crush Sedgwick if possible; so leaving Stuart with Jackson's corps in Hooker's front, he marched to McLaws and Early's assistance with Anderson's division. Anderson reached Salem Church about noon, but the attack did not begin until about six, owing, General Lee says, to the difficulty of getting the troops in position. When the signal was given, Anderson and Early moved forward at once in gallant style, driving Sedgwick across the plank road in the direction of the Rappahannock. The approaching darkness, we are told by General Lee, prevented McLaws from perceiving the success of the attack, until the enemy began to cross the river below Banks's Ford. When the morning of the 5th dawned, Sedgwick had made good his escape and removed his bridges. Fredericksburg was also evacuated. Early was left to hold the lines as before, while Anderson and McLaws returned to Chancellorsville, which place they reached on the afternoon of the 5th in a violent thunderstorm. At daylight on the 6th these two divisions were ordered to assail the enemy's works in conjunction with Jackson's corps, but during the storm of the night before, Hooker retired over the river. One can hardly conceive a greater risk than that taken by General Lee in these operations. For two days Hooker's immense army was kept in place by Jackson's corps, while General Lee assaulted Sedgwick.

The Confederate cavalry operations, from smallness of numbers, were much circumscribed. Stuart only had five regiments at Chancellorsville, three of them being on Lee's left and two on his right, while two more had been left to contend as best they could with Stoneman's ten thousand troopers. Stoneman accomplished nothing. Hooker's official report says that no officer ever made a greater mistake in construing his orders, and no one ever accomplished less in so doing. He returned to the army on the 4th, the day Sedgwick was disposed of. General Lee's official report said that "the conduct of the troops cannot be too highly praised. Attacking largely superior numbers in strongly intrenched positions, their heroic courage overcame every obstacle of Nature and of art, and achieved a triumph most honorable to our arms."

Hooker's General Order No. 49, of May 6th, congratulates his army on its achievements, saying that, in withdrawing from the south bank of the Rappahannock before delivering a general battle, the army has given renewed evidence of its confidence in itself and its fidelity to the principles it represents. That the Army of the Potomac was profoundly loyal, and confident of its strength, and would give or decline battle when its interests or its honor might demand. "The events of last week," said he, "might well swell with pride the heart of every officer and soldier of this army." And then in a letter to Mr. Lincoln, dated May 13th, 1863, Hooker says: "Is it asking too much to inquire your opinion of my Order No. 49? If so, do not answer me. Jackson is dead, and Lee beats McClellan with his untruthful bulletins." It is not known whether Mr. Lincoln ever answered this question. The truth is, the Army of the Potomac was woefully mismanaged. Its commander guided it into the mazes of the Wilderness and got it so mixed and tangled that no chance was afforded for a display of its mettle. General Paxton was killed while leading his brigade with conspicuous courage in the assault of the 3d. Generals A. P. Hill, Nichols, McGowan, Heth, Hoke, and Pender were wounded.

Chancellorsville is inseparably connected in its glory and gloom with Stonewall Jackson. General Lee officially writes: "I do not propose to speak here of the character of this illustrious man, since removed from the scene of his eminent usefulness by the hand of an inscrutable but all-wise Providence. I nevertheless desire to pay the tribute of my admiration to the matchless energy and skill that marked this last act of his life, forming, as it did, a worthy conclusion of that long series of splendid achievements which won for him the lasting gratitude and love of his country."

Jackson's purely military genius resembled Caesar's and Napoleon's. Like the latter, his success must be attributed to the rapid audacity of his movements and to his masterly control of the confidence and will of his men. He had the daring temper and fiery spirit of Caesar in battle. Caesar fell at the base of Pompey's statue, which had been restored by his magnanimity, pierced by twenty-three wounds at the hands of those he had done most for. Jackson fell at the hands of those who would have cheerfully joined their comrades in the dismal, silent bivouacks, if his life could have been spared. With Wolfe, Nelson, and Havelock he takes his place in the hearts of English-speaking people.

General Lee wrote Mrs. Lee from camp near Fredericksburg, May 11, 1863: "In addition to the death of friends and officers consequent upon the late battle, you will see we have to mourn the loss of the good and great Jackson. Any victory would be dear at such a price. His remains go to Richmond to-day. I know not how to replace him, but God's will be done. I trust He will raise someone in his place."

The battle of Chancellorsville increased immensely General Lee's fame. The difference in the numbers of the contestants was very marked. The three corps originally crossed to Lee's front at Fredericksburg were about equal in numbers to the whole of his army, so that Hooker's right flanking wing of four corps represented his numerical superiority.

The tactical and strategical operations of Chancellorsville is a remarkably interesting military study. Two armies seek, like the knight La Mancha, a foe to combat. One is much stronger than the other, and in quartermaster, commissary, and ordnance supplies is vastly superior. The larger army assumes the offensive, and plans to hold the smaller in place with one of its wings, while making a three or four days detour with the other and greater portion to attack it in reverse. The flanking movement is arrested, while the identical tactics proposed are adopted by the other army, which in turn successfully assails their flank and rear, and holds them in the close embrace of a portion of the assailing troops, while two divisions which had been in their original front are countermarched and added to the division left at Fredericksburg. The three then attack and drive over the river the troops which were attempting to get in their rear at Chancellorsville, after which they are marched back to join in the expected battle around Chancellorsville next day, which did not take place because their opponents retreated across the river during the night. The bold conception of Lee was faultlessly executed by officers and men. It is true the wretched terrene assisted him in holding the lines in front of Hooker, for his axes could quickly make it defensible; that the forest concealed Jackson's march, and that an unpardonable negligence permitted twenty-five or thirty thousand troops to pass near a line of battle for many hours and mass for attack a short distance behind one of its flanks.

Had Hooker kept the ten thousand sabers of Stoneman, which he sent away on a fruitless mission, and placed them on the right or in front of his flank, his infantry would not have been surprised; or had he continued his advance on Fredericksburg when first moving out of Chancellorsville, and, pushed his cavalry along the route toward Todd's Tavern and Spottsylvania Court House, the chances of success would have been in his favor. General Lee fought the battle in the only way it could have been won, but the risks assumed were very great. To say that he committed faults is only to say that he made war. Once more the armies surveyed each other from their old camps; twice had one of them attempted the offensive. It was but fair that the Confederates should make the next move.

Lee devoted the few weeks of rest and recuperation which now followed in placing his army in better condition and reorganizing it. He now divided it into three corps instead of two-three divisions to the corps — commanded respectively by Longstreet, Ewell, and A. P. Hill. Ewell had been next in command to Jackson, participating in the glories of his Valley campaign, and maintaining his reputation as an excellent assistant to his great chief. He graduated at West Point in 1840, and served twenty-one years in the United States Army; was in Mexico, and brevetted for gallantry at Contreras and Churubusco; served on the frontier in the dragoons; was forty-three years old; had lost a leg at second Manassas, and was just able to rejoin the army. He succeeded to much of Jackson's spirit and the quickness and ardor of his strokes in battle, was kind-hearted, eccentric, and absent-minded. It has been said this last trait came very near being fatal to him, for, forgetting he had lost his leg, he suddenly started one day to walk and came down on the stump, imperfectly healed, which produced a violent hemorrhage. "Virginia never had a truer gentleman, a braver soldier, nor an odder, more lovable fellow."

A. P. Hill's promotion to a corps commander was bestowed on account of meritorious service. He had graduated at West Point seven years later than Ewell, and was an artillery officer in the United States Army. His bravery at the first Manassas, around Richmond where he drew the first blood — at second Manassas, Harper's Ferry, and at Sharpsburg, had been conspicuous, and drew to him the attention of his commanding general.

The artillery arm consisted of fifteen battalions of four batteries each, besides the batteries of horse artillery, and to each infantry corps was assigned its own battalions of artillery, commanded by its own chief, while the reserve artillery of the whole army was in charge of General Pendleton, Lee's chief of artillery. This arm of the service was well commanded, and was rapidly asserting its claim to the front rank of the artillery armament of an army. Parrott, Napoleon, Whitworth, and Armstrong guns, acquired by capture and foreign purchase, were replacing the 6- and 12-pound howitzers. Longstreet's two absent divisions had returned under their distinguished commander. The cavalry had again been brought together, and was more numerous and effective than ever. At the end of May, Lee commanded a splendid army, numbering present for duty, by the returns of May 31, 1863, 54,356 infantry, 9,536 cavalry, and 4,460 artillery, or a total of 68,352, with over two hundred guns. Its efficiency, confidence, and morale made it worthy of being led by a great chief.

The time for active operations to be resumed had arrived. Lee would have preferred that Hooker should assume the offensive, but as he showed no disposition to do it, the financial condition of the South and the scarcity of supplies made time too precious to wait longer for such action on his part.

Moltke, with his impassive student face, his bent figure, and his periodic pinches of snuff, directing operations as if they were certain calculations, was not more diligent than Lee, as under his canvas shelter he planned the Pennsylvania campaign, and designated, it is said, Gettysburg or its vicinity as the place of battle. It is certain that at that time he foretold his enemy's movements, knew his own, and predicted a meeting in Pennsylvania east of the mountains. Among the results to be reached by a march to Pennsylvania was the relief of the Confederate commissariat. Indeed, when making requisition for a supply of rations, the commissary general is reported to have said, "If General Lee wants rations let him seek them in Pennsylvania." Among other results of a decisive successful battle on Northern soil, might be a recognition of the Confederacy by foreign powers and a lasting peace.

General Lee had been accustomed to expose himself unnecessarily on the field of battle, and about this time his son W. H. F. Lee wrote to him: "I hear from every one of your exposing yourself. You must recollect, if anything should happen to you the cause would be very much jeopardized. I want very much to see you. May God preserve you, my dear father, is the earnest prayer of your devoted son." Lee remarked upon one occasion, when remonstrated with about endangering his life: "I wish someone would tell me my proper place in battle. I am always told I should not be where I am." On May 20, 1863, from camp near Fredericksburg, the general writes to Mrs. Lee in Richmond: "I learn that our poor wounded are doing very well. General Hooker is airing himself north of the Rappahannock and again threatening us with a crossing. It was reported last night that he had brought his pontoons to the river, but I hear nothing of him this morning. I think he will consider it a few days. He has published a gratulatory order to his troops, telling them they have covered themselves with new laurels, have destroyed our stores, communications, thousands of our choice troops, captured prisoners in their fortifications, filling the country with fear and consternation. 'Profoundly loyal and conscious of its own strength, the Army of the Potomac will give or decline battle whenever its interests or honor may demand. It will also be the guardian of its own history and its own honor.' All of which is signed by our old friend S. Williams, A. A. G. It shows at least he is so far unhurt, and is so far good, but as to the truth of history I will not speak. May the great God have you all in his holy keeping and soon unite us again!" On the 31st of May, two days before he began his campaign, he writes: "Camp Fredericksburg, May 31, 1863. General Hooker has been very daring the past week, and quite active. He has not said what he intends to do, but is giving out by his movements that he designs crossing the Rappahannock. I hope we may be able to frustrate his plans in part if not in whole. He has General Heintzelman's corps now, on whom the Northern papers seem to place great reliance. I pray that our merciful Father in Heaven may protect and direct us! In that case I fear no odds and no numbers."

Three days before, Hooker had dispatched to Secretary Stanton that he was certain important movements were being made, and that he was in doubt as to the direction Lee would take, "but probably the one of last year, however desperate it may appear." As Hooker could not be attacked except at a disadvantage, General Lee determined to draw him from his position and transfer the scene of hostilities beyond the Potomac.

This embraced the expulsion from the Valley of Virginia of the Federal force under General Milroy. On the 2d of June Ewell's Corps marched for Culpeper Court House, and a day or two afterward Lee followed with Longstreet's Corps. Hill's Corps was left to watch Hooker and follow as soon as he should retire. A daring commencement of a campaign! Hill, with less than twenty thousand troops, was between Hooker and Richmond, sixty miles away, while Lee, with the other two corps, was at Culpeper Court House, some thirty miles distant in another direction.

Mr. Lincoln and Halleck would not let Hooker attack Hill, as General Lee supposed, because it was "perilous to allow Lee to move on the Potomac while your army is attacking an intrenched position on the other side of the Rappahannock," wrote Halleck. "If left to me," said Mr. Lincoln, "I would not go south of the Rappahannock upon Lee's moving north of it. Lee's army, not Richmond, is your true objective point. Fight him when opportunity offers; if he stays where he is, fret him and fret him."

Hill would have retarded Hooker's progress, falling back toward the defenses of Richmond, while Lee would have taken Washington before Hooker could have countermarched and interposed; or he could have placed his troops in Richmond from Culpeper by railroad in time to support Hill. "No," reiterated the Union President to Hooker, "I would not take any risk of being entangled upon the river like an ox jumped half over the fence and liable to be torn by dogs front and rear without a fair chance to gore one way or kick the other."

Lee's two infantry and his cavalry corps were concentrated around Culpeper by the 7th of June. Hooker knew Stuart was at Culpeper and thought he meant mischief, so determined to break him up, if possible, by sending all of his cavalry against him, stiffened by three thousand infantry.

General Lee reports that on the 9th of June the cavalry under General Stuart was attacked by a large force of Federal cavalry, supported by infantry, which crossed the Rappahannock at Beverly's and Kelly's Fords. After a severe engagement from early in the morning until late in the afternoon, "the enemy was compelled to recross the river with heavy loss, leaving about five hundred prisoners, three pieces of artillery, and several colors in our hands." On the other hand, Hooker dispatched that "Pleasonton pressed Stuart three miles, capturing two hundred prisoners and a battle flag. Our cavalry made many hand-to-hand combats, always driving the enemy before them."

General Lee wrote Mrs. Lee the day of the battle at Culpeper, June 9, 1863: "I reviewed the cavalry in this section yesterday. It was a splendid sight. The men and horses looked well. They had recuperated since last fall. Stuart was in all his glory. Your sons and nephews are well and flourishing. The country here looks very green and pretty, notwithstanding the ravages of war. What a beautiful world God in his loving kindness to his creatures has given us! What a shame that men endowed with reason and knowledge of right should mar his gifts!"

And again on the 11th of the month, from the same place, he wrote: "My supplications continue to ascend for you, my children, and my country. When I last wrote I did not suppose that Fitzhugh (his son) would so soon be sent to the rear disabled, and I hope it will be but for a short time. I saw him the night after the battle — indeed, met him on the field as they were bringing him from the front. He is young and healthy, and I trust will soon be up again. He seemed to be more concerned about his brave men and officers who had fallen in the battle than himself."

The day after the conflict between Pleasonton and Stuart, Ewell left Culpeper, and crossed the Shenandoah near Front Royal, where Jenkins's cavalry brigade joined him, while at the same time Imboden's cavalry was moved to Romney to keep the troops guarding the Baltimore and Ohio Railroad from re-enforcing Milroy. On the 13th Ewell was in line of battle in front of Winchester, and next day he stormed and carried the works there, Milroy, the Union commander, and a few of his men alone escaping. Four thousand prisoners, twenty-eight pieces of superior artillery, wagons, horses, small arms, ordnance, commissary and quartermaster stores were captured. Ewell then entered Maryland. How very daring these movements were! On June 12th, when Ewell was at Winchester, Longstreet was at Culpeper and Hill at Fredericksburg, while Hooker was still, with the larger part of his army, in front of Hill.

Hooker, having at last found that General Lee had left, determined to move too, and issued orders on the 13th for four corps to rendezvous at Manassas Junction. At five o'clock next afternoon Hooker was at Dumfries, some twenty miles north of Fredericksburg, on the road to Washington, and Mr. Lincoln asked him by telegraph if he thought it "possible that fifteen thousand of Ewell's men can now be at Winchester?" and later tells him that the enemy have Milroy surrounded at Winchester, and Tyler at Martinsburg, and asks him if he could help them if they could hold out a few days, and then with habitual humor said: "If the head of Lee's army is at Martinsburg, and the tail of it on the plank road between Fredericksburg and Chancellorsville, the animal must be very slim somewhere. Could you not break him?"

There was nothing now for the Union commander to do except to keep interposed between his enemy and Washington, and Hooker therefore concentrated his troops along the Orange and Alexandria Railroad. The movement of the Army of the Potomac depended on that of the Army of Northern Virginia. As Lee proceeded north, so did Hooker, on parallel lines. Five days after Ewell's departure from Culpeper Court House Longstreet left. His route was east of the Blue Ridge with Stuart's cavalry in his front and on his right flank to mask his position. Hill, who had joined Lee again, was then passed into the Valley behind Longstreet's lines. Hooker was mystified, and pushed his cavalry on Stuart to see what was going on. He thought Stuart was preparing for a raid, "which may be a cover to Lee's re-enforcing Bragg or moving troops to the west." Stuart and Pleasonton had frequent encounters for three days, but the cavalry mask was not torn away, and no information gained by Hooker.

General Lee wrote Stuart, June 22d, that he thought Pleasonton's efforts were made to arrest the progress of his army and ascertain its location, and that "perhaps he is satisfied" that he was afraid the Federals would "get across the Potomac before we are aware"; and that if he found Hooker moving northward, and "two brigades can guard the Blue Ridge and take care of your rear, you can move with the other three into Maryland and take position on General Ewell's right." The same day Ewell was ordered toward the Susquehanna and told "if Harrisburg comes within your means, capture it." Stuart was to go to Ewell's right flank on the Susquehanna, provided (Lee wrote Longstreet) he could be spared from his front, and that he could move across the Potomac if Longstreet thought he could do so without disclosing Lee's plans. He was then guarding Longstreet's front and flank, which brought him under that officer's command. General Lee suggested that Stuart move through Hopewell Gap in the Bull Run Mountains, pass in rear of Hooker, and then cross the Potomac. Longstreet wrote Stuart that if he "crossed by our rear at Shepherdstown it would in a measure disclose our plans," and that he "had better not leave us unless you can take the proposed route in rear of the enemy." The next day Stuart received from Lee an order to cross the Potomac with three brigades, either at Shepherdstown or "east of the mountains in rear of the enemy," and that he must "move on and feel the right of Ewell's troops," then marching toward the Susquehanna. Stuart marched through Hopewell Gap, as suggested by General Lee, and took the route in rear of the enemy as directed by Longstreet. He crossed the Potomac at Seneca, thirteen miles above Washington, the day Lee was at Chambersburg and Ewell at Carlisle. This officer has been unjustly criticized for not being in front of Lee's army at Gettysburg, but Lee and Longstreet must be held responsible for his route. Lee crossed the Potomac west of the Blue Ridge, Hooker east of it, and Stuart between him and Washington.

General Lee continued to march his columns over the river into Maryland and Pennsylvania. Ewell, the first of the invaders, with Jenkins's cavalry brigade and White's battalion under its fine commander, was in advance. His march was directed by Hagerstown to Chambersburg, Pa., and Carlisle, where he arrived on June 27th with two of his divisions. His remaining division, under Early, was sent to York to break the railroad between Harrisburg, Pa., and Baltimore, and seize the bridge over the Susquehanna at Wrightsville. Longstreet and Hill encamped near Chambersburg the day Ewell reached Carlisle. Lee was spreading over Northern territory in order to collect as large an amount of supplies as possible, as well as to draw the Army of the Potomac away from Washington before delivering battle. Under the supposition that the Union army was still in Virginia guarding the approaches to Washington, Lee had issued orders to move upon Harrisburg. Stuart captured a wagon train at Rockville, on the direct road from Washington to Hooker's army, the nearest wagon being taken four miles from Washington city, burned a large number, and marched away with two hundred wagons and their teams, burned the railroad bridge at Sykesville, cut the telegraph wires, drove the Delaware cavalry in confusion out of Westminster, fought Kilpatrick's cavalry at Hanover, Pa., prevented two infantry corps from reaching Meade until the second day at Gettysburg, and drew in pursuit of his three cavalry brigades two Federal cavalry divisions, and after ceaseless combats and night marches reached Dover, Pa., on July 1st. Whole regiments slept in their saddles, their faithful animals keeping the road unguided. Without rations for men, and with horses exhausted, Stuart arrived at Carlisle the day Hill and Ewell were engaged at Gettysburg. He wanted to levy a contribution for rations on Carlisle, but the Federal General "Baldy" Smith, with his Pennsylvania reserves, would not surrender the place. Its probable capture the next day was prevented by news received for the first time of General Lee's position and intentions. Stuart did not know until he received a dispatch from General Lee on the night of July 1st where he was, for the Union army had been between his march and his own army. Leaving Carlisle, he marched at once for Gettysburg, prevented a movement of the enemy's cavalry on Lee's rear by way of Hunterstown, and took his position on the York and Heidelburg roads on the left of his army late on the evening of July 2d.

Cavalry raids are dazzling, but do not generally accomplish enough to compensate for the number of broken-down horses and men. The cavalry chief could not tell Lee when and where Hooker's army crossed the Potomac, because, when it was crossing, he was in its rear, moving to cross the day afterward lower down the same stream, and after that he had no opportunity. It was left to an adventurous scout to report to General Lee, on the night of June 28th, that Hooker had crossed the Potomac and was approaching the south mountains. The information obliged him to draw in his advance and concentrate his army east of the mountain, to prevent his communications from being intercepted. Had Lee had all of his cavalry in Pennsylvania, the irrepressible conflict would not have taken place at Gettysburg, but possibly on Pipe Creek; and had Hooker not detached his cavalry out of his reach, the battle fought at Chancellorsville would possibly have taken place on the confines of Fredericksburg.

On the 29th Hill's corps was directed to move toward Cashtown and Longstreet to follow next day, leaving Pickett's division at Greenwood as a rear guard until Imboden should get up with his cavalry brigade, while Ewell was recalled from Carlisle to Cashtown or Gettysburg, as circumstances might require. As the Army of Northern Virginia was ordered to concentrate in a southerly direction, while Hooker slowly advanced his columns north, it was manifest the two armies must meet. Topographically, Gettysburg was a strategic point, available for concentration by both armies. Roads from Washington, Baltimore, and all points in the section south of it, where the Union army lay in its fan-shaped position, entered it, as well as the roads from Chambersburg, twenty miles off, via Cashtown, and from Carlisle and York.

Lee was coming south to guard his communications and fight if opportunity presented. Hooker was going north to prevent the occupation of so much territory by the detached parts of Lee's army and to deliver battle when opportunity offered. Each army was manoeuvring for defensive combat, but each was prepared to assume the offensive if occasion required, and neither intended to decline an encounter. There was a cry too for blood from noncombatants everywhere — as strong as once resounded in the Roman Coliseum.

The night that Lee heard of the Federal advance crossing the Potomac, a new commander was in the saddle. "Fighting Joe Hooker" had fought his last battle as an army commander. Halleck, after the battle of Chancellorsville, did not want to trust Hooker with the management of another battle, and had been sustained in his opinion by Mr. Lincoln and Secretary Stanton at a council held between them. It was even said that politics was dragged into the subject, and that the friends of Mr. Chase, a prospective presidential candidate, were bound up in the fortunes of Hooker, and that they interposed to prevent his removal, for "the general who should conquer the rebellion would have the disposal of the next presidency." The friends of presidential aspirants were on the lookout for the right military alliance, and it was stated that if it should be Hooker's fortune to bring the war to a successful close nothing would induce him to accept other than military honors in recognition of his services. At any rate, it is certain Hooker naturally resented interference in the field from a general safely shut up in his office in Washington, and properly contended that one man should command all the troops whose operations could be combined against Lee. Halleck not consenting, the difficulty culminated when Hooker requested that Maryland Heights, the gate to Harper's Ferry, be evacuated, that he might mobilize the ten thousand troops there. Halleck refused, and Hooker, now at Frederick, Maryland, finding he was not allowed to manoeuvre his army in the presence of the enemy, asked to be relieved from command, which, being in accordance with the views of the Washington authorities, was promptly done.

CHAPTER 12

GETTYSBURG.

The fifth commander of the Army of the Potomac was Major-General George Gordon Meade, then in command of the Fifth Corps. This officer was born in Cadiz, Spain, in December, 1815, and was consequently forty-six years old. He graduated at West Point in 1835, and was assigned to the artillery arm of the service. A year afterward he resigned from the army, but after six years was reappointed second lieutenant of the Topographical Engineers, and was in Mexico on General Patterson's staff. Meade's father served as a private soldier in the Pennsylvania troops to suppress the "Whisky Insurrection" in western Pennsylvania, and therefore was under General Lee's father, who commanded the forces raised for that purpose. He was afterward a merchant, a shipowner, and a navy agent in Cadiz, but shortly after his son's birth returned to the United States.

In justice to this officer, it may be said that he protested against being placed in command of an army that had been looking toward Reynolds as Hooker's successor, but, loyal to authority, he assumed the command in obedience to orders. His position was environed with difficulties, for he was ignorant of Hooker's plans. Awakened from sleep by General Hardee, the War Department messenger, he had not much time to get any knowledge of them from Hooker, while a battle in the next few days could not be avoided. He determined to continue the move northward through Maryland into Pennsylvania, and force Lee to give battle before he could cross the Susquehanna.

After two days march, he received information that Lee was concentrating and coming toward him, and he at once began to prepare the line of Pipe Creek to await his approach and fight a defensive battle. On the night of June 30th his headquarters and reserve artillery were at Taneytown; the First Corps, at Marsh Creek, six miles from Longstreet and Hill at Cashtown; the Eleventh Corps, at Emmittsburg; Third, at Bridgeport; Twelfth, at Littletown; Second, at Uniontown; Fifth, at Union Mill; Sixth, at Winchester, Md., with Gregg's cavalry, that being his extreme right. Kilpatrick's cavalry division was at Hanover, Pa., while Buford's cavalry guarded his left.

Lee was rapidly concentrating. Longstreet and Hill were then near Cashtown, Hill's advance (Heth's division) being seven miles from Gettysburg, and Ewell at Heidelburg, nine miles away. Had Lee known of the defensive position at Gettysburg, he could have easily massed his whole army on July 1st there; but he was in no hurry to precipitate a battle, and would have preferred to fight at some point not so far from his base.

On the 30th Pettigrew, commanding a brigade of Heth's division, Hill's corps, was directed to march to Gettysburg to get shoes for the barefooted men of the division, but returned the same evening without them and reported that Gettysburg was occupied by the Federal cavalry, and that drums were heard beating on the other side of the town. So Heth told Hill if he had no objection, he would take his whole division there the next day, July 1st, and "get the shoes," to which Hill replied, "None in the world."

Buford, with his cavalry division, reached Gettysburg on the day Pettigrew made his visit, and threw out his pickets toward Cashtown and Hunterstown. In an order of march for July 1st, Meade, not knowing Lee was so near, directed the First and Eleventh Corps, under that excellent officer Reynolds, to Gettysburg; Third, to Emmittsburg; Second, Taneytown; Fifth, Hanover; Twelfth to Two Taverns; while the Sixth was to remain at Manchester, thirty-four miles from Gettysburg, and await orders.

Heth, after his coveted shoes, reached McPherson's Heights, one mile west of Gettysburg, at 9 A. M. on July 1st, deployed two brigades on either side of the road, and advanced on the town. Promptly the few sputtering shots which first announced the skirmish line's opening told him that Buford's dismounted cavalry were blocking the way; and the great struggle which was to determine, like Waterloo, the fate of a continent, and whether there should be one or two republics on this continent, had commenced. Precipitance was neither desired by Meade nor Lee, but "shoes" took command that day, and opened a contest which drew in its bloody embrace one hundred and seventy thousand men. For Reynolds, hearing Buford's guns, hastened to him with the First Corps, Wadsworth's division leading. Hill, who had followed Heth with Pender's division, sent it rapidly to his support, while the Eleventh Corps hastened to the First Corps's assistance. Ewell, with his leading division (Rodes's), at 2.30 P. M. came to Heth's and Pender's support, while Early's division, at about 3.30 P. M., moved in such a way as to attack the Federal flank, and at 4 P. M. the Federal force was in full retreat through the town of Gettysburg, toward the heights to the south of it, where a brigade of Howard's had been posted as a reserve and rallying point in case of disaster when his corps marched to the battlefield. A well-contested combat had occurred between two infantry corps, a cavalry division, and the artillery on one side, and four divisions of infantry, with the artillery, on the other.

Fifty thousand men fought (after all were up), about equally divided in numbers between the contestants. For six hours the battle raged. General Lee reached McPherson Heights about 2.30 P. M., and, getting off his horse, swept with his field glasses the country in his front; he saw the Union troops retreating over the hills south of the town, and ordered Walter Taylor, of his staff, to ride to Ewell and tell him to move on and occupy them, but that he did not want to bring on a general engagement until Longstreet arrived. A false report, however, caused Ewell to send out first one, then another brigade to guard his flank, and while waiting for them and his remaining division under Johnson to get up, the shades of coming night covered his proposed field of operations. Lee had made a good beginning; his troops had captured more than five thousand prisoners, including two general officers, exclusive of a large number of the wounded, and three pieces of artillery. Heth had been slightly, General Scales seriously, wounded, and General Archer captured; his enemy had been driven through Gettysburg with great loss, and General Reynolds, their commander, killed.

The death of this splendid officer was regretted by friend and foe. Able, brave, with military talents of the highest order, his place could not well be filled. His Government recognized his merit, and he was next on the list for the command of the army. Napier's eulogy on Ridge has been happily applied to him: "No man died on that field with more glory than he, yet many died, and there was much glory!"

The Confederate success was not followed up. Lee wanted Longstreet's troops to be present before delivering a general battle, and, perhaps, did not make his order for pursuit positive. He says Ewell was directed to pursue "if practicable." Had Ewell decided to go forward on the 1st of July, the Southern troops would have been in line of battle on Cemetery Heights that afternoon, and Meade would have been occupied during the night in forming defensive lines on Pipe Creek, ten or twelve miles distant, or elsewhere. Heth lost on the 1st twenty-five hundred killed, wounded, and missing, which left him forty-three hundred. The losses in the other division were not so heavy. Allowing them forty-five hundred effectives at the close of the action, would give the four divisions seventeen thousand eight hundred to pursue.

A letter of Hancock's, the officer dispatched by Meade, on hearing of Reynolds's death, to supersede Howard, his senior in command at Gettysburg, says: "When I arrived upon the field, about 3 P. M. or between that and 3.30 P. M., I found the fighting about over; the rear of our troops were hurrying through the town, pursued by the Confederates. There had been an attempt to reform some of the Eleventh Corps as they passed over Cemetery Hill, but it had not been very successful. I presume there may have been one thousand or twelve hundred organized troops of that corps in position on the hill." Twenty-four hundred and fifty men, the shattered remains of the First Corps, were there too, and Buford's cavalry were drawn up upon the plain, making a total of six thousand troops, which could not have offered much resistance against the victorious seventeen thousand of Ewell and Hill, and two hours must elapse before they could receive re-enforcements, and then only at 6 P. M., of two divisions of the Twelfth Corps; but Johnson's division of Ewell's corps reached the town at six, and Anderson's, of Hill's, could have been there too if necessary, which would have maintained the original status.

At sunset two brigades of Sickles's Third Corps arrived; Sickles in person reached the field an hour earlier. They would have been too late, and would have been recalled to Pipe Creek, with all other troops then in motion toward Gettysburg. Two brigades of Pender's and one of Early's division had scarcely fired a shot. Dole's, Hoke's, and Hays's brigades were in good condition. "The artillery was up, and had an admirable position to cover an assault, which could have been pushed under cover of the houses to within a few rods of the Union position." The impartial military critic will admit Confederate camp fires would have blazed at night and Confederate banners waved in the afternoon from the high places south of Gettysburg had Ewell and Hill marched again on the broken and vanquished Federal battalions.

Gettysburg is a small town near the Pennsylvania and Maryland boundary line, ten miles east of the south range of mountains — "the eastern wall of the Cumberland Valley" — and through whose passes Lee's army debouched. The intervening section is described as full of long ridges running north and south, as the mountains do. On Lee's route from Cashtown to Gettysburg one of these ridges is crossed at right angles one and a half mile west of Gettysburg, and a little farther on another; Willoughby Run flows between them, and here the combat of July 1st opened. Closer to the town and about half a mile west of — it is the now famous Seminary Ridge, so called from a Lutheran theological seminary on it, upon which were located the battle lines of portions of two of Lee's corps on the 2d and 3d of July.

Directly south of Gettysburg is the beginning of another series of heights, hills, and depressions which, running in a southerly direction for three miles, terminate in "a lofty, wooded, rocky peak" called Round Top. Adjoining this peak on its north side is Weed's Hill, better known as Little Round Top — a spur to Round Top — "rough and bald." Round Top is at the southern extremity of this ridge. A cemetery at the northern point gives to the ridge its name. Upon this ridge the Federal line of battle was formed. An undulating valley stretches up to Seminary Ridge, a mile distant, and on the elevated tableland between the two runs the Emmittsburg road.

Gettysburg lies at the base of Cemetery Hill, where the ridge bends in a curve, east, and then southeast, to an elevation called Culp's Hill. On Culp's Hill and around this curve, and then south to Round Top for three miles, was the Union battle line. Its shape has been not inaptly compared to a fish hook, with long side and curve. The formation was convex, allowing the Union commander to operate tactically on interior lines, so that he could rapidly re-enforce along his rear the threatened points. The ground in rear of this splendid battle line fell in gradual slope to Rock Creek, affording capital shelter for reserves and trains.

Five hundred yards west of Little Round Top, and one hundred feet lower, is Devil's Den, "a bold, rocky height, steep on its eastern face, but prolonged as a ridge to the west." It lies between two streams in the angle where they meet. The northern extremity is covered with huge bowlders and rocks, forming crevices and holes, the largest of which gives the name to the ridge. Gettysburg is the hub of the wheel, and the Baltimore, York, Harrisburg, Carlisle, Mummasburg, Chambersburg, Millerstown, Emmittsburg, and Taneytown roads the spokes. Lee's troops were distributed over a larger "fishhook," surrounding the smaller or inner one; his extreme left was in front of Meade's refused right at Culp's Hill. Johnson's, Early's, and Rodes's divisions, in order named, were located on the curve and through the town to Seminary Ridge from left to right; then came Hill's corps, stretching south, and later, Longstreet's was formed on its right.

The army smallest in numbers had the longest or outside line, while the largest force occupied in its front a superb defensive position. Lee's army was practically concentrated on the night of the 1st, except his cavalry and Pickett's infantry division, Ewell and Hill in front of the enemy, and Longstreet in camp only four miles in the rear. Meade and his Second Corps were at Taneytown, in Maryland, when the sun went down on the 1st, thirteen miles distant; the Fifth Corps, at Union Mills, twenty-three miles distant and the Sixth Corps, sixteen thousand men, thought to be the largest and finest in the army, was at Manchester, thirty-four miles away. Both Meade and Lee would have preferred to postpone the battle a few days, but were face to face sooner than contemplated.

Meade received Hancock's report on the evening of the 1st, and determined in consequence to fight the battle at Gettysburg, and issued orders for the movement of his troops at 7.30 P. M. that evening. In two hours he left Taneytown, and arrived on Cemetery Ridge at 1 A. M. There is testimony that he did not like his position, and his chief of staff says he was directed to prepare an order to withdraw the army from it.

The Union commander was uncertain whether he could bring his two fine corps, the Fifth and Sixth, on the field in time, and was solicitous about his depot of supplies at Westminster.

As late as 3 P. M. on the 2d, and before he was attacked, he telegraphed in cipher to Halleck that if his enemy did not attack, and he "finds it hazardous to do so, or is satisfied the enemy is endeavoring to move to my rear and interpose between me and Washington, I shall fall back to my supplies at Westminster."

Lee, impressed with the idea of whipping his opponent in detail, on the other hand, was practically ready and eager for the contest next day, and so was his confident army. He was under no obligation, as has been affirmed, to any one to fight a defensive battle; he sought the enemy's soil to gain a victory, whether by offensive or defensive tactics, and his objective point was the Army of the Potomac. He knew the Union army had not yet concentrated, and was anxious to attack before it could. He had already talked with Longstreet, who, following Hill's corps, joined him, at 5 P. M., the afternoon of July 1st, on Seminary Ridge, where both made a careful survey with glasses of the hostile heights opposite, and, it is presumed, attempted to impress him with the importance of an early attack next day, and later that night saw him again. On the same evening he rode into the town of Gettysburg, and met, in an arbor attached to a small house on the Carlisle road north of the town, Ewell, Early, and Rodes.

The Confederate commander was anxious at first that Ewell and Hill should commence the battle, and seemed apprehensive that Longstreet might not get into position as soon as the conditions demanded, but finally yielded to the opinion expressed, that Longstreet should commence the battle by a forward movement on Hill's right, seize the commanding positions on the enemy's left, and envelop and enfilade the flank of the troops in front of the other two corps. Lee left the conference, Early states, with the "distinct understanding that Longstreet would be ordered to make the attack early next morning." General W. N. Pendleton, his chief of artillery and his honored and trusted friend, has put on record that General Lee told him that night, after he [Pendleton] returned from a reconnoissance on the right flank, that he "had ordered General Longstreet to attack on the flank at sunrise next morning."

Hill, in his official report, says, "General Longstreet was to attack the flank of the enemy and sweep down his line." And General Long, of Lee's staff, writes, in his opinion orders were issued for the movement to begin on the enemy's left as early as practicable.

Lee's plan of battle was simple. His purpose was to turn the enemy's left flank with his First Corps, and after the work began there, to demonstrate against his lines with the other two in order to prevent the threatened flank from being re-enforced, these demonstrations to be converted into a real attack as the flanking wave of battle rolled over the troops in their front.

Lee did not like Ewell's bent line — his left was too far around the curve of the fishhook — and decided to draw him more to his right. But that fine old soldier had seen that Culp's Hill was the key to the Federal right, and was told that it was unoccupied at dark, by two staff officers who said they were on its top at that time. At his request he was allowed to remain to secure the hill at daybreak. Hancock, however, reports that he ordered Wadsworth's division with a battery of artillery to take post there in the afternoon. The Federal right was very strong. The woods on Culp's Hill enabled its defenders, with a multitude of axes and spades, to convert it promptly into a fort.

When Lee went to sleep that night he was convinced that his dispositions for battle next day were understood by the corps commanders, for he had imparted them to each one in person. On the morning of July 2d Lee was up before light, breakfasted, and was "ready for the fray," but his chariot of war had hardly started before he found his corps team were not pulling together; the wheel horse selected to start it

141

was balky and stubborn, and, after stretching his traces, did not draw his share of the load with rapidity enough to be effective.

We hear from General Longstreet that on the evening of the 1st he was trying to induce Lee not to attack, but manoeuvre, and on the 2d he "went to General Lee's headquarters at daylight and renewed my views against making an attack; he seemed resolved, however, and we discussed results."

In consequence of the reluctance of the officer next in command to fire the opening gun, Lee was induced to send Colonel Venable, of his staff, to Ewell at sunrise to see whether, after viewing the position in his front by daylight, he could not attack from his flank, but the work of thousands of men during the night made the hills too strong to assault; indeed, Meade was then massing there to attack Ewell. Later, Lee rode there himself, not wishing to drive his right corps commander into battle when he did not want to go, but saw nothing could be done, so at eleven o'clock gave a positive order to Longstreet to move to his right and attack.

It was clearly the duty of Longstreet to carry out his commander's views and not lapse into refractoriness. Lee might possibly have moved toward Frederick on the 2d, and thus forced Meade to fall back to Westminster, but he could not hope to reach Baltimore or Washington, or a point between these cities before Meade. From Westminster cars could have conveyed the Union troops more rapidly than his could have marched, and if Meade had followed him toward Washington he would have been caught between the powerful works then defended by thirty or forty thousand troops and General Meade's army, while the change of base would have greatly endangered his lines of communication.

The closer the two armies approached Westminster the larger the numbers of the Unionists would grow. Lee could not move around now and manoeuvre, or scatter his legions to gather supplies as he had done, because his opponent was uncomfortably near. He could not march en masse, with a host subsisting by pillage, and to concentrate was to starve. There was no alternative, he must fight.

He was obliged to adopt the tactics of William the Conqueror when he invaded England, who, similarly situated, assumed the offensive and defeated Harold at Hastings. Napoleon waited at Waterloo for the ground to dry and lost hours, during which he might have defeated Wellington before the arrival of re-enforcements. Why should Lee lose the advantages of his more rapid concentration? His "superb equipoise" was not threatened by "subdued excitement." His unerring sagacity told him he would catch General Meade partially in position, but he was disturbed because one of his principal officers had not the faith and confidence necessary to win success.

Longstreet's troops not long after daybreak stacked arms near the battlefield. Hood reports he was in front of the heights of Gettysburg shortly after daybreak. General Lee was there walking up and down under the large trees near him, and seemed full of hope, but at times buried in deep thought. He seemed anxious that Longstreet should attack, says Hood. "The enemy is here," Lee said, "and if we don't whip him he will whip us." Hood states that Longstreet afterward said, seating himself near the trunk of a tree by his side: "The general is a little nervous this morning. He wishes me to attack. I do not want to do so without Pickett. I never like to go into battle with one boot off."

McLaws says that his orders were to leave his camp at 4 A. M., but were afterward changed to sunrise; that he reached Gettysburg at a very early hour, and halted the head of his column within a hundred yards of where General Lee was sitting on a fallen tree with a map beside him; that he went to Lee, who pointed out to him on the map the road to his right as the one he wanted him to place his division across, and that he wished him to get there, if possible, without being seen by the enemy; that the line pointed out was perpendicular to the Emmittsburg road, about the position he afterward occupied, and that "Longstreet was then walking back and forth some little distance from General Lee, but came up and, pointing to the map, showed him how he wanted his division located, to which General Lee replied: 'No, general, I wish it placed just the opposite,'" and "that Longstreet appeared as if he were irritated and annoyed, but the cause I did not ask."

McLaws, while waiting, reconnoitered in his front, and was soon convinced that by crossing the ridge where he was then his "command could reach the point indicated by General Lee in half an hour without being seen." McLaws then went back to the head of his column and sat on his horse, he says, and "saw in the distance the enemy coming, hour after hour, on to the battle ground." Wilcox's brigade of Anderson's division, Hill's corps, which had been left on picket on Marsh Creek, east of which stream Longstreet's corps bivouacked the night of the 1st, left its post after sunrise, passed through Hood's and McLaws's divisions, whose arms were stacked, and went into line of battle on Anderson's right at 9 A. M. Wilcox's right rested in a piece of woods, and seven hours afterward, at 4 P. M., McLaws formed in these same woods.

Longstreet admits that he was ordered at eleven to move to the right to attack with the portion of the command then up, but delayed, on his own responsibility, to await General Laws's brigade, which had been detached on picket. His disobedience of orders in failing to march at once with his command then present, many believe, lost to Lee the battle of Gettysburg. With a corps commander who knew the value of time, obeyed orders with promptness and without argument, Lee's movement on Meade's left could have commenced at seven or eight o'clock A. M., with all the chances for success, and there would probably have been no combat on the 3d. The Third Federal Corps was not all up at the hour the attack should have been made, or a division of the Fifth, or the reserve artillery, or the Sixth Corps.

When McLaws and Hood advanced, eight or nine hours afterward, the conditions had changed; Meade, having relinquished his design to attack from his right, had been steadily strengthening his left, and his whole army was concentrated on a splendid defensive line, for Lee had waited, as if he did not purpose to take advantage of his being first prepared to fight. The fine Federal position would have been useless to Meade had Longstreet attacked only a few hours earlier, as he might have done, for in that case he would have secured Round Top, six hundred and sixty-four feet high, and one hundred and sixteen feet higher than Little Round Top, one thousand yards north of it, and crowned it with artillery. "Little Round Top would have been untenable, and Little Round Top was the key point of my whole position," said Meade; "and if they" (his opponents) "had succeeded in occupying that, it would have prevented me from holding any of the ground I subsequently held to the last."

Lee to the strong courage of the man united the loving heart of the woman. His "nature was too epicene," said an English critic, "to be purely a military man." He had a reluctance to oppose the wishes of others, or to order them to do anything that would be disagreeable and to which they would not consent. "Had I Stonewall Jackson at Gettysburg, I would have won a great victory," he said to Professor White, of the Washington and Lee University, after the war, because he knew it would have been sufficient for Jackson to have known his general views without transmitting positive orders, and that Stonewall, quick and impatient, would have been driving in the enemy's flank ere the rays of the morning sun lifted the mists from the Round Tops. If Lee had issued by his chief of staff his battle order for the 2d in writing, as is customary, Longstreet would have carried it out probably in good faith, and not have wasted most valuable time in attempting to convince his commander it was faulty.

The attack on the right, commencing five or six hours after the positive order had been given, even then had some elements of success. Sickles, with the Third Corps, had become dissatisfied with his location, and had moved out about twelve o'clock nearly a mile in his front and taken a new alignment, which became a salient to the main line. Lee was deceived by it, and gave general orders to "attack up the Emmittsburg road, partially enveloping the enemy's left," which Longstreet "was to drive in." There was much behind Sickles, and Longstreet was attacking the Marye Hill of the position only. "Sickles's right was, three fourths of a mile in front of Hancock's left," says Meade, "and his left one quarter of a mile in front of the base of the Little Round Top, leaving that key point unoccupied," which should have been seized by Longstreet before Meade did so with the Fifth Corps.

Sickles's right rested on the Emmittsburg road, and then his line was refused in the direction of the Round Top, making an angle at that point, his corps facing westerly and southerly. Lee wanted to get possession of this point to assail and carry the more elevated ground beyond, but the Fifth Corps had then been placed on the ground referred to, and the Sixth Corps, under sturdy old Sedgwick, had arrived, having marched thirty-four miles since 9 P. M. the previous night, and was in position before the two divisions of Lee's First Corps, which were in bivouac only four miles in rear of the field. The tired troops of the Sixth Corps were massed on the Taneytown road, in the rear of Little Round Top. When that gallant officer, Hood, was informed by his Texas scouts, that instead of attacking Sickles's left he could turn Round Top, he sent three officers, at different intervals of time, to Longstreet, asking to do it, but in every case was answered, "General Lee's orders are to attack up the Emmittsburg road." As he was going into battle Longstreet rode up, and Hood again asked permission to make the move, but was told, "We must obey General Lee's orders." A strange acknowledgment from one who a few hours before had disregarded them.

In twenty minutes Hood was borne from the field badly wounded. The immense bowlders of stone so massed as to form narrow openings offered great obstruction to the advance of Hood's right, and he was exposed to a heavy fire from the crest of the high range adjoining Little Round Top. Had Lee known the situation Hood would have been thrown more to his right. He would not have succeeded in getting around the Union left rear, for the Sixth Corps would have blocked his way, but he would have secured and held Round Top, and in all probability Little Round Top too, for a plunging fire from big Round Top would have cleared its crest and sides of Federal troops.

The Fifteenth Alabama, under the brave Colonel Oates, was on the extreme right of Hood's line, and advanced up the southern slope of the Round Top in the face of an incessant fire from behind rocks and crags that covered the mountain side "thicker than gravestones in a city cemetery." Oates pushed forward until he reached the top of Round Top; the Forty-seventh, Alabama, on his left, also reached the top, where both regiments rested a short time, and were then ordered forward, and went down the north side of the mountain. Oates saw at a glance the great value of the position, but was obliged to obey orders and move on.

With the whole division there, some higher officer with authority to act would have quickly placed artillery on its summit, and the next day from that point Lee would have been master of the situation.

The Alabamians, after reaching the level ground, came upon a second line behind excellent fortifications of irregular rocks, from which was poured a murderous fire into their very faces. After a prolonged and most courageous contest, these brave men were forced back and retreated to the top of the mountain, losing out of six hundred and forty-two men and forty-two officers in the Fifteenth Alabama, three hundred and forty-three men and nineteen officers, killed and wounded. When nearly dark they fell back to the point from which they advanced. This is ample proof that big Round Top was not occupied by Northern troops at dark on the evening of the 2d. Buford's cavalry from that flank had been sent away early in the day to guard supplies at Westminster. Over the splendid scene of human courage and human sacrifice at Gettysburg there arises in the South an apparition, like Banquo's ghost at Macbeth's banquet, which says the battle was lost to the Confederates because "someone had blundered."

Longstreet's two divisions made a superb record, if late when they began to fight. The attack on Sickles's corps was bravely made and bravely resisted; Sickles's left was turned, and had it not been that Warren sent a brigade of the Fifth Corps and battery on Little Round Top, that most important point might have been seized, and, if held, decided the battle. For its possession there was furious fighting. Sickles first, and then Warren, Meade's chief engineer, called Meade's attention to Little Round Top, and Sykes's column, then in motion, was hurried forward to save it. Sykes, Meade reports, was fortunately able "to throw a strong force on Little Round Top, where a most desperate and bloody struggle ensued to drive the enemy from it and secure our foothold upon that important position." Longstreet did not engage Sickles alone, for the Fifth Corps, part of the Second, two regiments of the Twelfth, and a brigade of the First Corps re-enforced him, while he received assistance from Anderson's division of Hill's corps, which went into action with the left of McLaws's division. Lee intended Ewell to make a diversion in his front when he heard the guns of Longstreet, to be converted into a genuine attack if opportunity offered; but Ewell's infantry were under fire as soon as the bugles blew the advance, so a demonstration could only be made by artillery, which was done.

If an early attack on the Union right had been successful, and Ewell, in consequence, had discovered confusion in his front, or that his enemy had weakened his line in his front, then his orders required him to attack because the "opportunity offered"; but Longstreet had not enveloped the enemy's left, and the Federal main line behind Sickles's outlying corps was intact. After the partial success there, Lee directed Ewell to assault with his whole corps. Johnson on the slopes of Culp's Hill to start first, then Early up Cemetery Hill, and Rodes to advance on Early's right.

Johnson had in front a rugged and rocky mountain difficult of ascent — "a natural fortification, rendered more formidable by deep intrenchments and thick abatis." His left brigade carried a line of breastworks of the Twelfth Corps, which (with the exception of Greene's brigade) had gone to support Sickles against Longstreet's attack, and captured prisoners and colors. The firing continued until late at night.

Early had only two of his brigades in the attack, and they made a brilliant charge. His Louisianians and North Carolinians continued to ascend the hill in the face of a blaze of fire, reached and entered the Union works, and while fighting for the battery were attacked by Carroll's brigade and three regiments of fresh troops, and forced to retire, but not in disorder. Had Rodes, as expected, been on his right, with Hill's troops co-operating, permanent possession of the line might have resulted, for Hancock would have been kept busy in his own front, and could not have sent troops to help Howard to hold Culp's Hill.

Rodes reports: "He had commenced to make the necessary preparations, but he had to draw his troops out of town by the flank, change the direction of the line of battle, and traverse a distance of twelve or fourteen hundred yards, while Early had to move only half that distance, without change of front, and before he drove in the enemy's skirmishers General Early had been compelled to withdraw." Gregg, with a division of Federal cavalry and horse artillery, was in position east of Slocum, and with dismounted cavalry and artillery made Johnson detach Walker's brigade to meet him.

When night stopped Johnson he was but a short distance from Meade's headquarters and the Union reserve artillery. A strong night attack then in conjunction with Stuart, who had at last reached the battlefield, would have secured the Baltimore pike in Meade's rear, and perhaps been productive of great results, all of which is easy to see now, but was difficult to know then.

The sentinel stars set their watch over a ghastly field of dead, dying, and wounded soldiers, lying in blue and gray heaps everywhere. Both contestants sought rest, but battlefields are not pleasant couches when dyed in the blood of numerous brave men, who, sleeping their last sleep, lie cold and quiet, while the piteous moans of the wounded pierce the ear and reach the heart. The armies rested without pleasant anticipations of the morrow, knowing well that at the roll call next evening many would not respond. The pickets alone were on duty, the surgeons alone at work.

When Lee summed up his day's work he found on his right that he had gained possession of Devil's Den and its woods, the ridge on the Emmittsburg road with its fine positions for artillery, and made lodgments on the bases of the Round Tops. On his left he had occupied a portion of the Federal works, which gave him an outlet on the Baltimore pike, and was partially successful against the Federal center by penetrating it with Anderson's division of Hill's corps, though ultimately expelled. His cavalry was all up except Jones's and Robertson's brigades; and J. E. B. Stuart was again in the saddle near him. The result of the day's operations, Lee reported, "induced the belief that with proper concert of action, and with the increased support that the positions gained on the right would enable the artillery to render the assaulting columns, we should ultimately succeed, and it was accordingly determined to continue the attack."

His opponent was doubtful what he should do next day; his efforts to prevent an entrance into his lines had been, on the whole, successful, but there had been moments when an unwelcome intrusion seemed inevitable. So he called another council of war at night, having called one before the fighting began. In a little front room not twelve feet square in the Liester House his commanders assembled. "Should the army attack or wait the attack of the enemy?" was the written question they were required to answer; and they voted — as they should have done, being in superior position, with interior lines — to wait, as Lee had done at Fredericksburg, for another attack, and found him more accommodating than Burnside.

General Lee had a difficult task: the lines of his enemy had grown stronger during the night; Slocum, Howard, Newton (in Reynolds's place), Hancock, Sickles, Sykes, and Sedgwick's troops were all before him, and on his right and left flank was a division of cavalry under Gregg and Kilpatrick respectively. The Union flanks, five miles apart on Culp's Hill and the Round Tops, were almost impregnable and difficult to turn. Lee's strategy at Chancellorsville was bold, but his determination to assault the left center of the Union army with his right corps and its supports was consummate daring. "Longstreet, re-enforced by Pickett's three brigades, which arrived near the battlefield during the afternoon of the 2d, was ordered to attack next morning," said Lee, "and General Ewell was directed to assail the enemy's right at the same time." During the night General Johnson was re-enforced by two brigades from Rodes and one from Early.

"General Longstreet's dispositions were not completed as early as was expected," continues Lee, and before he could notify Ewell the enemy attacked Johnson, was repulsed, and Johnson, thinking the fighting was going on elsewhere, attacked in his turn and forced the Union troops to abandon part of their intrenchments, but "after a gallant and prolonged struggle" was not able to carry the strongly fortified crest of the hill. "The projected attack on the enemy's left not having been made," Lee states, "he was enabled to hold his right with a force largely superior to that of General Johnson, and finally to threaten his flank and rear, rendering it necessary for him to retire to his original position about 1 P. M." The delay to attack on the right was but a repetition of the preceding day's tactics. It was impossible to move from different flanks a slow officer and a prompt one "at the same time." Longstreet was delayed, General Lee's report tells us, by a force occupying the high rocky hills on the enemy's extreme left from which his troops could be attacked in reverse as they advanced, and he deemed it necessary to defend his flank and rear with the divisions of Hood and McLaws. "He was therefore re-enforced by Heth's division and two brigades of Pender's (Hill's corps), to the command of which Major-General Trimble was assigned, and General Hill was ordered to afford General Longstreet further assistance if requested, and avail himself of any success that might be gained."

Meade had sent Kilpatrick's division of cavalry — two brigades — under Merritt and Farnsworth, to his left; they arrived there about 12 M., and may have looked, mounted and dismounted, formidable on Longstreet's flank, but were not. Nothing could be gained by charging Longstreet's infantry in the position they held, and later the same day, when it was attempted, the cavalry were easily driven off and held at bay by two or three regiments of Law's brigade on the extreme right. Cavalry charges against infantry cannot be made as formerly, because the improved range and rapidity of fire of cannon and small arms mow them down before they get to close quarters.

The Federal cavalry rendered the greatest assistance, however, to Meade, and his thanks are due to them for keeping out of the fight the fine infantry divisions of Hood and McLaws. The assaulting column was at last formed: Pickett's division of three brigades, five thousand men, was formed in two lines, Kemper on the right, Garnett on his left, and Armistead in the rear. Hill's troops — six small brigades — having passed through the fiery furnace of two days battles, did not number seven thousand men; they were sent to support Longstreet's corps, but, curiously, were placed in an attacking column that had no support.

Four brigades — Pettigrew's, Davis's (a nephew of the Southern President), Brockenbrough's, and Archer's (of Heth's division, under that fine officer Pettigrew, Heth having been wounded the day before) — were placed on Pickett's left, and two, Lane's and Scales's, about twenty-five hundred men of Pender's division, under Trimble, in a second line, while Wilcox's was to march on the extreme right to protect their flank. Thirteen thousand five hundred, or at most fourteen thousand troops, had been massed to attack an army, but with no more hope of success than had the Spartans at Thermopylae, the English cavalry at Balaklava, or the Old guard of the French at Waterloo.

Pickett's division formed at 10.30 A. M. in line nearly parallel and in rear of the rise upon which runs the Emmittsburg road, but rather diagonally to the Union position at the contemplated point of attack. Kemper's right was one thousand eight hundred and sixty yards distant from it, while Pettigrew prolonged the line somewhat en echelon. Pickett's first formation was in one line, Armistead, Garnett, and Kemper from left to right. Garnett's troops were twenty yards only in rear of Wilcox's brigade of Anderson's division, which had been sent out to the front between daylight and sunrise to protect guns then being put in position by Colonel E. P. Alexander, of the artillery. Wilcox states that the four brigade commanders were together nearly all the time before the artillery opened "in the yard near the Spangler House," and that there was no officer present in that open field at any time higher in rank than a brigade general, which differs with an account by the right corps commander, who has said that Lee rode with him "twice over the line to see that everything was arranged according to his wishes, and that there was no room for a misconstruction of his orders." Lee's object was to cut the Federal army at its left center as Marlborough split that of Vendome in the same month one hundred and fifty-five years before, thinking perhaps its right wing could be destroyed first, or driven so far out of the way that he could turn in whole or part against the left wing before it could disentangle itself from the rocks and woods of the Round Tops.

It is fortunate three of General Lee's trusted staff officers — Taylor, Venable, and Long — have recorded that the plan of assault involved an attack by Longstreet's whole corps, supported by one half of Hill's, or all of it if he called for it, or upon the bright shield of the Southern chieftain there might have been a lasting blot. Taylor, the adjutant general of the army, says it was originally intended to make the attack with Hood and McLaws, re-enforced by Pickett, and it was only because of the apprehensions of General Longstreet that his corps was not strong enough that General Hill was called on to support him; and Hill, in an official report, states that his troops were sent to Longstreet "as a support to his corps." Lee "rode along a portion of the line held by A. P. Hill's corps, and finally took a position about the Confederate center on an elevated point, from which he could survey the field and watch the result of the movement." Long says the order for the assault by the whole corps was given verbally by General Lee in his presence and that of Major Venable and other officers of the army. Venerable states that he heard the orders given to support Pickett's attack by McLaws and Hood, and that when he called General Lee's attention to it afterward he said: "I know it, I know it."

A consummate master of war such as Lee would not drive en masse a column of fourteen thousand men across an open terrene thirteen or fourteen hundred yards, nearly every foot of it under a concentrated and converging fire of artillery, to attack an army, on fortified heights, of one hundred thousand, less its two days losses, and give his entering wedge no support! Why, if every man in that assault had been bullet proof, and if the whole of those fourteen thousand splendid troops had arrived unharmed on Cemetery Ridge, what could have been accomplished? Not being able to kill them, there would have been time for the Federals to have seized, tied, and taken them off in wagons, before their supports could have reached them. Amid the fire and smoke of this false move these troops did not know "someone had blundered," but had a right to feel that the movement had been well considered, and ordered because it had elements of success. But there was no chance to write victory upon their fluttering flags. The pages of history which record the magnificent exhibition of human courage drip with the useless sacrifice of blood.

At 1 P. M. on July 3, 1863, two signal guns were fired by the Washington Artillery, and instantly the brazen throats of nearly one hundred and fifty cannon barked defiance at the grim, blue battle line in the distance. Two hours before, Colonel E. P. Alexander, of Longstreet's artillery, reported he was ready to open fire. Seventy-five guns were in position from the peach orchard on the right to the woods on the left, where the Third Corps rested, and nearby, the other corps had as many more, under R. L. Walker. Salvos by battery were practiced, to secure greater deliberation and power. The Union batteries, under the alert and able chief of artillery, Hunt, were ready to return the greeting with seventy-seven guns (Meade had two hundred and twelve guns with his seven infantry corps, fifty with the cavalry, and one hundred and eight in reserve — three hundred and seventy in all), which were placed on the Second Corps line within the space of a mile. It was a grand spectacle, never before witnessed on this continent. Hunt reported he could see "from Cemetery Hill the Southern guns stretched, apparently in one unbroken mass, from opposite the town to the peach orchard, the ridges of which were planted thick with cannon. It was a cannonade to crush our batteries and shake our infantry previous to an assault." Most of the projectiles, he states, passed overhead and swept the ground in his rear. The Union batteries along the Second Corps front suffered heavily, however; wounded soldiers, dead and dying horses, and exploded caissons were on every side. Meade's headquarters, a little to the rear, had been plowed up by the swift-flying missiles, and had been abandoned, forcing Meade to go over to Powers Hill and seek shelter at Slocum's headquarters. The horses of many of his staff were killed. This sublime exhibition, with its great roar, throwing out huge black smoke clouds, was protracted for nearly two hours.

For waste of ammunition on both sides without compensating results it stands unequaled, and towers in unrivaled superiority above all similar displays. One hundred and fifty Southern guns raining metallic tons on the Northern infantry for two hours ought to have made a desert of their lines wide and broad enough to admit an army, but three days work on a strong, natural, and defensive ridge had placed the infantry under cover, and resting securely, they were not "shaken," as those who participated in the charging column can testify. Hunt, with a soldier's instinct, knew so much noise meant a fight with other arms. Anticipating Meade's orders, he gave instructions to cease firing, to let his guns cool, ran up fresh batteries, replenished his limber chests and caissons, and "cleared decks" for the real work to follow. Amid the clamor produced by fiery flashes from nearly three hundred guns, the gray heroes selected to destroy an army lay close under the cover of a friendly ridge.

Longstreet was disappointed when he received the order to make this attack, and wanted to move to the Federal left, but Lee knew his relations with Meade had been too intimate during the last two days and the relative hosts too close for such tactical folly. His right corps chief says he took Pickett, who was to command the charge, to the crest of Seminary Ridge, pointed out the direction to be taken and the point to be assaulted, that he "could see the desperate and hopeless nature of the charge and the cruel slaughter it would cause," and that his "heart was heavy" when he left Pickett; that his objections to Pickett's battle had been overruled, and that the day was one of the saddest of his life, for he foresaw what his men would meet, and would gladly have given up his position rather than share in the responsibilities of that day. Lee, au contraire, was impatiently waiting to see Longstreet's corps and one half of Hill's, or, if necessary, all of it, break, with the force of the tempest which strands navies, through the hostile lines, if the testimony of his staff officers is worthy of credence.

The details of the attack were properly left to the officer who was to make it. Lee did not care whether Hood and McLaws attacked, re-enforced by Pickett and Hill's troops, as at first intended, or whether Pickett led and the remainder followed; but he wanted the muskets numerous enough to plant the victory upon his standards. To fight to a finish a protracted struggle was a bold conception; to give in audacious form a coup de grace to his enemy was the acme of daring. But Lee, calm, quiet, conservative, and self-controlled, was fearless when occasion demanded, as a study of his campaigns will demonstrate.

Colonel E. P. Alexander, the commander of a battalion of artillery of a division of the First Corps, but whose functions had been enlarged that day, a well-equipped, intelligent, and active officer, was directed by Longstreet to station himself at a point where he could observe the effect of the great cannonade; and when he discovered the Federal batteries crippled or silenced to send word to Pickett, who, upon receipt of such notice, was to move forward. At twelve o'clock Alexander, with a courier of Pickett's, stood on a favorable spot on the left side of his guns, and was loaded, like them, with a terrible responsibility. In a short time a note from Longstreet told him if the artillery fire did not drive off the enemy or greatly demoralize them, he would "prefer he should not advise Pickett to make the charge," that he relied a great deal on his good judgment to determine the matter, and expected him to let Pickett know when the moment arrived. That the responsibility and fate of a great battle should be passed over to a lieutenant colonel of artillery, however meritorious he might be, is, and always will be, a subject of grave comment.

Alexander replied that he could only judge of the effect of the enemy's fire by the return fire, that his infantry was but little exposed to view, and that if there was any alteration to this attack it should be carefully considered before opening fire, for it would take all the artillery ammunition left to test this one, and leave none for another effort. To this Longstreet responded in another note that "the intention is to advance the infantry if the artillery has the desired effect of driving the enemy off, or the effect is such as to warrant us in making the attack; when the moment arrives, advise General Pickett, and of course advance such artillery as you can use in aiding the attack."

With Alexander at the time was General Wright, of Georgia, commanding a brigade in Anderson's division of Hill's corps, who practically told him to "brace up," that "it is not so hard to go there as it looks. I was nearly there with my brigade yesterday. The trouble is to stay. The whole Yankee army is there in a bunch." He was further stiffened by hearing "a camp rumor that General Lee had said he was going to send every man he had upon that hill." Afterward it occurred to him that he would ride over and see Pickett and feel his pulse, as it were, and how he felt about the charge. He ascertained that Pickett "seemed very sanguine, and thought himself in luck to have the chance."

By this time Alexander had risen to the height of the great occasion, and felt that he could not let the attack suffer through indecision on his part. "General," he then wrote to Longstreet, "when our artillery fire is at its best I shall order Pickett to charge." It was a fearful order for a subaltern to give, but what could he do? Pendleton, the chief of artillery of the army, offered him nine howitzers from Hill's corps, and Alexander put them in a safe place, to wait until he sent for them, intending to take these guns in advance of Pickett's infantry, nearly to musket range; but they could not be found when he wanted them.

General Pendleton had sent for a part of them, thinking Alexander would not need them; and those remaining had moved to another place, and his courier did not find them. At first Alexander thought he would turn the infantry loose in twenty minutes after the firing began; but when he looked at the enemy's batteries and knew his infantry was protected from the artillery by stone walls and swells of ground, "it seemed madness to launch men into that fire with three quarters of a mile to go at midday under a July sun," and he "could not bring himself to give the word." Then he wrote Pickett, who was in view and in rear of his observation point: "If you are coming at all you must come at once, or I cannot give you proper support; but the enemy's fire has not slackened."

Two minutes afterward the Federal fire ceased, and some of his guns limbered up and vacated their positions. Then he wrote to Pickett, "For God's sake, come quick." Pickett had taken his first note to Longstreet and asked him if the time for his advance had come, and Longstreet bowed his assent; he could not speak, because he says he was convinced that Pickett was going to lead his troops to useless slaughter. Longstreet then rode to Alexander's position, and, upon being told the artillery ammunition might not hold out, directed Alexander to stop Pickett and replenish it; but was told there "was very little to replenish with," and that the enemy would recover from the effect of the fire if there was further delay, and just then, says he, Pickett swept out and showed the full length of the gray ranks and shining bayonets — as grand a sight as ever man looked on — and that on the left Pettigrew stretched farther than he could see. General Garnett, just out of the sick ambulance and buttoned up in an old blue overcoat, riding at the head of his brigade, passed just then, and saluted Longstreet. Alexander had served with him on the Plains before the war, and they "wished each other luck and a good-by" — a last farewell for Garnett. Alexander followed Pickett with eighteen of his guns which had most ammunition, whose fire was very effective against Stanard's Vermont troops. The small thunderbolt had been discharged, and the red-crested wave of assault rolled forward, destined to break into fragments on the murderous rocks athwart its path.

At the word of command, in compact form, with flying banners and brave hearts, the Southern column sprang to the attack. It was a magnificent and thrilling spectacle. "It is well war is so terrible," said Lee at Fredericksburg; "we should grow too fond of it." No such inspiring sight was ever witnessed in this country. Two long lines of angry men, who for two days had been trying to destroy each other, lay within cannon range. Their mutual roar of defiance had ceased when suddenly there swept into the intermediate space nine small brigades of infantry, whose "tattered uniforms and bright muskets," as the smoke of the battle lifted, were plainly in view of both.

The divisions of Hood and McLaws, one half of Hill's corps, and the whole of Ewell's stood like the fixed stars in the heavens as their comrades marched into the "jaws of death." Over the ridge, then a slight wheel to the left, and down the slope with confident step they advanced. The Codori farm building had been passed, and the guides instructed to take a directing point for the Union left center held by the

Second Corps, exposing by the move their right flank to an enfilade fire from the batteries near and on little Round Top.

In an instant the masses in their front were preparing for the shock of battle. "Here they come! Here they come! Here comes the infantry!" was heard on every side. At an average of eleven hundred yards the Union batteries began to open, and solid shot first tore through their ranks, but with no more effect than firing a pistol at the rock of Gibraltar. The skirmish lines, composed of the Sixteenth Vermont and One Hundred and Sixty-sixth Pennsylvania, and parts of Hall's brigade, were next encountered and brushed from their front, as the hurricane sweeps the breast of the mountain.

Screaming shells broke in front, rear, on both sides, and among them; but the devoted band, with their objective point steadily in view, kept step to their music. The space between them and the Federal lines grew rapidly less, and soon they were in the "mouth of hell" within range of the well-protected infantry, and then there came a storm of bullets on every side, before which men dropped in their ranks as ripe fruit from a shaken tree. Still they closed the gaps and pressed forward, though canister was now raining on flanks and front with a terrible destructive fire. Brave men along the Union line could scarcely refrain from cheering at the perfect order and splendid courage exhibited by the Southern soldiers as they staggered on amid death and destruction, like a great pugilist, whose fast-failing strength denotes the loss of the contest, but resolves to stand in front of his antagonist to the last. What was left of the right of the assaulting troops struck the portion of the Federal lines held by Webb's brigade, Second Corps, and from the stone wall drove two Pennsylvania regiments, capturing the three guns in charge of Lieutenant A. H. Cushing and mortally wounding this brave young officer, who had been fighting for an hour and a half after being wounded in both thighs by the cannonade.

The Confederate advance had been thrust into the Federal works, and from the top of the stone wall their battle flags were victoriously flying; the wedge had entered, but the power to drive it through was nearly a mile distant and motionless. What could this handful of heroes accomplish? A second line and a second stone wall was in front of them, while from every side hostile regiments rushed to overwhelm them. Their three brigade commanders had fallen as the brave fall, every field officer, except one, killed or wounded, while their route was red with the blood of their dead and dying. Kemper had been shot down, Garnett killed within twenty-five yards of the stone wall, while Armistead and Lieutenant-Colonel Martin, of the Fifty-third Virginia, fell thirty-three yards beyond Webb's line, moving on with a few courageous followers to attack the second line, which had been hurriedly formed. Brave old Armistead's behavior deserves more than a passing word. When the troops halted at the captured line, seeing still another force in his front, he drew his sword for the first time and placed his hat on its point, so that his men could see it through the dense smoke of the unequal combat, and sprang over the wall, crying: "Boys, we must use the cold steel. Who will follow me?" It is said that when the head of what had been so grand an attack got within a few yards of the second defensive line it consisted of Armistead, his lieutenant, Colonel Martin, and five men; with the destruction of the head the body perished, and one half of those who crossed the road and followed Armistead were killed. To the left of Pickett the four brigades under Pettigrew and the two under Trimble charged. Archer's brigade, under Colonel B. D. Fry, of the Thirteenth Alabama, was on the right and was the directing brigade of the whole force. They made their assault in front of Hays's and Gibbon's division, Second Corps, in the vicinity of Ziegler's Grove. "Stormed at with shot and shell," this column moved steadily on, closing up the gaps made and preserving the alignment.

"They moved up splendidly," wrote a Northern officer, "deploying as they crossed the long sloping interval. The front of the column was nearly up the slope and within a few yards of the Second Corps's front and its batteries, when suddenly a terrific fire from every available gun on Cemetery Ridge burst upon them. Their graceful lines underwent an instantaneous transformation in a dense cloud of smoke and dust; arms, heads, blankets, guns, and knapsacks were tossed in the air, and the moan from the battlefield was heard amid the storm of battle." Sheets of missiles flew through what seemed a moving mass of smoke, human valor was powerless, and the death-dealing guns were everywhere throwing blazing projectiles in their very faces. No troops could advance and live. The fiery onslaught was repulsed as Pickett's division had been, and then the survivors of both came back to their former positions, but not one half of the fourteen thousand. The famous charge was over.

Pickett's column had gone to the front four hundred yards, when Wilcox, whose brigade had not formed part of the attacking column, was ordered by Longstreet to advance in rear of Pickett's right. His twelve hundred Alabamans moved promptly, but were soon subjected to a concentrated fire from the artillery of the Federals; the distance between his left and the smoke-enveloped force which had preceded them increased; his own flank was threatened; he could not see, he reports, what had become of Pickett, so halted and returned, losing two hundred and four killed, wounded, and missing of his five regiments.

Lee was bitterly disappointed at the day's results. He had confidently expected to hurl at least one half of his army on his enemy, cut him in two, and then with a portion of it wheel to the left, annihilate Meade's right, and before troops of his left could recover and unite with the remainder of the army he proposed to give support to that portion of the attacking column holding them at bay. He was playing for big stakes and a decisive victory, which would bring in its train peace to his people and success to his cause. Reasoning, doubtless, that the tendency of separated wings of an army is to seek a reunion in the rear, he had thrown J. E. B. Stuart, with four brigades of cavalry and three batteries of horse artillery, around the Union right rear, so as to be in position to reach his opponent's lines of communication when driven from Cemetery Heights. Between Stuart and the Baltimore pike, two and a half miles off, directly in the rear of General Meade's center were three brigades of Union cavalry, some five or six thousand troops, with horse batteries, under General Gregg, both commands being between the York and Hanover roads.

Stuart had hardly reached the point where he proposed to rest and await developments before he saw, advancing to his front, a heavy line of dismounted sharpshooters, and a cavalry combat followed, creditable to the courage and skill of the contestants. Charges and countercharges were made on both sides, and in the resulting melee there was hand-to-hand fighting, during which the brave and distinguished General Wade Hampton was seriously wounded twice. Both sides claim a victory, but neither were driven beyond the positions originally occupied, to which they mutually retired from a midway charging ground — Stuart to watch his opportunity if Pickett was successful, as first contemplated; Gregg to watch Stuart. One of Stuart's brigades, under Jenkins, had only ten rounds of ammunition, and was therefore ineffective. The great battle of Gettysburg should be an object lesson to students of military science — first, as illustrating the difficulty of carrying strong positions behind which sheltered troops shoot with the latest improved guns; second, the great advantage of celerity of execution after carefully considered plans have matured — a qualification so conspicuous in the careers of Napoleon and Stonewall Jackson.

"This has been a sad day to us," said Lee, "but we cannot always expect to win victories." It was a sad day for the South, for at that time it was "within a stone's throw of peace." Fate was against Lee; the high-water mark of Southern independence had been reached, and from that hour it began to ebb from the mountains of Pennsylvania until lost in the hills of Appomattox. "It is all my fault," Lee exclaimed, and proceeded in person to rally and reform his shattered troops. "There was much less noise, fuss, or confusion of orders than at any ordinary field day; the men were brought up in detachments, quietly and coolly," said an English colonel who rode by his side.

With that wonderful magnanimity which Lee so fully possessed he took all the responsibility on his own broad shoulders, and some of it must be put there. First, the discretion allowed, which separated him from his cavalry; second, the omission of positive orders to Ewell to advance on the evening of the 1st, and the failure to replace an officer who opposed his plans with one who would have entered into them heartily, and readily cooperated with him to "whip the enemy in detail."

In justice to Stuart, it may be said that he did not foresee that a marching, intervening, hostile army would keep him away from Lee so long, or that he would be required before he could get to the Susquehanna, and it is fair to Ewell to recall his instructions about not bringing on a general battle, the absence of a division of his corps, and the false alarm of an advance on his left, after the battle of the 1st was over; but it will be difficult to comprehend how two thirds of his right corps, which lay four miles behind a battlefield the night before, did not get into action until 4 P. M. on the succeeding day, in spite of the "subdued excitement," the earnest aggressiveness, and the reported utterances of the commanding general; and hard to palliate the conduct of a corps commander, who acknowledged the reception of a direct order at 11 A. M. to attack with his troops then up, and did not get into action for five hours thereafter, because he took the responsibility of waiting for one of his brigades to arrive — a delay which allowed the remaining Union troops to reach the battlefield before he did.

The delay in getting two or three miles to the right, after the early hour Longstreet's command got near Lee's headquarters, cannot be wholly laid at the door of his guide — Lee's engineer officer, Colonel S. P. Johnston. That officer states he called attention to the fact that the road they were following would pass over a hill in view of the Federal line, and pointed out a shorter route across a field screened from observation; but the corps commander preferred the road, and followed it to the top of the hill, then halted, and changed the position of his divisions in column. At that time the distance to the place Hood occupied was only a mile and a half, and could have been reached, Johnston says, in less than an hour. And, finally, if the positive assertions of Lee's staff officers can be believed — and they must be, from their well-known high character she disobeyed orders when he attacked with one third and not with his whole corps. Lee knew all the facts, for, in addition to what was said to Ewell, Early, and Pendleton, he told Governor Carroll, of Maryland, "that the battle would have been gained if General Longstreet had obeyed the order given him and attacked early instead of late; that Longstreet was a brilliant soldier when once engaged, but the hardest man to move in my army."

At 1 A. M. on the 4th General Imboden was sent for by Lee to get orders about the movements of the trains and ambulances which his command was to escort to the Potomac, and says that Lee, after expressing his admiration for the splendid behavior of the troops in "the grand charge," added, "and if they had been supported as they were to have been, but, for some reason not yet fully explained to me, were not, we would have held the position and the day would have been ours." Military critics are not able to understand why the official head of the officer did not "drop in the basket." They do not know Lee or his great heart, or that self-denying for himself, self-suffering for others, which made him live in a tent for fear of incommoding the occupants of houses, eat the most frugal food, or sit in the most uncomfortable chair, lest some other person might get it.

He could not harden himself to hew to the strict military line in whatever directions the chips might fall, but tried to believe that the reasons given for noncompliance with implied or direct instructions might possibly have some force, that the delays on the 2d could not be foreseen, and that the right flank of the assaulting column on the 3d might have suffered if not protected by two fine divisions of infantry. Captain Mangold, a German officer, Instructor of Artillery and Engineer in the Royal Academy, Berlin, and a distinguished and active military student, says the defect in General Lee's military character was a too kindly consideration for incompetent officers, resulting from an excess of good-nature.

The intelligent and impartial critic must admit the offensive dispositions of Lee skillful; the Union left on the 2d to a late hour was most vulnerable, and upon it the attack was designed; while the assault on the 3d, if not surrounded with as many chances of success as on the former day, was made at a point where, if successful, he would have secured the great roads to Baltimore and Washington. It was not unlike Napoleon's tactics at Waterloo; the artillery fire was opened there on the allied right, and Reille directed to carry Hougoumont, but the real plan of the great soldier was to break through Wellington's left center, which he ordered to be assaulted with D'Erlon's whole corps supported by Loban's, to drive back the allies on their own right, and secure the great road to Brussels before the helmets of the Prussian squadrons could be seen on the heights of St. Lambert. Lee, too, was infused with the confidence of the fighting power of an army "trembling with eagerness to rush upon the enemy," though occupying very strong positions and with a numerical superiority of at least thirty thousand.

The numbers on each side in this great contest have been variously given. Colonel Walter Taylor, Lee's adjutant general, among whose duties was the consolidation of the corps returns into the army returns, and who, after the war, examined the Federal archives with much care, puts Meade's army at one hundred and five thousand and Lee's at sixty-two thousand, and in his Four Years with General Lee gives his reasons. The difference in these numbers is forty-three thousand, so the statement that the Army of the Potomac had thirty thousand more than the Army of Northern Virginia at the battle of Gettysburg, seems conservative. Meade did not use them all. His largest corps — the Sixth, some sixteen thousand men — was in reserve and remained intact, only losing two hundred and forty-two in killed, wounded, and missing. Lee had no reserve.

The loss in each army was about the same, Meade's killed being 3,072; wounded, 14,477; missing, 5,434. Lee's report claims nearly 7,000 prisoners, which makes a total of 23,003. In Lee's, killed, 2,592; wounded, 12,709; missing, 5,150; total, 20,451. It will thus be seen that not only is the aggregate loss nearly equal, but that the killed, wounded, and missing respectively does not vary much. Lee's loss was the greatest on the two last days of the combat, Meade's the first day. In the great struggle thirty thousand men were killed and wounded in both armies. The killed, wounded, and missing of the French at Waterloo have been reported at twenty-five thousand, the Anglo-Belgians at fifteen thousand, Napoleon having seventy-two thousand men, and Wellington sixty-eight thousand, a total of one hundred and forty thousand, while the total of the Army of the Potomac and the Army of Northern Virginia was about one hundred and sixty thousand.

Both armies mourned the death of brave men and competent officers. In the Army of the Potomac four general officers were killed — Reynolds, Vincent, Weed, and Zook — and thirteen wounded, viz., Hancock, Sickles, Gibbon, Warren, Butterfield, Barlow, Doubleday, Paul, Brook, Barnes, Webb, Stanard, and Graham. In the Army of Northern Virginia five general officers were killed — Pender, Garnett, Armistead, Barksdale, and Semmesand nine wounded, viz., Hood, Hampton, Heth, J. M. Jones, G. T. Anderson, Kemper, Scales, and Jenkins.

Meade showed no disposition to assume the offensive after Pickett's repulse. Like Lee at Fredericksburg, he did not want to lose the advantages of position, and was not certain the battle was over. The relative numbers in each army were still about the same, for their losses did not vary much, and the greater part of Lee's army was ready to receive him; he might have been repulsed in turn, producing perhaps other combinations and other results. Lee's ammunition was short, it is true — a fact which was unknown to him when the assault was made, but there was sufficient to still make "many tongues of flame." The natal day of American liberty broke upon both armies occupying nearly the same position, except that Lee had drawn in his left and retired it to a new line out of the town covering his lines of communication, and at the same time strengthened his right by defensive works at right angles to his main line to guard against any flank attack there.

The Southern leader knew on the night of the 3d that he could no longer resume the offensive, and there was nothing to be done except to withdraw from Meade's front. While not declining but rather inviting an attack on the 4th, he had started his long trains, his prisoners and such of his wounded as could bear transportation, back to the Potomac at Williamsport under a cavalry escort, and was busy in burying his dead and gathering up the badly wounded for treatment. At dark, in the midst of a heavy rain storm, the army was put in motion by the Fairfield road which crossed the South Mountain range seven miles south of Cashtown, being the direct road to Williamsport; but the rain and mud so impeded progress that the rear corps — Ewell's — did not leave Gettysburg until late in the forenoon of the 5th. With the exception of the loss of some wagons and ambulances by cavalry attacks, there was no interruption to the retrograde movement.

Lee reached Hagerstown, Md., on the 6th, the same day his trains arrived at Williamsport, a few miles distant. On account of the swollen condition of the Potomac from recent rains, and the destruction of the pontoon bridge at Falling Waters, a short distance below, by a roving detachment sent by French at Harper's Ferry, Lee could not cross his impedimenta or his army over the river, but sent the wounded and prisoners over in boats. Calm and quiet as usual, he had a line of defense skillfully traced to cover the river from Williamsport to Falling Waters, and confidently awaited the subsidence of the angry flood and the approach of his opponent. His cavalry had guarded his flanks in the retreat and had saved his trains at Williamsport from an attack of the Union cavalry before his army reached there, and had a creditable affair at Hagerstown.

Six days after his arrival, Meade, marching from Gettysburg by a different route from that pursued by Lee, began to deploy his legions in his front. Lee's position was not altogether agreeable, a rapid, rolling, impassable river sweeping by his rear and a powerful army going into line of battle in his front. Meade was very deliberate and circumspect at Gettysburg, for he did not forget the bullet holes through his hat when he attacked on his left at Fredericksburg, or the knowledge gained of the unfavorable conditions always surrounding an attacking force. He was still waiting further demonstrations from Lee, and when night appeared without a movement he called a council of his corps commanders, and in writing asked: First, "Shall the army remain here?" Second, "If we remain here shall we assume the offensive?" And then wanted to know if they deemed it expedient to move toward Williamsport through Emmittsburg, or if his enemy was retreating, should he pursue on the direct line of his retreat. The majority of the responses to his first question were in favor of remaining at Gettysburg, but all voted against assuming the offensive, for councils of war rarely, if ever, decide to fight. Pleasonton, his cavalry commander, was very clamorous the day before, for he says he rode up to Meade after the repulse of Pickett and said: "General, I will give you an hour and a half to show yourself a great general; order the army to advance while I take the cavalry, get in Lee's rear, and we will finish the campaign in a week."

While this advice, if followed, might have been of great benefit to Lee, its most remarkable feature was its presumption. Thirty-six hours after Lee abandoned the field of Gettysburg, Meade, recalling Sedgwick, who had gone toward Fairfield, marched from Gettysburg south to Frederick, Md., thence slowly around by Middletown and the old Sharpsburg battlefield to Lee's position. While he was moving around the horseshoe, General Lee, with a good start, had gone across from heel to heel, and, had it not been for high water, would have been in Virginia before the last of the Army of the Potomac left the battlefield of Gettysburg.

Meade telegraphed Halleck on the 6th that if he could get the Army of the Potomac in hand he would attack Lee if he had not crossed the river, but hoped if misfortune overtook him that a sufficient number of his force would reach Washington and, with what was already there, make it secure. Halleck, from his office in Washington, urged him to "Push forward and fight Lee before he can cross the Potomac." And Mr. Lincoln was cramming him with the comforting information that Vicksburg, on the Mississippi, had surrendered to Grant on July 4th, and that if "Lee's army could be destroyed, the rebellion would be over."

While waiting at Williamsport General Lee received the news of the capture (by raiding Federal cavalry) of his son, General W. H. F. Lee, who was wounded at Brandy Station on June 10th, and had been taken to Hickory Hill, the residence of the Wickhams, near Hanover Court House. He wrote Mrs. Lee: "I have heard with great grief that Fitzhugh has been captured by the enemy. Had not expected that he would have been taken from his bed and carried off; but we must bear this additional affliction with fortitude and resignation, and not repine at the will of God. It will eventuate in some good that we know not of now. We must all bear our labors and hardships manfully. Our noble men are cheerful and confident. I constantly remember you in my thoughts and prayers."

On July 12th, in camp near Hagerstown, Lee heard his son had been carried to Fort Monroe, and wrote: "The consequences of war are horrid enough at best surrounded by all the amelioration of civilization and Christianity. I am very sorry for the injuries done the family at Hickory Hill, and particularly that our dear old Uncle Williams in his eightieth year should be subjected to such treatment. But we cannot help it and must endure it. You will, however, learn before this reaches you that our success at Gettysburg was not so great as reported. In fact, that we failed to drive the enemy from his position, and that our army withdrew to the Potomac. Had the river not unexpectedly risen all would have been well with us; but God in his all-wise providence willed otherwise, and our communications have been interrupted and almost cut off. The waters have subsided to about four feet, and if they continue, by to-morrow I hope our communications will be open. I trust that a merciful God, our only hope and refuge, will not desert us in this hour of need, and will deliver us by his almighty hand, that the whole world may recognize his power, and all hearts be lifted up in adoration and praise of his unbounded loving-kindness. We must, however, submit to his almighty will whatever that may be. May God guide and protect us all is my constant prayer."

The Federal commander could not decide to attack Lee, though he had been heavily re-enforced, and called another council of war on the 13th. All his corps commanders opposed attacking except two. Later that day Halleck telegraphed him to "call no council of war. It is proverbial that councils of war never fight. Don't let the enemy escape." The Washington assaults had been so continuous that the Union commander, in spite of the council's decision, advanced his army on the 14th with a view of attacking, if justified by a closer examination; but on the night of the 13th the Army of Northern Virginia recrossed the river at Williamsport, and on the pontoon bridge at Falling Water, which had been repaired. "The escape of Lee's army without another battle has created great dissatisfaction in the mind of the President," said Halleck, "and it will require an energetic pursuit on your part to remove the impression that it has not been sufficiently active heretofore." To a high — minded, meritorious, conscientious officer like Meade this censure was irritating. His request to be immediately relieved was declined on the ground that the dispatch was intended as a "stimulus."

The river was still deep though fordable. Ewell crossed by 8 A. M. on the 14th, but the passage of Longstreet and Hill was not completed until! P. M. Had Meade made a vigorous attack in the forenoon he might have defeated and captured the portion of Lee's army which had not yet crossed. About 1 A. M. his cavalry, supported by artillery, appeared in front of Heth's division, which, acting as rear guard, was first encountered, and Brigadier-General Pettigrew, "an officer of great promise and merit," was killed. As soon as the bridge was clear Hill began to cross. The advance of the Federals cut off some of Hill's troops, who fell into their hands, as well as men from various commands, who, Lee reported, "lingered behind overcome by previous labors and hardships and the fatigues of a most trying night march, supposed to amount in all to about five hundred men, together with a few broken-down wagons and two pieces of artillery which the horses were not able to draw through the mud."

The Union commander made no effort to follow the Army of Northern Virginia across the river, except with Gregg's cavalry, which was attacked by two of Stuart's brigades and driven back with loss. Lee proceeded to Bunker Hill and its vicinity, intending to cross the Shenandoah and move into Loudoun County, Va.; but that river was past fording, and when it subsided, Meade, who had crossed the Potomac east of the Blue Ridge, seized the passes Lee designed to use and moved along the eastern slope of the mountains, as if to cut off Lee's communications with his capital. To prevent this, Lee crossed Chester Gap and went into Culpeper, his advance reaching Culpeper Court House July 24th. Afterward, with a view of placing his force in a position to move readily to oppose the enemy, should he proceed south, and to better protect Richmond, he made the Rapidan his defensive line. While at Bunker Hill he wrote Mrs. Lee on July 15th: "The army has returned to Virginia. Its return is rather sooner than I had originally contemplated, but, having accomplished much of what I proposed on leaving the Rappahannock — namely, relieving the Valley of the presence of the enemy, and drawing his army north of the Potomac — I determined to recross the latter river. The enemy, after centering his forces in our front, began to fortify himself in his position and bring up his troops, militia, etc., and those around Washington and Alexandria. This gave him enormous odds. It also circumscribed our limits for procuring subsistence for men and animals, which, with the uncertain state of the river, rendered it hazardous for us to continue on the north side. It has been raining a great deal since we first crossed the Potomac, making the roads horrid and embarrassing our operations. The night we recrossed it rained terribly; yet we got all over safe, save such vehicles as broke down on the road from the mud, rocks, etc. We are all well. I hope we will yet be able to damage our adversaries when they meet us, and that all will go right with us. That it should be so we must implore the forgiveness of God for our sins and the continuance of his blessings. There is nothing but his almighty power that can sustain us. God bless you all."

And from Camp Culpeper, July 26, 1863: "After crossing the Potomac, finding that the Shenandoah was six feet above fording stage, and having waited a week for it to fall so that I might cross into Loudoun, fearing that the enemy might take advantage of our position and move upon Richmond, I determined to ascend the Valley and cross into Culpeper. Two corps are here with me. The third passed Thornton's Gap, and, I hope, will be in striking distance to-morrow. The army has labored hard, endured much, and behaved nobly. It has accomplished all that could be reasonably expected. It ought not to have been expected to perform impossibilities, or to have fulfilled the anticipations of the thoughtless and unreasonable." Meade crossed the Potomac at Harper's Ferry and Berlin on pontoon bridges, moved through Loudoun and Fauquier, forcing Lee to conform to his movements, so that when he eventually took up the line of the Rappahannock, Lee occupied a parallel line on the Rapidan. From his tent in Culpeper he wrote Mrs. Lee on August 2d: "I have heard of some doctor having reached Richmond who had seen our son at Fort Monroe. He said that his wound was improving, and that he himself was well and walking about on crutches. The exchange of prisoners that had been going on has for some cause been suspended, owing to some crotchet or other, but I hope will soon be resumed, and that we shall have him back soon. The armies are in such close proximity that frequent collisions are common along the outposts. Yesterday the enemy laid down two or three pontoon bridges across the Rappahannock and crossed his cavalry and a large force of his infantry. It looked at first as if it were the advance of his army, and, as I had not intended to deliver battle, I directed our cavalry to retire slowly before them and to check their too rapid pursuit. Finding later in the day that their army was not following, I ordered out the infantry and drove them back to the river. I suppose they intended to push on toward Richmond by this or some other route. I trust, however, they will never reach there."

The Army of the Potomac seeming reluctant to advance, General Lee, having made his campaign, did not then propose to do so. In the rest following, his thoughts turned to the operations at Gettysburg, and the difficulties and dangers of the campaign. He grew sensitive under press criticisms, it being charged that nothing had been accomplished, and began to depreciate himself and rate too low his high military abilities. He had voluntarily assumed the faults of his subordinates. "The twin disasters of Gettysburg and Vicksburg," with a surrender of thirty thousand men at Vicksburg, were dispiriting, and the thought that he was held in some degree responsible for one of them seized him.

Gradually the conclusion was reached that perhaps he was occupying a position which might be filled by one who could render greater service with the means at command. On August 8th, from his camp in Orange, General Lee wrote the Southern President "that the general remedy for the want of success in a military commander is his removal," and that his reflections had prompted him "to propose to your Excellency the propriety of selecting another commander for this army"; that he did not know how far the expressions of discontent in the public journals extended in the army; his brother officers had been too kind to report it, and so far the troops too generous to exhibit it. He begged Mr. Davis to take measures to supply his place, because he could not accomplish what he himself desired; how, then, could he fulfill the expectations of others? He confessed his sight was not good, and that he was so dull that in making use of the eyes of others he was frequently misled.

"Everything, therefore," he wrote, points to the advantages to be derived from a new commander, and I the more anxiously urge the matter upon your Excellency from my belief that a younger and abler man than myself can readily be obtained. I know that he will have as gallant and brave an army as ever existed to second his efforts, and it would be the happiest day of my life to see at its head a worthy leader — one that would accomplish more than I can perform and all that I have wished. I hope your Excellency will attribute my request to the true reason — the desire to serve my country and to do all in my power to insure the success of her righteous cause.

I have no complaints to make of any one but myself. I have received nothing but kindness from those above me, and the most considerate attention from my comrades and companions in arms. To your

Excellency I am specially indebted for uniform kindness and consideration. You have done everything in your power to aid me in the work committed to my charge without omitting anything to promote the general welfare. I pray that your efforts may at length be crowned with success, and that you may long live to enjoy the thanks of a grateful people.

The reply of Mr. Davis is refined in sentiment and tender in phrase:

I admit the propriety of your conclusions that an officer who loses the confidence of his troops should have his position changed, whatever may be his ability; but when I read the sentence I was not at all prepared for the application you were about to make. Expressions of discontent in the public journals furnish but little evidence of the sentiment of the army. I wish it were otherwise, even though all the abuse of myself should be accepted as the results of honest observation. Were you capable of stooping to it, you could easily surround yourself with those who would fill the press with your laudations, and seek to exalt you for what you had not done, rather than detract from the achievements which will make you and your army the subject of history and the object of the world's admiration for generations to come. But suppose, my dear friend, that I were to admit, with all their implications, the points which you present, where am I to find the new commander who is to possess the greater ability which you believe to be required? I do not doubt the readiness with which you would give way to one who could accomplish all that you have wished, and you will do me the justice to believe that if Providence should kindly offer such a person for our use I would not hesitate to avail myself of his services.

My sight is not sufficiently penetrating to discover such hidden merit, if it exists, and I have but used to you the language of sober earnestness when I have impressed upon you the propriety of avoiding all unnecessary exposure to danger, because I felt our country could not bear to lose you. To ask me to substitute you for someone, in my judgment, more fit to command, or who would possess more of the confidence of the army or of the reflecting men of the country, is to demand an impossibility. It only remains for me to hope that you will take all possible care of yourself, that your health and strength will be entirely restored, and that the Lord will preserve you for the important duties devolved upon you in the struggle of our suffering country for the independence which we have engaged in war to maintain.

The commanding generals of both armies, upright in character and scrupulous in the performance of their respective duties, were naturally sensitive to criticism, and the curious spectacle was presented that, after a gigantic and fierce contest against each other, both should ask to be relieved from their commands. Fancy the grim veterans of the Army of Northern Virginia paraded in their camp grounds in that month of August, 1863, to hear the announcement that Mr. Davis had accepted General Lee's resignation. There would have resounded from flank to flank "Le roi est mort!" but when the "younger and abler man" assumed command, the mummies of the Nile, or the bones beneath the ruins of Pompeii, could not be more silent than the refusal of these heroes to shout to Robert E. Lee's successor, "Vive le roi!" The Angel of Peace would have appeared in the hour General Lee bid farewell to the Army of Northern Virginia and mounted Traveler to ride away, for the rapid termination of the war would have simplified the duties of "the younger and abler man." Traveler, the most distinguished of the general's war horses, was born near the Blue Sulphur Springs, in West Virginia, and was purchased by General Lee from Major Thomas L. Broun, who bought him from Captain James W. Johnston, the son of the gentleman who reared him. General Lee saw him first in West Virginia and afterward in South Carolina, and was greatly pleased with his appearance. As soon as Major Broun ascertained that fact the horse was offered the general as a gift, but he declined, and Major Broun then sold him. He was four years old in the spring of 1861, and therefore only eight when the war closed. He was "greatly admired for his rapid, springy walk, high spirit, bold carriage, and muscular strength." When a colt he took the first premium at the Greenbrier Fair, under the name of Jeff Davis. The general changed his name to Traveler. He often rode him in Lexington after the war, and at his funeral Traveler followed the hearse. He was appraised by a board in August, 1864, at $4,600 in Confederate currency.

Though Lee was ready to cover his face with his mantle and die like the Athenian, it would have broken his heart to have separated himself from troops who, with empty haversacks, shoeless feet, tattered uniforms, but full cartridge boxes and bright bayonets, had with such undaunted courage nobly supported him at all times. And where would the Southern President have found an officer who was superior in vigorous strategy, fertility of resource, power of self-command, influence over others, patient endurance, or one more composed in victory or dignified in defeat?

An English officer described him in the Pennsylvania campaign as having courtly manners and being full of dignity; that he had none of the small vices — such as smoking, drinking, chewing — and his bitterest enemy never accused him of any of the greater ones; that Lee was the handsomest man of his age that he ever saw — "broad shoulders, well made, well set up, a thorough soldier in appearance." He generally wore a long gray jacket with three stars on the collar, blue pants tucked into his Wellington boots, and a high felt hat. He never carried arms, was always neat in dress and person, and on the most arduous marches looked smart and clean, and, "what is very pleasing to an Englishman, he rides a handsome horse, which is extremely well groomed." The removal from the command of the Union army of such an excellent officer as Meade would have been an act of kindness to the Confederates, the appreciation of which would have been increased if Halleck had been appointed his successor.

The season of repose which now followed was much enjoyed by both sides. Lee was employed in looking after the welfare of his troops, for their rations and clothing were both getting scarce. He took great interest in the religious progress of his soldiers, and did everything in his power to promote sacred exercises in his camps. The relative location of the hostile forces made partial reduction of their numbers comparatively safe. If the Army of the Potomac did not want a battle, it could fall back on the defenses of Washington. If the Army of Northern Virginia declined the encounter, it could withdraw to the Richmond line.

At this period it was determined to re-enforce General Bragg in the West with two divisions of Longstreet's corps, to enable him to defeat the Federal General Rosecrans, which he did at Chickamauga, while the third division — Pickett's — should be detached for duty south of the James River.

Meade then crossed over the Rappahannock and occupied Culpeper and the country between the two rivers, so as to be closer to Lee should he decide to resume offensive operations, but his plans were set aside by troops being detached from him also. The Eleventh and Twelfth Corps under Hooker were sent West, and a considerable number to South Carolina and New York — to this latter place to prevent riots resulting from an enforcement of the recruiting draft. Meade and Lee for some weeks, with reduced forces, simply observed each other. From his camp near Orange Court House, August 23, 1863, General Lee wrote Mrs. Lee that he hears his son is "doing well, is walking about, and has everything he wants except his liberty. You may see that a distinguished arrival at Washington is chronicled in the papers of that city — Miss Catherine Burke. She is reported to have given interesting accounts of the Lee family. (This was one of the colored servants from Arlington.) My camp is near Mr. Erasmus Taylor's house, who has been very kind in contributing to our comfort. His wife sends us every day buttermilk, loaf bread, ice, and such vegetables as she has. I cannot get her to desist, though I have made two special visits to that effect. All the brides have come on a visit to the army — Mrs. Ewell, Mrs. Walker, Mrs. Heth, etc. General Meade's army is north of the Rappahannock, along the Orange and Alexandria Railroad. He is very quiet." And again, September 4, 1863: "You see I am still here. When I last wrote, the indications were that the enemy would move against us any day; but this past week he has been very quiet, and seems at present to continue so. I was out looking at him yesterday from Clark's mountain. He has spread himself over a large surface, and looks immense, but I hope will not prove as formidable as he looks. He has, I believe, been sending off some of his troops to re-enforce Rosecrans, and has been getting up others; among them several negro regiments are reported. I can discover no diminution." And on September 18, 1863, from the same camp he tells her: "The enemy state that they have heard of a great reduction in our forces here, and are now going to drive us back to Richmond. I trust they will not succeed. But our hope and refuge is in our merciful Father in heaven."

CHAPTER 13

CAMPAIGN IN VIRGINIA. — BRISTOL STATION. — MINE RUN. —
WILDERNESS.

For three weeks Lee waited, hoping to be attacked, and then suddenly, on October 9th, put his own army in motion with a design of making a wide circuit around his antagonist's right, to manoeuvre him out of Culpeper to his rear, and force him to deliver battle by intercepting his march toward Washington. He left a small force of infantry and cavalry to hold his old line on the Rapidan, which the Union cavalry attacked the next day, and was repulsed and pursued rapidly toward Culpeper Court House, where Stuart was driving Meade's rear guard under Kilpatrick.

The Army of Northern Virginia, numbering, without Longstreet's corps, forty-four thousand, was placed by a wide swing, via Madison Court House, around Meade's right, and in forty-one miles reached Culpeper Court House to find the Army of the Potomac had been promptly withdrawn to the north bank of the Rappahannock. Lee then essayed another swing around the circle, and forced a passage over the Rappahannock at the White Sulphur Springs on the 12th, roughly handling Gregg's cavalry division, which guarded Meade's right, marching eighteen miles that day; but while Lee was moving north, Meade, not hearing from him, recrossed the river and moved south to Culpeper again, leaving one corps on the river. As soon as Gregg reported Lee's position, the Union troops were countermarched in haste, and on the morning of the 13th, after a night march, were again north of the Rappahannock. That morning Lee only went to Warrenton — seven miles. He was still the nearer to Washington, and ahead. A five-mile march from Warrenton to Auburn, or nine miles to Warrenton Junction, or fourteen to Bristoe, would have placed him in position to strike as Meade's columns marched South. The 13th, after a march of a few miles, was passed at Warrenton by Lee, while Meade's rear, under Warren, bivouacked five miles away at Auburn. That delay, which General Lee says was due to being out of rations, allowed Meade to pass beyond him.

The next morning, the 14th, Ewell was sent via Auburn to Bristoe, and A. P. Hill by New Baltimore to the same place. The former struck Warren's rear, the latter the head of his column at Bristoe, and attacked it with only two brigades, which were repulsed by the masterly management of Warren, who seized with Hays's division a cut on the railroad. So skillfully was this done that Warren captured from Hill four hundred and fifty prisoners, five pieces of artillery, and two stand of colors, and passed his whole corps across the broad run, following Meade's rear without further molestation, though one half of Lee's army might have been hammering his head and the other half his tail.

The adventurous Stuart got caught near Auburn on the night of the 13th between two marching parallel columns of Federal infantry, and, with a portion of his cavalry and some guns, lay perdue during the night within a mile or two of Meade's headquarters and some four hundred yards from General Warren's rear division, but dexterously extricated his whole command next morning.

While Lee lay at Warrenton on the 13th, Meade was twenty miles south of Bristoe, but, in spite of his night march on the 12th, succeeded in placing his whole army beyond Lee on the 13th, except Warren, who stopped opposite him and only a few miles away. Meade fell back to Centreville and its vicinity, where he prepared to offer battle. The position might have been turned, as in the case of Pope, but the immense works around Washington held out hospitable arms in case Meade again declined the contest. Nothing was accomplished except to demonstrate that the army which first left Gettysburg first assumed the offensive in Virginia. When General Lee retired, Meade followed, and his advance cavalry, under Kilpatrick, was routed by Stuart wheeling about and attacking it in front, while another portion of his horsemen assailed their flank at Buckland on the Warrenton road in an affair christened "Buckland races."

"I have returned to the Rappahannock," wrote General Lee to his wife, October 19, 1863; "I did not pursue with the main army beyond Bristoe or Broad Run. Our advance went as far as Bull Run, where the enemy was intrenched, extending his right as far as Chantilly, in the yard of which he was building a redoubt. I could have thrown him farther back, but I saw no chance of bringing him to battle, and it would have only served to fatigue our troops by advancing farther. If they had been properly provided with clothes I would certainly have endeavored to have thrown them north of the Potomac; but thousands were barefooted, thousands with fragments of shoes, and all without overcoats, blankets, or warm clothing. I could not bear to expose them to certain suffering on an uncertain issue." The Union troops around Warrenton waited for the railroad which the Confederates had torn up to be repaired.

From Camp Rappahannock, October 28, 1863, the General said to Mrs. Lee: "I moved yesterday into a nice pine thicket, and Perry is to-day engaged in constructing a chimney in front of my tent which will make it warm and comfortable. I have no idea when F. [his son, W. H. F. Lee] will be exchanged. The Federal authorities still resist all exchanges, because they think it is to our interest to make them. Any desire expressed on our part for the exchange of any individual magnifies the difficulty, as they at once think some great benefit is to result to us from it. His detention is very grievous to me, and, besides, I want his services. I am glad you have some socks for the army. Send them to me. They will come safely. Tell the girls to send all they can. I wish they could make some shoes, too. We have thousands of barefooted men. There is no news. General Meade, I believe, is repairing the railroad, and I presume will come on again. If I could only get some shoes and clothes for the men I would save him the trouble."

On November 1st Lee reviewed his cavalry corps, much to the delight of J. E. B. Stuart, who, like Murat, was not averse to the pomp of war. The cavalry chief was in all his glory with his "fighting jacket" and dancing plume. The cavalry corps numbered — by the returns of the day before — seven thousand nine hundred and seventeen. Many squadrons were absent on picket and other detached duty, but at least five thousand sabers passed his front. It was an inspiring sight. The privates, who were graceful riders, owned the horses, which were generally good.

From Camp Rappahannock, November 1, 1863, he wrote Mrs. Lee: "I have just had a visit from my nephews, Fitz, John, and Henry. They looked very well. The former is going on a little expedition. As soon as I was left alone I committed them in a fervent prayer to the care and guidance of our heavenly Father. I think my rheumatism is better to-day. I have been through a great deal with comparatively little suffering. I have been wanting to review the cavalry for some time, and appointed to-day with fear and trembling. I had not been on horseback for five days previously and feared I would not get through, but, to my surprise, I got along very well. The Governor was here and told me Mrs. Letcher had seen you recently."

Meade now decided to get closer to Lee so as to be in a position where he in turn could take the offensive, and began to advance on November 7th. His left wing of three corps, under French, was directed to cross the Rappahannock at Kelly's Ford; his right, under Sedgwick, at Rappahannock Station. French progressed without much opposition, but Sedgwick found a tete-de-pont with lines of rifle trenches on the north side of his crossing point. This was a fort or redoubt, being in part some old intrenchments, but without a ditch and open to the south, with which it was connected by a pontoon bridge. It was occupied by two of Early's brigades under Colonels Penn and Godwin, with four pieces of artillery. Daylight was fast disappearing; Russell's division of the Sixth Corps was in line of battle in its front, with Upton's brigade deployed as skirmishers. Russell thought he could carry the work, so Sedgwick gave the order. The conditions were favorable to success; the wind blowing strong from south to north, the firing could not be heard by the supporting batteries on the south side, so Russell stormed the redoubt with so much dash that it was captured before the Southern force on the south side knew it.

It was a brilliant coup de main, reflecting credit on those engaged, particularly the Maine and Wisconsin regiments. The troops assailed by a division amounted to one thousand six hundred and seventy-four, and so rapid was the Federal rush that only six were killed and thirty-nine wounded; eight captured flags were carried to Meade's headquarters by Russell and Upton, preceded by a band, and then sent in charge of Russell to the War Department at Washington, after the manner Napoleon's trophies went sometimes to Paris, but the Secretary sent the gallant officer word he was too busy to see him, so the concluding ceremony was not as ostentatious as planned. Lee withdrew on the night of the 8th to his lines behind the Rapidan, while Meade reoccupied his camp between the rivers. Both sides wanted a battle, but on ground of their own selection.

About this time the city of Richmond presented General Lee with a house. In consequence, the President of the City Council received the following letter, dated November 12, 1863: "I assure you, sir, that no want of the appreciation of the honor conferred upon me by this resolution, or insensibility of the kind feeling that prompted it, induces me to ask, as I most respectfully do, that no further proceedings be taken with reference to the subject. The house is not necessary for the use of my family, and my own duties will prevent my residence in Richmond. I shall therefore be compelled to decline the generous offer, and trust that whatever means the City Council may have to spare for this purpose may be devoted to the relief of the families of our soldiers in the field who are now in need of assistance, and more deserving of it than myself."

The general was still worried about his imprisoned son, who was an affectionate, lovable fellow, as well as a fine officer, and wrote: "Camp, November 21, 1863. I see by the papers that our son has been sent to Fort Lafayette. Any place would be better than Fort Monroe with Butler in command. His long confinement is very grievous to me, yet it may all turn out for the best."

The people of Richmond, not being able to do anything for General Lee, doubled their acts of kindness to his wife. She was deeply grateful for their love and friendship, and so informed her husband, who replied from camp, November 25, 1863: "The kindness exhibited toward you as well as myself by our people, in addition to exciting my gratitude, causes me to reflect how little I have done to merit it, and humbles me in my own eyes to a painful degree. I am very sorry the weather was so bad that I could not give the President a review. I wanted him to see the troops, and wanted them to see him."

Over two weeks elapsed, after the Army of the Potomac and the Army of Northern Virginia were face to face along the Rapidan, before Meade executed a well-considered plan to turn Lee's right and either throw him nearer to his capital or beat him before he could concentrate his force, which was much scattered, in order to secure supplies more easily. At dawn on November 26th his columns were put in motion to cross the Rapidan at its lower fords, reach the country south of the river and east of Orange Court House, and there be directed to Orange Court House on the roads leading from Fredericksburg to that point. He was in light marching order, well supplied with ten days rations, and his wagons were left north of the Rapidan; but around his Culpeper camp hovered Southern cavalry scouts, and Lee early knew Meade's preparations and movements.

Flowing northerly into the Rapidan and almost at right angles was Mine Run, on whose western banks Lee rapidly deployed a line of battle, his great engineering talent assisting him in locating his troops, and with great rapidity breastworks were constructed too strong to be assailed. When Meade reached the line of Mine Run en route to Orange Court House, Lee's army confidently blocked his way. He could not make a direct assault, so the Union commander resolved to attack both wings, by Sedgwick on Lee's left, by Warren on his right; but the latter, formerly an engineer officer, who was to begin, reported that closer reconnaissance disclosed his enemy's lines too were well defended. There was no alternative left Meade except to withdraw, which he did during the night.

To Mrs. Lee the general gave his account of the affair from Camp Rapidan, December 4, 1863: "You will probably have seen that General Meade has retired to his old positions on the Rappahannock without giving us battle. I had expected, from his movements and all that I had heard, that it was his intention to do so, and after the first day, when I thought it necessary to skirmish pretty sharply with him on both flanks to ascertain his views, I waited patiently his attack. On Tuesday, however, I thought he had changed his mind, and that night made preparations to move around his left next morning and attack him. But when day dawned he was nowhere to be seen. He had commenced to withdraw at dark Tuesday evening. We pursued to the Rapidan, but he was over. Owing to the nature of the ground it was to our advantage to receive rather than to make the attack, and as he about doubled us in numbers, I wished to have that advantage. I am greatly disappointed at his getting off with so little damage, but we do not know what is best for us. I believe a kind God has ordered all things for our good."

In the latter part of December General W. H. F. Lee, still in prison, was overtaken by a great calamity. His wife and his two children died. When General Lee was informed of their death he wrote:

Sunday Morning, December 27, 1863.

Custis's dispatch which I received last night demolished all the hopes in which I had been indulging during the day of dear Charlotte's recovery. It has pleased God to take from us one exceedingly dear to us, and we must be resigned to his holy will. She, I trust, will enjoy peace and happiness forever, while we must patiently struggle on under all the ills that may be in store for us. What a glorious thought it is that she has joined her little cherubs and our angel Annie [his daughter] in heaven! Thus is link by link of the strong chain broken that binds us to earth, and smoothes our passage to another world. Oh, that we may be at last united in that haven of rest, where trouble and sorrow never enter, to join in an everlasting chorus of praise and glory to our Lord and Saviour! I grieve for our lost darling as a father only can grieve for a daughter, and my sorrow is heightened by the thought of the anguish her death will cause our dear son, and the poignancy it will give to the bars of his prison. May God in his mercy enable him to bear the blow he has so suddenly dealt and sanctify it to his everlasting happiness!

Rations and clothing for his men and forage for his animals were sources of great anxiety to him. In the midst of winter many of his brave men were without blankets and barefooted. From camp, January 24, 1864, he wrote: "I have had to disperse the cavalry as much as possible to obtain forage for their horses, and it is that which causes trouble. Provisions for the men, too, are very scarce, and with very light diet and light clothing I fear they suffer; but still they are cheerful and uncomplaining. I received a report from one division the other day in which it was stated that over four hundred men were barefooted and over a thousand without blankets."

Difficulties surrounded him on every side! From camp, February 6, 1864, he wrote Mrs. Lee: "I received your letter some days ago, and last night your note accompanying a bag of gloves and socks and a box of coffee. Mrs. Devereux sent the coffee to you, not to me, and I shall have to send it back. It is so long since we have had the foreign bean that we no longer desire it. We have a domestic article, which we procure by the bushel, that answers very well. You must keep the good things for yourself. We have had to reduce our allowance of meat one half, and some days we have none. The gloves and socks are very acceptable, and I shall give them out this morning. The socks of Mrs. Shepherd are very nice, but I think it is better to give them to the soldiers than to dispose of them as you suggest. The soldiers are much in need. We have received some shoes lately, and the socks will be a great addition. Tell 'Life' [his youngest daughter] I think I hear her needles rattle as they fly through the meshes."

The very day after this letter was written these destitute men joyfully sprang to arms. General Butler, at Fort Monroe, but commanding the Department of Virginia and North Carolina, thought, from what he had heard, he could capture Richmond with cavalry from the Peninsula — the general ability of Butler was great, his military qualifications small. Brigadier-General Wister marched from New Kent Court House to the Chickahominy and marched back again. A portion of the Army of the Potomac, in pursuance of Butler's plan, were to cross the Rapidan and threaten Lee, to prevent him from dispatching troops to Richmond by rail. This Army-of-the-Potomac diversion was under gallant old Sedgwick, who was commanding the army during Meade's temporary absence.

General Lee gives his account of the diversion in a letter dated Camp, Orange County, February 14, 1864: "This day last week we were prepared for battle, but I believe the advance of the enemy was only intended to see where we were and whether they could injure us. They place their entire loss in killed, wounded, and missing at twelve hundred, but I think that is exaggerated. Our old friend Sedgwick was in command. In reference to Rob" (his youngest son, who was a private in the Rockbridge artillery battery, and who Mrs. Lee desired to be with his father), "his company would be a great pleasure and comfort to me, and he would be extremely useful in various ways, but I am opposed to officers surrounding themselves with their sons and relatives. It is wrong in principle, and in that case selections would be made from private and social relations rather than for the public good. There is the same objection to going with Fitz Lee. I should prefer Rob's being in the line in an independent position, where he could rise by his own merit and not through the recommendation of his relatives. I expect him here soon, when I can better see what he himself thinks. The young men have no fondness for the society of the old general. He is too heavy and sombre for them."

Again Lee's rest was disturbed by a diversion on his left flank by infantry and cavalry, in order to allow Kilpatrick, with some four thousand horsemen, to ride past his right, make a dash for Richmond, release the Union prisoners, and disturb the peace generally. It accomplished nothing. The idea originated in Washington, it is said, for Meade disapproved it. Upon one of Kilpatrick's officers — Colonel Ulric Dahlgren, who was killed — some remarkable papers were found, including a sort of an address to the soldiers to burn Richmond, "kill Jeff Davis and Cabinet," and do many other horrible things. The United States Government promptly disclaimed any knowledge of such orders, and so did Meade. Dahlgren was a daring, dashing young fellow, but was too enthusiastic. It is certain the papers published at the time were taken from his person. The Southern President laughed as he read over the originals in his office, and turning to Mr. Benjamin, his Secretary of State, who was with him, said, when he reached the word Cabinet, "That is intended for you, Mr. Benjamin."

Lee was now making every effort to promote the efficiency of his army for the great struggle he knew must come in the spring. On March 18, 1864, he wrote: "I arrived safely yesterday." (He had been on a short visit to Richmond.) "There were sixty-seven pairs of socks in the bag I brought up instead of sixty-four, as you supposed, and I found here three dozen pairs of beautiful white-yarn socks, sent over by our kind cousin Julia and sweet little Carrie, making one hundred and three pairs, all of which I sent to the Stonewall brigade. One dozen of the Stuart socks had double heels. Can you not teach Mildred [his daughter] that stitch? They sent me also some hams, which I had rather they had eaten. I pray that you may be preserved and relieved from all your troubles, and that we may all be again united here on earth and forever in heaven." His wife and daughter and other friends of the cause were knitting socks for the soldiers, and the commanding general had brought some of them back to the army himself.

The cavalry, for the better subsistence of men and horses, had been moved back to Charlottesville for the winter, and, not having much to do, some of the officers proposed to dance. General Lee wrote his son Robert, then belonging to that arm of service, from Camp Orange Court House, January 17, 1864: "I inclose a letter for you which has been sent to my care. I hope you are well and all around you. Tell Fitz I grieve over the hardships and sufferings of his men in their late expedition. I would have preferred his waiting for more favorable weather. He accomplished much under the circumstances, but would have done more in better weather. I am afraid he was anxious to get back to the ball. This is a bad time for such things. We have too grave subjects on hand to engage in such trivial amusements. I would rather his officers should entertain themselves in fattening their horses, healing their men, and recruiting their regiments. There are too many Lees on the committee. I like them all to be present at battles, but can excuse them at balls. But the saying is, 'Children will be children.' I think he had better move his camp farther from Charlottesville, and perhaps he will get more work and less play. He and I are too old for such assemblies. I want him to write me how his men are, his horses, and what I can do to fill up his ranks."

From camp, April 2, 1864, he wrote Mrs. Lee: "Your note with the socks arrived last evening. I have sent them to the Stonewall brigade; the number all right-thirty pairs. Including this last parcel of thirty pairs, I have sent to that brigade two hundred and sixty-three pairs. Still, there are about one hundred and forty whose homes are within the enemy's lines and who are without socks. I shall continue to furnish them till all are supplied. Tell the young women to work hard for the brave Stonewallers." And once more, from Orange County, April 21, 1864: "Your note with bag of socks reached me last evening. The number was correct — thirty-one pairs. I sent them to the Stonewall brigade, which is not yet supplied. Sixty-one pairs from the ladies in Fauquier have reached Charlottesville, and I hope will be distributed soon. Now that Miss Bettie Brander has come to the aid of my daughters, the supply will soon be increased."

The preparations of the Government of the United States for prosecuting the war in 1864 were on a vast scale. Stupendous efforts were made to crush armed resistance everywhere. An irresistible invasion was designed to destroy "rebellion" from center to circumference. The principal objective points were the two principal armies of the Confederacy — the one then at Dalton, Ga., under J. E. Johnston, and the other in Virginia under Robert E. Lee. The Washington authorities decided that there should be only one head to direct these immense plans of campaign, and it determined the head should be on the shoulders of General U. S. Grant. This officer was commissioned lieutenant general on March 9, 1864, and placed in the command of all the armies of the United States. His success in the West had brought him prominently to the notice of Mr. Lincoln. In the exercise of supreme command his especial attention was to be bestowed upon General Lee, and his headquarters were to be established with Meade's army. Hiram Ulysses, as christened, or Ulysses S. Grant, as he was registered at West Point, was a native of Ohio, who graduated at the United States Military Academy in 1843; was assigned to the Fourth Infantry and became regimental quartermaster; served with distinction in Mexico, and was bold and adventurous — for instance, at Molino del Rey he climbed to the roof of a house and demanded the surrender of Mexicans occupying it; and at another point placed howitzers in the belfry of a church to drive his enemy out of a defensive position near the City of Mexico. After eleven years in the United States Army he resigned, was afterward on a small farm near St. Louis, and then became a clerk in 1860 in the hardware and leather store of his father in Galena, Ill. When the war broke out he offered his services to his Government in writing, but received no reply, and was afterward made colonel of the Twenty-first Illinois Regiment by the Governor of that State. He was thirty-nine years old when he confronted Lee, and was not to be despised as a commander. He was fortunate in being placed in command at a time when the resources of men and means of the Confederacy were smaller than ever before, and his peculiar direct tactics could be employed in consequence of superiority in numbers, for he admitted to Meade he never manoeuvred. With two hostile armies of approximate strength commanded by Lee and Grant in a campaign demanding a high order of military sagacity and a familiarity with strategic science, the chances of success would be with Lee.

The Union chief had, however, many excellent qualities for a soldier. He was taciturn, sturdy, plucky, not afraid of public responsibility or affected by public opinion. There was no ostentation in his position, and to an outsider he was not as showy as a corporal of the guard. Meade had a Solferino flag with a golden eagle in a silver wreath for his headquarters. When General Grant first saw it unfurled, as they broke camp for the Wilderness campaign, he is reported to have exclaimed, "What's this? Is imperial Caesar anywhere about here?"

Lee, who had campaigned against McClellan, Pope, Burnside, Hooker, and Meade, had now to measure swords with Grant. Sheridan, too, made his first bow in Virginia at this time. He had served with distinction under Halleck in the West, and when Grant asked for the best officer that could be found to be his chief of cavalry, Halleck suggested Sheridan, and his suggestion was instantly adopted. This officer graduated in 1853 at West Point, was a classmate of McPherson, Schofield, and Hood, had served in the Fourth Infantry — Grant's old regiment — and was thirty years of age when he first drew his sabre in Virginia in 1864.

The Federal Government laid at the feet of Grant its unbounded treasures. His Virginia army was increased to one hundred and eighteen thousand men of all arms and three hundred and eighteen cannon, as some authorities have it; but the report of the Union Secretary of War to the first session of the Thirty-ninth Congress gave one hundred and forty-nine thousand one hundred and sixty men. Some idea of its vast proportions may be had by the statement that one hundred and eighteen thousand men, disposed for battle two ranks deep, would cover a front of thirty miles, while sixty-two thousand men, similarly disposed, would cover only sixteen miles. Grant says, in his Memoirs, his wagon train would have reached on a single road from the Rapidan to Richmond, sixty-five miles. To meet this grand "On to Richmond!" Lee had sixty-two thousand men and two hundred and twenty-four field guns.

At midnight on May 3d Grant began to cross the Rapidan at Ely's and Germanna fords, some distance below Lee's right, but at the very points Lee had predicted, a few days before, in a conference with his officers. The Army of the Potomac was now consolidated into four corps — Second, Fifth, and Sixth — commanded by Hancock, Warren, and Sedgwick, and the Ninth under Burnside. (Under the consolidation the First and Third Corps disappeared.) When the sun sank to rest on the 4th, Grant had crossed his whole army, and on the morning of the 5th confidently started across the Wilderness in a southerly direction to force Lee to accept battle.

Crossing the river without opposition relieved his mind from serious apprehensions; but it was no part of Lee's plan to resist him there. Indeed, he generally gave plenty of room on his side of a stream for his opponent to form, hoping to make it as difficult for him to get back as it was easy for him to get over. It is safe to say he would never have formed his troops at the water edge of the Bull Run fords as Beauregard did at the first Manassas, but upon commanding positions back, with only sufficient force to delay and give notice of the crossing. Had Beauregard done this, he would not have had his left turned, for the opportune arrival of Johnston alone gave him the battle. Grant's move did not, as he expected, compel Lee to fall back toward Richmond and fight a defensive battle; but hardly had he filled the Wilderness with men as thick as "raging locusts" than Lee marched to meet and attack him.

Early on the morning of May 4th he bade adieu to the three or four tents near Orange Court House which had been the winter home of himself and personal staff, and with Ewell's corps, two detached brigades, and two divisions of Hill's corps, with artillery and cavalry, marched by the most direct course for Grant's army. Longstreet, who was near Gordonsville then with two divisions (Pickett's was south of James River), was directed to follow, as well as Anderson's division of Hill's corps which was on Rapidan Heights. On the 5th, in two columns, Lee advanced by the old turnpike and plank roads, which, leading east from Orange Court House via Chancellorsville to Fredericksburg, were being crossed by Grant at right angles, who was marching south. Ewell was on the former and Hill moved on the latter road, and by Hill's side at the head of the column rode Lee, while his cavalry marched still farther to the right. Grant did not know of the proximity of the Confederates, though Ewell's advance had bivouacked on the night of the 4th three miles from Warren's corps, which was at the intersection of the Germanna road with the old turnpike, called Wilderness Tavern. So on the 5th Grant gave orders for his army to move in two columns — Fifth and Sixth Corps from Wilderness Tavern to Parker's Store, where their route intersected the plank road, and Hancock from Chancellorsville to Shady Grove Church. Warren, as a military precaution, threw Griffin's division up the old turnpike toward Orange Court House to protect his moving column, and Ewell, coming down the pike about this time, met and engaged Griffin, and the battle of the Wilderness began, for shortly thereafter Hill became engaged with a force at Parker's Store.

Hancock, whose troops formed Grant's left advance, was stopped, and the heads of his columns turned toward Parker's Store to meet Hill. Grant discovered that he had Lee's army on his right marching flank and would have to fight in the Wilderness.

As Ewell and Warren became more engaged, lines of battle were formed — Warren in the center and Sedgwick on his right, and afterward Hancock on his left. On the plank road Hill's left did not connect with Ewell's right. Getty's division, Sixth Union Corps, was sent first to retard Hill's progress, and then Hancock's corps arrived. Ewell and Warren had their encounter, and then Hancock and Hill took up the fighting. Warren gained ground at first against Ewell, but was in turn driven back with the loss of three thousand men, while Hancock's vigorous assaults on Hill's two divisions on the plank road were successfully resisted.

Night came and both sides prepared for the morrow's desperate battle, when Lee and Grant each proposed to assume the offensive. It was a terrible region to receive or deliver battle: thousands of acres of tangled forest, interlaced undergrowth, scrub oaks, dwarf pine and cedar, were on every side, with here and there a few narrow roads. Grant did not manoeuvre, so it suited him in that respect; but his preponderance of numbers could not be made effective, and his men were in each other's way, just as Hooker's had been in this same Wilderness nearer to Chancellorsville. Artillery was of but little service, mounted cavalry none; no man could command the battle, because no man saw but a few yards around him. Two hundred thousand men were mixed up in a wild, weird struggle, like a hole full of snakes with their tails intertwined. On the morning of the 6th, Sedgwick, Warren, Burnside (now up), and Hancock faced Ewell and Hill, while Longstreet was rapidly marching to Hill's position.

Lee's plan was to feign attack on Grant's right and assail his left flank, Grant's to attack along his whole line. Sedgwick was attacked before his orders required him to attack; but Longstreet was not yet up, nor was Anderson's division of Hill's corps. So Lee had to wait on his right; but Hancock with nearly forty thousand men did not wait, but rushed on Heth and Wilcox's division of Hill's corps, and finally carried their whole front and drove their right back in some confusion. Lee's right wing was threatened with disaster; neither Longstreet's corps nor Anderson's division of Hill's had arrived. The former left his camp near Gordonsville at 4 P. M. on the 4th, and marched that afternoon sixteen miles. The next day, when Hill and Ewell were fighting, he resumed his march, lost his way, had to retrace his steps, and finally went into camp on the night of the 5th near Verdiersville, some ten miles in the rear of where Hill and Ewell had been fighting, broke camp at 12.30 A. M. on the 6th, and reached Hill, whose two divisions had been assailed by six Federal divisions under Hancock, just in time to save Lee's right.

Lee has stated since the war that he sent an officer to Longstreet to stay with him and show him the roads, anticipating he would move him when Grant crossed the Rapidan, but Longstreet discharged him, and, by taking the wrong road, did not get up to his position until May 6th, when he might have joined him on the 5th. Gordonsville was only ten miles from Orange Court House and the court house thirteen from Verdiersville, where Longstreet bivouacked the night of the 5th. By the route he should have marched he could have reached Verdiersville in twenty miles. He consumed one day and a half of precious time in getting there. Though late in his arrival, no one could have made dispositions to assume the offensive with more celerity, or have attacked with more promptness. Hancock was now in turn assailed. Holding his front with three brigades under Gregg, Benning, and Law, Longstreet threw four — viz., Mahone's, G. T. Anderson's, Wofford's, and Davis's around Hancock's left flank. Attacked in flank and front, Hancock's troops were routed and driven rapidly back three quarters of a mile to his line of works.

It was a well-planned, well-executed movement. As Longstreet rode down the plank road at the head of his column he came opposite to his brigades, which had made the flank movement, and were drawn up parallel to the plank road and some sixty feet from it. He was mistaken in the thick woods for the Federals, and a volley was fired at him by his own men, which severely wounded him and killed General Jenkins by his side. It was most unfortunate. Jackson at Chancellorsville had been shot down by his troops at the moment of victory, and here in the Wilderness in the midst of a deserved success, and when Longstreet had given orders for the advance of his whole force, he, too, fell by the fire of his own men. His fall arrested the movement. R. H. Anderson was taken from Hill's corps and put in command of Longstreet's, and Mahone given Anderson's division; but the change required time.

Lee had in person been in the midst of Hill's troops, restoring confidence and order, and his presence, as he rode along the lines on his gray horse, was most inspiring. In splendid style the troops of Longstreet went into battle. As the Texans swept by with enthusiastic cheers Lee rode with them in the charge until those brave fellows insisted he should go back. A sergeant actually seized his horse, and just then Colonel Venable, of his staff, called his attention to Longstreet sitting on his horse on a little knoll not far away, and he rode off and joined him. The Texas soldiers were, like "Scipio's veterans, ready to die for him if he would only spare himself." General Lee had served in Texas when in the United States Army, and was familiar with the State and her people; he had the highest admiration for the Texas troops, as the whole army had. They were descendants of the adventurous spirits who first settled Texas, were good marksmen, and their eyes could look down a gun barrel without a tremor of the lid. He asked Senator Wigfall, of Texas, to get him more Texans, and said after Sharpsburg if he had more of them he would feel more certain of results.

Hancock's troops were driven behind their log breastworks, upon which a later attack failed. The same afternoon Gordon, with three brigades of Ewell's corps, made a successful assault on Sedgwick's line, Wright's division; but night stopped the contest. During the day severe combats had taken place between the cavalry of the two armies on the Furnace and Brock roads and at Todd's Tavern, with no decisive results. Both armies were locked in their temporary breastworks. Lee could no longer hope to successfully assail the immense masses of Grant, and on Grant, imperturbable and calm, the impression had been made that to again "attack along the whole line" would be hopeless. It was a terrible field for a battle — a region of tangled underbrush, ragged foliage, and knotted trunks. "You hear the saturnalia, gloomy, hideous, desperate, raging unconfined. You see nothing, and the very mystery augments the horror; nothing was visible, and from out the depths came the ruin that had been wrought in bleeding shapes borne in blankets or on stretchers." The Wilderness was a tract of gloom, and over all was the shadow of death. Grant had lost seventeen thousand six hundred and sixty-six men, his opponent one half that number. Science had little to do with such a struggle. "Two wild animals were hunting for each other; when they heard each other's footsteps they sprang and grappled." It was like a huge Indian fight, and different from any other battle. The two days contest on this unique ground can be compared to nothing in military records, ancient or modern. "Charges were made and repulsed, the men in the lines scarcely seeing each other. Soldiers fell, writhed, and died unseen, their bodies lost in the bushes, their death groans drowned in the steady, continuous, never-ceasing crash."

To add to the horrors, the woods caught fire and many wounded men perished in the flames. Lee's army was Grant's objective point, but the objective point sought Grant, and the latter, after remaining in its front all of the 7th, deliberately marched away during the night and attempted to interpose between it and Richmond at the strategic point of Spottsylvania Court House, fifteen miles southeast of the battlefield. His infantry did not begin to march until 9 P. M.; but during the afternoon a portion of his wagon train was first moved toward Chancellorsville, and the watchful Stuart, who had cavalry on all sides, at once reported the fact. Lee divined Grant's plans, and promptly ordered Anderson, commanding Longstreet's corps, to move around General Hancock's left to the same point.

Warren, the Union van, was much delayed during the night. Meade's large escort was first in his way, and then Merritt's cavalry, which was preceding his march, failed to drive the Confederate cavalry in his front, but finally gave the right of way to Warren; it was then daylight. Indeed, so effectual was the resistance of a dismounted division of Confederate cavalry that Warren's leading division, Robinson's, did not get in sight of Spottsylvania Court House until after 8 A. M., and then found Anderson's troops in his front, which, marching by a parallel road, had replaced the cavalry and received Robinson with a savage musketry fire, severely wounding him and driving back his line. As the Union troops came up they formed on Warren, while Anderson formed the nucleus for Lee's lines. The race had been finished, and Lee, between Grant and Richmond, cried Check!

Both armies intrenched, and two formidable lines of earthworks sprang into existence. For twelve days Grant repeatedly and vainly assaulted at different points his opponent's position. The small army in gray stood as immovable as the mountains. Twice Grant assailed on the 8th of May, five times on the 10th, and on the 12th, when he succeeded in carrying a salient. On the 18th and 19th he attacked again. Grant lost eighteen thousand three hundred and ninety-nine men, making forty thousand in the two weeks of overland travel, or in numbers equal to two thirds of Lee's whole army. The "hammering" process was costly, but might ultimately succeed as long as General Lee lost one man to his three, because the Federal reservoir of human supply was so much greater.

Here the Union commander lost one of his best and bravest corps commanders — John Sedgwick, of the Sixth Corps. On the 11th, while walking along a portion of his line, a ball from the gun of a Confederate sharpshooter pierced his cheek under the left eye. A soldier in front of him a moment before dodged to the ground as he heard the shrill whistle of a bullet. Sedgwick touched him gently with his foot, telling him to get up, he was ashamed of him, and remarked, "They could not hit an elephant at this distance." The man rose, saluted, and said, "General, I dodged a shell once, and if I hadn't it would have taken my head off." Sedgwick laughed and told him to go to his place in line, and was immediately afterward killed. He had two mourners — his friend and his foe. With Lee and others who had served with him before the war he was a great favorite; he was so true, so faithful in all of life's relations. In his death the Army of the Potomac lost an arm. General Horatio G. Wright succeeded to the command of his corps.

The Union assault of the 12th was partially successful. There was a salient on Ewell's works, and its V-shape was enwrapped by the Federals. Hancock's corps was brought from Grant's right during the stormy night before and massed twelve hundred yards from the work, and at half-past 4 in the morning, with Barlow's and Birney's divisions in advance, successfully and gallantly stormed the position, capturing General Edward Johnson, one of Ewell's division commanders, between three and four thousand prisoners, and twenty pieces of artillery.

Lee had detected the weak point, and had already commenced a line across the base of the triangle. It was well conceived, as his right center would have been pierced and his army divided. This second line received the victorious rush of the Federals, who were in turn driven back with great slaughter to the salient, where the fiercest and most deadly fighting in the war took place. Lee concentrated his efforts to retake the salient, Grant to hold it. The musketry fire with its terrific leaden hail was, beyond comparison, the heaviest of the four years of war. In the bitter struggle, trees large and small fell, cut down by bullets. Grant re-enforced Hancock by the Sixth Corps and by two of Warren's divisions, after failing to get Warren and Burnside in at other points. He then had over half of his army — over fifty thousand men — holding on to the advantage gained, while Lee, equally as determined, purposed to retake the position. Rodes's, Ramseur's, and Gordon's troops, three brigades under McGowan, Perrin, and Harris, and two battalions of artillery were "put in," and all day the savage contest raged.

Late in the night Lee drew back his troops on the new line. On the 11th he thought Grant was preparing for another move, and that night ordered most of the cannon out of the salient so as to be ready for a counter move, all of which a deserter from Johnson's line reported, and which may account for the assault which, though favored by a climatic condition, was courageously executed. Johnson during the night, becoming suspicious of ominous sounds in his front, ordered them back, but was attacked before getting them in position. The famous salient has been called the "bloody angle." Some trenches almost ran with blood, while others had to be cleared of dead bodies. The lips of the dead were incrusted with powder from biting cartridges. It was a horrible scene. Two days before Upton's brigade of the Sixth Corps broke through the Confederate lines. General Lee was very sensitive about his lines being broken. It made him more than ever personally pugnacious, and ready and desirous to lead in their recapture.

On this occasion the general rode to the head of the column forming for the charge, took off his hat, and pointed to the captured line; but General John B. Gordon proposed to lead his own men, and no one in the army could do it better, for he was in dash and daring inferior to none. "These are Virginians and Georgians who have never failed," said Gordon. "Go to the rear, General Lee." And appealing to his men, he cried: "Is it necessary for General Lee to lead this charge?" "No, no," they exclaimed; "we will drive them back if General Lee will go to the rear." The Union troops were hurled back in the charge that followed and the line re-established. Grant again had no alternative but to flank-or fall back. He had written Halleck, addressing him as "Chief of the staff of the army," that he was sending back his wagons for a fresh supply of provisions and ammunition, and proposed "to fight it out on this line if it takes all the summer," and asking that "re-enforcements be sent as fast as possible, and in as great numbers." Grant, who said he never manoeuvred, states in his official report that from the 12th to the 18th "was consumed in manoeuvring and awaiting the arrival of re-enforcements," which to the number of some thirty-five thousand were sent to him from the Middle and Washington Departments.

When Grant reached Spottsylvania Court House he determined to throw Sheridan's cavalry corps between Lee and Richmond, tear up his communication, and be in position to dispatch what was left of

Lee after he had crushed him in Spottsylvania, just as Hooker had proposed to use Stoneman at Chancellorsville. So on the 9th of May, at 6 A. M., Sheridan, clearing widely Lee's right, turned toward Richmond. Ten thousand horsemen riding on a single road in columns of fours made a column thirteen miles in length, and with flashing sabres and fluttering guidons were an imposing array. Stuart was not long in ascertaining and following the movement, but had only three brigades available for that purpose, one of which, a small North Carolina brigade, was directed to follow Sheridan's rear, while the other two, riding over the chord of the arc traveled by Sheridan, reached Yellow Tavern, six miles from Richmond, on the 11th, before Sheridan, and were thrown directly across his route. Here a fierce though most unequal cavalry combat ensued, the numbers of the contestants being as ten thousand to three thousand. Nearly all day these two cavalry brigades held their ground in Sheridan's front, while General James B. Gordon's small force attacked his rear, losing their gallant commander, giving General Bragg, commanding the Richmond defenses, ample time to get some troops from below Richmond, so that when Sheridan finally broke through them and arrived in front of the defenses his valor was replaced by prudence, and he marched around them, making a long circuit, and rejoined his army after an absence of over two weeks. It would have been the usual record of nothing accomplished and a broken down command, except that at Yellow Tavern the Confederate cavalry chieftain was mortally wounded, and died the following day in Richmond. This sad occurrence was more valuable to the Union cause than anything that could have happened, and his loss to Lee irreparable. Stuart was the "best cavalry officer," said General Sedgwick, the late Sixth Corps commander, who had been an officer in that arm of service, "ever foaled in America." He was the army's eyes and ears vigilant always, bold to a fault; of great vigor and ceaseless activity, he was the best type of a beau sabreur. He had a heart ever loyal to his superiors, and "duty" was "the sublimest word in the language" to him.

In a letter from Spottsylvania Court House, May 16, 1864, General Lee said to his wife: "As I write I am expecting the sound of the guns every moment. I grieve the loss of our gallant officers and men, and miss their aid and sympathy. A more zealous, ardent, brave, and devoted soldier than Stuart the Confederacy cannot have. Praise be to God for having sustained us so far. I have thought of you very often in these eventful days. God bless and preserve you." And in his order, May 20th, announcing the death of Stuart to the army, he said: "Among the gallant soldiers who have fallen in this war, General Stuart was second to none in valor, in zeal, and in unflinching devotion to his country. His achievements form a conspicuous part of the history of this army, with which his name and services will be forever associated. To military capacity of a high order and to the nobler virtues of the soldier he added the brighter graces of a pure life, guided and sustained by the Christian's faith and hope. The mysterious hand of an all-wise God has removed him from the scene of his usefulness and fame. His grateful countrymen will mourn his loss and cherish his memory. To his comrades in arms he has left the proud recollections of his deeds and the inspiring influence of his example."

Lee was much attached to Stuart and greatly lamented his death; he had been a classmate and friend at West Point of his son Custis, and his whole family were fond of him. In his tent in the hours of the night, when he knew not what the morrow would bring forth, his thoughts constantly turned to the great cavalryman whose saber had been sheathed forever. Stuart's superb personal gallantry was conspicuous to the last. His death wound was received while from the back of his horse he was steadying dismounted men by words of encouragement, and firing his pistol over their heads at the Federal cavalry in close proximity.

Once more General Grant, "deeming it impracticable," he said, to make any further attack upon the enemy at Spottsylvania Court House, drew his troops from Lee's front on the night of the 20th and started on another flank march, this time for the North Anna; but when his leading corps, the Fifth, reached that stream on the afternoon of the 23d Lee was there too, still between his capital and his enemy, where he again exclaimed, Check! To Mrs. Lee, from Hanover Junction, May 23, 1864, the general wrote: "General Grant, having apparently become tired of forcing his passage through, began on the night of the 20th to move around our right toward Bowling Green, placing the Mattapony River between us. Fearing he might unite with Sheridan and make a sudden and rapid move upon Richmond, I determined to march to this point so as to be in striking distance of Richmond, and be able to intercept him. The army is now south of the North Anna. We have the advantage of being nearer our supplies and less liable to have our communication trains, etc., cut by his cavalry, and he is getting farther from his base. Still, I begrudge every step he takes toward Richmond." Lee's position south of the North Anna River was an admirable one, and his defensive lines showed the skill of the engineer. Grant crossed his army at two points some miles apart. Lee kept his center on the river, but retired his wings so that the Union forces in front of them were separated from each other, and could only hold communication by crossing the river twice or by breaking through his army. It was his intention to assume the offensive here, and to strike Grant a stunning blow; but, unfortunately, he was taken ill. Colonel Venable, of his staff, writes that as he lay in his tent he would say in his impatience: "We must strike them. We must never let them pass us again." He wanted to seize the advantage of his position. Warren, on the right of Grant's army and Hancock on the left, supposed, after crossing the river, they could unite, but were totally unprepared to find Lee's lines of battle between them. The Confederate army was posted upon two long lines of an obtuse-angle, whose strong apex rested on the river. It had received its first re-enforcements in the force under Breckinridge and Pickett's division, and Hoke's brigade of Early's division — in all seventy-five hundred men. And the whole army was in good condition; but its commanding general was ill, and so was one of his corps commanders, while another had been disabled by wounds. Lee's sickness made it "manifest he was the head and front, the very life and soul of his army."

Grant did not like his North Anna situation. He said he found Lee's position stronger than either of the two previous ones, so he withdrew "during the night of the 26th and moved via Hanovertown to turn the enemy's position by his right." Hanovertown is on the Pamunkey River, which is formed by the North Anna and South Anna; the Mattapony is formed by the junction of the Mat, Ta, Po, and Ny, and the two make the York. When Grant crossed the Pamunkey and marched south he was on the Peninsula, and when his advance reached Cold Harbor on May 31st he was on McClellan's former grounds. Across his path, and once more between him and Richmond, was the Army of Northern Virginia. Its commander was again in the saddle, and again he heard Check! The duty of keeping from his capital an army nearly three times as great in number as his own was an occupation sufficient to employ all the military skill of Lee; but so great were the resources of the United States Government that it was able to converge several armies on the one objective — Richmond. Butler was to concentrate the troops of his department, largely reenforced from detachments hitherto operating in the South, and march on Petersburg, twenty miles south of Richmond, destroy the railroads running south, and invest the Confederate capital from his side of the James, so as to be in position to co-operate with Grant when his conquering banners should wave from the other side. The columns of Crook and Averell were to debouch from West Virginia, and Sigel to advance up the great Valley of Virginia, capture Staunton, Charlottesville, and Lynchburg, and then be guided by future instructions.

But the co-operating armies did not co-operate; Butler, with an army of over thirty thousand men, "marched up the hill and then marched down again." On transports he conveyed his troops up the James River, landed them at City Point, and above, at Bermuda Hundred, in the angle between the junction of the Appomattox River flowing from Petersburg and the James from Richmond, and intrenched across the narrow neck of land on a line some three miles only from the Richmond and Petersburg Railroad, less than ten from Petersburg and twenty from Richmond. Here he established his entrepot of supplies, and from this base proceeded to play his part in the campaign drama. He was too slow, for after some preliminary success, just as he was about to achieve fame, he was attacked by Beauregard on the morning of the 16th, and driven within his fortified lines, in front of which Beauregard threw up works stretching from river to river. He was caged, so far as any further advance from that point could be made, for Beauregard had locked him up and put the key in his pocket, or, as General Barnard, Grant's chief engineer, expressed it — and General Grant adopted the phrase in his report — he was in a bottle which Beauregard had corked, and with a small force could hold the cork in place. Beauregard had been brought from the Southern Department, and his command consisted of detachments from South Carolina, Georgia, and other points. His plans to defeat Butler were most skillfully arranged, and would have been crowned with great success but for the unpardonable and admitted nonaction of one of his division generals, to whom had been confided the duty of cutting off General Butler's retreat.

Sigel, the Valley co-operator, with sixty-five hundred men, was defeated by Breckinridge with five thousand troops on May 15th at New Market, the day before Beauregard beat Butler, in which he was greatly assisted by a battalion of cadets from the Virginia Military Institute at Lexington, Va. The boys were transformed by the crash of arms, roar of cannon, and shouts of combatants, into young heroes, and displayed marked heroism. The cadets of the Virginia Military Institute are responsible for the fact that many soldiers fought for the last time "mit Sigel." Breckinridge was then called to Lee, and General David Hunter replaced Sigel in command in the Valley, with whom Crook and Averell later united.

When General Lee faced Grant at Cold Harbor, Butler was still "bottled up"; but twelve thousand five hundred of his force under General "Baldy" Smith, as he was called, had been taken out from the bottom of the bottle, placed on transports, carried down the James and up the York, landed, and marched to Grant. Lee was also re-enforced by a division of North Carolinians. On June 1st, at 5 P. M., Smith's command and the Sixth Corps attacked, the other corps being held by Grant in readiness to advance on receipt of orders. The Confederate thick skirmish or preliminary line was carried, but the main position was immovable, of which, after the loss of two thousand men, Smith and Wright became convinced. "The 2d of June," says Grant, "was spent in getting troops into position for attack on the 3d; on the 3d of June we again assaulted the enemy's work in the hope of driving him from his position. In this attempt our loss was heavy while that of the enemy, I have reason to believe, was comparatively light."

This remarkable assault deserves more attention than the brief statement in which Grant disposes of it. Its isolation on the pages of history as the most extraordinary blunder in military annals will alone make it famous. Nearly all of the one hundred and thirteen thousand troops then at Cold Harbor, in double lines of battle six miles long, sprang to arms at half-past 4 on the morning of the 3d, and, in obedience to the customary order "to attack along the whole line," assailed the army of Lee and were terribly slaughtered at every point. There has been no instance of such destructive firing attended with such small loss to the men who were shooting from stationary lines. The troops went forward, said Hancock, "as far as the example of their officers could carry them"; but that was not far, for eight or ten minutes was the time of actual advance sixty minutes of battle from first to last. Grant seemed willing to submit everything to the "nice hazard of a doubtful hour." Death and destruction everywhere enveloped charging columns, and direct and cross fires tore them to pieces. Lee's men were hungry and mad: three hard biscuits and one piece of fat pork were all the rations many had obtained since leaving the North Anna, and the pork was eaten raw because cooking involved waste. One cracker to a man, with no meat, became a luxury, and the lament of a poor fellow who had his shot out of his hand before he could eat it was ludicrous: "The next time I'll put my cracker in a safe place down by the breastworks where it won't get wounded, poor thing!" said he.

In front of the Confederate defenses the scene was heartrending. The ground was strewn with the dead, dying, and wounded Federals, and yet at 8 A. M. an order came from the chief of staff of the Army of the Potomac for the corps to assault again, each without reference to the other's advance. It is known that "Baldy" Smith positively refused to obey it, while some of the other corps commanders went through the form of opening fire, but there was no advance. Again the order was given for a general assault. It was transmitted to corps commanders, from them to the division chiefs, down through brigades to regiments; but immobile ranks entered a solemn protest against human butchery, and men who had charged to the cannon's mouth when there was a chance for victory lay in long lines as still as their dead comrades. The rank and file knew the hopelessness of another attack upon Lee's lines; they had been there, and did not propose to make another useless, bloody experiment. In an incredibly short time twelve thousand seven hundred and thirty-seven of their number had dropped from their ranks. Who knew how many would fail to answer roll call after another attack? "Cold Harbor," said General Grant after the war, "is the only battle I ever fought that I would not fight over again under the circumstances." Wellington, victorious at

Waterloo, said to Lord Fitzroy: "I have never fought such a battle, and I trust I shall never fight such another." Lee proudly stood at the gate of his capital. If Grant was going to fight it out on that line, he must enter there. Another flank move would carry him farther from his objective, so he determined to lay siege to Lee's position and dig up to it, and began the construction of parallels united by zigzag trenches, the work on which had to be done at night; but he soon gave up the substitution of spades and picks for guns and determined to move his army south of James River, and on the night of June 12th began the movement.

Five days before, he sent Sheridan on an expedition against the railroad which runs from Richmond to Charlottesville and Staunton, as well as to meet Hunter, who was expected from the Valley, and conduct him to the Army of the Potomac. Sheridan started on the 7th with the divisions of Gregg and Torbert, ten thousand strong, in light marching order; two days "short forage," three days rations, and one hundred rounds of ammunition were carried by each trooper. On the evening of the 10th Sheridan bivouacked three miles from Trevilian's Station in Louisa County. Hampton, with a division of cavalry, moved at once after him, while another division speedily followed; with these two divisions Hampton intercepted Sheridan at Trevilian's, and interposed between him and Charlottesville. Here he was attacked on the 12th by Sheridan, all of whose assaults — principally upon General Butler's command were handsomely repulsed, and that night Sheridan started back to his army, having accomplished nothing. Hampton, with half of his numbers, was not strong enough to seriously interrupt his retrograde movement.

After the battle of Cold Harbor, Lee had such great confidence in his ability to keep Grant from getting closer to Richmond that he detached Breckinridge to meet Hunter, who, having defeated the small Confederate force in the Valley, under W. E. Jones, was advancing via Staunton and Lexington to Lynchburg. On the 13th he sent Early with the Second Corps (Ewell's), eight thousand muskets and twenty-four pieces of artillery, to join him. Lee then crossed the James, and on that night his tent was pitched near Drewry's Bluff. Grant had sent Smith's troops around by water, down the York and up the James to City Point, with orders to try and capture Petersburg, and on the morning of the 15th Smith was in front of the lines there. He was slow and cautious. That afternoon Lee's army began to arrive, any opportunity to capture the city by a coup de main was gone, and the siege of Petersburg, destined to last ten long, weary months, began. The campaign from the Wilderness to Petersburg was brilliantly conducted on Lee's part. It was a magnificent exhibition of defensive warfare.

For one month his gigantic opponent fought him over nearly every mile between the Rapidan and the James. Practically every soldier in Lee's army placed hors de combat a soldier in Grant's, for the latter's losses equaled in numbers the strength of the former's command. Colonel Taylor, General Lee's able adjutant general, places the number of re-enforcements Lee received in the thirty days campaign at fourteen thousand four hundred men, which, added to his original strength, gives seventy-eight thousand four hundred as the aggregate of all troops under his command from the Wilderness to Cold Harbor. And to Grant, Taylor assigns fifty-one thousand during the same period, giving him an aggregate under his command from the Wilderness to Cold Harbor of one hundred and ninety-two thousand one hundred and sixty men. This is a marvelous monument to the skill of Lee and the courage of his troops. Grant's hammering process was expensive in time and men. It took him thirty days to march seventy-five miles, at a loss of sixty odd thousand men, and then he was only on ground reached by McClellan without firing a gun, if we except the affair at Williamsburg.

CHAPTER 14

SIEGE OF PETERSBURG.

Richmond, on the left bank of the James, and Petersburg, on the right bank of the Appomattox, were strategic twin cities twenty-one miles apart. The capture of one embraced the fall of the other. Richmond proper, from a point on the river below to a position on the river above, was easily defended. Its investment would still leave the Weldon, Lynchburg, or Southside, and Danville Railroad open for supplies. Circumvallating lines around Petersburg would ultimately close all of them; this done, Richmond must be evacuated. But were it possible to capture Richmond first, to Burkeville, the junction of the Southside and Danville roads, the Southern army must retreat, not to Petersburg.

Grant, though not remarkable as a strategist, promptly saw the way to reach the Confederate capital. To reach Richmond it was necessary to batter down the gates of Petersburg. Butler made several attempts to capture the city before Grant took him under his charge, but failed. Grant, having decided to cross the Army of the Potomac to the south side of the James, determined to essay the capture of Petersburg before Lee — who had drawn most of Beauregard's force to him on the north side — could prevent it, and would have been successful if he had not lost a day in getting his pontoons ready; and even then it could have been done if General Smith, of the Eighteenth Corps, to whom the duty was confided, had attacked when he arrived before it. Beauregard was in peril. He had re-enforced Lee, but Lee had not yet returned the compliment, and when "Baldy" Smith began to deploy on his front, about ten o'clock on the morning of June 15th, with eighteen thousand men, he had but twenty-two hundred soldiers to return his greetings, and had to station them so as to allow one man for every four yards and a half of his works. At 7 P. M. Smith carried with a "cloud of tirailleurs" the lines on a portion of his front, in spite of the heroic resistance of General Henry A. Wise, and held on to them during the night. Had Hancock, who was on the morning of the 15th on the south side of the James, been ordered to Petersburg, he could have been there by twelve or one o'clock, and Petersburg would have certainly fallen. Meade knew nothing of Smith's proposed coup de main, nor did Hancock, until he received orders at half-past 5 that afternoon to join General Smith, reaching his position about dark, after he had made a lodgment.

About the same time Hoke's division, from Drewry's Bluff, re-enforced Beauregard. On the morning of the 16th Hancock was in command of the operating troops, but was instructed by Meade not to attack until Burnside arrived with his corps. He reached the field at 10 A. M., but Hancock did not attack until after 5 P. M. In the meantime Beauregard drew to him Bushrod Johnson's division, who had been playing the cork to the Butler bottle in front of the Bermuda lines. But the inequality in numbers was still very great — Beauregard then having ten thousand, and Hancock fifty-three thousand. For three hours the battle raged, and at night the result was a serious loss on the Southern right, but Beauregard gained some advantage on the left. Warren had now arrived, but too late for the attack, making the Federal army in front of Petersburg sixty-seven thousand. All day on the 17th the contest was maintained with no decisive results. About dusk a portion of the Confederate lines was wholly broken, which might have ended in irreparable disaster; but at the opportune moment a fine brigade, under General Gracie, an excellent officer, reached the scene from Chaffin's Bluff, leaped the breastworks captured by Burnside, and drove out his troops, capturing two thousand prisoners.

Petersburg was still in danger. Fortunately, Beauregard's engineering skill, as well as that of his chief of engineers, Colonel D. B. Harris, was brought into requisition, and during the day selected the site of another and shorter line of defense, near Taylor's Creek, to his rear, and at midnight successfully made a retrograde movement, occupied and began fortifying his new line. On the 18th a general assault on the Southern lines was ordered at an early hour, but finding the old line had been abandoned, it was not made until noon — then only partially; but about 6 P. M. the "predetermined great attack," as Beauregard called it, was made by the Second Corps and everywhere repulsed, as were like attempts later by the Fifth and Ninth. Hancock's, Burnside's, and Warren's corps, Martindale's division of Smith's, and Neill's division from the Sixth Corps — or ninety thousand effectives — were present, while on that day Beauregard had been re-enforced by Kershaw's and Field's division of Longstreet's corps, making his total twenty thousand.

At half-past 11 General Lee rode up and was warmly welcomed by Beauregard, who had been anxiously hoping to see him for three days. He had been very slow in giving credence to Beauregard's telegrams about Grant's movements, and even as late as the night of the 17th dispatched, "Am not yet satisfied as to General Grant's movements, but upon your representations will move at once on Petersburg." And it was well he did, for the remarkable resistance of Beauregard's troops alone saved the city from capture on the 15th, 16th, and 17th. It was very difficult for Lee to ascertain on the north side of the James what troops Grant was crossing to its southern side, because his crossing was masked by the presence of troops interposed between the point of crossing and Lee's position; and he had to be most careful lest, in his anxiety to save Petersburg, he would lose Richmond. He could not afford to take the risk of denuding the Richmond lines until it had been demonstrated beyond doubt that the real battle was to be delivered at Petersburg. The admirably selected new line of Beauregard was strengthened, and maintained until the end of the war.

The next day the main portion of the Army of Northern Virginia arrived, and Beauregard wanted to throw the entire disposable force on the Union left and rear before they began to fortify; but General Lee pronounced against the plan. Grant and Meade, satisfied that nothing more could be gained by direct assaults — ten thousand men had been lost in three days — decided to play another game for the prize in which spades should be trumps, and the siege of Petersburg began. In an incredibly short time high, impregnable, bastioned works began to erect their crests. It was designed to make the Union defensive lines so formidable as to be unassailable. A system of redans chained together by powerful parapets, whose approaches were to be obstructed by abatis, were constructed. Behind these gigantic earthworks a small force could safely remain, and thus the "loyal legions" could be drawn out at any time for other work. The Federal plan, wisely adopted, was to extend their ramparts south, then west, to seize and retain the Weldon Railroad and cut off Lee's communication with the coast States, then gradually work westerly toward the Lynchburg Railroad, which once in Grant's possession, would have confined Lee to the Danville and Richmond Railroads to supply his army. The short road from Petersburg to Richmond connected him with it and the Staunton road, running north from Richmond. It was intended to throw a huge steel cordon around Petersburg, which would force Lee with his limited numbers to so extend his lines that they would snap or be weak enough to break under blows.

Grant had now established his troops in the best location for the achievement of his purpose. With bloody hands he had reached the confines of the object of his campaign; but he was there and most excellently situated; his water line of communication down the James and up the Potomac with Washington and the North was absolutely free from hostile interruption. His headquarters — City Point, at the junction of the Appomattox and the James — was connected with his army by rail, and from a point on that road a field railroad, moving in the rear of his lines, made the transportation of supplies from his water base easy in sunshine or storm. Field telegraph connected army headquarters with those of subordinate commanders; so with plenty of commissary, quartermaster, and medical supplies, and plenty of men, he anticipated with confidence future success. At Deep Bottom, on the James, he had thrown a pontoon bridge and protected it by strongly fortified works on the north side, manned by a sufficient force to defend them, thus always securing a debouch on the Richmond side of the river. He could thus make a mock assault on Richmond and a real attack at Petersburg, or the reverse.

General Lee was uneasy; he was defending two cities and a line of intrenchments enveloping both thirty-five miles long, and could not know with certainty at what point on them the real blow would be delivered. Grant's troops withdrawn from one portion of his front at night, could appear at another before the sun lifted the mists of morning. Lee too had communication with the Richmond defenses by a pontoon bridge above Grant's at Drewry's Bluff, but in any movement of troops across the river Grant, if the aggressor, would move first and thereby gain a start. Then, too, Lee's days were full of other troubles: the question of supplies, always a serious one, was growing daily more so. The subjugation of productive portions of the South and the devastation of other sections made the collection of food for men and forage for animals more difficult than ever. The supply of men was exhausted. Conscription in 1862 first placed on the rolls all men between eighteen and thirty-five, and later between thirty-five and forty. After Gettysburg and Vicksburg, a call was made for men between forty and forty-five, and in February, 1864, the Conscript Act was more stringent, and the population between seventeen and fifty were made subject to call — "a robbery," designated at the time, "of the cradle and the grave." The end of conscription had been reached. The currency in the Confederate Treasury was in value as sixty to one of coin. A deficiency in supply of arms and ammunition was imminent. The Ordnance Department contained only twenty-five thousand stand of small arms for the whole Confederacy; the foreign market supplied one half of the arms used, but that market was nearly cut off; many workshops had been destroyed, and the usefulness of others much impaired by the withdrawal of details of men.

Then General Lee was distressed at the condition of his army. It had been exposed in a violent campaign against overwhelming numbers, was badly fed — a pound of flour and a quarter of a pound of meat to the man — badly paid and cared for in camp and hospital, and every letter brought news of the families of the troops suffering at home. As his resources diminished, those of his opponent seemed to increase. He was too weak to assume the offensive against fortification, and yet something must be attempted. In the midst of the gathering gloom, Lee once more attempted to diminish the troops in his front by threatening the Federal capital.

Ewell, suffering from the loss of his leg, had relinquished the command of his corps to Early, and with eight thousand muskets this officer had been sent, as already stated, to Lynchburg, to re-enforce Breckinridge in Hunter's front. Hunter had retreated from Lynchburg to the mountains of West Virginia before Early could strike him. Then General Lee submitted to Early the question whether the condition of his troops would permit him to threaten Washington as originally contemplated; if not, to return to his army. Early determined to take the responsibility of carrying out the original plan, so he turned the head of his column toward the Potomac. On June 26th he was at Staunton, July 2d at Winchester, crossing the Potomac on the 6th, fought and defeated six thousand troops under General Lew Wallace on the Monocacy on the 9th, and arrived in front of the works at Washington at noon on July Sixth with about ten thousand men and forty pieces of artillery. That afternoon his army was placed in position with orders to assail the works at daylight next morning; but learning during the night that the Sixth Corps from the Army of the Potomac and the Nineteenth, under Emory, from New Orleans, had arrived, he countermanded the order, remained in front of Washington during the 12th, and that night withdrew and began his march back to Virginia, reaching Strasburg, in the Valley of Virginia, on the 22d. General Early could not have held Washington if he had entered its gates with his small force. No re-enforcements were nearer to him than Richmond, and from the North and General Grant's army a large force could have been speedily assembled.

Grant, in consequence of the opportune arrival of Emory, only detached the Sixth Corps from his lines, which did not materially reduce his great numbers in Lee's front, and hence Lee did not dare to weaken his lines by re-enforcing Early. Early's presence in the lower valley was menacing to Washington, preserved a threatening attitude toward Pennsylvania and Maryland, prevented the use of the Baltimore and Ohio Railroad and the Chesapeake and Ohio Canal, and kept a large force from Grant's army to defend the Federal capital.

The greater part of this force was moved south of the Potomac, organized into the Army of the Shenandoah, and the command of it given, on August 7th, to General Sheridan. With the Sixth and Nineteenth Corps, and the Army of West Virginia, as General George Crook's force was called, Sheridan had a total present for duty on September 10th, including Averill's cavalry, of forty-eight thousand men and officers. He was abundantly able to assume the offensive, for he had in addition garrisons of seven thousand men at Harper's Ferry, Martinsburg, and other points, making his whole force about fifty-five thousand. General Lee was very anxious to win a battle in the lower valley — it was the only way he could relieve Petersburg — and so re-enforced Early by a division of cavalry and one of infantry, both under General Anderson, the commander of Longstreet's corps. This officer was selected to produce the impression, the remaining divisions of his corps were to follow, in order to induce Grant to send troops to Sheridan equivalent to Longstreet's whole corps. In that case Lee would again re-enforce Early and transfer the principal scene of hostilities to the Potomac, just as he had successfully drawn McClellan from the James and Hooker from the Rappahannock at Fredericksburg by similar movements; but Grant refused to follow the precedent. Sheridan had already an army numerically equal to the one Lee commanded on the Petersburg lines, and was strong enough to stand alone. Lee could not detach more troops, but instead was obliged to recall Anderson and his infantry. The failure to transfer the seat of war from in front of Petersburg was due to the decreasing Confederate strength and the increase of that of their opponents.

Lee could only wait, watch, and frustrate Grant's plans as far as possible. After Anderson's departure from the Valley Sheridan assumed the offensive, and on September 19th, with nearly fifty thousand troops, fought and defeated, at Winchester, fourteen thousand under Early, the Confederate loss being about four thousand, the Federal five thousand, of which nearly forty-four hundred were killed or wounded. On the 22d Early was again defeated at Fisher's Hill, but, being reenforced near Port Republic by Kershaw's division of infantry and Cutshaw's battalion of artillery, and later by Rosser's brigade of cavalry, he assumed the offensive and again moved down the Valley to Fisher's Hill, Sheridan retiring in his front to Cedar Creek. Here he was attacked by Early on the 19th of October before daybreak and defeated, but afterward, rallying his troops, he in turn attacked and routed Early, who lost twenty-three pieces of artillery, eighteen hundred and sixty in killed and wounded, and over one thousand prisoners.

Major-General Ramseur, one of Early's best and bravest officers, was mortally wounded. The operations here were practically over, and both Grant and Lee called to them the greater part of their respective troops. The beautiful Valley of Virginia was a barren waste, and from the breasts of its mountains was reflected the light of two thousand burning barns, seventy mills filled with wheat and farming utensils, while in front of the victorious army were driven thousands of head of stock. In the expressive language of the Federal commander — "A crow flying across the Valley would have to carry its rations."

General Lee's duties were very exacting, and he was constantly called upon to meet some movement of his enemy. He was closer to his family in Richmond than he had been, and the citizens around him were very kind, considerate, and generous. In a note to Mrs. Lee, dated Petersburg, June 19th, he says: "I am much obliged to the kind people for the clothes; but if they are not gray they are of no use to me in the field. I hope to go to church this blessed day, and shall remember you all in my poor prayers." The ladies were always contributing to his comfort. He writes from Camp Petersburg, July 24, 1864: "The ladies of Petersburg have sent me a nice set of shirts. They were given to me by Mrs. James R. Branch, and her mother, Mrs. Thomas Branch. In fact, they have given everything — which I fear they cannot spare — vegetables, bread, milk, ice cream. To-day one of them sent me a nice peach — the first one I think I have seen for two years. I sent it to Mrs. Shippen. Mr. Platt held services again to-day under the trees near my camp. We had quite a large congregation of citizens, ladies and gentlemen, and our usual number of soldiers. During the services I constantly heard the shells crashing among the houses of Petersburg. Tell Life [his youngest daughter] I send her a song composed by a French soldier. As she is so learned in that language I want her to send me a reply in verse." And from Camp Petersburg, June 26, 1864: "I hope it is not as hot in Richmond as here. The men suffer a great deal in the trenches; and this condition of things, with the heat of the sun, nearly puts an end to military operations."

And again: "Camp Petersburg, June 30, 1864. I was very glad to receive your letter yesterday, and to hear that you were better. I trust you will continue to improve and soon be as well as usual. God grant that you may be entirely restored in his own good time! Do you recollect what a happy day thirty-three years ago this was? How many hopes and pleasures it gave birth to! God has been very merciful and kind to us, and how thankless and sinful I have been! I pray that he may continue his mercies and blessings to us and give us a little peace and rest together in this world, and finally gather us and all he has given us around his throne in the world to come. The President has just arrived, and I must bring my letter to a close. God bless you all."

And on July 10, 1864: "I was pleased, on the arrival of my little courier this morning, to hear that you were better, and that Custis Morgan (a pet squirrel) was still among the missing. I think the farther he gets from you the better you will be. The shells have scattered the poor inhabitants in Petersburg, so that many of the churches are closed. Indeed, they have been visited by the enemy's shells. Mr. Platt, pastor of the principal Episcopal Church, had services at my headquarters today. The services were under the trees, and the discourse on the subject of salvation."

Lee and Grant, dissimilar in many characteristics, were similar in others: both were quiet and self-possessed, both sometimes restless — Grant to break through Lee's works somewhere, Lee impatient to improve any opportunity that might be offered. By mere chance both were gratified. The Forty-eighth Pennsylvania Regiment, Burnside's corps, was largely composed of Schuylkill coal miners, and its lieutenant colonel, Pleasants, had been a mining engineer. One hundred and thirty yards in front, on General Johnson's front, at the center of General Elliott's brigade, was a salient in the Confederate lines. It was a re-entrant commanded by a flank from either side; in its rear was a deep hollow. The mining men, with the instinct of their profession, conceived the idea of blowing it up. Burnside approved it, and work was commenced on June 25th. Lee knew what was going on and directed countermining, but abandoned it and threw up intrenchments at the gorge of the salient, and established 8- and 10-inch mortar batteries to give a front and cross fire on it. It was prosecuted under many difficulties. Meade, and his chief engineer, Duane, did not believe such a mine for military purposes could be excavated. The former did not think the location selected was the proper one. The part of the line containing the works to be blown up could not be assaulted with success, because it was commanded in both flanks by the fire of the Southern troops, and could be taken in reverse from their position on the Jerusalem plank road and from their works opposite the Hare House.

Pleasants deserves great credit for his perseverance. Burnside, his corps, and Potter, his division commander, of the officers of high rank, alone encouraged his efforts. On July 23d the mine was ready for the powder; for forty workmen, even with inferior implements, can move much dirt in a month. Imagine a main gallery five hundred and ten and eight tenths feet long, with lateral galleries thirty-seven and thirty-eight feet each, into which eight magazines were placed, filled with a total charge of eight thousand pounds of powder. The theodolite had accurately measured the distance; the powder was directly under the fort. To Burnside, of course, was assigned the honor of making the grand assault. He had three white divisions and one division of negro troops in his corps, and determined to charge in column of divisions on all men and guns not blown up, and directed that the negroes should lead in what was expected to be a finishing stroke to a great war, and thus give the goddess Fame the opportunity to crown the colored brow.

Burnside thought the colored division would make a better charge at that time than the white division, because the latter had been for forty days in the trenches, had few opportunities of washing, and were not in condition to make a vigorous charge. Meade and Grant objected, the former because "they were untried and could not be trusted," while the latter directed the leading column of assault to be formed of white, not black troops. The negro was a sensitive plant in the Northern greenhouses at that time; and if he had been butchered in the attack there it would have been charged by some, as Meade expressed it, that "we were shoving these people ahead to get killed because we did not care anything about them."

There was only one negro division then in the Army of the Potomac, and the fact that in over one hundred thousand men it had been selected to lead the "On-to-petersburg!" charge would have been a striking and unique stricture upon the rest of the army. The sight of forty-three hundred howling, charging black men at the head of the column would have been a red rag to the Southern bull, and the contest would have been butcherly, bloody, and brief. A humorous picture has been drawn of these negro troops on the night they learned Burnside was going to give them the advance. They were represented sitting in circles in their company streets, intently and solemnly "studying," when all at once a heavy voice began to sing:

We-e looks li-ike me-en a-a-marching on,

We looks li-ike men-er war, and shortly thereafter a thousand voices were upraised to swell the refrain. The dark men with white eyes and teeth and red lips crouching over smoldering fires, the rays of lanterns piercing the gloom, made a picturesque scene. The heroes "carved in ebony" being ruled out, Burnside made his three white division commanders "pull straws" to ascertain who should lead the attack when the mine was sprung, and General Ledlie, commanding the first division, "was the unlucky victim." At 3.30 A. M. on the morning of the 30th Ledlie was in position, and ready to follow him were the other divisions.

Meade had made every preparation for a general assault, the whole army, if necessary, was to be thrust through the broken works into the city. Warren's Fifth Corps, and General Ord, commanding the Eighteenth Corps, was to support Burnside. Hancock, who had been moved to the north side of the James River to threaten an attack upon Richmond to draw troops from Lee to that side, and thus weaken his Petersburg lines, was to move back during the night and be in position at daylight to follow up the assaulting column, and Sheridan, with the cavalry corps, was to move on Petersburg by the roads leading from the southward and westward.

The great mine upon whose explosion this comprehensive wholesale battle plan pivoted was to be sprung at half-past 3 in the morning; but, owing to a defect in the fuse, the wreck of matter did not begin until an hour and a quarter afterward. Then the earth trembled and heaved and opened over the powder, and cannon, caissons, sandbags, timbers, men; smoke and fire went up in the mass of earth to a high altitude, spread out like an immense cloud, which "flushed to an angry crimson and floated away to meet the morning sun." The solid part began to fall. The troops waiting to make the charge thought the great descending mass was aimed at them, and, without the word of command, broke and scattered to the rear, and a little time, most valuable to the Confederates, was lost in reforming them. When the order for the advance was given, more time was consumed in climbing over their own breastworks, which broke their ranks, and in irregular order they pushed on for the crater one hundred and thirty yards distant, the debris having covered up the Confederate abatis and chevaux-de-frise in front of it. An enormous hole in the ground here confronted them — one hundred and seventy feet long, sixty feet wide, and thirty feet deep — "filled with dust, great blocks of clay, guns, broken gun-carriages, projecting timbers, and men buried up to their necks, others to their waists, and some with only their feet and legs protruding from the earth." Two hundred and fifty-six South Carolinians — the Eighteenth and part of the Twenty-third — and twenty-two men and officers of Pegram's Petersburg battery, were buried beneath "the jagged rocks of blackened clay."

The two advance brigades became inextricably mixed in the one great desire to look into the hole; and then, when the Confederates on either side of the crater began to take in the situation and to fire from the traverses, there was an uncontrollable and natural desire to get in the hole. General Elliott, while forming his command on the higher ground in the rear of the crater, was severely wounded; but Colonel McMaster, who succeeded to the command, got part of his troops in the ravine in the rear, and their front fire, and the flank fire from the remainder, and Ransom's troops to the Confederate left, repulsed all attempts of the Union troops to advance. The crest of the crater was now being swept by canister, for Lieutenant-Colonel John Haskell had with great promptness brought up two light batteries, and Pegram's guns were rapidly coming up. Wright's four guns, six hundred yards to the southern left of the salient, concealed in the woods and covered by traverses, and two guns to the right of the crater, opened a destructive fire and covered the ground between the big hole and the Union lines. The artillery alone stood between the crater and Cemetery Hill, which, if occupied and held as had been intended, would have resulted in the fall of Petersburg. Ledlie was in the rear ensconced in a "bomb-proof" protected angle of his own works, his division in the crater, and his orders to move forward were not obeyed. "It was as utterly impracticable to reform brigades outside of the crater under the severe fire of front and rear as it would be to marshal bees into line after upsetting the hive, or to hold dress parade in front of a charging enemy," wrote a Federal officer.

Griffin's brigade of Potter's division was advanced, but, meeting a severe fire, fell back in the crater. Every organization melted away, as soon as it entered this hole in the ground, into a mass of human beings clinging to the almost perpendicular sides. The other brigade of Potter's division now advanced, but got no farther than the abandoned traverses and intrenchments; and then Wilcox, with the third and last division of Burnside's white troops, started forward. The crater was filled with men at this time, the thermometer above ninety degrees, and the sun beating down in the great hole caused much suffering. No more troops could get in. Wilcox was left out, and with a part of his command attempted to carry some of the works on the Confederate right of the crater, but only held them a short time. Orders were being constantly sent to push forward and occupy Cemetery Hill, but were not relished and not obeyed. It was now two hours after the explosion of the mine; Burnside determined to let loose the real dogs of war, and ordered General Edward Ferrero with his black division to advance, pass the white troops, and carry the crest of Cemetery Hill at all hazards. Ferrero did not think it advisable to move his troops in, as there were already three divisions of white troops in his front "huddled together"; but Burnside said the order was peremptory.

The colored division moved out to death or glory; its commander did not, but sought the "bomb-proof" where Ledlie was. These troops, moving by the flank, passed around the crater and attempted to advance, but a deadly fire enveloped them and they broke in disorder, some falling back to the crater, while a majority ran back to the Union defenses. General Ord's Eighteenth Corps was now ordered to go forward. He had difficulty in getting through the Ninth Corps intrenchments; the parapets and abatis were not prepared for an exit, and the covered ways were crowded with the soldiers of the Ninth Corps. Turner's, his leading division, succeeded in advancing to the Confederate works, but would not stay, and fell back to the starting point. The object now was to get the men in and around the crater back to the Union lines. The ground was so thoroughly combed with showers of shot that it was proposed to dig a covered way; but not many spades or picks were available, though it was commenced. Any advance was now hopeless, and Meade, at 1.30 P. M., gave orders for the troops to be withdrawn from the crater — a difficult undertaking. Burnside thought they should stay there until night.

In the meantime the Confederates were massing for the attack. Lee heard what had been done about 6 A. M., promptly took steps to retake the position, and sent a staff officer for troops to do it. Traveler carried him rapidly to Gee House, a commanding position five hundred yards in the rear of the crater. Beauregard was already there, and soon Mahone with two brigades — Weiseger's and Wright's — arrived, and formed in a ravine in the rear of the crater. The Virginia brigade had formed for the attack, and the Georgia troops were in the act of forming when suddenly Lieutenant-Colonel John A. Bross, of the Thirty-first United States Colored Troops, sprang upon the crater crest waving a flag and calling upon his men to follow him.

Brigadier-General Weiseger, commanding the Virginia brigade, saw him, and, thinking his position would be assailed, determined to move first, and appealed, he says, to Captain Girardy, of Mahone's staff, to give the order, for he had been directed by Mahone to wait until he or Girardy ordered him forward. The order was given, and the lines were captured by a most gallant charge. The crater remained crammed with human beings, living and dead, into which huge missiles from mortars were bursting. The Georgia brigade advanced and attempted to dislodge the Union troops in the lines south of the crater, but failed. Later the Alabama brigade came up, when a general assault by these and other troops on the lines upon either side of the crater was made, and everywhere successfully; and just then a white handkerchief on the end of a ramrod was projected above the crater, in token of the surrender of the men there.

Altogether it was a horrible affair; and what promised, Grant said, "to be the most successful assault of the campaign terminated in disaster" — a disaster in which the Federals lost four thousand men. "The operation was not successful," Meade states, "for a coup de main depends for success upon the utmost promptitude of movement." Fifty thousand troops were ready to support it, but proper debouches had not been prepared. The Ninth Corps had great difficulty in getting over the high works in their front, and the space was too contracted to deploy troops, preventing rapidity of execution and cordial co-operation essential to success.

From camp, July 31, 1864, General Lee wrote: "Yesterday morning the enemy sprung a mine on one of our batteries on the line and got possession of a portion of our intrenchments. It was the part defended by General Beauregard's troops. I sent General Mahone with two brigades of Hill's corps, who charged into them handsomely, recapturing the intrenchments and guns, twelve stand of colors, seventy-three officers, including General Bartlett, his staff, three colonels, and eight hundred and fifty-five enlisted men. There were upward of five hundred of his dead unburied in the trenches, among them many officers and blacks. He suffered severely. He has withdrawn his troops from the north side of the James. I do not know what he will attempt next. He is mining on other points along our line. I trust he will not succeed in bettering his last attempt." The vigilance of the Southern general was daily displayed, and his remarkable talent for promptly disregarding the feint and locating the real attack had to be incessantly exercised. If at first he was in doubt of Grant's designs, he was patient, knowing that as they developed he would fathom his purpose.

From camp, August 14, 1864, he wrote his wife: "I have been kept from church to-day by the enemy's crossing to the north side of the James River, and the necessity of moving troops to meet him. I do not know what his intentions are. He is said to be cutting a canal across the Dutch Gap — a point in the river — but I cannot as yet discover it. I was up there yesterday, and saw nothing to indicate it. We shall ascertain in a day or two. I received to-day a kind letter from the Rev. Mr. Cole, of Culpeper Court House. He is a most excellent man in all the relations of life. He says there is not a church standing in all that country within the lines formerly occupied by the enemy. All are razed to the ground, and the materials used often for the vilest purposes. Two of the churches at the Court House barely escaped destruction. The pews were all taken out to make seats for the theater. The fact was reported to the commanding officer, General Newton (from Norfolk), by their own men of the Christian Commission, but he took no steps to rebuke or arrest it. We must suffer patiently to the end, when all things will be made right."

Hancock kept Lee from attending divine services. By Grant's direction, he left City Point with the Second and Tenth Corps on steamers, at ten o'clock Saturday night, the 13th of August, to produce the impression he was going to Washington, but disembarked at the lower pontoon bridge at Deep Bottom and marched toward Richmond. Gregg's cavalry division and the artillery of the two corps went by land and across the usual pontoon bridge. The movement was made to prevent further detachments of Lee's army going to the Valley, and if possible call back those sent, and under the impression the remaining divisions of Longstreet's corps had followed Kershaw. It involved the capture of Chaffin's Bluff, one of the chief fortifications guarding the river approach to Richmond. Field's and Wilcox's divisions, re-enforced by Mahone's division of infantry, and Hampton's and W. H. F. Lee's cavalry divisions sent from the south side, interposed an effective barrier to Hancock's advance. This officer, after making one unsuccessful assault, remained quiet for four days, and then during the night withdrew to the south side with a loss of twenty-seven hundred and eighty-six men.

In a combat on the 16th between the Confederate and Gregg's Federal cavalry, General John R. Chambliss, a bold, enterprising Southern brigadier of cavalry, was killed. While Hancock was demonstrating on the north side, Warren with his Fifth Corps was withdrawn from his lines and sent to destroy, with Kautz's cavalry, the Weldon Railroad. He struck it a point four miles from Petersburg, at Globe Tavern, and was soon afterward re-enforced by three divisions of the Ninth Corps. Dearing's Confederate cavalry was there and reported to Beauregard the occupation of the railroad by infantry, who sent Heth with two brigades to attack him. A sharp encounter between Ayers's division and Heth followed, in which both sides lost heavily. On the 19th the fighting was renewed, both sides being re-enforced. Hill attacked with five brigades under Heth and Mahone, a division of cavalry, and Pegram's batteries, at the intersection of the Vaughn road with the railroad. Heth and Mahone made a fine effort, meeting with deserved success, but were later in turn repulsed. Warren lost three thousand men, and on the 20th fell back a mile and a half and intrenched. On the 21st Hill again attacked, but was unsuccessful. General Sanders, of Mahone's brigade, was killed.

Hancock was now brought up with instructions to destroy the Weldon Railroad south of Ream's Station. He was attacked by Hill on the 25th at 5 P. M. with eight infantry brigades and two divisions of cavalry under Hampton, and beaten, capturing three batteries of artillery. A disorderly rout was avoided by the personal bearing and example of General Hancock and the good behavior of a part of his first division under Miles. Gibbon's division had been so roughly handled that their commanders, said Humphreys, could not get the troops to advance; they were driven from the breastworks by Hampton's dismounted cavalry; Gregg's cavalry division was also driven back by these troopers, and during the night Hancock retreated, having lost twenty-three hundred and seventy-two men, while Hill's loss only amounted to seven hundred and twenty. Hill captured twelve stand of colors, nine guns and ten caissons, thirty-one hundred stand of small arms, and twenty-one hundred and fifty prisoners.

General Lee's labors were incessant; as soon as one attempt on his lines failed another began. His power of endurance was great, but anxiety, fatigue, and loss of rest must make inroads. Mrs. Lee, growing uneasy for fear the great strain upon him would be too heavy, remonstrated and begged him to look more to his comfort and health. From Camp Petersburg, September 18, 1864, he replies: "But what care can a man give to himself in time of war? It is from no desire of exposure or hazard that I live in a tent, but from necessity. I must be where I can speedily at all times attend to the duties of my position, and be near or accessible to the officers with whom I have to act. I have been offered rooms in the houses of our citizens, but I could not turn the dwellings of my kind hosts into a barrack, where officers, couriers, distressed women, etc., would be entering day and night."

Warren was still intrenched across the Weldon Railroad on the left of the Union lines. Ten days after Hancock and Hill had their battle, Grant next endeavored to break the Southern lines on the Richmond side. Ord and Birney, with the Tenth and Eighteenth Corps, crossed the James the night of September 28th, moved rapidly up the River and New Market roads, while Kautz's cavalry marched on the Darby road. The sixteen thousand troops sought to assail and capture the Confederate works, which were feebly garrisoned, before they could be re-enforced from the south side. Ord, nearest the river, succeeded in capturing Fort Harrison, a strong work on the Southern main line of intrenchments about a mile and a quarter from the river, with its sixteen guns and a number of prisoners, as well as two adjoining lunettes with their artillery — six guns. But Birney's attack on Fort Gilmer, three quarters of a mile north of Harrison, was repulsed with great loss to him. Grant was present urging Birney forward, but the canister and musketry fire broke his advancing lines and caused them to fall back in confusion.

Ewell was in command of the local troops on the north side, Lee joined him during the day, and at 2 P. M. on the 30th directed an assault on Fort Harrison with five brigades under Anderson, commanding Longstreet's corps; but during the night before, large working parties had made Fort Harrison an inclosed work and too strong to be carried. After this Grant's left on the south side was further extended to the Peebles farm, and cooperative movements on both Lee's flanks followed without practical results. Longstreet returned to duty on the 19th of October, and was assigned to the command of the troops on the north side and on the Bermuda Hundred front. General Weitzel was given the command of the Eighteenth Federal Corps, and General Hancock was called to Washington to organize, out of abundant material, another fresh corps to take the field in the spring.

The picture of the winter of 1864 and 1865 has a somber background. The Confederate commander had displayed "every art by which genius and courage can make good the lack of numbers and resources," but could not gather hope from coming days; clothing, food, ammunition, and forage for animals were so scarce, suffering and distress so plentiful. The leader of a brave people must fight until the war clouds of misfortune enveloped him on so many sides he could fight no longer. "I say that, if the event had been manifest to the whole world beforehand, not even then ought Athens to have forsaken this course, if she had any regard for her glory or for her past, or for the ages to come," exclaimed Demosthenes.

Self-possessed and calm, Lee struggled to solve the huge military problem, and make the sum of smaller numbers equal to that of greater numbers. It was the old heathen picture of "man sublimely contending with Fate to the admiration of the gods, accepting the last test of endurance, and with the smile of a sublime resolution risking the last defiance of fortune." His thoughts ever turned upon the soldiers of his army — the ragged, gallant fellows around him, whose pinched cheeks told hunger was their portion, and whose shivering forms denoted the absence of proper clothing. Mrs. Lee, in her invalid chair in Richmond, with large heart and small means, assisted by friends, was busy knitting socks and sending them to him. He writes her from Petersburg, November 30, 1864: "I received yesterday your letter of the 27th, and am glad to learn your supply of socks is so large. If two or three hundred would send an equal number we should have a sufficiency. I will endeavor to have them distributed to the most needy." And again on December 17, 1864: "I received day before yesterday the box with hat, gloves, and socks; also the barrel of apples. You had better have kept the latter, as it would have been more useful to you than to me, and I should have enjoyed its consumption by yourself and the girls more than by me." And on December 30, 1864, he tells her: "The Lyons furs and fur robe have also arrived safely, but I can learn nothing of the saddle of mutton. Bryan, of whom I inquired as to its arrival, is greatly alarmed lest it has been sent to the soldiers' dinner. If the soldiers get it I shall be content. I can do very well without it. In fact, I should rather they would have it than I." And on January 10, 1865, after stating how the socks which Mrs. Lee had sent had been distributed to the army, the general writes: "Yesterday afternoon three little girls walked into my room, each with a small basket. The eldest carried some fresh eggs laid by her own hens; the second, some pickles made by her mother; the third, some pop corn which had grown in her garden. They were accompanied by a young maid with a block of soap made by her mother. They were the daughters of a Mrs. Nottingham, a refugee from Northampton County, who lived near Eastville, not far from old Arlington. The eldest of the girls, whose age did not exceed eight years, had a small wheel on which she spun for her mother, who wove all the cloth for her two brothers — boys of twelve and fourteen years. I have not had so pleasant a visit for a long time. I fortunately was able to fill their baskets with apples, which distressed poor Bryan [his steward], and begged them to bring me nothing but kisses and to keep the eggs, corn, etc., for themselves. I pray daily, and almost hourly, to our heavenly Father to come to the relief of you (Mrs. Lee was sick) and our afflicted country. I know he will order all things for our good, and we must be content."

Children always held the key which would unlock the heart of Lee, and his description of the little girls bringing him presents is a charming illustration of his fondness for them.

In spite of the wonderful success attending Lee's efforts, at every attempt Grant made to get toward Lynchburg or Southside Railroad, the Union line of contravallation continued to stretch, and it was evident, unless Lee could get more men, he would lose that line of railroad. A lodgment once effected, enormous intrenchments would follow, which could not be assailed with success; but where were men to come from when the end of conscription had been reached and exchange of prisoners stopped? Lee did not believe the white population could supply the necessities of a long war without overtaxing its capacity, and thought the time had come to enlist the negroes as soldiers, and so wrote Hon. E. Barksdale, a member of the Confederate States House of Representatives, on February 18, 1865. Six months before, he had advocated their employment as teamsters, laborers, and mechanics, in place of whites, who, being replaced, could be restored to the ranks. He thought, too, that the negroes would be used against the South as fast as the Federals got possession of them; that he could make as good soldiers of them as his enemy, who attached great importance to their assistance; that the negroes furnished more promising material than many armies mentioned in history, possessed the requisite physical qualifications, and their habits of obedience constituted a good foundation for discipline; and that those who were employed should be freed. Congress passed a bill for the purpose; but it was now too late to experiment with new measures.

The Southern chief not only wanted more men, but supplies for those he already commanded. "The struggle now is," said he, "to keep the army fed and clothed. Only fifty men," he wrote, "in some regiments had shoes, and bacon is only issued once in a few days."

On January 11, 1865, he tells Mr. Seddon, the Secretary of War, that his army had only two days supplies, the country was swept clear, and the sole reliance was on the railroads. And the next day he issued an appeal to the "farmers east of the Blue Ridge and south of the James to send food for the army, for which he would pay, or return in kind." Many months before, flour was quoted at two hundred and fifty dollars per barrel in Confederate money; meal fifty dollars, corn forty, and oats twenty-five dollars per bushel; hay twenty-five dollars per pound; beans fifty dollars, and black-eyed peas, forty-five dollars per bushel. Brown sugar, ten dollars, coffee, twelve dollars, and tea, thirty-five dollars per pound, and very scarce. Sorghum, a substitute for sugar and meat, forty dollars per gallon. In Richmond a relative offered General Lee a cup of tea, and to prevent him from knowing one cup was all she had, filled her own cup with James River water, colored by mud from recent rains, which she unconcernedly sipped with a spoon.

The capture of Fort Fisher, North Carolina, on January 15, 1865, closed the last gateway between the Southern States and the outside world. Sherman with a powerful army reached Savannah, on his march from Atlanta to the sea, on December 21, 1864, from which point he could unite with Grant by land or water. On February 1st he crossed into South Carolina, and on March 23d was at Goldsborough, N. C., one hundred and fifty miles from Petersburg.

Lee had now been made commander in chief of all the armies of the Confederacy, and assumed charge in General Orders No. 1, February 9th. He could have had practical control of military operations throughout the South before, for his suggestions would have been complied with by the constitutional commander in chief, but he always attended to his own affairs and let those of others alone. Five days after he was commissioned commander in chief he issued General Orders No. 2, exhorting Southern soldiers to respond to the call of honor and duty, pardoning deserters and those improperly absent if they returned in twenty days — except those who deserted to the enemy — and saying, "Let us oppose constancy to adversity, fortitude to suffering, and courage to danger, with the firm assurance that He who gave freedom to our fathers will bless the efforts of their children to preserve it."

The day before this order was issued "was the most inclement day of winter." Lee dispatched to Seddon, Secretary of War, that his troops "were greatly exposed in line of battle two days, had been without meat for three days, and in scant clothing took the cold hail and sleet." The commissary general reported not a pound of meat at his disposal. "The physical strength of the men," said Lee, "if their courage survives, must fail under this treatment;" that his "cavalry had to be dispersed for want of forage; with these facts, taken in connection with paucity of numbers, you must not be surprised if calamity befalls us." General John C. Breckinridge, who had been appointed Secretary of War in Mr. Seddon's place, received and referred General Lee's letter to Mr. Davis, who indorsed upon it: "This is too sad to be patiently considered." Want of supplies, want of men, was indeed a grievous calamity. In the numerous recent combats many of his best men and officers had fallen, among the latter, General John Pegram, who was endeared to him by many personal ties. It seemed difficult to get the simplest necessaries — even soap became scarce, and, as a consequence, many of his soldiers had cutaneous diseases. "The supply from the Commissary Department is wholly inadequate," he wrote, "notwithstanding the materials for making it are found in every household and the art is familiar to all well-trained domestics." The equipments for cavalrymen were so greatly wanted that Lee issued a circular requesting the citizens to send him any saddles, revolvers, pistols, and carbines that might be in their possession. His scant battalions grew smaller and smaller, the lines to be guarded longer and longer. "Cold and hunger struck them down in the trenches, while from the desolate track of triumphant armies in their rear came the cries of starving and unprotected homes." On all sides difficulties and dangers multiplied. Beauregard had been sent South to concentrate such troops as he could in Sherman's front, and had reported that Sherman would move via Greensborough and Weldon to Petersburg, or unite with Schofield at Raleigh.

"Beauregard has a difficult task to perform," said Lee to Breckinridge, Secretary of War, "and one of his best officers, General Hardee, is incapacitated by sickness. I have heard his own health is indifferent; should his health give way there is no one in the department to replace him, nor have I any one to send there. General J. E. Johnston is the only officer I know who has the confidence of the army and the people, and if he were ordered to report to me I would place him there on duty." Lee had no troops to send Beauregard, and yet it was all-important to retard Sherman's march. The troops in the Valley, under General L. L. Lomax, were scattered for subsistence, and could not be concentrated. "You may expect," said Lee to Breckinridge on February 21st, "Sheridan to move up the Valley, and Stoneman from Knoxville. What, then, will become of those sections of the country? Bragg will be forced back by Schofield, I fear, and until I abandon James River nothing can be sent from the army. Grant is preparing to draw out by his left with the intent of enveloping me; he may be preparing to anticipate my withdrawal. Everything of value should be removed from Richmond. The cavalry and artillery are still scattered for want of provender, and our supply and ammunition trains, which ought to be with the army in case of a sudden movement, are absent collecting provisions and forage in West Virginia and North Carolina. You will see to what straits we are reduced."

On the same day he wrote Mrs. Lee: "After sending my note this morning I received from the express office a bag of socks. You will have to send down your offerings as soon as you can and bring your work to a close, for I think General Grant will move against us soon — within a week if nothing prevents — and no man can tell what may be the result; but, trusting to a merciful God, who does not always give the battle to the strong, I pray we may not be overwhelmed. I shall, however, endeavor to do my duty and fight to the last. Should it be necessary to abandon our position to prevent being surrounded, what will you do? Will you remain, or leave the city? You must consider the question and make up your mind. It is a fearful condition, and we must rely for guidance and protection upon a kind Providence."

General Lee determined to make one more effort by a bold stroke to break the chains forged to confine him. Grant had so extended his left that he thought he might break through his works near the Appomattox below and east of Petersburg, and hence determined to assault Fort Stedman, two miles from the city, where the opposing lines were one hundred and fifty yards and the respective pickets fifty yards apart. General Gordon, an officer always crammed with courage and fond of enterprise, was selected to make the attack with his corps (formerly Ewell's) and parts of Longstreet's and Hill's and a detachment of cavalry. His object was to capture the fort, thrust the storming party through the gap, and seize three forts on the high ground beyond and the lines on the right and left of it, under the impression that the forts were opened at the gorge. But there were no such forts. The redoubts that had a commanding fire on Fort Stedman were on the main line in the rear, and in front were a line of intrenchments. At about half-past 4 on the morning of March 25th Gordon made his daring sortie, broke through the trench guards, overpowered the garrison, and captured Fort Stedman, or Hare's Hill, and two adjacent batteries; but, after a most gallant struggle, was forced to retire, losing nineteen hundred and forty-nine prisoners and one thousand killed and wounded, but bringing back five hundred and sixty prisoners and Brigadier-General McLaughlin.

On February 27th Sheridan, with two divisions of cavalry, ten thousand sabers, moved up the Valley to Staunton, pushed from his front at Waynesborough a small force under Early, and, marching via Charlottesville, joined Grant on March 27th. Lee now recalled Rosser's cavalry division, and his cavalry corps embraced that division, W. H. F. Lee's and Fitz Lee's old division under Munford, Fitz Lee being assigned to the command of the cavalry corps — in all, about five thousand five hundred troopers.

During the winter General Lee had given careful consideration to the question of evacuating Petersburg and Richmond. It was attended with many embarrassments. Richmond was the capital city, the machinery of the Confederate Government was in motion there, and the abandonment of a country's capital was a serious step; there, too, were the workshops, iron works, rolling mills, and foundries, which were so essential. Their loss would be a deprivation; and then, too, there was sorrow in turning away and leaving to their fate the noble women, children, and old men of the two cities, whose hearths and homes he had been so long defending. The question of withdrawal was discussed with Mr. Davis, who consented to it, the line of retreat was decided, and Danville, in Virginia, selected as the point to retire upon. It was determined to collect supplies at that point, so that Lee, rapidly moving from his lines, could form a junction with General Joseph E. Johnston, who on February 23d had been instructed to assume the command of the Army of the Tennessee, and all troops in the Department of South Carolina, Georgia, and Florida. Lee and Johnston were then to assail Sherman before Grant could get to his relief, as the question of supplying his enormous army, moving from its base to the interior, would retard him after the first few days' march.

Sherman, after his junction with Schofield at Goldsborough, had nearly ninety thousand men of the three arms. Johnston, having only eighteen thousand seven hundred and sixty-one, telegraphed Lee that with his small force he could only annoy Sherman, not stop him, adding: "You have only to decide where to meet Sherman; I will be near him." It is possible Lee, with his army out of the trenches, gaining strength from other quarters as he marched to Danville, and with absentees returning, as in that event many would, could have carried to Johnston fifty or sixty thousand fighting men making their combined force over seventy thousand effectives, as against Sherman's ninety thousand. The South would have gladly staked its fortunes upon a battle, when Lee and Johnston rode boot to boot and directed the tactical details. Sherman by water visited Grant on March 27th, told him he would be ready to move from Goldsborough by April 10th, would threaten Raleigh and march for Weldon, sixty miles south of Petersburg, and to General Grant in the direction deemed best.

Grant, apprehensive that Lee would certainly abandon his intrenchments as soon as he heard Sherman had crossed the Roanoke, determined to take the initiative. He could easily do it, for he had an army numbering one hundred and twenty-four thousand seven hundred men for duty. The returns of February 28, 1865, gives as the strength of General Lee's army, total effective of all arms, fifty-nine thousand and ninety-three. His losses in March were great at Fort Stedman — nearly three thousand — and desertions were numerous. Colonel Taylor, on March 31st, estimates that Lee had thirty-three thousand muskets to defend a line thirty-five miles in length, or a thousand men to the mile. Lee told the writer he had at that time thirty-five thousand; but after Five Forks, and in the encounters of March 31st, April 1st and 2d, he had only twenty thousand muskets available, and of all arms not over twenty-five thousand, when he began the retreat that terminated at Appomattox Court House.

The opposing horsemen, commanded by General Wesley Merritt, were composed of three divisions, under Thomas C. Devin, Custer, and Crook and formed part of the mixed command of Sheridan. From the morning report of March 31, 1865, they numbered thirteen thousand two hundred and nine present for duty, exclusive of a division under General Ronalds Mackenzie — about two thousand effectives. The cavalry corps of the Army of the Potomac numbered over fifteen thousand men in the saddle. In other words, where Lee had one infantry or cavalry or artillery soldier Grant had three! He possessed the enormous advantage, too, of being able to hold his formidable works with a force equal to the whole of Lee's army and still manoeuvre nearly one hundred thousand men outside of them, either to extend his left or for other purposes. Fully aware of his great advantage, he waited impatiently to commence the spring campaign.

He was apprehensive that Lee would quietly draw out from his front at night and, gaining a good start, appear in Sherman's front before he could reach him. Having plenty of men, why should he wait for Sherman to join him? "I have had a feeling that it is better," said he to Mr. Lincoln, "to let Lee's old antagonist give his army the final blow and finish up the job. If the Western armies were ever to put in an appearance against Lee's army, it might give some of our politicians a chance to stir up sectional feeling in claiming everything for the troops from their own section of the country." "I see, I see," replied Mr. Lincoln; "in fact, my anxiety has been so great that I didn't care where the help came from so the work was perfectly done." Lee, chained to his trenches by his necessities, and waiting for better roads on account of the weak condition of his artillery and transportation animals, gave General Grant the opportunity to get around his lines west of Petersburg, for which he had so long waited.

On March 28th Grant sounded the laissez aller, as a writer puts it, and the next day great turning columns were put in motion to swing around the flank of Lee, and get possession of his remaining lines of transportation, the Lynchburg or Southside Railroad, and the Danville Railroad at Burkesville, the junction of the two. It was calculated that Lee would largely draw troops from his lines to avert such a disaster, and in that event they could be successfully assailed by the troops on their front. On that day General Lee wrote Mrs. Lee: "I have received your note with a bag of socks. I return the bag and receipt. The count is all right this time. I have put in the bag General Scott's autobiography, which I thought you might like to read. The general, of course, stands out very prominently, and does not hide his light under a bushel, but he appears the bold, sagacious, truthful man that he is. I inclose a note for little Agnes. I shall be very glad to see her to-morrow, but cannot recommend pleasure trips now."

The Southern lines south of James River stretched from the Appomattox below Petersburg along the territory south of the city, then ran in a southwest direction parallel and protecting the Lynchburg Railroad, then bending west and northwest, terminated on Hatcher's Run, a little over a mile from Sutherland Station on the railroad. From this point the White Oak road runs west to Five Forks, four miles distant, where it is crossed by the Ford road at right angles; a road from Dinwiddie courthouse joins the intersection of the two. A person at that point could therefore travel in five different directions — east or west, north or south, or southeast — to the courthouse, eight miles away, from which the location probably derives its name. Five Forks, in front of the Southern right, became a strategic point. If Grant occupied it he could tear up the Southside Railroad west of Sutherland Station, and, while holding Lee in his lines, detach infantry and cavalry, and destroy the Danville Railroad, the only connecting link with the Southern States.

Sheridan's large cavalry corps, supported by Warren's Fifth and Humphreys's Second Corps, was directed, on the 29th, to Dinwiddie Court House, the infantry to occupy the country between the courthouse and Federal left, the cavalry the courthouse. Parke, who had succeeded to the command of Burnside's Ninth Corps, Wright with his Sixth, and Ord with the Army of the James, held the line in the order named from the Appomattox to Lee's right. Ord, in command of the Twenty-fourth (Gibbon's) and Twenty-fifth (Weitzel's) Army Corps, Butler's old army, had placed Weitzel in charge of the defenses at Bermuda Hundred and on the north side of the James.

The purpose of the Union commander to get around his right rear and break up his railroad connections was promptly perceived by Lee. General Anderson was sent at once, with Bushrod Johnson's division and Wise's brigade, to his extreme right. Pickett's division was also transferred to that point, and Fitz Lee's division of cavalry was brought from the north side of James River to Five Forks, reaching there on the morning of the 30th; this division was at once advanced toward Dinwiddie Court House, and met, fought, and checked the Union cavalry under Merritt, advancing from that point to Five Forks. General W. H. Payne, whose conspicuous daring and gallant conduct on every battlefield had made him so well known to the public and the army, was here severely wounded. At sunset Pickett, with Corse's, Terry's, and Stuart's brigades of his own division, and Ransom's and Wallace's of Johnson's division, arrived at Five Forks, and so did the cavalry divisions of W. H. F. Lee and Rosser. The five infantry brigades under Pickett and the three cavalry divisions of Fitz Lee moved out on the Dinwiddie Court House road on the 31st, and attacked and drove Sheridan's cavalry corps back to the courthouse. Night put an end to the contest. The Confederates fell back early on the morning of April 1st to Five Forks, to prevent Warren's Fifth Corps, which had moved during the night to Sheridan's assistance, from attacking their left rear. Sheridan followed with Warren's infantry and his cavalry; Pickett's line of battle ran along the White Oak road, Munford's cavalry division was on his left, W. H. F. Lee's on his right, and Rosser in the rear, north of Hatcher's Run, guarding the wagon trains. About 4 P. M. Sheridan, having succeeded in massing the Fifth Corps, concealed by the woods beyond Pickett's left, attacked by seizing the White Oak road between Pickett and General Lee's lines, four miles away, with Warren's infantry, which enabled him to flank Pickett's line with the Fifth Corps, while he assailed his front and right with his cavalry corps.

Pickett was connected with the main line of his army by the cavalry pickets of Roberts's brigade, and was cut off from support and badly defeated, in spite of his right making a gallant resistance, in which W. H. F. Lee, with one of his cavalry brigades, in a brilliant encounter, repulsed two brigades under Custer. The Confederates lost between three and four thousand men, thirteen colors, and six guns. Pickett's isolated position was unfortunately selected. A line behind Hatcher's Run or at Sutherland Station could not have been flanked, but might been maintained until re-enforced by troops drawn from the Southern right at the Claiborne road crossing of Hatcher's Run. The Confederate cavalry were withdrawn during the night to the Southside Railroad, and were joined there by Hunton's brigade of Pickett's division and by General Bushrod Johnson, with Wise's, Gracies's, and Fulton's brigade, all under the command of General R. H. Anderson.

The disaster at Five Forks was the beginning of the end. Two large infantry and one cavalry corps, making a total of fifty thousand officers and men, with a roving commission in front of Lee's extreme right, imperiled his communications most seriously, as well as the safety of his lines. The Southern general could not risk another attack outside of his works, and, in order to strengthen that portion of them sufficiently to resist assault, had so weakened what remained that it became vulnerable. From the Appomattox to the right center the thin gray line was so stretched that it was not as formidable as a well-prepared skirmish line. Though holding with tenacity to his right, Lee must let the bars down elsewhere. Thirty-five thousand muskets were guarding thirty-seven miles of intrenchments.

Grant on the night of April 1st was at Dabney's Mill, a mile or two south of Boydton plank road, which runs from Dinwiddie Court House to Petersburg. Colonel Horace Porter, his aid-de-camp, first gave him the news of Sheridan's success at 9 P. M. that night as he was sitting before "a blazing camp fire with his blue cavalry overcoat on and the ever-present cigar in his mouth." He sent over the field-wires at once orders for an immediate assault along the lines, but subsequently directed the attack to be made at 4 A. M. the next day. All during the night a bombardment was kept up on all portions of the Confederate lines. At dawn on Sunday, April 2d, Parke and Wright, with the Ninth and Sixth Corps, and Ord, with the Army of the James, successfully assaulted the attenuated lines in their front. The task was easy, and while handfuls of brave men heroically resisted, like shooting stars their course was brilliant but brief. The storming pioneer parties everywhere cut away the abatis and chevaux-de-frise, and through the opening the blue masses poured into the works. There were high parapets and high relief and deep ditches; but the troops had been drawn away to the Southern right, and except here and there, notably at Fort Gregg, it was only a matter of physical agility to climb over them. Only small garrisons were in the forts, and very few men in the connecting lines.

Four small brigades, Wilcox's division, Hill's corps — viz., Thomas's, Lane's, Davis's, and McCombs's — held the entire line in the front of the armies of Ord and Wright, while Gordon, with a few thousand troops, held in front of Parke's Ninth Corps. Lee's troops were forced back to an inner line whose flanks rested on the river above and below Petersburg, and there resisted all further attempts to break through them. Before 10 A. M., Lee knew he could only hope to cling to his trenches until night, and that the longer defense of Richmond and Petersburg was not possible. All his skill would be required to extricate his army and get it out and away from the old lines. Longstreet reached Lee from the north side of the James about 10 A. M. on the 2d, with Field's division. It is stated that he had not perceived that the Federal lines in front of Richmond had been weakened by transferring troops to the vicinity of Petersburg, and hence did not move to Lee earlier, as he had been instructed to do in that event. In the midst of the turmoil, excitement, and danger, Lee was as calm and collected as ever. When the Sixth Corps broke over A. P. Hill's lines, that officer was at General Lee's headquarters at the Turnbull House, and rode at once rapidly to his front, where he was killed by some stragglers who had crossed the Boydton road in the direction of the railroad, whose presence in that vicinity he did not expect. Hill in many respects was a good officer — earnest, dashing, zealous, and prompt to execute; he had rendered marked service throughout the whole war, and his light division had written many victories upon its proud standards.

CHAPTER 15

*EVACUATION OF RICHMOND AND THE PETERSBURG LINES. —
RETREAT AND SURRENDER.*

General Lee on the morning of April 2d telegraphed Breckinridge, Secretary of War, that it was necessary his position should be abandoned that night, "or run the risk of being cut off in the morning; it will be a difficult but I hope not an impracticable operation. The troops will all be directed to Amelia Court House." He advised that all preparations be made for leaving Richmond that night. The Southern President was kept informed on all subjects connected with the army, and of course knew that a crisis in its affairs was approaching, which involved the evacuation of its position; but he was not prepared for a precipitate announcement to that effect, or indeed for any change of affairs for two weeks. On April 2d he occupied his accustomed seat, about the center of the middle aisle, in St. Paul's Episcopal Church, Richmond, much interested as usual in the services conducted by his friend, the Rev. Dr. Minnigerode. There he received a dispatch. Upon reading it, he quietly rose and left the church. The telegram was from General Lee, announcing his speedy withdrawal from Petersburg. Lee's decision quickly became generally known in the two cities, and the feeling produced can readily be imagined. Women prayed, men wept, children wondered. Three exits remained only for the Army of Northern Virginia — one north of Richmond, one west, and one southwest. No object could now be achieved by marching in the first two directions, but by the remaining one Johnston might be reached, and his communications by the Danville Railroad with the South be maintained. On the afternoon of April 2d Lee issued orders for his troops to leave their lines everywhere at 8 P. M., and take up the line of march for Amelia Court House.

This little village is on the Richmond and Danville Railroad, thirty-eight miles southwest of Richmond. At that point it was determined to concentrate, issue — wonderful to relate — abundant rations to the troops, and get them again in shape after the heavy work of the past few days and the night march. As Grant's army was stretched to the Appomattox on the south side above Petersburg, Lee must march up its north side. Longstreet's, Hill's, and Gordon's corps crossed the Appomattox that night, the two former at Battersea factory pontoon bridge, the latter at Pocahontas and Railroad bridge, and moved — via Bevel's and Goode's bridges on the Appomattox below where it is crossed by the Danville Railroad — to Amelia Court House. Mahone's division was directed to the same point, via Chesterfield Court House. Ewell, commanding the troops in front of Richmond, Kershaw's and Custis Lee's divisions, and the naval brigade, was instructed to cross to the south side of James River, cross the Appomattox at Goode's bridge, and join the army at Amelia Court House. The commands of Pickett and Bushrod Johnson and the cavalry, being west of Petersburg and of the Federal lines, moved up the south bank of the Appomattox. General Lee was not able to concentrate all his troops at Amelia Court House until midday on the 5th, Ewell being the last to arrive. The small army was now divided into four small infantry corps or commands, and a cavalry corps commanded respectively by Longstreet, Ewell, R. H. Anderson, Gordon, and Fitzhugh Lee. Mahone's division was assigned to Longstreet's corps, and the naval battalion of Commodore Tucker to General Custis Lee's division.

The troops, though suffering for food and raiment, want of sleep, and marching over roads heavy from copious rains, were buoyant in spirit, brave in heart, and of undoubted morale; nearly every one of them was a survivor of bloody battles and a veteran of years of terrible war. They were soldiers of no "ordinary mold, who had an abiding faith amounting to fanaticism that the God of battles would in the end send their cause safe deliverance, and they followed Lee with an almost childlike faith, which set no bounds to his genius and power of achievement." Shut up so long in dismal, dangerous trenches, the fields, running streams, trees thick with bursting buds of spring, grass growing green under the kisses of the sun, and new scenes, were to them most refreshing and exhilarating.

In obedience to a law of Congress, Ewell, in command at Richmond, had made arrangements to burn the tobacco there whenever the evacuation of the city should render that necessary to prevent it from falling into the hands of the enemy. After the departure of the Southern troops, the fire got beyond local control. Mrs. Lee's house, in the center of the square on Franklin Street between Seventh and Eighth, was at one time in danger from the conflagration, a large church on the opposite side having caught fire from flying sparks, and many offers were made by persons rushing to her room to move her elsewhere. which she resisted. In the midst of the excitement a gentleman cried that the only way to save the square in which she lived was to blow up every other house, and all were so agitated that they readily acquiesced in the remarkable suggestion, and seemed much pleased at the ready ability of the person who could devise at such a time a remedy; while the poor property holder immediately began to calculate if his dwelling would be the "every other house." Graphic pictures have been painted in well-chosen phrase of the exciting scenes of April 3d. On one side the retreating march of the Confederates, on the other the triumphant advance of the Federals; while between the two, great pillars of fire rose draped in the smoke of a burning city. The tattered, brown, weather-beaten army is marching away through woods and over roads with straggling trains; the faces of the soldiers are turned from Richmond. The victorious legions, glistening with steel, with clashing music and waving banners, are pouring into the city, marching through the streets, and stacking arms in the Public Square, where "stood the dumb walls of the Capitol of the Confederacy." White clouds of dense smoke with the light of the fire woven in their folds, reaching from the island — dotted river to the tall trees on the hill of the Public Square, hung in the sky above the fated city.

At the same time Grant rode into Petersburg between rows of closed houses and deserted streets, cheered here and there by a few groups of negroes, until he came to a comfortable-looking brick house with a yard in front, where he dismounted and with his staff took seats on the piazza. There Mr. Lincoln, who had been for some days at City Point, joined him. "I doubt," said an eye witness, "whether Mr. Lincoln ever experienced a happier moment in his life," as, seizing General Grant's hand, he congratulated him on his success. The Union commander then set out for Sutherland Station, above Petersburg, where he and Meade passed the night of the 3d. Mr. Lincoln afterward went to Richmond; he was curious to see the house Mr. Davis had lived in. With a stride described as long and careless he walked its streets, and asked "Is it far to President Davis's house?" Upon reaching the house, Captain Graves, aide-de-camp to General Weitzel, whose Twenty-fifth Corps first entered the city, states that he took a seat in a chair, remarking, "This must have been President Davis's chair," and then jumped up and said in a boyish manner, "Come, let us look at the house." Mr. Davis was then in Danville, from which place on the 5th he published a proclamation in which he tells his countrymen not to despond, "but, relying on God, meet the foe with fresh defiance and with unconquered and unconquerable hearts."

Grant gave orders for a vigorous pursuit in two columns south of Appomattox parallel to Lee's route north of it — one under Ord up the Southside or Lynchburg Railroad to Burkeville Junction, fifty-two miles from Petersburg; the other under Sheridan, who had the cavalry corps and Second, Fifth, and Sixth Infantry Corps, on a route between Ord and Lee. These movements directly west, if properly made, would plant the Army of the Potomac across the Danville road at Burkeville, as well as at another point between there and Amelia Court House, twenty miles northeast of Burkeville. In that case Lee's withdrawal to Danville would be blocked, his junction with Johnston foiled, and the use of the Danville Railroad taken away from him. Sheridan arrived at Jetersville — on the Danville Railroad, seven miles from Amelia Court House, where Lee was that morning on the afternoon of the 4th, with some eighteen thousand troops of all arms, and intrenched. Meade did not reach him until late in the afternoon of the 5th. The last of Lee's force, Ewell, it will be remembered, did not reach Amelia Court House until noon that day. Still, if Lee's supplies had been there as ordered, he might have moved against Sheridan at Jetersville very early on the 5th with his whole force except Ewell, over twenty thousand men, and defeated him and reached Burkeville, thirteen miles farther, before Ord, who arrived there late that night.

Had Lee once passed beyond Burkeville, the Danville road could have supplied his army, its trains transported them to Danville, and via Greensborough to Raleigh and Goldsborough, or wherever Johnston was, or Johnston's force could have been rapidly brought to the Army of Northern Virginia. "Not finding the supplies ordered to be placed at Amelia Court House," says Lee, "nearly twenty-four hours were lost in endeavoring to collect in the country subsistence for men and horses. The delay was fatal, and could not be retrieved." There is some mystery about these supplies. Lee ordered them to be sent there from Danville, for he has so stated; and General J. M. St. John, then commissary general, states that on April 1, 1865, there were five hundred thousand rations of bread and one million five hundred thousand rations of meat at Danville, and three hundred thousand rations of bread and meat in Richmond, and that he received no orders to send supplies to Amelia Court House either from Richmond or Danville; and Mr. Lewis Harvie, then the president of the Richmond and Danville Railroad, has testified that no orders were ever given to his officers to transport any rations to Amelia Court House. It has been stated that on that famous Sunday a train-load of supplies arrived at Amelia Court House from Danville, but the officer in charge was met there by an order to bring the train to Richmond, because the cars were needed for the transportation of the personal property of the Confederate authorities. Mr. Davis was in ignorance of any such instruction, and would be the last man to place his personal wants or desires ahead of the necessities of the soldiers, and the commissary general and the railroad president also testify that they knew nothing of any such orders.

Cut off from Danville, the Southern troops were directed on Farmville, thirty-five miles west, and broke camp on the night of the 5th. Meade had proposed to attack Lee with the Second, Fifth, and Sixth Corps and Sheridan's cavalry at Amelia Court House early on the morning of the 6th, and did not know he had moved until he had proceeded within a few miles of that village. Longstreet, in the advance, reached Rice Station, on the Lynchburg Railroad, on the morning of the 6th, and formed line of battle; he was followed by the commands of R. H. Anderson, Ewell, and Gordon, and W. H. F. Lee's cavalry division in the order named. The remainder of the cavalry, under Rosser, had been passed to the front to protect the High Bridge between Rice Station and Farmville, and were just in time, as General Ord had sent out two regiments of infantry and his headquarters cavalry to burn that bridge and the one above at Farmville.

General Theodore Read, of Ord's staff, conducted the party. A fight ensued, in which General Read and Colonel Washburn, commanding the infantry, and all the cavalry officers were killed on the Federal side, and General Dearing, commanding a brigade of Rosser's division; Colonel Boston, the Fifth Virginia Cavalry; and Major Thompson, commanding Rosser's horse artillery, were killed on the Confederate side. The Federal force surrendered. The three Southern officers killed were exceptionally fine soldiers, and their loss was greatly deplored.

Anderson's march was much interrupted by the attack of the Federal cavalry on his flank. Halting to repel them and save the trains, a gap was made between the head of his column and the rear of Longstreet's, into which, after he had crossed Sailor's Creek — a small tributary flowing north into the Appomattox — the large force of Union cavalry was thrust, and mounted and dismounted cavalry stopped him and compelled him to deploy in their front. Ewell followed Anderson across Sailor's Creek, but Gordon, guarding an immense wagon train, turned to his right down the creek before crossing it on a road running to High Bridge. The Sixth Corps getting up on Ewell's rear, made him face his two divisions about — Kershaw on the right of the road and Custis Lee on the left, the navy battalion in rear of his right. Anderson and Ewell were facing in opposite directions, and neither had any artillery. Enveloped on both flanks and front in the combat which followed, Ewell was overwhelmed, not more than three hundred men of his three thousand escaping. Anderson was simultaneously attacked on front and flank, and also defeated. Both commands lost, in killed, wounded, and prisoners nearly six thousand men. Among the prisoners were Generals Corse and Hunton, of Pickett's division, and Generals Ewell, Custis Lee, Kershaw, and Dubose, of Ewell's.

Humphreys's Second Corps in the meantime closely followed Gordon, and had a running contest with his rear for some miles, capturing thirteen flags, four guns, and some seventeen hundred prisoners. Gordon reached High Bridge that night, but lost a large part of a wagon train which had given the Confederates much trouble on the whole march and greatly delayed their progress, because drawn by weak animals over roads soft and muddy from the recent rains. Longstreet, after waiting in vain for the other commands to join him at Rice Station, under instructions marched with the divisions of Heth, Wilcox, and Field for Farmville, and that night crossed to the north side of the Appomattox. He had crossed that river twice already — once at Petersburg and once at Goode's Bridge. Fitz Lee's cavalry corps followed him, crossing the river above Farmville by a deep ford, leaving a force to burn the bridge. Gordon, to whose command Bushrod Johnson's division had been assigned, crossed at High Bridge, below Farmville, and so did Mahone with his fine division.

At Farmville the Confederates feasted. It was the first occasion since leaving Richmond that rations had been issued, and their outdoor exercise had given them an appetite. Previous to this, organized bodies had been marched up to the corn houses en route, and each soldier given a dozen ears of corn, with a suggestion that he parch the grains on getting into camp. An enthusiastic young Irishman from Belturbet, County of Cavan, named Llewellyn Saunderson, reached the country in one of the last vessels running the blockade, and, being a Southern sympathizer, reported to the War Department, asking to be commissioned and sent to the field. It was done, and he was ordered to report to General Fitz Lee. His pockets were full of gold, and he quickly purchased a fine horse, the gray uniform of the staff officer, and joined the staff but a short time before the final attack. The rear guard of cavalry from Petersburg to Appomattox was obliged to pass over ground gleaned by the preceding infantry and artillery. Occasionally a trooper would secure a can of buttermilk, but corn, divided between horses and troopers, was the "solid comfort." Saunderson was bold, bright, and witty of course, behaving admirably under fire, and cheerfully under the treatment he received. He was paroled at Appomattox Court House, and returned to the "Green Isle" loaded with war experience. When asked in Richmond what he would say to his countrymen about the Confederates, he replied, "Oh, I never saw men fight better, but they don't ate enough."

The once great Army of Northern Virginia was now composed of two small corps of infantry and the cavalry corps, and resumed the march toward Lynchburg on the old stage road, but after going four miles stopped; and was formed into line of battle in a well-chosen position to give the trains time to get ahead. It was attacked by two divisions of Humphreys's Second Corps, which had been long hanging on its rear, but repulsed them, Mahone handling Miles very roughly. Humphreys lost five hundred and seventy-one men killed, wounded, and missing. Preceding this attack, Crook's cavalry division crossed the river above Farmville, and was immediately charged with great success by the Southern cavalry and driven back. The Federal General Gregg and a large number of prisoners were taken. General Lee was talking to the commander of his cavalry when Crook appeared, saw the combat, and expressed great pleasure at the result.

Had Lee not stopped to fight he could have reached Appomattox Station on the afternoon of the 8th, obtained rations, and moved that evening to Lynchburg. The delay allowed Sheridan — with two divisions of cavalry, followed by Ord's infantry and Fifth Corps, marching by Prince Edward Court House — to reach Appomattox Station on the evening of the 8th, where he captured trains with Lee's supplies and obstructed his march. Ord's infantry did not arrive in front of Appomattox Court House until 10 A. M. on the 9th. Having demonstrated that what was left of his proud army would rush to battle as of old, Lee on the night of the 7th continued his retreat — Gordon in advance, next Longstreet, then the cavalry — and on the evening of the 8th halted in the vicinity of Appomattox Court House. The Second and Sixth Corps resumed the direct pursuit at half-past five on the morning of the 8th, and that night went into camp three miles in the rear of Longstreet. The Confederate cavalry had marched from the rear to the front during the night, with orders to resume the march at one o'clock, on the morning of the 9th. "Fitz Lee, with the cavalry supported by Gordon," says General Lee, "was ordered to drive the enemy from his front, wheel to the left, and cover the passage of the trains, while Longstreet should close up and hold the position. During the night there were indications of a large force massing on our left and front. Fitz Lee was directed to ascertain its strength, and to suspend his advance until daylight if necessary." It was General Lee's intention to move by Campbell Court House through Pittsylvania County toward Danville. Two battalions of artillery and the ammunition wagons were directed to accompany the army, the rest of the artillery and wagons to move toward Lynchburg; but the plan could not be executed. Sheridan had been joined by Crook, and had thrown the immense cavalry corps directly across his path, between Appomattox Station and the Court House, the two places being five miles apart; and Ord, with the Army of the James and the Fifth Corps, was rapidly marching to his support, joining him at 9 or 10 A. M. on the 9th. The greater part of Gibbon's Twenty-fourth Corps, a portion of Weitzel's Twenty-fifth Corps, the Fifth Corps, and four divisions of cavalry, including Mackenzie, formed a living rampart of over forty thousand troops to the advance of Gordon and Fitz Lee's five thousand. Directly behind Lee were the Second and Sixth Corps, over twenty-five thousand troops.

Gracefully General Lee yielded to the inevitable. The splendid army, with whose courage and heroism a world was familiar, was reduced to a fragment of brave men, many of whom, from exposure and want of food, could not lift a musket to the shoulder. The end which Lee feared and Grant expected had come. For some days the latter had been thinking how best he could introduce the subject of surrender to Lee, to relieve him from initiating an embarrassing proposition. The Union commander arrived at Farmville a little before noon on April 7th, establishing headquarters at the village hotel. He told Ord, Gibbon, and Wright, who had called at the hotel, that he was thinking of sending a communication to General Lee "to pave the way to the stopping of further bloodshed"; he had heard, too, that Ewell, then a prisoner, had said that "it was the duty of the authorities to negotiate for peace now, and that for every man killed somebody would be responsible, and it would be little better than murder." Influenced by such reflections, he wrote the following communication:

April 7, 1865.

General: The result of the last week must convince you of the hopelessness of further resistance on the part of the Army of Northern Virginia in this struggle. I feel that it is so, and regard it as my duty to shift from myself the responsibility of any further effusion of blood, by asking of you the surrender of that portion of the Confederate States army known as the Army of Northern Virginia.

U. S. Grant, Lieutenant General. General R. E. Lee.

General Seth Williams, his adjutant general, a former intimate friend of General Lee's and his adjutant when he was superintendent at West Point, carried this communication across the river to Humphreys, who sent it at once through his lines to Lee, who was still in the position from which he had repulsed Humphreys's attack that day. Humphreys received Grant's note at 8.30 P. M., and Grant, Lee's reply after midnight, which read:

April 7, 1865.

General: I have received your note of this date. Though not entertaining the opinion you express on the hopelessness of further resistance on the part of the Army of Northern Virginia. I reciprocate your desire to avoid useless effusion of blood, and therefore, before considering your proposition, ask the terms you will offer on condition of its surrender.

R. E. Lee, General. Lieutenant-General U. S. Grant.

The next morning a reply was given to General Williams, who again went to Humphreys front to have it transmitted to Lee's. Williams overtook Humphreys on the march; his letter was sent at once through the cavalry rear guard, close to General Humphreys's front, to General Lee, whose reply was not received until dusk by Humphreys, and did not reach General Grant until after midnight, at a large, white farmhouse at Curdsville, ten miles in his rear. The two notes of that day (8th) are as follows:

April 8, 1865.

General: Your note of last evening, in reply to mine of the same date, asking the condition on which I will accept the surrender of the Army of Northern Virginia, is just received. In reply, I would say that, peace being my great desire, there is but one condition that I would insist upon — namely, that the men and officers surrendered shall be disqualified for taking up arms again against the Government of the United States until properly exchanged. I will meet you, or will designate officers to meet any officers you may name for the same purpose, at any point agreeable to you, for the purpose of arranging definitely the terms upon which the surrender of the Army of Northern Virginia will be received.

U. S. Grant, Lieutenant General. General R. E. Lee.

April 8, 1868.

General: I received at a late hour your note of to-day. In mine of yesterday I did not intend to propose the surrender of the Army of Northern Virginia, but to ask the terms of your proposition. To be frank, I do not think the emergency has arisen to call for the surrender of this army, but as the restoration of peace should be the sole object of all, I desire to know whether your proposal would lead to that end. I cannot, therefore, meet you with a view to surrender the Army of Northern Virginia, but as far as your proposal may affect the Confederate States forces under my command, and tend to the restoration of peace, I should be pleased to meet you at To A. M. to-morrow on the old stage road to Richmond, between the picket lines of the two armies.

R. E. Lee, General. Lieutenant-General U. S. Grant.

The Federal flag of truce accompanying Williams when he bore Grant's first communication appeared in front of General Sorrel's Georgia brigade, formerly Wright's, of Mahone's division, about 9 P. M. Sorrel had been dangerously wounded at Petersburg, and the brigade was commanded by Colonel G. E. Tayloe. This officer sent Colonel Herman H. Perry, his adjutant general, to meet the flag, who advanced some distance from his lines, and met a very handsomely dressed officer, who introduced himself as General Seth Williams, of General Grant's staff. Perry's worn Confederate uniform and slouch hat did not compare favorably by moonlight with the magnificence of Williams's, but, being six feet high and a fine-looking fellow, he drew himself up proudly, as if perfectly satisfied with his personal exterior.

"After I had introduced myself," says Perry, "he felt in his side pocket for documents, as I thought, but the document was a very nice-looking silver flask, as well as I could distinguish. He remarked that he hoped I would not think it was unsoldierly if he offered me some very fine brandy. I will own up now that I wanted that drink awfully. Worn down, hungry, and dispirited, it would have been a gracious godsend if some old Confederate and I could have emptied that flask between us in that dreadful hour of misfortune. But I raised myself about an inch higher, if possible, bowed, and refused politely, trying to produce the ridiculous appearance of having feasted on champagne and pound-cake not ten minutes before, and I had not the slightest use for as plebeian a drink as 'fine brandy.'"

"He was a true gentleman, begged pardon, and placed the flask in his pocket again without touching the contents in my presence. If he had taken a drink, and my Confederate olfactories had obtained a whiff of the odor of it, it is possible that I should have 'caved.' The truth is, I had not eaten two ounces in two days, and I had my coat tail then full of corn, waiting to parch it as soon as an opportunity might present itself. I did not leave it behind me, because I had nobody I could trust it with. As an excuse which I felt I ought to make for refusing his proffered courtesy, I rather haughtily said that I had been sent forward only to receive any communication that was offered, and could not properly accept or offer any courtesies. In fact, if I had offered what I could, it would have taken my corn." Grant's note to Lee being then transferred from Williams to Perry, the Confederate colonel and Federal general bowed profoundly to each other and separated.

On the morning of the 9th General Grant dispatched another note to General Lee as follows:

April 9, 1865.

General: Your note of yesterday is received. I have no authority to treat on the subject of peace; the meeting proposed for 10 A. M. to-day could lead to no good. I will state, however, General, that I am equally anxious for peace with yourself, and the whole North entertains the same feeling. The terms upon which peace can be had are well understood. By the South laying down their arms they will hasten that most desirable event, save thousands of human lives, and hundreds of millions of property not yet destroyed. Seriously hoping that all our difficulties may be settled without the loss of another life, I subscribe myself, etc.,

U. S. Grant, Lieutenant General. General R. E. Lee.

Humphreys sent it forward by Colonel Whittier, his adjutant general, who met Colonel Marshall, of Lee's staff, by whom he was conducted to the general. To this note Lee replied:

April 9, 1865.

General: I received your note of this morning on the picket line whither I had come to meet you and ascertain definitely what terms were embraced in your proposal of yesterday with reference to the surrender of the army. I now ask an interview in accordance with the offer contained in your letter of yesterday for that purpose.

R. E. Lee, General. Lieutenant-General U. S. Grant.

Grant, who received this note eight or nine miles from Appomattox, at once answered it.

April 9, 1865.

General R. E. Lee, commanding C. S. A.: Your note of this date is but this moment (I 1.50 A. M.) received. In consequence of my having passed from the Richmond and Lynchburg road to the Farmville and Lynchburg road, I am, at this writing, about four miles west of Walker's Church, and will push forward to the front for the purpose of meeting you. Notice sent to me on this road where you wish the interview to take place will meet me.

Very respectfully, your obedient servant, U. S. Grant, Lieutenant General.

The reply was sent direct to General Lee by Colonel Babcock, of his staff. Lee was obliged to confront a painful issue. His duty had been performed, but so earnest was he in trying to extricate his troops, and carry them South, that he had failed to recognize the hopelessness of further resistance, or the emergency that called for the surrender of his army. At the suggestion of some of his higher officers, General Pendleton, the commander of his reserve artillery, went to Lee on the 7th to say that their united judgment agreed that it was wrong to have more men on either side killed, and that they did not wish that he should bear the entire trial of reaching that conclusion. But Lee replied that he had too many brave men to think of laying down his arms, and that they still fought with great spirit; that if he should first intimate to Grant that he would listen to terms, an unconditional surrender might be demanded, and "sooner than that I am resolved to die." Lee had not altogether abandoned the purpose to march South, even after the notes of the 7th and 8th had been exchanged. Longstreet, Gordon, and Fitz Lee, commanding his corps, were summoned to his headquarters bivouac fires on the night of the 8th, near Appomattox Court House. The situation was explained freely, and the correspondence with Grant alluded to. It was decided that Gordon and Fitz Lee should attack Sheridan's cavalry at daylight on the 9th and open the way; but in case the cavalry was reenforced by heavy bodies of infantry, the commanding general must be at once notified, as surrender was inevitable. The attack was made at sunrise, and the Federal cavalry driven back with the loss of two guns and a number of prisoners; the arrival at this time of two corps of Federal infantry necessitated the retirement of the Southern lines. General Ord states that he was "barely in time, for, in spite of General Sheridan's attempts, the cavalry was falling back in confusion." A white flag went out from the Southern ranks, the firing ceased; the war in Virginia was over. Colonel Babcock, the bearer of General Grant's last note, found General Lee near Appomattox Court House, lying under an apple tree upon a blanket spread on some rails, from which circumstance the widespread report originated that the surrender took place under an apple tree.

General Lee, Colonel Marshall, of his staff, Colonel Babcock, of General Grant's, and a mounted orderly rode to the village, and found Mr. Wilmer McLean, a resident, who, upon being told that General Lee wanted the use of a room in some house, conducted the party to his dwelling, a comfortable two-story brick, with a porch in front running the length of the house. General Lee was ushered into the room on the left of the hall as you enter, and about one o'clock was joined by General Grant, his staff, and Generals

Sheridan and Ord. Grant sat at a marble-topped table in the center of the room, Lee at a small oval table near the front window. "The contrast between the commanders," said one who was present, "was striking." Grant, not yet forty-three years old, five feet eight inches tall, shoulders slightly stooped, hair and beard nut brown, wearing a dark-blue flannel blouse unbuttoned, showing vest beneath; ordinary top boots, trousers inside; dark-yellow thread gloves; without spurs or sword, and no marks of rank except a general's shoulder straps. Lee, fifty-eight years old, six feet tall, hair and beard silver gray; a handsome uniform of Confederate gray buttoned to the throat, with three stars on each side of the turned-down collar, fine top boots with handsome spurs, elegant gauntlets, and at his side a splendid sword. With a magnificent physique, not a pound of superfluous flesh, ruddy cheeks bronzed by exposure, grave and dignified, he was the focus for all eyes. "His demeanor was that of a thoroughly possessed gentleman who had a disagreeable duty to perform, but was determined to get through it as well and as soon as he could" without the exhibition of temper or mortification. Generals Lee and Grant had met once, eighteen years before, when both were fighting for the same cause in Mexico — one an engineer officer on the staff of Scott, the commanding general, the other a subaltern of infantry in Garland's brigade. After a pleasant reference to that event, Lee promptly drew attention to the business before them, the terms of surrender were arranged, and at General Lee's request reduced to writing, as follows:

Appomattox Court House, Va., April 9, 1865.

General: In accordance with the substance of my letter to you of the 8th inst., I propose to receive the surrender of the Army of Northern Virginia on the following terms, to wit: Rolls of all the officers and men to be made in duplicate, one copy to be given to an officer to be designated by me, the other to be retained by such officer or officers as you may designate. The officers to give their individual paroles not to take up arms against the Government of the United States until properly exchanged; and each company and regimental commander sign a like parole for the men of their commands. The arms, artillery, and public property to be parked and stacked, and turned over to the officers appointed by me to receive them. This will not embrace the sidearms of the officers nor the private horses or baggage. This done, each officer and man will be allowed to return to his home, not to be disturbed by United States authority so long as he observes his parole, and the laws in force where he may reside.

U. S. Grant, Lieutenant General R. E. Lee.

"Unless you have some suggestion to make, I will have a copy of the letter made in ink and sign it," said Grant; and it gave Lee the opportunity to tell him that the cavalrymen and many of the artillerymen owned their own horses, and he wished to know whether these men would be permitted to retain their horses. The terms gave to the officers only that privilege, and so Grant stated; but seeing that Lee's face showed plainly that he would like that concession made, the former said feelingly that he supposed that most of the men in ranks were small farmers, that their horses would be useful in putting in a crop to carry themselves and families through the next winter, and that he would give instructions "to let all men who claim to own a horse or mule take the animals home with them to work their little farms." The Union commander was in touch with his President. General Weitzel, who had entered Richmond with his Twenty-fifth Corps and received its formal capitulation, asked Mr. Lincoln what he "should do in regard to the conquered people?" The latter is reported to have replied that he did not wish to give any orders on that subject, but added, "If I were in your place I'd let 'em up easy, I'd let 'em up easy." It was the fear of his men losing their horses in case of surrender that made the Confederate cavalry commander ask permission at the council the night before to extricate his cavalry in case of surrender, provided it was done before the flag of truce changed the status. To Grant's written propositions for the surrender of the Army of Northern Virginia, General Lee replied:

Headquarters Army of Northern Virginia, April 9, 1865.

General: I received your letter of this date, containing the terms of the surrender of the Army of Northern Virginia as proposed by you. As they are substantially the same as those expressed in your letter of the 8th instant, they are accepted. I will proceed to designate the proper officers to carry the stipulation into effect.

R. E. Lee, General.

Lieutenant-General U. S. Grant.

The formalities were concluded without dramatic accessories, and then Lee's thoughts turned to his hungry veterans and to his prisoners. "I have a thousand or more of your men and officers, whom we have required to march along with us for several days," said Lee to Grant. "I shall be glad to send them to your lines as soon as it can be arranged, for I have no provisions for them. My own men have been living for the last few days principally upon parched corn, and we are badly in need of both rations and forage." The rations sent from Lynchburg to the Southerners were captured. When Grant suggested that he should send Lee twenty-five thousand rations, the latter told him it would be ample, and assured him it would be a great relief. The Confederate commander then left, and rode away to break the sad news to the brave troops he had so long commanded.

His presence in their midst was an exhibition of the devotion of soldier to commander. The troops crowded around him, eagerly desiring to shake his hand. They had seen him when his eye calmly surveyed miles of fierce, raging conflict; had closely observed him when, tranquil, composed, undisturbed, he had heard the wild shout of victory rend the air; now they saw their beloved chieftain a prisoner of war, and sympathy, boundless admiration, and love for him filled their brave hearts. They pressed up to him, anxious to touch his person or even his horse, and copious tears washed from strong men's cheeks the stains of powder. Slowly and painfully he turned to his soldiers, and, with voice quivering with emotion, said: "Men, we have fought through the war together; I have done my best for you; my heart is too full to say more." It was a simple but most affecting scene. On the next day a formal leave of his army was taken by General Lee.

Headquarters Army of Northern Virginia, April 10, 1865.

After four years of arduous service, marked by unsurpassed courage and fortitude, the Army of Northern Virginia has been compelled to yield to overwhelming numbers and resources. I need not tell the survivors of so many hard-fought battles, who have remained steadfast to the last, that I have consented to this result from no distrust of them; but feeling that valor and devotion could accomplish nothing that could compensate for the loss that would have attended the continuation of the contest, I have determined to avoid the useless sacrifice of those whose past services have endeared them to their countrymen. By the terms of agreement, officers and men can return to their homes and remain there until exchanged. You will take with you the satisfaction that proceeds from the consciousness of duty faithfully performed; and I earnestly pray that a merciful God will extend to you his blessing and protection. With an unceasing admiration of your constancy and devotion to your country, and a grateful remembrance of your kind and generous consideration of myself, I bid you an affectionate farewell.

R. E. Lee, General.

And then in silence, with lifted hat, he rode through a weeping army to his home in Richmond. He was not present at the final act of surrender; the details were prepared by three officers on each side, and were as follows:

Agreement entered into this day in regard to the surrender of the army of Northern Virginia to the United States authorities:

Appomattox Court House, Va., April 10, 1865.

1. The troops shall march by brigades and detachments to a designated point; stack their arms, deposit their flags, sabers, pistols, etc., and thence march to their homes, under charge of their officers, superintended by their respective division and corps commanders, officers retaining their side arms and the authorized number of private horses.

2. All public horses, and public property of all kinds, to be turned over to staff officers to be designated by the United States authorities.

3. Such transportation as may be agreed upon as necessary for the transportation of the private baggage of officers will be allowed to accompany the officers, to be turned over, at the end of the trip, to the nearest United States quartermaster, receipts being taken for the same.

4. Couriers and mounted men of the artillery and cavalry, whose horses are their own private property, will be allowed to retain them.

5. The surrender of the Army of Northern Virginia shall be construed to include all the forces operating with that army on the 8th instant, the date of the commencement of the negotiations for surrender, except such bodies of cavalry as actually made their escape previous to the surrender, and except, also, such pieces of artillery as were more than twenty miles from Appomattox Court House at the time of the surrender on the 9th instant.

(Signed) John Gibbon, Major General Volunteers. Charles Griffin, Brevet Major General U. S. Volunteers. W. Merritt, Brevet Major General. J. Longstreet, Lieutenant General. J. B. Gordon, Major General. W. N. Pendleton, Brigadier General and Chief of Artillery.

General Grant's behavior at Appomattox was marked by a desire to spare the feelings of his great opponent. There was no theatrical display; his troops were not paraded with bands playing and banners flying, before whose lines the Confederates must march and stack arms. He did not demand Lee's sword, as is customary, but actually apologized to him for not having his own, saying it had been left behind in the wagon; promptly stopped salutes from being fired to mark the event, and the terms granted were liberal and generous. "No man could have behaved better than General Grant did under the circumstances," said Lee to a friend in Richmond. "He did not touch my sword; the usual custom is for the sword to be received when tendered, and then handed back, but he did not touch mine." Neither did the Union chief enter the Southern lines to show himself or to parade his victory, or go to Richmond or Petersburg to exult over a fallen people, but mounted his horse and with his staff started for Washington. Washington, at Yorktown, was not as considerate and thoughtful of the feelings of Cornwallis or his men.

Charges were now withdrawn from the guns, flags furled, and the Army of the Potomac and the Army of Northern Virginia turned their backs upon each other for the first time in four long, bloody years. The Southern soldiers, wrapped in faded, tattered uniforms, shoeless and weather-beaten, but proud as when they first rushed to battle, returned to desolate fields, homes in some cases in ashes, blight, blast, and want on every side. A few days afterward General Lee rode into Richmond, accompanied by his staff, and the cheering crowds which quickly gathered told in thunder tones that a paroled prisoner of war was still loved by his people. It was a demonstration in which men forgot their own sorrow and gave way to the glory and gratitude of the past. They adored him most, not in the glare of his brilliant victories, but in the hour of his deepest humiliation.

CHAPTER 16

RETURN TO RICHMOND. — PRESIDENT OF WASHINGTON
COLLEGE. — DEATH AND BURIAL.

Personally it was a great relief to General Lee to be transferred to domestic life and the company of his wife and children. For forty years, including his cadetship, he had been a soldier whose movements and duties were directed by others; now he was independent of all war departments and military orders. He was a private citizen for the first time during his manhood, and would not be disturbed as long as he observed his parole and the laws in force wherever he might reside. He had denounced the assassination of Mr. Lincoln as a crime previously unknown to the country, and one that must be deprecated by every American; and when President Johnson proclaimed his policy of May 29th, in the restoration of peace, he applied on June 13th to be embraced within its provisions, and tendered his allegiance to the only government in existence, under whose flag he must resume the duties of citizenship. He cited to his friends the example of Washington, who fought against the French in the service of the King of Great Britain, and then with the French against the English, under the orders of the Continental Congress. "If you intend to reside in this country," he wrote a friend in New Orleans, "and wish to do your part in the restoration of your State and in the Government of the country, which I think is the duty of every citizen to do, I know of no objection to your taking the amnesty oath." In the same month he was indicted by the United States grand jury, with Mr. Davis and others, for treason. With a clear conscience, he made up his mind, he said, "to let the authorities take their course. I have no wish to avoid any trial the Government may order; I hope others may be unmolested."

Reverdy Johnson, the distinguished Maryland lawyer, who did not agree with General Lee's political views, hearing that he was to be prosecuted in court for the alleged crime of treason, placed the fifty years of his great study and profound experience at his command, because, as he states, "in saving him I would be saving the honor of my country." General Lee wrote General Grant to withdraw his application for amnesty under the President's proclamation, if steps were to be taken for his prosecution, as he was willing to stand the test. Grant saw the President, and protested against a procedure against General Lee, informing him that he considered his honor and the honor of the nation pledged to him, and no proceedings were taken.

General Lee's enjoyment of the society of his family and friends in Richmond was much broken into by visitors from all sections of the country. Many persons were attracted to the city because it had been the Southern capital, whose lines had for so long kept great hosts from entering her gates, and a visit to or a sight of General Lee was always on their programme. Numbers of people stood on the street and gazed at the house, hoping to catch a glimpse of its occupant. Not desiring to make a public exhibition of himself, the paroled soldier was a prisoner in his own house; and his condition produced the desire to move to more secluded quarters. Mrs. Lee's health, too, would be benefited by going out of town during the coming summer months. The house he lived in belonged to Mr. John Stewart, of Brook Hill, a fine specimen of the kind-hearted, benevolent Scotch gentleman. He had rented it to General Lee's son, General G. W. C. Lee, some time before the war closed.

The general felt that he should make post-war terms with his excellent landlord; but, before he could take any steps, Mrs. Lee received a note from Mr. Stewart which read: "I am not presuming on your good opinion when I feel that you will believe me — first, that you and yours are heartily welcome to the house as long as your convenience leads you to stay in Richmond; and, next, that you owe me nothing, but, if you insist on pay, that the payment must be in Confederate currency, for which alone it was rented to your son. You do not know how much gratification it is, and it will afford me and my whole family, during the remainder of our lives, to reflect that we have been brought into contact and to know and to appreciate you and all that are dear to you."

In looking beyond Richmond for quarters, General Lee was much in favor of purchasing a farm in Orange County, in the beautiful section near the railroad crossing of the Rapidan, with which he was so familiar; but about that time Mrs. Elizabeth Randolph Cocke, of Cumberland County, Virginia, granddaughter of Edmund Randolph, offered him the use of a dwelling house situated on a portion of her estate in Powhatan County. As it was known that he had been dispossessed of his old home at Arlington, numerous offers of money, houses, and lands almost daily reached him, as well as requests to become the president of business associations and chartered corporations. Mrs. Cocke's kind, cordial manner, for which she was proverbial, and the retired situation of the dwelling offered, induced him to put all others aside and accept her hospitable and thoughtful invitation. The spring and early summer of 1865 were spent by the great soldier in the full fruition of a well-earned and long-needed repose.

In the meantime the trustees of Washington College, at Lexington, Va., determined to reorganize the institution, pledging their personal credit to provide means to repair the ravages of war. A member of the board had accidentally heard that a daughter of General Lee had said she thought her father would like to be connected with an institution of learning, and this casual remark first directed the attention of the trustees to General Lee in connection with the presidency of their college; but, as one of them said, it was unmingled impudence to tender to General Lee the head of an institution which had nothing then, and must start at the bottom round of the collegiate educational ladder. The temerarious trustees were equal to the emergency, and boldly grappled with the subject, doubtless encouraged and inspired by the strong advice of ex-Governor John Letcher, who suggested that if the college had nothing then, its condition would instantaneously change at the moment General Lee accepted the presidency. The name of Robert E. Lee was duly proposed for the office, and the letter informing him of his unanimous election, signed by the rector, Judge John W. Brockenbrough, and the committee, was consigned to the rector, to be delivered in person rather than by mail, because its contents could be strengthened by the well-known persuasive powers of the learned judge. At this point the trustees were confronted with a fresh and apparently insurmountable obstruction. Neither the rector nor any one of them, owing to the disasters of cruel war, had raiment of sufficient texture, shape, and freshness to wear in making a trip from home, more especially when it comprised a personal interview with the great soldier upon which so much depended. After laborious search, the best-dressed citizen of that section since the war was found, whose clothes fortunately came near enough to fitting the rector to encourage him to make his appearance in them as ambassador to the county of Powhatan, where the general was then residing. The sigh of relief that this obstacle had been so successfully overcome was scarcely audible before the trustees encountered still greater trials. Neither the rector nor anyone else had any finances, or possibly even financial standing. Money was as absolutely necessary, when rectors traveled so soon after the war, as it is now, and Confederate money for some time before the surrender had not been worth ten cents per yard. Finally, however, by the supreme exertion of one of the trustees, fifty dollars of "good money" was secured, and the representative of Washington College was safely started. The public and private monetary stringency was not confined at that period to Lexington.

In the letter dated August 5, 1865, carried by Judge Brockenbrough, General Lee was told that Washington College, though a great sufferer from havoc and devastation, "is still blessed with a vigorous vitality, and needs only the aid of your illustrious character and transcendent scientific attainments to reanimate her drooping fortunes and restore her to more than her pristine usefulness and prosperity." General Lee had already declined the presidency of the Suwanee University of Tennessee, and shrank from any connection with the University of Virginia, on the ground that one was a denominational and the other a State university. He considered this matter nineteen days, and then wrote that he feared he would be unable to "discharge the duties to the satisfaction of the trustees or to the benefit of the country." Then, too, he was excluded from the terms of amnesty in the proclamation of the President of the United States, he said, and "an object of censure to a portion of the country," and he was afraid he might draw upon the college a feeling of hostility, and therefore cause injury to an institution which it would be his highest desire to advance, and concluded by saying, "I think it is the duty of every citizen, in the present condition of the country, to do all in his power to aid in the restoration of peace and harmony, and in no way to oppose the policy of the State or General Government directed to that object"; and that, after what had been written, if the board should still think his services would be advantageous to the college and country, he would yield to their judgment and accept.

The trustees on August 31st adopted and transmitted to General Lee resolutions that, in spite of his objections, in their opinion, "his connection with the institution will greatly promote its prosperity and advance the general interest of education," and solicited him to enter upon the duties of the presidency of the college at his earliest convenience. The "happy audacity," as one of the professors of the Virginia Military Institute termed it, of the trustees gave to them the victory. That General Lee should put aside the many large and lucrative offers and accept this position at the salary then offered — fifteen hundred dollars per annum — was but in keeping with his great character. Washington College had descended from a classical school taught in the Valley of Virginia as early as the year 1749, known as the Augusta Academy. On May 13, 1776, nearly two months before the Declaration of Independence, in response to the patriotic sentiment of the times, the name was changed to 1 "Liberty Hall Academy." The institution was removed successively to different places, and was finally established in Lexington, Va., a town founded in 1778 as the county seat of Rockbridge County and called after Lexington, Mass., where the "embattled farmers stood and fired the shot heard round the world."

In 1784 Virginia, desiring to testify her appreciation of the services and character of her great son Washington, directed the Treasurer of the State to subscribe to one hundred shares of the par value of two hundred dollars in the stock of a company organized for the improvement of the navigation of James River, and vested the same in General Washington. The Legislature agreed to the condition upon which alone he would receive the gift — viz., that he would be permitted to present it to objects of a public nature, such as "the education of the poor, particularly the children of such as have fallen in the defense of the country." He gave this stock in 1796 to Liberty Hall Academy in Rockbridge County, first presided over by William Graham, an old Princeton classmate and friend of General Lee's father. "Liberty Hall" was now Washington College, that name having been adopted in 1812.

Perhaps past associations had something to do with General Lee's accepting the presidency of the college, as well as a desire to contribute his part toward laying the only true foundation upon which a republic can rest the Christian education of its youth. His object now, as in 1861, was to render the best service he could to his native State, and to that purpose he had never been unfaithful. By the intelligent and judicious management of sums donated, principally by the patriots of the Revolution, the endowment fund, in 1861, had nearly reached one hundred thousand dollars, and the college had secured ample buildings, apparatus, and libraries, while its alumni had already richly adorned pulpit, bench, bar, medical profession, halls of legislation, seats of learning, and all the walks of life. It might have escaped war's devastation had any other Federal officer than General David Hunter marched upon its campus. This officer had no respect for colleges, or the peaceful pursuits of professors and students, or the private dwellings of citizens, though occupied by women and children only, and during his three days occupancy of Lexington in June, 1864, the college buildings were dismantled, apparatus destroyed, and the books mutilated.

At the end of the fiscal year 1865 there was a balance in the hands of the college treasurer of two thousand four hundred and fifty-eight dollars and twenty cents in Confederate money. The assets of the college were not available, nor could the interest upon its bonds or State securities be collected. There was a balance due professors and others of nearly two thousand dollars, and the Finance Committee of the Board of Trustees recommended that the college borrow at once, to meet pressing demands, four thousand six hundred dollars. The trustees proved equal to the encounter with these discouraging difficulties, and with "happy audacity" promptly sent their rector to offer General Lee the presidency at a salary at that time not in sight of the college's treasury! General Lee's favorite war horse, Traveler, the famous gray which had borne him so faithfully amid the flying bolts of battle, now carried him to peaceful pursuits. Unheralded and unattended, having ridden from Powhatan County in four days, his simple entree was made into the little mountain town of Lexington. As he drew rein in front of the village hotel, an old soldier recognized him, gave the military salute, placed one hand upon the bridle, the other upon the stirrup, and stood, waiting for him to dismount.

The general's wish for a quiet, informal inauguration was gratified, and on October 2, 1865, in the presence of the faculty, students, and board of trustees, subscribed before William White, Esq., justice of the peace, the oath prescribed by law. During the ceremony the general, dressed in a plain but elegant suit of gray, remained standing, his arms folded, calmly and steadfastly looking into the eyes of the speaker, Judge Brockenbrough. The warrior had been transformed into a college president, who was to discharge his duties there as conscientiously as when his simple mandate sent thousands of men into fierce battle. "I have," said he, "a self-imposed task, which I cannot forsake." The college to which he was called was broken in fortune; "the war had practically closed its doors; its buildings had been pillaged and defaced and its library scattered." He had the profoundest convictions of the importance of educational influence and the deepest sense of personal responsibility. Year by year the conception of his duty grew stronger, and year by year, as its instrument, the college grew dearer. He was no figurehead, kept in position for the attraction of his name; his energy, zeal, and administrative ability surmounted all difficulties. His great labors were directed to making Washington College the seat of science, art, and literature. Far-reaching plans laid for its success were wisely conceived.

A scholastic monument was slowly responding to his noble influence and wise administration, which would be as illustrious as his most brilliant military achievements. He mastered all details, observing the students, becoming personally acquainted with them, their aspirations and hopes; his interest followed them everywhere, and their associations, dispositions, and habits were well known to him. He never grew imperious, or tried to force a measure upon the faculty, but modestly said he had but one vote and wished to know the opinion of his colleagues, and leave the decision to be determined by the whole body. Sustained by the loftiest principles of virtue and religion, an exalted character, and a conscientious sense of duty, General Lee suffered no complaint to escape his lips during the eventful years from 1865 to 1870, though troubled by much that was taking place.

He manifested much interest in the case of Captain Wirtz, on trial for his life, accused of cruelty to the Federal prisoners of war committed to him. He knew the captain had done all that was possible with the resources at his disposal; subsistence for them had been most difficult to procure, their exchange for an equal number of Southerners had been refused, while the Federal blockade kept out medical supplies. A portion of the Northern press charged Lee with being responsible for the alleged suffering of the Union prisoners. He declined to make a public reply unless the accusation came from a responsible source, but said that he was in no way responsible for the condition of prisoners after they had been sent from his army. When the commissary general said to him, upon one occasion, that it would be necessary to reduce either the rations of the Federal prisoners or those of his men in the field, he replied, "While I have no authority in the case, my desire is that the prisoners shall have equal rations with my men." He was summoned to Washington in March, 1866, as a witness before a congressional committee which was inquiring into the condition of things in the South. His testimony was simple, direct, dignified, and elicited the admiration of all who heard or read it. It was his first appearance in any of the cities since the war, and, being at a time of public political excitement, his visit was an occasion of absorbing interest. The day after his return he proposed a walk with one of his daughters, who playfully objected to a new hat he was about to put on. "You do not like my hat?" said he; "why, there were a thousand people on Pennsylvania Avenue in Washington the other day admiring this hat!" It was his only reference to the crowds of persons who gathered around him wherever he went in the city.

General Lee was still receiving numerous letters, filled with offers of remunerative positions, to which he always replied that he preferred to continue the educational work he had undertaken; but still they came, coupled often with the condition that he should not relinquish his self-imposed task, and should not resign the college presidency. On one occasion the general said to a particular friend in his office: "My friend Mr.— has been to see me, and offers me twenty thousand dollars per annum to take the presidency of — Company. I would like to make some money for Mrs. Lee, as she has not much left, and he does not require me to leave the college; what do you think of my accepting it?" The irony of the question was appreciated, but his friend took him at his word, and expressed his opinion adversely, saying, as modestly as possible, that if he "allowed himself to be influenced by filthy lucre he would begin to gravitate." With the winsome way so characteristic of him the general replied: "I am glad to find that you agree with me. I told Mr. — yesterday that I must decline his offer."

About this time the subject of the removal of the remains of the Southern dead from the field of Gettysburg was being considered. General Lee replied to a letter calling his attention to it:

Lexington, Va., December 15, 1868.

My dear Fitz: I have considered the subject of your letter, which has been unaccountably delayed on the journey; and though I have no desire that my views should govern in the decision of a question in which others are equally interested, I will give them for your consideration. In the first place, I have no fears that our dead will receive disrespectful treatment at the hands of the Gettysburg association. If they do so, it will then be time, as it will also furnish the occasion, for us to apply for their transfer to our care. I am not in favor of disturbing the ashes of the dead unless for a worthy object, and I know of no fitter resting-place for a soldier than the field on which he has nobly laid down his life. If our State governments could reflect the wishes of their citizens, and each State could receive its own dead, I think it would be very appropriate to return them to their native soil for final interment, if possible; and I know it would be soothing to the feelings of their friends to have their sacred dead committed to their affectionate keeping.

The General was only induced to take the presidency of the Valley Railroad because it did not require him to leave Lexington, and because he was so interested in obtaining railroad facilities for his college. He really loved his work, in which his interest increased rather than diminished. Occasionally he would administer admonition to the students or make public his directions by circulars, which were called by them "General orders"; for example:

Washington College, Va., December 24, 1869.

Academic exercises will be suspended from the 25th to the 27th inclusive, to enable the students to join in the rites and services appropriate to the occasion; and while enjoying these privileges with grateful hearts, all are urged to do or countenance nothing which may disturb the peace, harmony, and happiness that should pervade a Christian community.

R. E. Lee, President.

The labors, exposure, and responsibilities of his campaigns laid the foundation for bodily distress. Rheumatism of the heart sac and of other portions of his body was creeping by gradual approach to assault the vitals. He was reluctantly persuaded to go south in March, 1870, to look upon other scenes and enjoy the fragrant breezes in the "land of sun and flowers." In Richmond, en route, in response to an invitation tendering the privileges of the legislative floor, he wrote:

Richmond, Va., March 26, 1870.

Hon. J. S. Marye, President of the Senate of Virginia.

Sir: It would afford me great pleasure to be able to avail myself of the privileges of the floor of the Senate extended to me by the resolution of that body to-day, but the condition of my health is such as to require me to reach a milder climate as soon as practicable. With a due sense of the honor conferred on me by the resolution of the Senate, I have the honor to be your most obedient servant,

R. E. Lee.

His sweet daughter Agnes, who did not long survive her father, accompanied him. On the trip he embraced the opportunity to see once more his father's grave, on an island off the coast of Georgia.

General Henry Lee (or "Light-horse Harry"), in returning from the West Indies, where he had been, hoping to restore his health, was, it may be remembered, taken ill, and begged to be put ashore at General Greene's mansion, then occupied by his daughter, where he died, and where his remains now lie. From Savannah, Ga., April 18, 1870, the general wrote Mrs. Lee: "We visited Cumberland Island, and Agnes decorated my father's grave with beautiful fresh flowers. I presume it is the last time I shall be able to pay it my tribute of respect. The cemetery is unharmed and the graves are in good order, though the house of 'Dungeness' has been burned and the island devastated. I hope I am better. I know that I am stronger, but I still have the pain in my chest whenever I walk. I have felt it, too, occasionally recently, when quiescent."

He returned benefited by the trip, but the steady progress of his disease had not been checked. While absent, the college trustees appropriated money to present him with a house and settle an annuity of three thousand dollars per annum on his family, all of which he firmly declined. "I am unwilling that my family should become a tax to the college," he wrote to the board, "but desire that all its funds should be devoted to the purposes of education. I feel assured that, in case a competency should not be left to my wife, her children would never suffer her to want."

When the fall session of 1870 of the college opened, General Lee was at his post of duty, but "his step had lost something of its elasticity, the shoulders began to stoop as if under a growing burden, and the ruddy glow of health upon his countenance changed to a feverish flush." A noble life was drawing to a close. The morning of September 28, 1870, found him faithfully performing the duties of his office; the afternoon, engaged with his brother members of the vestry of Grace Episcopal Church in work congenial to the true Christian, and the autumn evening shadows fell upon a couch over which the heavenly angels were bending. The important question of rebuilding the church and increasing his faithful friend and pastor's compensation had interested him so deeply at the vestry meeting, that the cold church and the outside storm were forgotten, and it was only after a protracted session of over three hours, as he proceeded to his house, a short distance off, that weariness and weakness overtook him, and his wavering steps indicated increasing feebleness. Entering his private office as usual, he took off his hat, military cloak, and overshoes, and then proceeded to join his family, who had been waiting tea for him. Quietly he stood in his accustomed place in the dining-room, while his family with bowed heads waited to hear the well-known grace, but no sound came from his lips. Speechless the great soldier stood; an expression of despair spread over his face; and from his eyes came a dreamy, far-away look which denoted the approaching summons from his Creator.

"My husband came in," wrote Mrs. Lee, "and I asked where he had been, remarking that he had kept us waiting a long time. He did not reply, but stood up as if to say grace. No word proceeded from his lips, but with a sublime look of resignation he sat down in his chair." With intense anxiety the family went to his assistance. A bed was brought to the dining-room, in which he was placed, and Dr. B. L. Madison and Dr. H. T. Barton were quickly summoned. For two weeks,

'Twixt night and morn upon the horizon's verge,
Between two worlds life hovered like a star.

Mrs. Lee tells us that his whole demeanor during his sickness was that of one who had taken leave of earth. He never smiled and rarely attempted to speak except in his dreams, and then, she says, "he wandered to those dreadful battlefields." "You must get out and ride your faithful gray," the doctor said. He shook his head and looked upward; and once when his daughter Agnes urged him to take medicine, he looked at her and said, "It is no use." Human love was powerful, human aid powerless. Hope and Despair were twin watchers by his bedside. At first, as his disease seemed to yield to treatment, Hope brightened, but soon Despair alone kept watch. During the afternoon and night of October 10th shadowy clouds of approaching dissolution began to gather, a creeping lethargy captured the faculties, and the massive grandeur of form and face began to contract. During the succeeding day he rapidly grew worse; his thoughts wandered to the fields where he had so often led his gray battalions to victory; and like the greatest of his captains, Stonewall Jackson, whose expiring utterance told "A. P. Hill to prepare for action," he too, in death's delirium, said, "Tell Hill he must come up!" "For the last forty-eight hours he seemed quite insensible of our presence," Mrs. Lee states; "he breathed more heavily, and at last gently sank to rest with one deep-drawn sigh, and oh, what a glorious rest was in store for him!"

Robert Edward Lee died at half-past 9, on the morning of October 12, 1870, in the sixty-fourth year of his age. His physicians stated as the cause, "mental and physical fatigue inducing venous congestion of the brain, which, however, never proceeded as apoplexy or paralysis, but gradually caused cerebral exhaustion and death." On the 14th the casket containing the body of the dead warrior was removed to the college chapel, and on the 15th buried in the area of the chapel in a brick vault prepared for it. Upon the marble capping on the top of the vault, and on a level with the library floor is this simple inscription: "Robert Edward Lee,

Born January 19, 1807,

Died October 12, 1870."

Tolling bells first proclaimed the sad intelligence to the citizens of Lexington, electric wires to the world. Throughout the South business was suspended, schools closed, societies and associations of all sorts assembled, where eulogistic speeches were made, and resolutions passed laudatory of General Lee's life and lamenting his death. In those adopted by the faculty of the college it was declared that "his executive ability, his enlarged views of liberal culture, his extraordinary powers in the government of men, his wonderful influence over the minds of the young, and his steady and earnest devotion to duty, made the college spring, as if by the touch of magic, from its depressions after the war to its present firm condition of permanent and widespread usefulness"; that it was "a deep satisfaction to receive his remains beneath the chapel he had built"; and that the "memory of his noble life will remain as an abiding inspiration to the young of the country as they gather at the last scene of his labors, to emulate his virtues and to follow his great example."

The board of college trustees by resolution extolled General Lee for his great military services, and for the victories won by him in the classic shades of Washington College, saying that the two most renowned names in their respective centuries were Washington and Lee, and that they "be hereafter associated indissolubly as founder and restorer of our beloved college"; that the charter be so amended as to hereafter express in fit conjunction the immortal names of Washington and Lee; that the anniversary of his birth should always be celebrated in the college; and that, with the co-operation of the faculty, measures should be taken and plans prepared for the erection within the college grounds of a suitable monument to his memory. The sorrowing students met and resolved: "We deeply mourn the loss of one who in his public career had endeared himself to us by all the virtues that adorn the character of the patriot and Christian, and who in his official and private relations with ourselves has also won our peculiar affection and confidence by his paternal sympathy and his tender regard for our interest as students." The academic board of the Virginia Military Institute, at Lexington, put on record that his life is a part of the history of the world, and that his moral excellences inspired love and admiration in the hearts of all the good.

At 12.30 P. M., October 15th, 1870, one of the most solemn, imposing, and impressive funeral processions ever assembled moved with slow tread from the late president's home, through the streets of Lexington, and thence to the college chapel. At its head, as the escort of honor, marched the old Confederate soldiers who had gathered from many quarters to pay a last tribute to their commander. In its ranks were the representatives of the Virginia Legislature, State officials, distinguished visitors, members of numerous organizations, trustees, faculty, students, alumni, cadets of the Virginia Military Institute, and citizens. At the chapel the beautiful service of the Episcopal Church was read with great solemnity by the Rev. Dr. W. N. Pendleton, the distinguished officer who had for forty-five years been the comrade and fellow-soldier of the dead chieftain. The mournful ceremonies were concluded outside the chapel in the presence of a vast throng who were unable to enter. The coffin was then removed to the vault. The large assemblage sang one of the general's favorite hymns, "How firm a foundation, ye saints of the Lord," and all that was mortal of the Christian soldier was consigned to the grave.

Traveler, who had borne in so many battles the great Confederate leader, led by two old soldiers, slowly walking, riderless, behind the hearse, covered with the sable trappings of mourning, was a tender and touching sight. He survived his master but two years.

The college pledge was sacredly kept, and a sleeping marble recumbent statue of exquisite workmanship, the production of Valentine, a Virginia sculptor, after "Rauch's figure of Louise of Prussia," is a superb monument to the memory of its president. The Washington and Lee, a great university, under the wise management of General Lee's eldest son, has linked two names which spring spontaneously to every mind. Of these two men, exemplars of a country's character, born almost a century apart, but similar in the history of their boyhood, earnest, grave, studious, alike in noble carriage and commanding dignity, it has been said that in the remarkable combination and symmetry of their intellectual qualities — all so equal, so well developed, no faculty of the mind overlapping any other — you are almost persuaded to deny them greatness, because no single attribute of the mind was projected upon itself. Well may Virginia be proud of sons who shine upon the pages of the world's history "like binary stars which open their glory and shed their splendor on the darkness of the world."

In Virginia's capital city now stand two splendid equestrian statues to George Washington and Robert E. Lee. Riding side by side in calm majesty, they are henceforth contemporaries in all the ages to come. The mother State mourned for the departed soldier, and her General Assembly passed a bill making January 19th, the birthday of General Robert E. Lee, a legal holiday in Virginia. In the universal mourning for him the sympathies of the world first flew to the smitten family. The final parting from her husband after a most happy married life was a great shock to Mrs. Lee. She had been a sufferer for years from rheumatism, unable to move without assistance, and was described at that time as having "a sad but noble countenance, her features much resembling those of her great-grandmother Martha, the wife of Washington, her expression firm, her eyes beautiful and sparkling with the uncommon intelligence which marks her conversation, her almost snowy-white, fine, soft hair, in waves and curls framing her full forehead. She sits in her widow's cap a grand and lovely picture, combining in itself much of the history and glory of the immortal past with the modern events of our history." When the South sent her sons to fight under her husband's command, she devoted every energy to the cause in which he had enlisted.

A very few extracts from communications which reached her from all sections in great numbers can be given: A cousin of the general's, Mr. Edmund I. Lee, from Shepherdstown, October 31, 1870, writes Mrs. Lee: "I cannot find language to convey the distress I felt when I first read the announcement of Robert's death in the papers. The most pleasant recollections of my youth are connected with him and his mother's family. How often have I called to mind the evenings and the mornings spent in their company! — our English rabbits fed together, and our daily visits to the markets in Alexandria to procure meat and vegetables for our mothers, each carrying his own basket; his rescuing me on one occasion from the fangs of his father's mastiff, Killbuck, and the grief of his mother and sisters when your aunt — Mrs. Lewis — having procured from President Jackson a cadet warrant (which was given upon her application, as a personal favor to her), it became necessary to send him to West Point; and my proffering my own services to attend in Robert's place to his mother's business — for his gentle, affectionate manners had attached all his relations to him in early life."

From Savannah, Ga., October 15, 1870, General Joseph E. Johnston wrote her:

My dear Madam: Although you are receiving the strongest proofs that a whole people are sharing in your great sorrow, I venture to write, not merely to say how I, General Lee's earliest and most devoted friend, lament his death and how sadly the event will visit my memory while I stay on earth, but, still more, to assure you of my deep sympathy in this greatest bereavement a human being can know, and of my fervent prayers to our merciful God that he may grant his help to you and your children.

Most sincerely and truly your friend, (Signed) J. E. Johnston.

A dear little girl wrote:

I have heard of General Lee, your husband, and of all his great and noble deeds during the war. I have also heard lately of his death. I have read in the papers that collections are being made for the Lee monument. I have asked my mother to let me send some money — not money that she gave me, but money that I earned myself. I made some of my money by keeping the door shut last winter, and the rest I made by digging up grass in the garden. I send you all I have. I wish it was more. I am nine now.

Respectfully, Maggie McIntyre.

Rev. R. S. Stewart wrote to Mrs. Lee from Baltimore, December 29, 1872: "Accident a few weeks ago led me to read over again after fifty years the Scottish Chiefs, and I have been so struck with the identity of character between Sir William Wallace and General Lee that I cannot help mentioning it to you and asking you to read this book again, if you have not done so, since the late struggle for Southern liberty commenced. In reading it myself, I find every noble sentiment of religion, of patriotism, and of humanity expressed that we all heard from the lips or pen of your noble husband, and so similar are the natures of the two men that I could almost believe in the transmigration of souls. As a descendant of an old Scottish family I have always felt proud of Wallace and cherished his memory."

The Hon. Beresford Hope, A. B., wrote from Bedgebery Park, Cranbrook, England, November 25, 1872, to Mrs. Lee, thanking her for photographs of General Lee, and added, "They embody to us heroic virtue and purest patriotism, the most exalted military genius, the highest and purest domestic excellence, while the impress of your pencil and your autograph doubles their value."

From Aldenham Bridge, North Shropshire, England, a lady sent Mrs. Lee a copy of a lecture delivered by her husband, and wrote, January 24, 1866, that she did it "in order to add one to the many testimonies which you must have received of the sympathy and veneration which have been inspired in Europe by the illustrious career of General Lee. I have less difficulty in presuming to do so, because the passages in which those feelings were most strongly expressed are omitted in this report. They were received with enthusiasm by a Shropshire audience who believed (I know not with what justice, though we should be proud if it were true) that the family of the general once belonged to this country." The Southland — plowed with graves and reddened with blood, that can look the proudest nation fearlessly in the face, and whose sons he led to battle joined in the lamentation over her distinguished son.

The Hon. Jefferson Davis, eloquently speaking at the memorial meeting in Richmond, said that "this day we unite our words of sorrow with those of the good and great throughout Christendom, for his fame has gone over the water; and when the monument we build shall have crumbled into dust, his virtues will still live — a high model for the imitations of generations yet unborn." And Benjamin Hill, of Georgia, in beautiful phrase declaimed: "He was a foe without hate, a friend without treachery, a soldier without cruelty, and a victim without murmuring. He was a public officer without vices, a private citizen without wrong, a neighbor without reproach, a Christian without hypocrisy, and a man without guilt. He was Caesar without his ambition, Frederick without his tyranny, Napoleon without his selfishness, and Washington without his reward. He was as obedient to authority as a servant and royal in authority as a king. He was as gentle as a woman in life, pure and modest as a virgin in thought, watchful as a Roman vestal, submissive to law as Socrates, and grand in battle as Achilles."

The Southern leader had no ambition except the consciousness of duty faithfully performed. Far removed from political or civic ambition, he would have declined the presidency of the Confederate States if his sword had carved their independence as readily as he did positions carrying great salaries. He once said that the only public office he ever might be inclined to accept would be the chief magistracy of his beloved native State; and yet when Judge Robert Ould, of Richmond, wrote him that there was a universal demand that he should become Governor of Virginia, he replied, after expressing his high appreciation of the position and the desires of the people: "I candidly confess, however, that my feelings induce me to prefer private life, which I think more suitable to my condition and age, and where I believe I can better subserve the interests of my State than in that you propose. This is no time for the indulgence of personal or political considerations in selecting individuals for supposed former services. Believing that there are many men in the State more capable than I of filling the position, and who could do more to promote the interests of the people, I most respectfully decline to be considered a candidate for the office." He thought that his election would excite hostility toward the State and injure its inhabitants in the eyes of the country, and he therefore refused to consent to become an instrument of bringing distress upon those whose prosperity and happiness were so dear to him. He adds: "If my disfranchisement and prohibition of civil rights would secure to the citizens of the State the enjoyment of civil liberty and equal rights under the Constitution, I would willingly accept them in their stead." It is perhaps well that he was not launched into public life, where all his actions would have passed in review before a hostile political party. After his sword was sheathed, the serene patience and quiet self-consecration of his latest years have filled the world with admiration.

CHAPTER 17

MILITARY CHARACTER.

It is difficult to accurately compare Lee's military genius even with that of the more modern great captains of war, except in strategical science, for he believed with them that "in planning all dangers should be seen, in execution none, unless very formidable." The great improvements in firearms have changed the tactics of the battlefield. Troops are no longer brought to a halt in the polite phrase of the French, "Halt your banners, in the name of God, the king, and St. Denis," but by bugle notes. Armies are no longer unable to contest because the strings of crossbows are slackened by rain; short lances have been replaced by bayonets on revolving breech-loading rifles; arbalest, phalanx, and other former military terms are no longer heard, and wonderful transformation has taken place since the day on which the blind King of Bohemia was led on the field of Crecy that he might deal one blow of his sword in battle. Marvelous metamorphoses have taken place even since 1815. Imagine the Federal and Confederate armies in a campaign in Belgium in 1861-1865, and that the Federal commander had accepted battle on the field of Waterloo and taken up the line of defense adopted by Wellington. He would not have compressed sixty-seven thousand six hundred and sixty-one men in battle lines within a space of two miles on the Wavre road, on a slope void of intrenchments. The chateau of Hougoumont and its inclosures might have been strongly occupied to add increased strength to the right of the line of battle; but it is improbable that La Haye Sainte, three hundred yards in front of the center on the Charleroi turnpike, and the little villages of Papelotte, La Haie, and Smohain, from a quarter to a half mile in front of the left, would have been occupied except by skirmishers. The flanks of a Federal army equal in numbers to the English would have been twice as far apart, and the whole line well protected by earthworks. Lee would not have attacked as Napoleon did if the Union troops had been placed precisely as Wellington arranged his, nor would his seventy-one thousand nine hundred and forty-seven troops (number of the French) been tactically formed like the Emperor's.

The battle of Gettysburg was fought forty-eight years after that of Waterloo. A comparison of the two strikingly shows the changes in the art of war in a half-century only. There was a similarity of purpose on the part of Lee on the third day's encounter at Gettysburg and the French emperor at Waterloo. The sun rises in Belgium in June at 3.48 A. M., in Pennsylvania in July at 4.30 A. M. Napoleon, at 11.30 A. M., ordered Reille, on his left, to attack Hougoumont on the English right with his left division as a diversion, while his main intention was to attack the British center and left center by his first corps, under D'Erlon, and brought up seventy-eight cannon to fire an hour and a half, at less than a third of a mile from the crest which the English occupied; but D'Erlon was not ordered forward until half-past one. Ewell, on Lee's left, was ordered to make a demonstration on the Federal right; cannon fired for hours, and then Pickett's assaulting column attempted to pierce the center and left center of the Union lines. Count Reille managed to get nearly the whole of his corps engaged, but effected nothing. Ewell got his troops early in action, but with no results. The fighting of both had terminated before the main operations began. Napoleon's object was to seize Mont St. Jean, in rear of Wellington's center, so as to possess himself of the principal avenue of retreat open to the British the road to Brussels. Lee's object was to get possession of the Baltimore pike and road to Westminster, Meade's chief route of retreat to his base of supplies. D'Erlon was unsuccessful; so was Pickett. Before the former moved out, the Prussians of Blucher were seen on the heights of St. Lambert; and the Sixth French Corps, instead of supporting the operations of the First Corps, as had been intended, was taken away and employed in resisting their progress. The troops ordered to support General Pickett lay on their arms waiting orders from a corps commander charged with the assault, which were never given.

The formation of Count d'Erlon's corps for the charge in 1815, and that of Pickett in 1863, is an apt illustration of tactical mutability. D'Erlon's attack was made in four columns in echelon, the left in advance; the first or left column was composed of two brigades, each brigade of four battalions, one behind the other; each battalion was in three ranks, and the distance between the battalions five paces; the next column had nine battalions, and the other two eight each — twenty-nine battalions in all. Sixteen thousand men in twenty-nine battalions would give approximately six hundred men to the battalion; and when in three ranks a front of two hundred men for each one of the four charging columns. If the front of each column had been on the same line, instead of in echelon, eight hundred men would have been in the front rank. It was intended that this force should break through by impact, for only the few men in front could fire. Pickett, with nearly as many troops, had nine brigades in two ranks, in two long lines — six brigades in the first and three in the second. The front line had some ten thousand men, which in two ranks would give a front of five thousand men instead of eight hundred! The dense masses of D'Erlon's corps would have been butchered by the concentrated, converging, rapid fire of modern breech-loading guns, big and small, before their banners could have been shaken to the breeze. We say, therefore, it is not easy to compare Lee with the great soldiers of former ages, except as a strategist.

In strategy it is certain Lee stands in the front rank of the great warriors of the world. He was a greater soldier than Sir Henry Havelock, and equally as devout a Christian. "There was not a heart in England," it was said, when Havelock died, thirteen years before Lee, at about the same age, "that did not feel it to be a subject for private as well as public mourning"; and so the South felt toward Lee. It is stated that it was impossible to gauge the full measure of Moltke's potentialities as a strategist and organizer, but perhaps Lee with the same opportunities would have been equally as skillful and far-seeing. The success of the former and failure of the latter does not prevent comparison. Kossuth failed in Hungary, but the close of his long life has been strewn with flowers. Scotland may never become an independent country, but Scotchmen everywhere cherish with pride the fame of Wallace and Bruce. If given an opportunity, said General Scott, who commanded the army of the United States in 1861, Lee "will prove himself the greatest captain of history." He had the swift intuition to discern the purpose of his opponent, and the power of rapid combination to oppose to it prompt resistance. The very essence of modern war was comprised in the four years campaign, demanding a greater tax upon the mental and physical qualifications of a leader than the fifteen years of Hannibal in the remote past. Military misconceptions have been charged to him; but Marshal Turenne has said, "Show me the man who never made mistakes, and I will show you one who has never made war."

The impartial historian, in reviewing Lee's campaigns and the difficult conditions with which he was always confronted, must at least declare that no commander could have accomplished more. In his favor was, however, that ponderous force known as the spirit of the army, which counterbalanced his enemy's excess of men and guns. Important battles are sometimes lost in spite of the best-conceived plans of the general commanding. The battle of Ligny, with the fate of a great campaign trembling on the result, was not made a decisive victory because Ney, at Quatre-Bras, showed a distrust of his emperor's judgment, was unwilling to take the most obvious step, and finally disobeyed orders; and like behavior of a corps commander at Gettysburg defeated the well-devised designs of Lee.

It has been wisely said that man is under no circumstance so nearly independent as he is when the next step is for life or death; and an infinite number of such independent forces influences the course of a battle — a course which can never be foreseen, and can never coincide with that which it would take under the impulsion of a single force. There are always inevitable conditions under which a commander in chief carries on his operations. The world places Lee by the side of its greatest captains, because surrounded on all sides by conflicting anxieties, interests, and the gravity of issues involved, he only surrendered his battle-stained, bullet-riddled banners after demonstrating that all had been done that mortal could accomplish. The profession of the soldier has been honored by his renown, the cause of education by his virtues, religion by his piety.

The greatest gift the hero leaves his race.

Is to have been a hero.

Made in the USA
Columbia, SC
01 February 2022

55187110R00126